James David Marwick, Helen Armet

**Extracts from the Records of the Burgh of Edinburgh**

Vol. 3

James David Marwick, Helen Armet

**Extracts from the Records of the Burgh of Edinburgh**
*Vol. 3*

ISBN/EAN: 9783337429539

Printed in Europe, USA, Canada, Australia, Japan

Cover: Foto ©Thomas Meinert / pixelio.de

More available books at **www.hansebooks.com**

# EXTRACTS

FROM

## THE RECORDS OF
## THE BURGH OF EDINBURGH.
### 1557—1571.

# EXTRACTS

FROM

# THE RECORDS OF
# THE BURGH OF EDINBURGH.

A.D. 1557—1571.

EDINBURGH:
PRINTED FOR THE SCOTTISH BURGH RECORDS SOCIETY.
MDCCCLXXV.

# PREFACE.

# PREFACE.

HE present volume, which forms the third of the series of "Extracts from the Records of the Burgh of Edinburgh," contains a selection, mainly from the Council Register, of extracts relating to matters of national interest, or illustrative of the history of the Scottish Capital from 1557 till 1571.

The volume opens with the imposition on Edinburgh of its proportion of a national tax to defray the expenses of the marriage of Queen Mary with the Dauphin of France. It closes with the Queen deposed and a prisoner in England; Scotland distracted by two factions, one professing allegiance to the Queen, the other supporting the cause of her son; the Castle of Edinburgh held for her by Sir William Kirkcaldy of Grange, and the Regent Lennox preparing to besiege it.

As might be expected, the records of the Burgh during these fourteen years contain frequent references to the important events that were taking place, many of them in the City and in its immediate vicinity; and it is hoped that the present volume which contains everything of general interest in the records during the period over which the selections extend, will be found to possess some interest as a contribution to the history not only of Edinburgh, but of Scotland.

It is curious to notice the ordinary stream of every-day life in the town flowing on during these years, side by side with that great current of human thought which was undermining and sweeping away old forms of faith and venerable institutions, and changing the whole aspect of Scottish character and history. When England and France were both prosecuting their schemes for attaching Scotland, and the issues of their diplomacy could not fail to exercise a momentous influence over the future of the country, the burgesses are to be found in these pages occupied in building the Newhaven; in discussing, with much keenness and not little acrimony, the relative rights and privileges of merchants and craftsmen; in extending civic hospitalities to distinguished strangers; in legislating as to the prices of victuals and the situation of markets, the repair of public buildings and highways, and all the varied details of every-day burghal life. The frequent references to "our auld enemies of England," and to the precautions to be observed against invasion by them; the ordinances as to providing armour, and as to weaponshawings and musters, as to building up approaches to the town through closes and wynds, as to furnishing artillery and gunners, and as to removing the charters and evidents of the Burgh to the Castle for safety,—all recall vividly the unhappy relations which then existed between England and Scotland. But still, absorbing as such interests must have been, appealing directly to instincts of self-preservation, as well as to sentiments of national honour, the citizens seem at no time to have been inattentive to the concerns of their daily trade within and without the Burgh. Monopoly was the order of that day, and the privileged trader was very jealous of his rights, and very careful to prevent their being invaded by those who did not possess the freedom of the town as burgesses, and the freedom of the merchant-guild or of a handicraft. As strictly, also, did the community guard its corporate rights from encroachment by adjoining and less-favoured districts. Leith, the port of the capital, to which Edinburgh then stood in a position of feudal superiority, had not the valuable and much-coveted privileges of trade. These belonged exclusively to Edinburgh, by whom they were guarded with a strictness and severity scarcely intelligible at the present day, but quite consistent with the policy and practice of the sixteenth century. Of the relations between the City and its dependency this volume affords abundant illustration. But it would be as unwarrantable to estimate the action of the citizens and authorities of the Edinburgh of that time towards Leith by the standard of the received notions of the present day, as it would now be to foster or perpetuate the jealousies of those times. The real interests of the two communities can never be antagonistic: a wise policy of mutual respect and conciliation, and a drawing together on all matters of common concern, will, it is to be

PREFACE.

hoped, lead ultimately to permanent union on the basis of common rights, interests, and privileges.

Unfortunately, the records of most of the Scottish Burghs previous to 1571 are not now extant; and as those of Edinburgh are, by reason of its being the capital, peculiarly interesting, it has been resolved to proceed forthwith with the publication of a fourth volume. The requisite transcripts are being made, and will be placed without delay in the hands of the printer.

It was intended that this volume should have contained selections from the accounts of the Treasurers and Deans of Guild for the period over which it extends, and its publication has been delayed for some time in the hope that this intention might be carried into effect. The City Chamberlain, Mr. Adam, whose intimate acquaintance with these accounts fits him beyond any other person for making the requisite selections and transcripts, kindly undertook the work, and has made considerable progress with it, but has been prevented from completing it by the pressure of other and more important duties. The fourth volume of extracts from the Records will probably be ready in the course of the present year, and the selections from the accounts from 1557 till the last date of the forthcoming volume will accompany it.

The Historical Preface, which was also intended to accompany the present volume, will be reserved for the next, or for the concluding volume, should it be resolved to carry down the selections from the Edinburgh Records to a still more recent date.

Since the first volume of Edinburgh Records was published, further investigation has enabled the List of Provosts, Presidents, Bailies, and Office-Bearers to be rendered more complete subsequent to 1500. The List appended to the present volume includes all the information which has been obtained on this subject from 1527-28, down to and including 1570-71.

J. D. MARWICK.

2 GREAT WESTERN TERRACE,
GLASGOW, *April* 1875.

# TABLE

OF

# THE CONTENTS.

# LIST OF ABBREVIATIONS.

*C.R.*—Council Records of the City.

*Inventory of City Charters.*—Inventory of the Writings in the Charter House of the City; 6 volumes.

*Reg. Mag. Sig.*—Registrum Magni Sigilli, in the General Register House, Edinburgh.

*A.P.S.*—Acts of the Parliaments of Scotland (Record Edition); 11 volumes.

*Balfour's Practicks.*—Practicks, or a System of the more Ancient Law of Scotland, compiled by Sir James Balfour of Pittendreich, late President of the Court of Session, 1754.

# TABLE OF THE CONTENTS.

PREFACE.

|   |   |   |   | PAGE |
|---|---|---|---|---|
| 1557, | March | 31. | Money to be expended in bigging the Newhaven, [*C.R. Vol. II. fol.* 95.] | 1 |
| — | April | 2. | Answer to Queen's letter as to craftsmen, [*Ib.*] | 1 |
| — | — | 9. | Forms to be provided for Magdalene Chapel, [*Ib.*] | 1 |
| — | — | 14. | Extent for expenses of Queen's marriage, [*Ib.*] | 2 |
| — | — | 18. | Landward fleshers to have liberty to sell flesh above Tolbooth, [*Ib. fol.* 97 ; *Inventory of City Charters, Vol. I. fol.* 21.] | 4 |
| — | June | 5. | Act discharging Thomas Makcalyeane, assessor, to be deleted, [*C.R. Vol. II. fol.* 98.] | 5 |
| — | — | 18. | Proclamation of weaponschawing, [*Ib. fol.* 98.] | 5 |
| — | — | 25. | Proclamation as to price of flesh ; halberts to officers, [*Ib. fol.* 99.] | 6 |
| — | July | 24. | St Rowkis chapel to be inspected, [*Ib.*] | 7 |
| — | — | 31. | Newhaven to be inspected, [*Ib.*] | 7 |
| — | August | 11. | Works at Newhaven and St Rokis chapel, [*Ib. fol.* 100.] | 7 |
| — | — | 13. | Payment for spears use of inhabitants, [*Ib.*] | 8 |
| — | — | 14. | Act as to weaponschawing, [*Ib.*] | 8 |
| — | — | 17. | Locks and keys for clerks' chamber ; proclamation of weaponschawing ; a bedrelship of St Mary's Wynd granted, [*Ib. fol.* 101.] | 9 |
| — | September | 17. | Men furnished to army, conform to Queen's writing, [*Ib. fol.* 102.] | 9 |

## TABLE OF CONTENTS.

|  |  |  | | PAGE |
|---|---|---|---|---|
| 1557, September | 18. | Craftsmen consent to be stented; clerk's expenses to Hamilton for artillery; signet to Queen's letters, [*C.R. Vol. II. fol.* 103.] | | 10 |
| — | — | — | Annual acts as to bread, &c.; acts as to regraters, beggars, and weapons in booths, [*Ib. fol.* 105-6.] | 11 |
| — | November | 5. | Grant of a benefice of St Andrew's altar; town walls, &c., to be repaired; wine escheat and given to serjeants, [*Ib. fol.* 109.] | 12 |
| — | — | 12. | Grant of burgesships, [*Ib. fol.* 110.] | 13 |
| — | — | 23. | Meetings of council, [*Ib. fol.* 113.] | 13 |
| — | — | 26. | Taxes of sons of burgesses, [*Ib.*] | 13 |
| — | December | 10. | Gift to the Queen and her servitors, [*Ib. fol.* 114.] | 14 |
| — | — | 15. | Absentees from musters unlawed, [*Ib.*] | 14 |
| — | — | 29. | Town to be fortified, [*Ib.*] | 15 |
| 1557-8, January | 19. | President chosen to act in Provost's absence, [*Ib.*] | 15 |
| — | — | 21. | Licence for obtaining alms for repair of Magdalene bridge, [*Ib. fol.* 116.] | 16 |
| — | February | 9. | Payment to chirurgeon for mending a leg; clothmarket restored to former site above Tolbooth, [*Ib. fol.* 117-8.] | 16 |
| — | — | 11. | A candlemaker ordered not to melt tallow near lord president's house; market of hides and skins, [*Ib. fol.* 118.] | 17 |
| — | March | 6. | Lime for town walls; powder and bullets for artillery, [*Ib. fol.* 119.] | 18 |
| 1558, April | 16. | Payment of taxes by merchants or free burgesses, [*Ib. fol.* 121.] | 18 |
| — | May | 9. | Proceedings taken for defence of burgh, [*Ib. fol.* 122-3.] | 19 |
| — | — | 11. | Concerning extenters and gentlemen heritors, [*Ib. fol.* 123.] | 20 |
| — | — | 21. | Gunners to be hired; close-foots to be built up; ports; preparations for defence; artillery to be bought, [*Ib. fol.* 124-5.] | 20 |
| — | — | 27. | Town's evidents and writings and silverwork of St Giles' kirk to be removed to castle; as to men to be furnished by crafts, [*Ib. fol.* 125.] | 22 |

## TABLE OF CONTENTS.

| | | | | PAGE |
|---|---|---|---|---|
| 1558, | May | 30. | Ordinance for defence of the town [*C.R. Vol. II fol.* 125.] | 22 |
| — | June | 5. | Hiring servants in time of war; merchants and craftsmen to be consulted as to number of men they may furnish; men to be furnished by merchants, [*Ib. fol.* 126.] | 23 |
| — | — | 10. | Roll of mason craftsmen to be given in; complaint by skinner craft as to unfreemen of St Johnston; men to be furnished by crafts, [*Ib. fol.* 131-2.] | 24 |
| — | — | 17. | Privileges obtained by Edinburgh against Leith, [*Balfour's Practicks, p.* 51.] | 25 |
| — | — | 23. | On complaint of bonnet makers, unfreemen not to sell bonnets except on market and fair days, [*C.R. Vol. II. fol.* 132.] | 25 |
| — | | | Celebration of Queen's marriage, [*Ib.*] | 26 |
| — | December | 15. | Gift of wine and wax to the Queen, [*C.R. Vol. III. fol.* 1.] | 26 |
| — | — | 29. | Passage and causeway of Cowgait to be repaired, [*Ib. fol.* 2.] | 26 |
| 1558-9, January | | 7. | Gift of bedrelship; jewels in kirk of St Giles, [*Ib.*] | 27 |
| — | February | 3. | Triumph and banquet to the Queen; licence to procurator-fiscal to vent and have wine in his house free of stent [*Ib. fol.* 4, 5.] | 28 |
| — | — | 12. | Price of wine; letters of Queen giving licence to a merchant of Flanders as to selling his goods, [*Ib. fol.* 5, 6.] | 29 |
| — | — | 13. | Charge by Queen to liberate merchant from ward, [*Ib. fol.* 7.] | 29 |
| — | — | 14. | Letter from Queen as to the merchant's goods, [*Ib. fol.* 7.] | 30 |
| — | March | 8. | Weight of kirk jewels, [*Ib. fol.* 3.] | 30 |
| — | — | 24. | Persons appointed for attending to matters between the town and Leith, [*Ib. fol.* 9.] | 30 |
| 1559, | April | 12. | Gifts of chaplainries in St Giles' Kirk. [*Ib. fol.* 10, 11.] | 31 |
| — | — | 20. | Complaint against Lord Seyton for putting a bailie and the common clerk in ward, [*Ib. fol.* 11.] | 31 |
| — | — | 22. | Message by Lord Seyton to the bailies, [*Ib. fol.* 12.] | 33 |

## TABLE OF CONTENTS.

| | | | | PAGE |
|---|---|---|---|---|
| 1559, | April | 26. | A prisoner set at liberty, [*C.R. Vol. III., fol.* 12.] | 34 |
| — | — | 28. | At desire of the Queen, actions between the town and Leith to be suspended; proposal to erect three shops at kirk gavil to be rejected, [*Ib. fol.* 13.] | 34 |
| — | May | 10. | Stents of Inverkeithing and Kinghorn, [*Ib.*] | 36 |
| — | — | 14. | Letter from Queen as to keeping rule and defending religious places, [*Ib. fol.* 14.] | 36 |
| — | — | 20. | Artillery to be ready and watch kept; gift of a bedrelship, [*Ib.*] | 37 |
| — | — | 24. | Imprisonment of a bailie; provost to write to Queen thereanent, [*Ib. fol.* 14, 15.] | 37 |
| — | — | 26. | Against unfreemen occupying the liberty of burgesses, [*Ib. fol.* 15.] | 39 |
| — | — | 28. | Letter from Queen as to defence of town, [*Ib.*] | 39 |
| — | June | 3. | Watchman casting stones at Blackfriars and Greyfriars windows, [*Ib. fol.* 16.] | 40 |
| — | — | 14. | Protest by dean of guild as to safe keeping of jewels and ornaments, [*Ib.*] | 40 |
| — | — | 16. | Watch and keepers of the ports; commission against Archbishop of St Andrews, [*Ib. fol.* 17.] | 41 |
| — | — | 21. | Gifts of beadmanships; keepers of St Giles' kirk; playing "sweis" at weapponschaw; mending causeways; gathering alms through town, [*Ib. fol.* 17, 18.] | 41 |
| — | — | 27. | Custody of jewels and vestments; names of persons to whom gear and vestments given in keeping, [*Ib. fol.* 18.] | 42 |
| — | — | 29. | Commission to treat with the congregation; preservation of St Giles' kirk; protest against deacon of hammermen, [*Ib. fol.* 18.] | 44 |
| — | July | 12. | Removal of stalls of choir; mending of walls and ports; proposition of the lords of the congregation, [*Ib. fol.* 19, 20.] | 45 |
| — | — | 29. | Negotiations between commissioners for the Queen Regent and brethren of the congregation; protest by provost, [*Ib. fol.* 20, 21.] | 46 |

## TABLE OF CONTENTS.

| | | | | PAGE |
|---|---|---|---|---|
| 1559, | August | 2. | Repairing of town wall and ports; payments for watching kirk, etc., [*C.R. Vol. III. fol.* 21.] | 49 |
| — | — | 4. | Payment of prebendaries; mending ports; acts as to beggars, [*Ib. fol.* 21, 22.] | 49 |
| — | — | 14. | Nightly watch to be kept, [*Ib. fol.* 22.] | 50 |
| — | — | 18. | Gift of a bedrelship; coal and candle furnished to lords of session; act as to beggars and the poor, [*Ib.*] | 51 |
| — | September | 4. | Repair of wells; removal of skin market, [*Ib.*] | 51 |
| — | — | 14. | Convening lords of session; answer to Queen's writing to be destroyed, [*Ib.*] | 52 |
| — | — | 20. | Commissioners to lords of secret council; election of persons to vote for absent members of town council; council summoned to appear before Queen; ratification by provost of proceedings in his absence; protest by crafts as to their privileges; refusal by council to allow crafts to vote in election, and protest by them thereanent, [*Ib. fol.* 22-5.] | 52 |
| — | — | 22. | Crafts not allowed to vote in election; letter by Queen as to election, [*Ib. fol.* 25.] | 56 |
| — | — | 26. | Payment for playing a "quhissal" at the watch, [*Ib.*] | 57 |
| — | — | 30. | Repair of tolbooth; preservation of town's evidents; gunners to be hired; keeping of the ports, [*Ib. fol.* 25, 26.] | 57 |
| — | October | 6. | Preservation of evidents, [*Ib. fol.* 26.] | 58 |
| — | — | 14. | Artillery to be taken to castle, [*Ib.*] | 58 |
| — | — | 27. | Extent for raising soldiers, [*Ib.*] | 58 |
| — | — | 29. | Extent; St Giles' arm; receipt for artillery, [*Ib. fol.* 27.] | 59 |
| — | November | 13. | Kirk gear, vestments and ornaments to be replaced, [*Ib.*] | 59 |
| — | — | 21. | Set of customs and tron; protest as to vestments, [*Ib. fol.* 27, 28.] | 60 |
| — | December | 12. | Gifts to Queen and provost; delivery of vestments, [*Ib. fol.* 28.] | 60 |
| — | — | 24. | Watch to be kept, [*Ib.*] | 61 |

## TABLE OF CONTENTS.

| | | | | PAGE |
|---|---|---|---|---|
| 1559-60, January | 10. | Ratification of certain statutes; wild adventures; officers and members of council to remain in town, [*C.R. Vol. III. fol.* 28.] | | 61 |
| — — | 19. | Lodging for lord provost, [*Ib.*] | | 62 |
| — February | 16. | Payments to prebendaries; farmers of customs and tron, [*Ib. fol.* 31.] | | 62 |
| 1560, April | 16. | Repairs on kirk; appointment of a bailie, [*Ib. fol.* 33.] | | 62 |
| — — | 30. | Tax for raising soldiers, [*Ib.*] | | 63 |
| — May | 1. | Repairs on walls, [*Ib.*] | | 63 |
| — — | 4. | Payment for playing on "sweseche and quhissill," [*Ib.*] | | 63 |
| — — | 6. | Disobedience to a bailie, [*Ib. fol.* 34.] | | 63 |
| — — | 8. | Furnishings to John Knox; pensions to kirkmen discharged; removal of a bell, [*Ib.*] | | 63 |
| — — | 10. | Money to be borrowed, [*Ib.*] | | 64 |
| — — | 15. | Keys to a port and John Knox's loging, [*Ib. fol.* 35.] | | 64 |
| — — | 26. | Watching prisoners; bell and brasen pillars of kirk to be made into artillery; duties payable to kirkmen, [*Ib.*] | | 64 |
| — June | 1. | Furnishings to John Willok, [*Ib. fol.* 36.] | | 65 |
| — — | 10. | Act as to idolaters, whoremasters, and harlots, [*Ib. fol.* 37.] | | 65 |
| — — | 12. | Stones of kirks not to be removed, [*Ib.*] | | 66 |
| — — | 19. | Tolbooth, school, and clerks' chamber to be fitted up in kirk; repairing of causeways, wells, and walls; seats for kirk; new keys for ports; collector of annuals, etc., to St Paul's work, [*Ib. fol.* 37, 38.] | | 66 |
| — — | 26. | Furnishings to ministers, [*Ib. fol.* 39.] | | 68 |
| — July | 12. | Annuals formerly pertaining to friars, etc.; iron rods and shackles, [*Ib.*] | | 68 |
| — — | 19. | Prices of bread and ale; acts as to beggars, musicians, and vagabonds, [*Ib. fol.* 41.] | | 68 |
| — — | 23. | Walls and fortress of Leith, [*Ib. fol.* 40.] | | 69 |
| — August | 1. | Silver work and repairs on kirk; articles to be given in to parliament; order of precedence in the kirk; repairs on town wall; against unfreemen using privileges, [*Ib. fol.* 42, 43.] | | 70 |

## TABLE OF CONTENTS.

vii

| | | | | PAGE |
|---|---|---|---|---|
| 1560, | August | 16. | Furnishings to minister; complaint against constable-depute for levying dues; as to courts held by constable, [*C.R. Vol. III. fol.* 13.] | 72 |
| — | — | 21. | Down casting walls and filling trenches of Leith; obligation by constable as to holding courts, [*Ib. fol.* 44.] | 74 |
| — | — | 24. | Payment to musicians, [*Ib.*] | 74 |
| — | — | 30. | Delivery of certain jewels; payment to minister; burgesses' oath, [*Ib. fol.* 44, 45.] | 74 |
| — | September | 4. | Lodging for John Knox; slander, parson of Pennecuke; delivery of jewels, [*Ib. fol.* 45.] | 76 |
| — | — | 5. | Parson of Pennecuke; silver work undelivered: maintaining officers in execution of duty; iron house; silver work, [*Ib. fol.* 46, 47.] | 76 |
| — | — | 6. | Delivery of silver work; masters of Haly Blude and St Anthony's, [*Ib. fol.* 47.] | 78 |
| — | — | 9. | Laird of Restalrig put in ward; proclamation as to idle men, [*Ib.*] | 79 |
| — | — | 10. | Watch ordered for sure keeping of the laird of Restalrig; search to be made for his concubine, [*Ib. fol.* 48.] | 80 |
| — | — | 11. | Laird of Restalrig's writing registered; he to be kept in ward till he find caution; payment for damage in building town hall, [*Ib.*] | 80 |
| — | — | 16. | Precautions for keeping Laird of Restalrig in prison; admission to Flesher craft, [*Ib. fol.* 48, 49.] | 81 |
| — | — | 20. | Proclamation as to blasphemers and idolaters; Nether kirk yard; beds furnished to Englishmen, [*Ib. fol.* 49.] | 82 |
| — | — | 26. | Two craftsmen to be on the council, [*Ib. fol.* 50.] | 83 |
| — | October | 14. | Acts as to bread, malt and ale, brewsters, poultry, candle, hay, and wine; corn market; stones of the Black and Grey Friars, [*Ib. fol.* 51-3.] | 84 |
| — | — | 20. | Sale of bell and brazen pillars; slander against minister, [*Ib. fol.* 54.] | 85 |

## TABLE OF CONTENTS.

|  |  |  | | PAGE |
|---|---|---|---|---|
| 1560, | October | 30. | Act as to keeping the Sabbath day; against blasphemers; iniquity of women "taverners"; duty of wine pertaining to fraternity of St Anthony; sundry acts; burgesses to be resident; payments to John Knox; fee to gild officer, [*C.R. Vol. III. fol.* 55-77.] . . . . . . . | 85 |
| — | November | 15. | Payments to provost and council; but at Nether Bow, [*Ib. fol.* 58.] . . . . . . . | 88 |
| — | — | 16. | Building of wall at North Loch side, [*Ib.*] . . | 88 |
| — | — | 20. | Market at House of Muir; price of wine; merchants to be burgesses and guild brethren, [*Ib. fol.* 59, 60.] . | 89 |
| — | — | 22. | Sentence against a flesher for adultery, [*Ib. fol.* 60.] . | 89 |
| — | — | 23. | Dissent by deacons of crafts against sentence; council refuse to set prisoner at liberty on caution; complaint against craftsmen taking flesher furth of ward, [*Ib.*] . . . . . . . . | 90 |
| — | — | 28. | Supplication by deacons, masters, and principal brethren of crafts as to disobedience of craftsmen in setting prisoner at liberty; certain persons to be summoned for their conspiracy, [*Ib. fol.* 60.] . . . | 90 |
| — | December | 6. | Proclamation as to proceedings of craftsmen; disobedience to magistrates and officers; craftsmen called to the laws; craftsmen's servants to be punished; delivery of vestments; money for repairing kirk; extent for furnishing of ambassadors; bell of St Paul's work; merchants and craftsmen to become freemen; building of the walls, [*Ib. fol.* 61-3.] . . . . . . . . | 93 |
| — | — | 20. | Vestments and jewels; down-casting dike at Leith; payment to John Knox, [*Ib. fol.* 63-4.] . . | 96 |
| — | — | 26. | Kirk doors to be kept shut, [*Ib. fol.* 64.] . . . | 97 |
| 1560-1, January | | 3. | Payment of burgess and gildships; down-casting of the Friars; payment to John Cairns, [*Ib. fol.* 67, 68.] | 97 |
| — | — | 15. | Rent of grammar school, [*Ib. fol.* 69.] . . . . | 98 |
| — | — | 17. | Delivery of jewels and ornaments, [*Ib.*] . . . | 98 |

TABLE OF CONTENTS.

|  |  |  | | PAGE |
|---|---|---|---|---|
| 1560-1, | February | 1. | Delivery of ornaments; payment to provost; beidmen of St Andrew's hospital; mending of causeways, [*C.R. Vol. III. fol.* 71-2.] | 98 |
| — | — | 7. | Gavil at St Giles' Kirk to be completed; town wall at Blackfriars, [*Ib. fol.* 73.] | 99 |
| — | — | 12. | Payments to John Knox, minister, [*Ib. fol.* 74.] | 99 |
| — | — | 19. | Repairing of town wall, [*Ib.*] | 100 |
| — | — | 21. | Delivery of silver chalice; dean of guild to be charged in account with pillars and bells, [*Ib.*] | 100 |
| — | March | 5. | Money received for bells and pillars, [*Ib. fol.* 75.] | 100 |
| — | — | 12. | Repair of town wall; stones taken from kirks to be restored; French ambassador, [*Ib. fol.* 75.] | 100 |
| — | — | 24. | Proclamation as to priests, monks, and friars; donations to poor; fleshers and fleshmarket, [*Ib. fol.* 75, 76.] | 101 |
| 1561, | April | 2. | Deacons to be convened to advise as to certain statutes; delivery of vestments; distribution of alms to the poor, [*Ib. fol.* 76, 77.] | 103 |
| — | — | 5. | Delivery and sale of vestments; payment to John Knox; place of fleshmarket, [*Ib. fol.* 77.] | 104 |
| — | — | 9. | Consent of deacons to removal of fleshmarket; disobedience of fleshers; removal of victualmarket; place to be acquired for fleshmarket, [*C.R. Vol. IV. fol.* 1-3.] | 104 |
| — | — | 23. | Extent for town walls; articles proposed to council as to rents and annuals payable to papists, deceased persons' goods, duty on wine, burial place, games, swearers and blasphemers, prayers and preaching; town's artillery to be received from castle; proclamation against celebration of play of Robin Hood; proclamation as to duty on wine, [*Ib. fol.* 3, 4.] | 105 |
| — | — | 24. | Lands to be acquired for fleshmarket; payment to John Cairns, [*Ib. fol.* 4, 5.] | 108 |
| — | — | 25. | Act as to registering of testaments and making inventory of deceased persons' goods; repairs on Grey- | |

TABLE OF CONTENTS.

| | | | | PAGE |
|---|---|---|---|---|
| 1561, | April | 25. | friars yard; duty on wine to be given to the poor; discharge of confraternities, [*C.R. Vol. IV. fol.* 4, 5.] | 109 |
| — | May | 10. | Proclamation as to prizes; insurrection of servants and apprentices in celebrating Robin Hood, [*Ib. fol.* 6.] | 111 |
| — | — | 13. | Answer of deacons of crafts as to punishing offenders, [*Ib. fol.* 7.] | 113 |
| — | — | 14. | Apprentices to be apprehended, [*Ib.*] | 113 |
| — | — | 21. | Precautions for keeping order in time of parliament, [*Ib.*] | 114 |
| — | — | 23. | Chaplain of St Katherine's altar authorised to feu lands, [*Ib.*] | 114 |
| — | — | 27. | Vestments and ornaments to be sold; gift to captain of the castle, [*Ib. fol.* 8.] | 115 |
| — | — | 30. | An advocate accused of receiving the priest's sacrament; quarterly payment to John Knox; artillery to be got back from castle, [*Ib. fol.* 9.] | 115 |
| — | June | 11. | Apprentices imprisoned; as to artillery being brought back from castle, [*Ib.*] | 116 |
| — | — | 16. | Alexander Skene, advocate, set at liberty; a priest banished; apprentices to be tried, [*Ib. fol.* 10, 11.] | 117 |
| — | July | 11. | " Succhis " to be taken from players; " crafts childer " to be apprehended, [*Ib. fol.* 12.] | 118 |
| — | — | 18. | A tailor imprisoned for allowing his servants to go forth with armour, [*Ib.*] | 118 |
| — | — | 25. | An officer discharged; town council besieged; guard to be asked for, [*Ib.*] | 118 |
| — | — | 30. | James Barroun authorised to pay wages to the guard, [*Ib.*] | 119 |
| — | August | 13. | Payment to James Barroun, [*Ib.*] | 119 |
| — | — | 22. | Payments to bailies, [*Ib.*] | 119 |
| — | — | 25. | Reward for services while provost and others were besieged, [*Ib. fol.* 13.] | 119 |
| — | — | 26. | Banquet and triumph to be made on Queen's entry, [*Ib.*] | 119 |
| — | — | 27. | Preparations for banquet and triumph, [*Ib. fol.* 13.] | 120 |

## TABLE OF CONTENTS.

|   |   |   | | PAGE |
|---|---|---|---|---|
| 1561, | August | 28. | Farther preparations, [*C.R. Vol. IV. fol.* 13, 14.] | 121 |
| — | — | 29. | Proclamation charging persons to give in accounts, [*Ib. fol.* 14.] | 122 |
| — | September | 3. | Extent for expenses of banquet, triumph, and gift to Queen, [*Ib.*] | 122 |
| — | — | 24. | Leet for election of two craftsmen as councillors, [*Ib. fol.* 15.] | 122 |
| — | — | 26. | Payment to "actour" of morning prayers; questions with crafts as to elections, [*Ib.*] | 123 |
| — | October | 2. | Proclamation charging priests and others to remove from town, [*Ib.*] | 125 |
| — | — | 5. | Order by Queen to deprive provost and bailies of their offices, [*Ib.*] | 125 |
| — | — | 8. | Provost and bailies discharged and others elected; protests thereanent, [*Ib. fol.* 16.] | 126 |
| — | — | 22. | A bailie fined for not accepting office, [*Ib.*] | 127 |
| — | November | 5. | Prices of bread and candles; a study to be made for minister, [*Ib. fol.* 17.] | 128 |
| — | — | 8. | Keeper of kirk; reader of common prayers, [*Ib.*] | 128 |
| — | — | 21. | Regulation as to markets, [*Ib. fol.* 18.] | 128 |
| — | — | 25. | Election of a treasurer; protest by deacons, [*Ib.*] | 129 |
| — | — | 26. | Banishment of an adulteress, [*Ib.*] | 129 |
| — | — | 27. | Extent for expenses of banquet and triumph, [*Ib.*] | 129 |
| — | December | 31. | John Knox sent to Angus and Mearns, [*Ib. fol.* 20.] | 129 |
| 1561-2, | January | 30. | Action by bailies of Kinghorn against inhabitants of Leith, [*Ib. fol.* 21.] | 129 |
| — | February | 10. | Letter by Queen as to ruinous state of Tolbooth, [*Ib. fol.* 22.] | 130 |
| — | — | 11. | Roup of mills; extent for building walls; a craftsman elected to be on the council, [*Ib.*] | 130 |
| — | — | 24. | Order for taking down Tolbooth, [*Ib. fol.* 23.] | 131 |
| 1562, | April | 8. | Friar Black to be kept in ward; John Craig to bear with John Knox half charge of preaching; proposal to remove master of High School; building of a college and hospitals; gift of annuals and | |

## TABLE OF CONTENTS.

|   |   |   |   | PAGE |
|---|---|---|---|---|
| 1562, | April | 8. | altarages to be asked; slander against John Knox, [*C.R. Vol. IV. 1b. fol.* 26.] | 131 |
| — | — | 11. | Price of wine; rumoured unjust dealings of websters; an adulteress to be kept in ward; letter by Queen as to Friar Black; master of grammar school required to produce his right; house for lords of session, [*1b. fol.* 26, 27.] | 132 |
| — | — | 30. | Proclamation against play of Robin Hood, [*1b. fol.* 29.] | 134 |
| — | May | 3. | Election of deacon of hammermen, [*1b. fol.* 30.] | 134 |
| — | — | 22. | Hole in North Loch to be prepared for dipping fornicators, [*1b. fol.* 31.] | 135 |
| — | June | 10. | Defences by master of grammar school, [*1b. fol.* 32.] | 135 |
| — | — | 19. | Another minister to be elected, [*1b. fol.* 33.] | 135 |
| — | — | 24. | Answers of deacons of crafts as to sustaining ministers; danger of tumult at weaponschawing; letter by Queen as to seditious and rebellious persons; the town's standard; sustenance of ministers; commissioners to the kirk, [*1b. fol.* 33-5.] | 136 |
| — | — | 28. | John Gordon of Fynlater and others put in prison, [*1b. fol.* 35.] | 138 |
| — | — | 29. | Letter from Queen as to variance between Lord Ogilvy and John Gordon, [*1b.*] | 138 |
| — | — | 30. | Proceedings against master of High School, [*1b. fol.* 36.] | 139 |
| — | July | 3. | Selling of leather, [*1b.*] | 140 |
| — | — | 15. | Extent for new tolbooth, [*1b. fol.* 37.] | 140 |
| — | — | 17. | Act as to who shall bear office in burgh; act deleted at command of Queen, [*1b.*] | 140 |
| — July 22, 24, 25. August 6, 11. | | | Proceedings against William Robertoun, master of the High School, [*1b. fol.* 38, 39, 40.] | 141-5 |
| — | — | 17. | Town's supplication to the Queen as to the poor, schools, hospitals, and burial place; grant by Queen of Greyfriars yard, [*1b. fol.* 41.] | 145 |
| — | — | 27. | Gift of a gildship; town walls; corns sown in Greyfriars yard; master of works; works at Greyfriars yard, [*1b. fol.* 41, 42.] | 147 |

## TABLE OF CONTENTS.

xiii

|  |  |  | | PAGE |
|---|---|---|---|---|
| 1562, September | 18. | Complaint by bonnetmakers of others taking away their servants, [*C.R. Vol. IV. fol.* 42.] | | 148 |
| — | — | 25. | Letter by Queen as to election of provost, [*Ib. fol.* 43.] | 148 |
| — | October | 3. | Decreet against master of High School, [*Ib. fol.* 44.] | 149 |
| — | — | 6. | Deacons not to have vote in choosing leet for provost; delay in answering Queen's letter, [*Ib. fol.* 43, 44.] | 150 |
| — | — | 21. | Convening of council, [*Ib. fol.* 46.] | 151 |
| — | November | 6. | Delivery of keys; act against adulterers and fornicators, [*Ib. fol.* 47.] | 151 |
| — | — | 9. | Pasturing of common muir and links, [*Ib.*] | 152 |
| — | — | 11. | Flesh not to be eaten on Friday or Saturday, [*Ib. fol.* 48.] | 152 |
| — | — | 12. | Baptism of children, [*Ib. fol.* 48.] | 152 |
| — | — | 18. | Usurpation of privileges by inhabitants of Leith; assessors and scribe, [*Ib. fol.* 48, 49.] | 153 |
| — | December | 5. | Prison for adulterers; payment for land on which new tolbooth is built, [*Ib. fol.* 50.] | 154 |
| — | — | 8. | Prices of tallow, candle, bread, ale, and hay, [*Ib.* 50, 51.] | 154 |
| — | — | 11. | Payment for necessaries of minister's lodging, [*Ib. fol.* 54.] | 154 |
| — | — | 22. | Yule duty to bedrels of St. Mary's Wynd, [*Ib.*] | 154 |
| 1562-63, January | 6. | Discharge of extents to Murray of Blackbarony; prices for work of cordiners, [*Ib. fol.* 56.] | | 154 |
| — | — | 15. | Porters at Queen's gate; sale of hides; sasines in town's lands, [*Ib. fol.* 57, 58.] | 155 |
| — | — | 22. | Surgeons and barbers discharged, [*Ib. fol.* 58.] | 155 |
| — | — | 27. | Prices of wines and cordiners' work, [*Ib.*] | 155 |
| — | February | 5. | Ordinance for convening deacons, [*Ib. fol.* 60.] | 156 |
| — | — | 6. | Mastership of high school, [*Ib.*] | 157 |
| — | — | 23. | Letter from Queen as to setting a prisoner free, [*Ib. fol.* 61.] | 157 |
| — | March | 5. | Chapel in Nether Kirkyard; banquet to commissioners of burghs; Kirk of Field and buildings thereof, [*Ib. fol.* 63, 64.] | 157 |

## TABLE OF CONTENTS.

|  |  |  |  | PAGE |
|---|---|---|---|---|
| 1562-63, March | 10. | Kiln and barns at King's Stables, [*C.R. Vol. IV. fol.* 64.] | | 158 |
| — — | 11. | Beidmanship in St Paul's Work, [*Ib. fol.* 65.] | . | . 158 |
| 1563, April | | Causeway opposite Cardinal's lodging, [*Ib. fol.* 67.] | | . 159 |
| — — | 23. | Convening inhabitants in time of need; promise of a burgesship to a mason on marriage, [*Ib.*] | . | . 159 |
| — — | 30. | Clerks' chamber in St Giles' Kirk, [*Ib. fol.* 68,] | . | . 160 |
| — May | 11. | Beidmanship in St Paul's Work, [*Ib. fol.* 69.] | . | . 160 |
| — — | 17. | Trial of Bishop of St Andrews and other kirkmen, [*Ib.*] | | 160 |
| — June | 11. | Support of minister and reader, [*Ib.*] | . | . 161 |
| — — | 18. | Commissioners to kirk; proposed hospital at the Blackfriars; accusations against John Knox and other ministers, and against doctrine now preached, [*Ib. fol.* 69, 70.] | . | . 161 |
| — — | 21. | Agreement with the parson of Pennycuke as to Kirk of Field; money borrowed for completing tolbooth, [*Ib. fol.* 70, 71.] | . | . 163 |
| — — | 25. | Tower of old tolbooth; slander against John Knox, [*Ib. fol.* 71.] | . | . 164 |
| — — | 30. | Bonnetmakers not to exercise their crafts in open places in High Street, [*Ib.*] | . | . 164 |
| — July | 2. | Proposed hospital at Blackfriars, [*Ib. fol.* 73.] | . | . 165 |
| — — | 4. | Markets on Sunday forbidden, [*Ib.*] | . | . 165 |
| — — | 6. | Reward to a surgeon for raising a dead woman and effecting certain cures, [*Ib.*] | . | . 165 |
| — — | 12. | Making of causeways and sewers, [*Ib. fol.* 74.] | . | . 166 |
| — — | 23. | Lodging for King of Sweden's ambassador; gift to Robert Norvell, of the kirk, yard, and croft of the Greenside, previously occupied by the friars, on certain conditions, [*Ib. fol.* 74-75.] | . | . 166 |
| — August | 15. | Men of Leith and new tolbooth, [*Ib. fol.* 77.] | . | . 169 |
| — — | 27. | Corn growing in Blackfriars yard; tack of yard challenged; price of ale and bread, [*Ib.*] | . | . 169 |
| — September | 11. | Action between Edinburgh and Leith as to new tolbooth; price of malt, [*Ib. fol.* 78, 79.] | . | . 169 |
| — — | 18. | Commissioners sent to Queen at Stirling, [*Ib. fol.* 79.] | | 170 |

TABLE OF CONTENTS.          xv

| | | | | PAGE |
|---|---|---|---|---|
| 1563, September | 26. | Printing irons and letters ; nothing to be printed with them without licence, [*C.R. Vol. IV.*] . | | 170 |
| — | October | 2. | Building of a wall at Leith Port stopped ; burials, [*Ib.* 80, 81.] . . . . . . | 171 |
| — | — | 8. | Evidents of the Kirk of Field, [*Ib. fol.* 82.] . . | 171 |
| — | — | 13. | Order of speaking in council house ; commissioners sent to Queen as to writings in favour of Leith, etc. ; benefices to be disponed, [*Ib.*] . . . . | 172 |
| — | — | 15. | Letters against Leith ; water bailie of Leith ; a bailie fined for leaving without licence ; ordinance as to office-bearers leaving town ; rental of prebendaries ; gift of benefice of Craigcruke, [*Ib. fol.* 83, 84.] . | 172 |
| — | November | 5. | Encroachments on commonty to be removed ; space at High Church to be set for shops, [*Ib. fol.* 85.] . | 173 |
| — | — | 10. | Seat and desk to be put in kirk ; imprisonment of adulterers and fornicators, [*Ib.*] . . . . | 173 |
| — | — | 26. | Sustenance of minister, reader, and others ; visitation of the Greenside ; payment to treasurer, [*Ib. fol.* 86, 87.] . . . . . . | 174 |
| — | December | 1. | Evidents concerning port and haven of Leith, [*Ib. fol.* 87.] | 174 |
| — | — | 24. | Gift of a burgess and gildship ; no burgesship to be given free for a year ; commissioners to convention of the kirk, [*Ib. fol.* 88.] . . . | 175 |
| — | — | 29. | Gift to the Queen, [*Ib. fol.* 89.] . . . . | 175 |
| 1563-4. January | | 7. | Money for building of hospital, [*Ib. fol.* 90.] . . | 175 |
| — | — | 21. | Payment to reader, [*Ib. fol.* 91.] . . . . | 176 |
| — | February | 16. | Timber bought for building hospital, [*Ib. fol.* 92.] . | 176 |
| — | — | 18. | Payment of feu-duty to a sister of the Senys, [*Ib. fol.* 93.] | 176 |
| — | March | 22. | Act as to cloth making, [*Ib. fol.* 96.] . . . | 177 |
| 1564, | — | 28. | Extent for furnishing ambassador to Denmark, [*Ib. fol.* 97.] . . . . . . | 177 |
| — | April | 24. | Sustaining of ministers, [*Ib. fol.* 99.] . . . | 177 |
| — | — | 28. | Extent payable by Inverkeithing, [*Ib. fol.* 99.] . | 178 |
| — | May | 1. | Gifts to the Queen and her " sumbeleir," [*Ib. fol.* 100.] | 178 |
| — | — | 3. | Sustaining of Ministers, [*Ib. fol.* 100.] . . . | 178 |

TABLE OF CONTENTS.

|  |  |  |  | PAGE |
|---|---|---|---|---|
| 1564, | May | 11. | Banquet to ambassador of Denmark, [*C.R. Vol. IV. fol.* 101.] | 179 |
| — | — | 15. | Payment for banquet, [*Ib.*] | 179 |
| — | — | 24. | Delivery of town's ammunition to the laird of Wittingham, [*Ib. fol.* 102.] | 179 |
| — | — | 31. | Gift to ambassador to King of Denmark, [*Ib.*] | 179 |
| — | June | 2. | Price of bread and mutton; duty on wine, [*Ib. fol.* 103.] | 180 |
| — | — | 16. | Charge by Queen as to building of tolbooth at Leith, [*Ib. fol.* 104.] | 180 |
| — | July | 9. | Prices of ale, mutton, and bread; annual payable to a chaplain, [*Ib. fol.* 106.] | 181 |
| — | — | 15. | Removal of stones near coal market; lint sown in the hospital yards; ships suspected of pest, [*Ib.*] | 181 |
| — | August | 2. | Clearing of haven of Leith, [*Ib.*] | 182 |
| — | — | 9. | Acquisition of Kirk of Field, [*Ib. fol.* 107.] | 182 |
| — | — | 11. | Watch over persons suspected of pest; repair of town walls, [*Ib. fol.* 107, 108.] | 182 |
| — | — | 18. | Substitute minister during absence of John Knox and John Craig, [*Ib. fol.* 108.] | 183 |
| — | — | 25. | Agreement as to Kirk of Field; a person cleansed of the pest; disladening of ships, [*Ib. fol.* 109.] | 184 |
| — | September | 1. | Against narrowing of common passages, [*Ib.*] | 184 |
| — | — | 8. | Payment for minister and of expenses to St. Andrews, [*Ib. fol.* 110.] | 185 |
| — | — | 18. | Watch over merchandise taken from a ship, [*Ib.*] | 185 |
| — | — | 20. | Leet of craftsmen for council, [*Ib. fol.* 111.] | 185 |
| — | — | 27. | Act as to election, and protest by craftsman, [*Ib.*] | 186 |
| — | — | 28. | Crafts ordained to present new tickets, [*Ib. fol.* 112.] | 186 |
| — | — | 30. | Other ticket produced by crafts; claim of deacon of candlemakers; as to assessors voting, [*Ib.*] | 186 |
| — | October | 8. | Price of ale and bread, [*Ib. fol.* 113.] | 187 |
| — | — | 30. | Act as to working cloth, etc., [*Ib. fol.* 114.] | 187 |
| — | November | 3. | Obligation by litsters; regulations as to their trade, [*Ib. fol.* 114.] | 187 |
| — | — | 8. | Admission of burgesses, [*Ib. fol.* 115.] | 188 |

## TABLE OF CONTENTS. xvii

|  |  |  | | PAGE |
|---|---|---|---|---|
| 1564, November | 17. | Passage to Kirk of Field port. [*C.R. Vol. IV. fol.* 115.] | | 189 |
| — | — | 25. | Kirk and kirkyard, [*Ib. fol.* 117.] | 189 |
| — | — | 28. | Place of hide, wool, and skin market, [*Ib. fol.* 118-9.] | 189 |
| — | — | 29. | Claim by schoolmaster for rent and fee; rent of John Knox's house; lighting of streets, [*Ib. fol.* 119.] | 190 |
| — | — | 30. | Collection of ministers' stipend, [*Ib. fol.* 120.] | 191 |
| — | December | 12. | Price of wine, [*Ib. fol.* 120.] | 191 |
| — | — | 25. | Sustentation of ministers and poor, [*Ib.* 121-2.] | 191 |
| 1564-5, January | 2. | Obligation by crafts as to sustaining ministers and poor; gift to Queen, [*Ib. fol.* 122-3.] | | 192 |
| — | — | 6. | Sustaining of poor and ministers; an arrow maker, [*Ib. fol.* 123.] | 193 |
| — | — | 17. | Charge by Queen to pay schoolmaster his annual fee, [*Ib.*] | 193 |
| — | — | 24. | Set of house to officer in Leith; eating flesh on Friday and Saturday; keeping order at kirk door, [*Ib. fol.* 124.] | 194 |
| — | February | 3. | Sword to be used as heading sword, [*Ib. fol.* 125.] | 194 |
| — | — | 7. | Order in the council house, [*Ib.*] | 195 |
| — | — | 21. | Ordinance as to sustaining the poor, [*Ib. fol.* 126.] | 195 |
| — | March | 2. | Poinding of goods for sustaining the poor, [*Ib.*] | 195 |
| 1565, | April | 30. | Accusation of assaulting a priest, [*Ib. fol.* 128.] | 195 |
| — | May | 11. | Writings by Queen as to master of grammar school; rent and fees to be paid him, [*Ib.*] | 196 |
| — | — | 12. | Commissioners to Queen as to contribution to the poor, [*Ib. fol.* 129.] | 197 |
| — | — | 31. | Commissioners to convention at Perth, [*Ib.*] | 198 |
| — | June | 22. | Price of wine, [*Ib. fol.* 130.] | 198 |
| — | — | 30. | Armour and weapons for inhabitants, [*Ib.*] | 198 |
| — | August | 3. | Completion of wall at Leith Wynd, [*Ib.*] | 198 |
| — | — | 4. | Extent for furnishing soldiers, [*Ib.*] | 198 |
| — | — | 23. | Charge by Queen to depose provost; his resignation; commissioners to Queen; discharge of John Knox, [*Ib. fol.* 130-1.] | 199 |

c

TABLE OF CONTENTS.

|  |  |  |  | PAGE |
|---|---|---|---|---|
| 1565, | August | 24. | The laird of Craigmillar accepted as provost and admitted burgess; extent for licence to abide from army; charge by King and Queen to set a Frenchman at liberty, [*C.R. Vol. IV. fol.* 131-2.] | 200 |
| — | — | 25. | Money to be raised for licence to abide from army, [*Ib. fol.* 132.] | 201 |
| — | — | 26. | Licence to inhabitants to abide from army; charge to pay composition; instructions and ordinances by King and Queen; [*Ib. fol.* 132-3.] | 202 |
| — | — | 28. | Nightly watch appointed, [*Ib. fol.* 133.] | 204 |
| — | September | 3. | Instructions by King and Queen as to rebels, etc., [*Ib. fol.* 134.] | 204 |
| — | — | 7. | Command by King and Queen as to hanging two soldiers, [*Ib. fol.* 135.] | 206 |
| — | — | 12. | Fee to session clerk, [*Ib.*] | 206 |
| — | — | 17. | Extent for licence to abide from army, [*Ib.*] | 206 |
| — | — | 26. | Charge by King and Queen as to election of new council, [*Ib.*] | 207 |
| — | — | 28. | Money borrowed for loan to King and Queen, [*Ib. fol.* 136.] | 207 |
| — | October | 12. | Inventory of property formerly belonging to priests, etc.; act as to convening of council, [*Ib. fol.* 139.] | 208 |
| — | November | 14. | Pudding and sheep head market; delivery of charters, etc., [*Ib. fol.* 141.] | 209 |
| — | — | 15. | Stipend to John Knox, [*Ib.*] | 210 |
| — | December | 4. | Gifts to the Queen and the provost, [*Ib. fol.* 142.] | 210 |
| — | — | 11. | Prices of wild meat; imposition on wines, [*Ib. fol.* 143.] | 210 |
| — | — | 21. | Commissioners to the Kirk; prices of wines, [*Ib.*] | 211 |
| 1565-6, | March | 19. | Expenses of two bailies to Dunbar, [*Ib. fol.* 145.] | 211 |
| — | — | 20. | Expenses of officer to Dunbar; payments to musicians, [*Ib.*] | 211 |
| 1566, | April | 5. | Gift to David Chalmer of clerkship of burgh, [*Ib.*] | 212 |
| — | — | 15. | Letter by Queen as to superiority of Leith; supplication as to intromission with town of Leith, [*Ib. fol.* 147.] | 213 |

## TABLE OF CONTENTS.

| | | | | PAGE |
|---|---|---|---|---|
| 1566, | May | 8. | Gift of a chaplainry; books for Queen's lodging, [*C.R. Vol. IV. fol.* 148.] | 214 |
| — | — | 17. | Payment for torches used in visiting Queen after slaughter of David Ricio, [*Ib.*] | 214 |
| — | — | 29. | Gift of wine to provost, [*Ib. fol.* 150.] | 215 |
| — | June | 8. | Bedrels of St Mary's wynd, [*Ib.*] | 215 |
| — | — | 19. | Payments to master of High School, [*Ib. fol.* 151.] | 215 |
| — | — | 21. | A papist set at liberty at command of Queen, [*Ib.*] | 215 |
| — | July | 19. | Alms to Trinity College; price of malt, [*Ib. fol.* 152.] | 216 |
| — | — | 24. | Payments for "convoying" a highlandman, [*Ib.*] | 216 |
| — | August | 2. | Gift to provost of excheit of a convict; expenses of scaffold, [*Ib. fol.* 152.] | 216 |
| — | September | 13. | Letter by Queen as to punishment of fornicators; keeping of the Greyfriars yard, [*Ib. fol.* 154.] | 217 |
| — | — | 18. | Rejoicings at the Prince's birth, [*Ib. fol.* 156.] | 219 |
| — | — | 25. | Payment of rent of minister's house, [*Ib.*] | 219 |
| — | October | 1. | Letter by Queen as to choosing of provost, bailies, and others, [*Ib.*] | 219 |
| — | — | 3. | Another letter as to election, [*Ib. fol.* 157.] | 220 |
| — | — | 4. | Election of councillors and office-bearers; keepers of the kirk, [*Ib.*] | 220 |
| — | — | 9. | Gallows at the Burgh Muir, [*Ib. fol.* 158.] | 221 |
| — | — | 11. | Persons to be admitted within the bar, [*Ib.*] | 221 |
| — | — | 14. | Sundry annual acts passed; closets; curing skins; waulkers; adulterers and fornicators; extent for expenses of baptism of Prince; payment to trumpeter, [*Ib. fol.* 158-164.] | 222 |
| — | — | 18. | Acts as to neighbourhoods or new buildings, [*Ib. fol.* 165.] | 22 |
| — | — | 22. | Price of wine, [*Ib.*] | 224 |
| — | — | 23. | Breaking of common muir, [*Ib. fol.* 166.] | 224 |
| — | — | 30. | Letter by Queen as to superiority of Leith, [*Ib. fol.* 167.] | 224 |
| — | November | 13. | Repair of a beacon, [*Ib. fol.* 170.] | 225 |
| — | — | 27. | Weight of mace; repair of sun horologe, [*Ib. fol.* 172-3.] | 225 |
| — | December | . | Regulations as to skinning sheep and bringing skins to market, [*Ib. fol.* 175.] | 225 |

## TABLE OF CONTENTS.

|  |  |  | PAGE |
|---|---|---|---|
| 1566, December | 16. | Refreshments for extenters, [*C.R. Vol. IV. fol.* 177.] | 226 |
| — — | 20. | Commissioners to general assembly; headmanship of St Paul's work; lock for prison; fee to schoolmaster, [*Ib.*] | 226 |
| 1566-7, January | 10. | Request by Queen to delay taking possession of Leith, [*Ib. fol.* 179.] | 227 |
| — — | 31. | Provost's ox; against children playing in kirk; yearly pension to procurator fiscal, [*Ib. fol.* 180.] | 227 |
| — February | 11. | Back door at Kirk of Field to be built up, [*Ib. fol.* 181.] | 228 |
| — — | 26. | Death of treasurer, and election of another, [*Ib. fol.* 182.] | 228 |
| — March | 8. | Receipt of money disbursed for superiority of Leith, [*Ib. fol.* 183.] | 228 |
| — — | 12. | Grant of annuals for sustaining ministers, [*Ib.*] | 229 |
| — — | 19. | Provost and bailies desired to get artillery from castle, [*Ib.*] | 229 |
| 1567, April | 4. | Kirk and kirk yard to be kept clean, [*Ib. fol.* 184.] | 229 |
| — — | 11. | Proclamation against "bickeraris," [*Ib. fol.* 185.] | 229 |
| — — | 24. | Repair of a horologe and purchase of another, [*Ib.*] | 230 |
| — May | 7. | Building of town wall at the Kirk of Field, [*Ib. fol.* 186.] | 230 |
| — — | 12. | Ground at Newhaven to be set to salt makers, [*Ib.*] | 230 |
| — — | 16. | Ground desired by salt makers to be visited; gift of burgess-ship to porter of castle, [*Ib. fol.* 187.] | 230 |
| — June | 4. | Set to three Englishmen of ground at Newhaven to make salt on, [*Ib. fol.* 191.] | 231 |
| — — | 11. | Incoming to town of lords convened in arms for avenging king's murder, etc., [*Ib.*] | 231 |
| — — | 18. | Act as to making of burgesses, [*Ib.*] | 231 |
| — — | 20. | A prisoner set at liberty at Queen's request, [*Ib. fol.* 192.] | 232 |
| — July | 2. | Court of superiority of Leith; general weaponschawing; bond by nobility for avenging King's murder, [*Ib. fol.* 192-3.] | 233 |
| — — | 9. | Mounting of artillery, [*Ib. fol.* 194.] | 236 |

## TABLE OF CONTENTS.

| | | | | PAGE |
|---|---|---|---|---|
| 1567, | July | 23. | Bailie of south-west quarter; defence of the town; bond to be made betwixt the town and the council; preventing passage over walls, [*C.R. Vol. IV. fol.* 195-6.] | 237 |
| — | — | 25. | Bond between castle and town; commissioners to attend at coronation of King; night watch, [*Ib. fol.* 197.] | 238 |
| — | — | 30. | Persons unlawed for not setting forth fires at coronation, [*Ib.*] | 238 |
| — | August | 1. | Repair of town wall; contract for building town wall, [*Ib. fol.* 198.] | 239 |
| — | — | 8. | Repairing walls, [*Ib. fol.* 199.] | 240 |
| — | — | 13. | Loan of munition to laird of Grange, [*Ib.*] | 240 |
| — | — | 20. | Apothecaries to desist from selling spices, [*Ib.*] | 240 |
| — | — | 27. | Inventory of annuals; collector appointed; payment to trumpeters, [*Ib. fol.* 199, 200.] | 240 |
| — | September | 11. | Appointment of collector of duties and annuals, [*Ib. fol.* 201.] | 241 |
| — | October | 1. | Locks and keys of new well, [*Ib. fol.* 203.] | 242 |
| — | — | 3. | Stones of Blackfriars to be restored for building hospital; penalty for drawing blood in fighting, [*Ib. fol.* 204-5.] | 242 |
| — | — | 10. | Visitation of kirk, [*Ib. fol.* 205.] | 243 |
| — | November | 7. | Officer of Leith to receive button with town's mark, [*Ib. fol.* 206.] | 243 |
| — | — | 10. | Gift of Trinity College to Edinburgh; master of work of hospital appointed, [*Ib.*] | 243 |
| — | — | 14. | Building of hospital, [*Ib. fol.* 207.] | 244 |
| — | — | 20. | Blackfriars lands feued, [*Ib. fol.* 208.] | 244 |
| — | December | 10. | "Ansenyeis" to be made; players on musical instruments, [*Ib. fol.* 211.] | 244 |
| — | — | 24. | Equipment of burgesses, [*Ib. fol.* 212.] | 244 |
| 1567-8, February | | 18. | Altarage of St. Anthony, [*Ib.*] | 245 |
| — | — | 20. | John Knox's house rent, [*Ib. fol.* 213.] | 245 |
| — | March | 3. | Feu-duty payable to chaplain of St. James' altar and the hospital, [*Ib. fol.* 214.] | 245 |

TABLE OF CONTENTS.

| | | | | PAGE |
|---|---|---|---|---|
| 1567-8, March | | 19. | Fines payable to hospital; repair of pier, causeways, and kirk; price of material in Blackfriars yard, [*C.R. Vol. IV. fol.* 215.] | 245 |
| — | — | 24. | Money expended on pier, causeways, and kirk, [*Ib.*] | 246 |
| 1568, March | | 27. | Repairs on kirk, [*Ib. fol.* 217.] | 247 |
| — | April | 7. | Pension to an aged Black-friar, [*Ib.*] | 247 |
| — | — | 9. | Commission to Regent as to licences to carry victuals out of realm, [*Ib.*] | 247 |
| — | — | 13. | Collector of contributions to hospital, [*Ib.*] | 247 |
| — | — | 20. | Gift of two beidmanships; gift of a burgess and guildship, [*Ib.*] | 248 |
| — | May | 8. | Supplication of the deacon and brethren of the hammermen; extent for defence of town; weaponshawing, [*Ib.*] | 248 |
| — | — | 12. | Nightly watch to be kept; "sweschis" to pass nightly through town, [*Ib. fol.* 218.] | 249 |
| — | — | 19. | Writing to magistrates of Campheir as to Scotchmen dwelling there; deacon to advise with crafts as to passing to army, [*Ib.*] | 249 |
| — | June | 2. | Licence to abide from army to be craved, [*Ib. fol.* 219.] | 249 |
| — | — | 4. | A burgesship gratis; extent for furnishing soldiers, [*Ib.*] | 249 |
| — | July | 17. | Work at North Loch; repair of wells, [*Ib. fol.* 220.] | 250 |
| — | — | 28. | Master of High School, [*Ib.*] | 250 |
| — | August | 6. | Repair of town walls, [*Ib.*] | 250 |
| — | — | 11. | Crafts to be convened; artillery borrowed; nightly watch, [*Ib. fol.* 221.] | 251 |
| — | — | 26. | Appointment of schoolmaster; stent for expenses of down-getting duty on wine, [*Ib. fol.* 221-2.] | 251 |
| — | September | 5. | Stones from Dunbar to shore of Leith, [*Ib. fol.* 222.] | 252 |
| — | October | 5. | Letter from Lord Regent as to election of council, [*Ib.*] | 252 |
| — | — | 13. | Visitation of sick persons at the Burghmuir, [*Ib. fol.* 223.] | 253 |
| — | — | 15. | Statutes for the bailies of the muir and ordering of the pest; a bailie urged to continue in office; statutes as to the pest; gift of two beadmanships; gift of a benefice, [*Ib. fol.* 223-6.] | 253 |

## TABLE OF CONTENTS.    xxiii

| | | | | PAGE |
|---|---|---|---|---|
| 1568, October | | 16. | Appointment of bailies depute to judge upon annuals and duties, [*C.R. Vol. IV. fol.* 225.] | . 256 |
| — | — | 17. | Payment for pikes, [*Ib.*] | . 256 |
| — | — | 21. | Burgesses required to remain within town, [*Ib. fol.* 226.] | 256 |
| — | November | 10. | People cleansed of pest; extent for sustaining poor; complaint by Lawson of Hierigs against council for building dike at South Loch, [*Ib. fol.* 226.] | . 257 |
| — | — | 14. | Inhabitants required to repair injury to South Loch by Lawson of Hierigs, [*Ib.*] | . 257 |
| — | — | 18. | Watch of eighteen persons; houses adjoining town walls to be demolished; renewing of causeway, [*Ib. fol.* 226-7.] | . 257 |
| — | — | 19. | Repair of John Knox's dwelling-house; victuals for poor infected with pest, [*Ib. fol.* 227.] | . 258 |
| — | December | 17. | Nightly Watch, [*Ib. fol.* 229.] | . 258 |
| — | — | 22. | Officers of the muir discharged, pest having abated, [*Ib.*] | 259 |
| 1568-9, January | | 1. | Threatened attack by lords of west country, [*Ib. fol.* 229.] | 259 |
| — | — | 7. | Pulpit in Over Tolbooth for preaching to papists; taverns to be closed in time of preaching, [*Ib.*] | . 259 |
| — | February | 11. | Entry of schoolmaster, [*Ib. fol.* 231.] | . 259 |
| — | — | 17. | Extent for furnishing men to the Regent, [*Ib.*] | . 259 |
| — | March | 4. | Rent of house occupied by John Knox, [*Ib. fol.* 232.] | . 260 |
| 1569, | April | 1. | Annuals of the "Senys," [*Ib. fol.* 235.] | . 260 |
| — | — | 6. | Pest St. Andrews; eschaet goods; kirk gear, [*Ib.*] | . 260 |
| — | — | 9. | Money to be clipped, [*Ib. fol.* 237.] | . 261 |
| — | May | 28. | Attendance of cleansers; burial of dead, [*Ib. fol.* 240.] | 261 |
| — | June | 1. | Stones taken from Kirk of Leith to bulwark, [*Ib.*] | . 262 |
| — | — | 15. | Water gate in Leith Wynd, [*Ib. fol.* 241.] | . 262 |
| — | July | 29. | Stipend of reader, [*Ib. fol.* 243.] | . 262 |
| — | August | 10. | Annuals payable to hospital and minister, [*Ib. fol.* 244.] | 262 |
| — | — | 12. | Collector for the ministry accepts office, [*Ib.*] | . 262 |
| — | September | 7. | Inquiry as to encroachments on North Loch, [*Ib.*] | . 262 |
| — | — | 16. | Pikes to be gathered and put in munition house, [*Ib. fol.* 245.] | . 263 |
| — | — | 21. | Arrival of ships suspected of pest, [*Ib.*] | . 263 |

| | | | | PAGE |
|---|---|---|---|---|
| 1569, September | 23. | As to what craftsmen should be admitted to the council, [C.R.Vol. IV. fol. 246.] | | 263 |
| — October | 7. | Removal from town of excommunicated persons, [Ib. fol. 246.] | | 264 |
| — — | 14. | Letter from Regent asking council to depose the laird of Grange from office of provost, [Ib. fol. 247.] | | 264 |
| — — | 21. | Prices of ale and bread, [Ib. fol. 248.] | | 265 |
| — — | 26. | Master of "foul muir" to be cleansed and discharged, [Ib.] | | 265 |
| — November | 16. | Provost's ox at Alhallowmas fair, [Ib.] | | 265 |
| — December | 2. | Desire of candlemakers to choose a deacon, [Ib. fol. 249.] | | 266 |
| — — | 16. | Inhabitants of Leith to desist from selling wine, [Ib. fol. 250.] | | 266 |
| — — | 30. | Delivery of town from pest; payment to officers, [Ib.] | | 267 |
| 1569-70, January | 20. | Duty of "clerk male" to be given to reader; privileges of gratis burgesses, [Ib. fol. 252.] | | 267 |
| — — | 25. | Troubles after murder of Regent; watch appointed; keeping of ports; proclamation as to weapons, [Ib.] | | 267 |
| — — | 27. | Commissioners to promise assistance to Lord Morton; as to removal of lords of session; ports and artillery to be put in order, [Ib. fol. 252-3.] | | 268 |
| — February | 1. | Commissioners to convene with lords of nobility, [Ib. fol. 253.] | | 269 |
| — March | 3. | Commission of 27th January ratified, [Ib. fol. 254.] | | 269 |
| — — | 8. | Guard during time of convention; officers to await on bailies, [Ib.] | | 269 |
| — — | 22. | Watch to be continued; South Loch to be repaired; keeping of ports, [Ib. fol. 254-5.] | | 270 |
| — — | 24. | Rent of grammar school in Friar Wynd, [Ib. fol. 255.] | | 270 |
| 1570, April | 12. | Answer giving welcome to lords of west country, [Ib.] | | 271 |
| — — | 14. | Addition to night watch, [Ib.] | | 271 |
| — — | 19. | Upholding of town clock, [Ib.] | | 271 |

TABLE OF CONTENTS.

| | | | | PAGE |
|---|---|---|---|---|
| 1570, | May | 11. | Gift to laird of Grange, captain of the castle, [*Ib. fol.* 256.] | 271 |
| — | May | 17. | Proclamation of weaponshawing, [*C.R. Vol. IV. fol.* 256.] | 272 |
| — | — | 26. | Missives to burghs as to Scots ships in France, [*Ib.*] | 272 |
| — | June | 2. | Surety for a printer not printing books without licence, [*Ib.*] | 272 |
| — | — | 16. | Writing sent to Earl of Huntly, [*Ib. fol.* 257.] | 272 |
| — | July | 12. | Commissioners to convention for electing a Regent; decreet as to usurping offices of deacons of crafts in town of Leith and Barony of Restalrig, [*Ib. fol.* 259.] | 272 |
| — | — | 14. | Contract between council and Captain Cokburne as to discharge of proclamation against merchandice with France, [*Ib. fol.* 258.] | 274 |
| — | — | 19. | Proclamation against buying certain prizes brought in French ships; meeting of commissioners of burghs, [*Ib. fol.* 260.] | 275 |
| — | August | 5. | Artillery lent to Jedburgh, [*Ib.*] | 275 |
| — | — | 9. | Watch during Regent's absence, [*Ib. fol.* 261.] | 276 |
| — | — | 11. | Deacons to bewarned to consult as to common affairs, [*Ib.*] | 276 |
| — | — | 15. | Regulations as to watch, [*Ib.*] | 276 |
| — | — | 23. | A carter fined for breaking the Sabbath, [*Ib. fol.* 262.] | 276 |
| — | — | 24. | Money for support of ministers, [*Ib.*] | 277 |
| — | September | 8. | Old holes of Muse well to be opened, [*Ib. fol.* 263.] | 277 |
| — | — | 27. | List of craftsmen for election of two councillors, [*Ib.*] | 277 |
| — | October | 18. | Stance for cranes; booth doors to be shut up, [*Ib. fol.* 265.] | 277 |
| — | — | 20. | Protest by provost as to his election; extent for expenses of ambassadors to England, [*Ib.*] | 277 |
| — | — | 25. | Deacons to be convened as to support of ministers; loosing arrestments of ships in France, [*Ib.*] | 278 |
| — | November | 1. | Answer by deacons as to support of ministers, [*Ib. fol.* 266.] | 278 |

TABLE OF CONTENTS.

|  |  |  |  | PAGE |
|---|---|---|---|---|
| 1570, November | 8. | Commissioner sent to King of France, [Ib.] | . | . 279 |
| — — | 15. | Collectors of ministers' stipends, [Ib.] | . . | . 279 |
| — — | 18. | Barrier of timber to be built before Regent's gate, C.R. Vol. IV. fol. 266.] | . . . | . 279 |
| — — | 29. | Repair of shore, pier and bulwarks of Leith, [Ib. fol. 267.] | | 279 |
| — December | 1. | Duty granted by master mariners for repair of pier and havin of Leith, [Ib.] | . . . | . 280 |
| — — | 6. | Statute imposing the duty; decreet against craftsmen of Leith, [Ib. fol. 267, 269.] | . . . | . 280 |
| — — | 8. | Claim by farmers of common muir, it having been "flayne" by captain of the castle, [Ib. fol. 269] | | 281 |
| — — | 27. | Nightly watch; keeping of ports, [Ib. fol. 270.] | . | . 281 |
| 1570-1, February | 2. | Captain of castle to be consulted as to defence of town, [Ib. fol. 271.] | | . 282 |
| — — | 3. | Report of captain's answer, [Ib. fol. 271.] | . | . 282 |
| — — | 7. | Prices of burgesships and gildships, [Ib. fol. 271-2] | | . 282 |
| — — | 9. | Proclamation against excommunicated persons; a bailie and the treasurer sent to the Regent, [Ib. fol. 272.] | | 283 |
| — — | 16. | Liberty to be asked for ships to pass to France, [Ib.] | | 283 |
| — March | 14. | Proclamation against trafficking with ships arrived in Leith with prizes, [Ib. fol. 273.] | . . . | . 283 |
| 1571, — | 30. | Protest against setting a prisoner at liberty; extent for expenses in getting down duty on wine and in obtaining liberty for ships, [Ib. fol. 274.] | . | . 284 |
| — April | 14. | Price of Dutch beer; writings sent to Regent, [Ib. fol. 275.] | . . . . . . | . 284 |
| — — | 20. | Thanks to the Earl of Morton, Lord Dunfermline and the provost for their services, [Ib.] | . . . | . 285 |
| — — | 28. | Captain of the castle asked not to suffer inhabitants to be molested, [Ib.] | . . . . . | . 285 |
| — May | 1. | Writings sent to Regent intimating arrangement between the town and the captain of the castle, [Ib.] . | . | . 285 |

## APPENDIX.

List of the Aldermen or Provosts, Presidents, Bailies, and other Office-Bearers of the City, from A.D. 1527 to A.D. 1571, . . . . 287

# EXTRACTS

FROM THE

# RECORDS OF THE BURGH OF EDINBURGH.

### 31 *March* 1557.

THE prouest baillies and counsale consentit that thair suld be warit vpoun the bigging of the Newhavin, of the commoun gudis this yeir, fyve hundreth pundis vsuall money of this realm. *Anent the Newhavin.*

### 2 *April* 1557.

In presens of Alexander Barroun and William Ker baillies sittand in jugement, Dauid Kinloch desyret ansuer of the wryting producit be him the xxiiij day of Merche last bypast fra the Quenis grace, and the saidis baillies declarit that thai wald obey the Quenis grace wryting, and thairupoun the said Dauid askit instrumentis. *Kinloch, bailies*

### 9 *April* 1557.

The baillies and counsale ordanis the thesaurer, Alexander Park, to caus mak on the townis expensis foure formes to the Magdalene Chapell, that the lordis and auditouris that cummis thair daylie to the cessoun may sitt thairon. *Precept anent the formes.*

*14th April* 1557.

Extent of jᵐ li. Queen's marriage.

The prouest baillies and counsall convenit at the command of the wryting vndirwrittin and presentit to thame be the Justice Clerk, off the quhilk the tenour followis : Apud Edinburgh ix die mensis Aprilis 1557. The quhilk day, forsamekill as the lordis being assemblit at the last conventioun in Striueling the last day of Marche last bypast for the honorabill mariage to be completit betuix our Souerane and the Dolphin of France, and setting fordwart of the hie and weehtie caussis thairof, and for performnyng of the honorabill chargis and expens thairof and of the nobillitie quhilk salhappin to be present at the doing of the samyn, and for vther resonabill and effectuous caussis contenit in the acts maid be the said lordis, hes concludit devysit and ordanit that ane taxt of thre scoir thowsand pundis be rasit and vpliftit vpoun this realme, that ane half thairof be the spirituall estait and the vther half be the temporall estait, quhairof the burrowis pairt of the samyn extendis to the sowme of ten thousand pundis to be payit at the termes following, that is to say, the sowme of ijᵐ vᶜ li. at the xv day of Julij nixt to cum, vther ijᵐ vᶜ li. at the feist of Pasche nyxt thairefter following, vther ijᵐ vᶜ li. at the feist of Michaelmes nixt thairefter followand, and the sowm of ijᵐ vᶜ li. in compleitt payment of the said sowm of xᵐ li. at the feist of Pasche nixt thairefter followand, and hes ordanit letteres to be direct to command and charge the prouestis aldermen and baillies of all the borrowis of this realme that thai inbring and deliuer the said sowme of ijᵐ vᶜ li. at euery ane of the termes foresaidis to [*blank*], collectour thairto and his deputtis, vndir the payne of rebellioun, and failyeing thairof ony of the saidis termes being bypast to put thame to the horne, as at mair lenth is contenit in the saidis acts maid be the said lordis thairupoun. Thairfoir the lordis of secreit counsall ordanis commandis and chairgis the prouest baillies and counsall of the burgh of Edinburgh that thai with all diligence convene and taxt all and sindry the borrowis within this realme, ilk ane efferand to thair pairtis of the foresaid sowme of xᵐ li. to be payit at the termes respectiue aboue specifiit, and the samyn being maid ordanis letteres to be direct chargeing all and syndry the prouestis aldermen and baillies of the saidis burrowis that thai and ilk of ane of thame respectiue inbring and delyuer thair pairtis of the said sowme quhilk thai salhappin to be taxt to at euery ane of the termes foirsaidis to the foirsaid collectour and his deputtis, vndir the said pane of rebellioun and putting of thaim to our horne, and failyeing thairof, ony of the saidis termes being bypast, to denunce the disobeyares our Souerane Ladyis rebellis and putt thaim to the horne; provyding alwys that ye tak consideratioun of the greit ruyne poverte and decay of the burgh of Hadingtoun and mak modeficatioun of thair taxt and augment and lay the samyn vpoun vthers burrowes nocht brynt nor destroyit, and conforme to the Quenis Grace and lordis mynd declarit thairvpoun. *Sequuntur subscriptiones Dominorum:* CASSILLIS, Thesaurer; Ro. ORCHADENSIS episcopus; J., clericus registri; BALLENDEN. Quhilk heand considerit be thame and efter diuers consultationis had thairupoun, and specialie anent the supplie to be done to the said burgh of Hadingtoun conform to the tenour of the said wryting, fyndis that of the haill extent mentionat in the said wryting to be vpliftit of the hail borrowis extending to x$^m$ li. the towne of Hadingtoun may pay thairof iij$^c$ iij li. xij s., and for support of the said towne of Hadingtoun beand brynt and destroyit the saidis prouest baillies and counsall hes extentit aboue the haill sowme of x$^m$ li. vpoun all the borrowis, ilk ane efferand to thair pairt except Edinburgh, the sowme of j$^e$ vj li. iij s., quhilk superexcrescence the saidis prouest baillies and counsale ordanis to be vpliftit and samekill tane of the extent of Hadingtoun, and becaus thair is na superexcrescence on the burgh of Edinburgh by thair just ferd pairt, and haifland consideratioun of the poverty and dekey of Hadingtoun, ordanis vther l li. to be tane of the extent of Hadingtoun and samekill augmentit to the extent of Edinburgh at this tyme alanerlie, and sua the extent of Hadingtoun to be alanerlie, of the haill x$^m$ li., j$^c$ xlvij li. ix s. Anent the rest of the borrowis thair particulare extentis followis, viz. :—

Margin note: Extent of j$^m$ li. Queen's marriage.

| | | | | |
|---|---|---|---|---|
| Edinburgh | ij$^m$ v$^c$ l li. | | Abirdene | ix$^c$ xlv li. |
| Strinelling | ij$^c$ lij li. xij s. vj d. | | Dunde | j$^m$ ij$^c$ lxv li. xj s. |
| Linlythqw | j$^c$ lj li. xvij s. vj d. | | Perth | vij$^c$ xlij li. x s. |
| Rothesay | lxvij li. x s. | | Banff | lxvij li. x s. |
| Dumbartane | lxxxiiij li. xviij d. | | Dunfermling | j$^e$ j li. v s. |
| Renfrew | j$^e$ j li. v s. | | Crail | lx li. |

4   EXTRACTS FROM THE RECORDS   [1557.

Extent of jᵐ li. Queen's marriage.

| | | | | | |
|---|---|---|---|---|---|
| Ruglin | . . | lxvij li. x s. | Forfar | . . . | 1 li. xij s. vj d. |
| Air | . . | ijᶜ xxxvj li. v s. | Brechane | | jᶜ lxviij li. xv s. |
| Irwyne | . | jᶜ xxxv li. | Montros | . . | ijᶜ lxx li. |
| Glasqw | . . | ijᶜ ij li. x s. | Elgyin | . . . | jᶜ j li. v s. |
| Kirkenbrycht | . | jᶜ li. v s. | Innernes | . jᶜ lxviij li. xv s. |
| Wigtoun | . . . | jᶜ j li. v s. | Abirbrothok | jᶜ xxxv li. |
| Quhithorn | . . | jᶜ j li. v s. | Sanctandrois | . iijᶜ li. |
| Lanerk | . | lxxxiiij li. xviij d. | Cowpar | . . | ijᶜ lxx li. |
| Jedburgh | . . | jᶜ j li. v s. | Culane | . . | xxxiiij li. x s. |
| Selkirk | . . | lxvij li. x s. | Fores | . . | lxxxiiij li. xviij d. |
| Peblis | . . | lxvij li. x s. | Nairn | . . | xxxiiij li. x s. |
| Hadingtoun | jᶜ xlvij li. ix s. | Thane | . . . . | 1 li. xij s. vj d. |
| Northberwik | xxxiiij li. x s. | Dysart | . . | jᶜ xviij li. ij s. vj d. |
| Dunbar | . . | lxvij li. x s. | Kirkealdy | . . | lxvij li. x s. |
| Lawder | . . | lxvij li. x s. | | | |
| Dumfries | jᶜ lxxiiij li. xviij s. | | | |

18 *April* 1557.

Flescheouris.
The quhilk day, James Kennedy of [*blank*], brother to the erle of Cassillis, presentit ane writting to the baillies and counsale of the burgh, direct to the provest and baillies thairof be our Soverane Ladeyis mother, Mary Quene Drowrar and Regent of this realm, subscrynit be hir grace hand of the quhilk the tennour followis:—Provest and bailyeis of our burgh of Edinburgh: Forsamekill as it is perfytlie wnderstand to ws that ye haue dischargeit the landwart flescheouris of all selling and breking of flesche aboue the tolbuth of Edinburgh, quhilk is expres aganis the commoun weill: Quhairfor we charge yow that, incontinent efter the sicht heirof, ye caus proclamatioun and ordinance be maid that all maner of flescheouris haif priuelege and liberte to slay sell and brek flesche aboue the said tolbuth as thai haif done in tymes bygane, and discharge all maner of actis and statutis gif ye ony haif maid in the contrar thairof for the caus aboue writtin as ye will ansuer to ws thairupon. Subscriuit with our hand, at Striueling the xvj day of Aprile 1557. MARIE. R. Quhairfoir the saidis baillies and counsale ordanis that na

maner of persone, flescheour nor vtheris, tak vpoun hand to stope trubill or Flescheouris.
mak impediment to oney of the saidis landwart flescheouris aboun the
tollbuith to slay sell and breke flesche as thai haif done in tyme bygane,
conforme to the said writting, vnder all hiest pane and charge that thai or
oney of thame may incur thairthrow.

### 5 June 1557.

In presens of the baillies, Alexander Barroun, William Ker and Alane Litera Regine,
Dikkyesoun, sittand in jugement, maister Thomas Makcalyeane advocat, Makcalyeane.
presentit the writting vnder writtin, subscriuit be the Quenis Grace, and
desirit the samyn to be registrat in thir buikis, and the act thairin contenit
to be deleitt conforme to the said writting, of the quhilk the tennour
followis: Prouest baillies and counsale of Edinburgh, greting: Oure will is
that the act maid be yow in Nouember that last wes, discharging and
removing oure seruitour maister Thomas Makcalyeane fra the office of
assissorie quhilk he had of your burgh during our will, ceis expyre and be
deleit. Be thir presentis subscryuit with oure hand, at Edinburgh the
penult day of Maii the yeir of God jm fyve hundreth fifty sewin.

### 18 June 1557.

We do yon to witt: Forsamekle as oure Souerane Ladeis letteres direct Wappin
be the Lordis of Counsale ar direct to the prouest and baillies of this burgh, schawin.
chargeing thame to sett and proclame wappynschawingis within thair
boundis and jurisdictioun betuix this and the xxij day of Julii nixttocum,
and to that effect that thai limit and prefix ane conuenient place thairto,
that knawlege may be had quhat diligence euery man hes done within the
boundis and jurisdictioun of the said prouest and baillies sen the last
wappynschawing, for recouering of wappynis and armour, sik as is requirit
for thair estait, and gif ony persoun wer fund negligent and nocht sufficientlie prouidit in armour [as] said is, thai suld execute the painis contenit
in the act of parliament aganis thame with all rigour, conform to the
tennour thairof, as at mair lenth is contenit in the saidis letteres direct to
thame thairupoun; quhairfor the saidis prouest and baillies hes assignit
and assignis wappynschawing of the nychthouris and inhabitaris of this

## EXTRACTS FROM THE RECORDS [1557.

**Wappin-schawin.**

burgh, merchandis craftismen and all vtheris, to be haldin the xviij day of Julij nixttocum at twa efternone on the Borrowmyre and west end thairof, quhairfor I command and charge in our Soucrane Ladeis name hir gracis moder Marie Quene Drowriar and Regent of this realme, and in name and behalf of the proucst and baillies of this burgh, that all maner of personis induellaris within this burgh, merchandis craftismen and all vtheris, convene the said day place and hour foirsaid boddin in feir of weir in thair best array, ilk persoun efferand to his estait, conform to the tennour of the said act of parliament and vnder the panis contenit in the samin.

### 25 June 1557.

**Flescheouris.**

The quhilk day, the ballies and assassouris, vpoun the complaint maid be certane of the lordis of our Soucrane Ladeis sessioun and vtheris hir Hienes lieges, inhabitanttis of this burgh, vpoun the flescheouris of the samyn, for the oppressioun committit vpoun thame and hale inhabitanttis foresaidis be the saidis flescheouris in contrair the tenour of our Soucrane Ladeis ordinance maid vpoun the prices of flesche, ordanit the proclamatioun following to be maid be the belman through the toun, quhilk wes proclamyt be him in maner following: We do yow to wyt. Forsamekill as it is havelie menit to the proucst and baillies of this burgh be the inhabitanttis of the samyn and vtheris oure Soucrane Ladeis liegis resortand thairto, vpoun the exhorbitant prices vsit vpoun thame be the flescheouris and vtheris slaerris and braikerris of flesche within this burgh, contrair the tennour of oure Soucrane Ladeis actis and statutis maid vpoun the prices of flesche of before, heirfor I command and charge in oure Soucrane Ladeis name, the proucst and baillies of this burgh, that na maner of flescheour braikaris slaerris or sellaris of flesche, fremen or vtheris, tak vpoun hand fra this day furth to sell onye mwttoun of onye hiear prices nor the best mwttoun bowk for aucht schillingis, and the secundar for sex schillingis, with certificatioun to thame that failyeis thair hale flesche salbe escheit and disponit to the pure for the first falt, the second falt to be spanyt fra the libertie of thair said craft for yeir and day, and for the thrid and last falt to be dischargeit of thair fredom for evir.

and to be reput and haldin in all tymes cuming as wilful contempnaris and Flescheouris.
dissobeyaris of oure Soucrane Ladeis actis and ordinances; and this
proclamatioun maid the day foresaid.

The prouest baillies and counsale ordanis Alexander Park, Halberttis to
thesaurer, to by tua halberttis and deliuer the samyn to maister Alex- Wyndegaittis,
ander Logye and Danid Wyndegaittis, seriandis, in consideratioun seriandis.
the said Danidis halbertt wes brokin in the thrang at the banket maid
be the gude toun to ane greit man of Moscovia, quha wes schip brokin
at Petslego in his vayege towert Ingland, and to the said maister
Alexander becaus he hes had nane fra the begynning.

### 21 July 1557.

The baillies and counsale ordanis Alexander Park, thesaurer, and Sir Sanct Rowkis
William M'Dougall, maister of wark, to pas vpoun Monunday nixt and Chapell.
vesye Sanct Rowkis chapell quhilk is allegeit to thame to be rewynous and
falling doun, and to tak consideratioun quhat will mend the samyn, and
mak report thairof to the counsale vpoun Wedinsday nixt.

### 31 July 1557.

The prouest baillies and counsale ordanis Alexander Park, thesaurair, Newhavin.
and Sir Williame M'Dougall, maister of wark, to pas the morne and vesie
the wark of the Newhavin, and the laubouris maid thairnpoun be the men
laubouraris thairat, and quhat beting and repairing the samin misteris at
this tyme for vphalding and susteuing of samekle thairof as is ellis biggit,
and to tak consideratioun quhat money will satefie the samin, and mak
report thairof to the counsale vpoun Monunday nixt.

### 11 August 1557.

The prouest [bailies and council] being convenit in the ovir counsale Precept.
hous, ordanis the said thesaurer to deliuer to Sir Jhoun Wilsoun the sowme Wilsoun.
of fourtye twa pundis xij s. iij d. ob., as for the expenssis maid be the said
Sir Johnn, at the command of the prouest baillies and counsale, vpoun the
Newhavin, fra the xix day of Junii in the yeir of God j$^m$ v$^c$ lvij yeris vnto
the last day of Julii in the said yeir, . . . . . and discharges the said
werk in the menetyme.

8                 EXTRACTS FROM THE RECORDS              [1557.

Precept, Sanct Rowk.

The prouest baillies dene of gild and counsale foresaid ordanis the thesaurer, Alexander Park, with the avise of Sir William M'Dougall, maister of wark, to wair the sowme of ten pundis vpoun the beting and mending of Sanct Rokis chapell for this present yeir.

13 *August* 1557.

Precept for speris.

The prouest, William Kar and Allane Dickesoun baillies, James Carmychell dene of gild, Jhonn Young, Jhonn Sym, Richart Carmychell, and Archibald Lech, of the counsale, decernit and ordanit Alexander Park thesaurer, him self being present, to mak payment to Andro Kylle, speir makar in Sanct Jhonstoun, for thre hundreth speris bocht and arllit be the said prouest for seruing of the lieges and inhabitanttis of this burgh, and to pay for euery speir with the heid the sowme of vj s., and that this be done with diligence becaus of the wappinschawing that is at hand.

14 *August* 1557.

Wappinschewing.

The quhilk day, our Soverane Ladeis letteris being direct to the prouest and baillies of this burgh, bering in effect forsamekill as hir hienes with auise of hir darrest moder, etc., had direct letteris of before chargeing all and sindrye scherefflis stewarttis baillies prouestis aldermen etc, euery ane within his awin jurisdictioun, to set wappinschawingis at tymes prefixt, to the effect that it mycht be considerit how the lieges were providit in armour and wappinnis and faling of sufficient armour to poynd conforme to the actis of parliament, nochtwithstanding the quhilkis charges it is vnderstand to our said Soueranis derrest moder and lordis of counsale that the maist pairt of the liges of this realme at all wappinschewing wer destitut of sufficient armour and nocht sufficientlie prouidit, nor thairfor na pvnischment maid nor vnlawis vptaikin conforme to the saidis actis of parliament, quhairfor charge wes gevin be the saidis letteris to the prouest and baillies of this burgh that thay within viij dayin following causit set wappinschewing of new within the boundis of thair jurisdictioun, with certificatioun to euerye inhabitant thairof that war nocht sufficientlie providit in fensible armour at the said day efferring to thair estait that thay sould be poyndit conforme to the saidis actis, and gyf the saidis prouest and baillies

foresaidis faillit in vptaking of the saidis vnlawis that thay sould be  Wappinschew-
pvnist thairfor in thair persoun and guddis with all rigour; quhilkis letteris  ing.
being red and effect thairof considerrit be the saidis provest baillies and
counsale, causit William Douglas ane of thair seriandis pas to the mercat
croce of this burgh, and efter forme and tenour of the saidis letteris in our
said Soncrane Ladeis name, provest and baillies of this burgh as said is,
and command and charge all and sindry the inhabitantis foresaidis to
convene vpoun the west end of the Burrow Mwre vpoun the xxix day of
August instant at twa efter none providit as aboue, ilk persoun vnder the
pane of x li., and witnes William Stewert, Johnn Freir, Jhoun Charteris,
with vtheris diuerssis.

### 17 *August* 1557.

The provest baillies and counsale ordanis Alexander Park, thesaurer,  Precept.
to deliuer to Thomas Pettegrew, smyth, xx s., for lokis bandis and keyis
to the almereis in the clerkis chalmer.

[Proclamation made to all indwellers within the bounds, liberty, and jurisdic-
tion, to " convene vpoun Sonday nixt at twa eftir none vpoun the Burrow Muir of
this burgh at the oist parte of the samin be cist the Sister of the Senis, well bodin
in feir of weir, with sufficient armour, lang wappynnis, sik as pik speir and vtheris
fensabill lang armour, conforme to the auld consuetude of the realm."]

The provest baillies counsale and dekynnis, sittand in jugement, hes  Strang, bedrall.
gevin and grantis to Cristiane Strang, relict of vmquhile Bartilmo Fairlie,
the bedrelschip of Sanct Marie Wynde now vacand in thair handis throw
deces of vmquhile Jonett Gottersoun, with all proflittis emolimentis and
pertinentis thairof during all the dayis of hir lyfetyme.

### 17 *September* 1557.

In presens of the provest baillies counsale and dekynnis of craftis,  Regina, anent
comperit ane worschipfull man maister James M'Gill of Rankelour Nether  the furnessing of iije men.
clerk of register, and produceit the Quenis grace writting subscriuit with
hir hienes hand of the quhilk the tennour followis : Apud Edinburgh xvij°
Septembris 1557. Forsameckle as it is vnderstand to the Quenis grace and

10        EXTRACTS FROM THE RECORDS       [1557.

Regina, anent the furnessing of iije men

lordis of secreit counsale that to the proclamatioun of the army the mennis personis ar subject and thaim selflis haldin to pas furth conforme to the charge, thairfoir it is thocht resonable that gif the Quenis grace grantis licence to ony burrowis to remane at hame, and to that effect takis ordour with thame, that the inhabitanttis be nocht stentit of the auld fassioun of stenting within burgh, bot that ilk man be taxt conforme to his abilite and guidis be him self, quhither he be craftismen or merchant, without respect. MARIE, *Regina*.

iije men furnest.

The provest baillies counsale and dekynnis of craftis, all in ane voce, consentis and grantis that thre hundreth men be raisit within this burgh, furneist vpoun the expenssis of the inhabitantis of the samin, ilk ane efferand to thair awin pairtis respective eftir thair substance and abilite, eftir the forme of the Quenis grace writting aboue specifeit; quhilkis iije men salbe reddy to depairt fordwart to Fala Muir with the army of this realme vpoun the secund day of October nixt, conforme to the proclamatioun maid thair-upon.

18 *September* 1557.

Protestatioun of the craftis.

The quhilk day, in presens of the provest Archbald Dowglas of Kilspindie, James Carmichell dene of gild, of the counsale: James Batroun, Richard Carmichell, maister James Watsone, Robert Fleming, John Sym, Archbald Leich, and dekynnis of craftis, compeirit Robert Hendersone in name and behalf of the hale craftismen of this burgh and exponet and schew that forsamekle as the Quenis grace be hir writting, subscrivit with hir hienes hand, direct, chargeing the provest baillies and counsale of every burgh within this realme to stent every persoun dwelling within the samin conforme to his abilite and guidis be him self, quhether he be craftisman or merchant, and nocht of the auld maner, in this present charge laid to the burrowis that he in name of the rest of his brethir craftismen of this burgh wald be content to be stentit at this instant tyme conforme to the tennour of the Quenis grace writting, provyding alwayis that the samin hurt nocht thair privilegeis nor be nocht ane preparative in tyme cuming to caus thaim stent in lyke maner in tyme cuming.

The prouest baillies and counsale ordanis Alexander Park, thesaurair, to content and pay to Alexander Guthre, for the expenssis maid be him the tyme he raid to Hammyltoun at thair command for desyring of artelyerie to the defence of the toun, the sowme of xxx s., and v s. for ane signett quhilk wes put to the Quenis grace letteres for chargeing of the inhabitantis of this burgh to pay thair taxt, quhilk being payit salbe allowit. *Precept. Guthre.*

It is statute and ordanit be the rycht honorable maister James M'Gill of Rankelour, clerk of our Soucrane Ladeis register, and maister Thomas Mariorbankis of Ratho, ane of the lordis of our Soucrane Ladeis sessioun, president depute be our Soucrane Ladeis darest mother to have the charge reule and gouernment of this burgh and caussis thairof to hir hienes returning fra this present armie and certane space thairefter, as at mair lenth is contenit in hir hienes commissioun dirrect to thame tharvpone, with awys of the counsale off this burgh :—[Here follow acts relative to "breid, malt, broustaris, meil mercat, fische, poultre, flesche, candilmakeris, fleschcouris, stabillaris, vagaboundis, middingis, assyssis, standis on the Hegait," in terms similar to those of October in previous years. The following are the prices fixed:—The fourpence loaf of bread, baked by baxters within burgh, to weigh 22½ ounces ; and that sold by outland baxters and other unfreemen to weigh 26 ounces ; malt, 9 firlots for £3 ; ale, 3d per pint ; best mutton "bouke" 8s., and the second, 6s. ; a pound of candles, viij d. the "rag weik," and vij d. the "hard weik," best corn to be sold by "stabillaris" at 1 s. per peck, and the second, 10 d. ; wine, 1 s. 4 d. per pint.] *Acts anent breid, etc.*

Item, that na maner of persoun, man nor woman, regratouris of fische eggis butter cheis breid and frute or vther sic stuffe, hald ony maner of burdes or crames to sell siclike stuffe vpone the Hiegait nor vndir stairris, bot in thair awn houssis fra this tyme furth, vndir the pane of banesing of the town, and that nane of the saidis ragratours be sene in the merket amangis byaris or sellaris vnto the tyme of the houre of [tuelf] at none and quhill vj houris at ewin be past, vnder the pane of banesing, and that na regratour by ony butter or cheis bot in the Monunday and in the merkat and nocht quhill tuelf houris at none be streikin vndir the pane of banesing. *Regratouris.*

| | |
|---|---|
| Beggaris. | Item, it is statute and ordanit that na beggaris be tholit within this burgh bot thai that are borne within the samin, and nane of thaim be sufferit to beg except thai be ald crnikit lame or debilitat be greit seiknes, quhilkis may nocht labour nor wirk for thair lewing, and gif ony other be at this present within this burgh that thai dispesche thame of the samin betuix and Sonday nixttocum, vndir the pane of birning of thair chiek and baneseing of this town for euir; and that nane of the portaris of this burgh suffer ony outlandis beggar to hawe entres within the samin, vndir the pane of extreme punischment of thame in thair persouis and deprewatioun of thair offices. |
| Waippinis. | Item, that all maner of persouis, merchandis craftismen and vthers haifand buythis or dwelling houssis vpone the fore gait, be sufficientlie providit of lang waippinis in thair buythis and houssis, sic as the aichis, hallartis, jedburgh staiflis, for stopping of tuilye, conforme to the statute maid of before, vndir the pane of xl s. to be taikin of ilk persoun that beis fundin desolat thairof. |

5 *November* 1557.

| | |
|---|---|
| Despositioun of ane prebendrye. | [The council disponed the benifice of St Andrew's altar in St Giles' Kirk to Robert Craig, son to Robert Craig, goldsmith, "quha promist him to be ane prist within twa yeirs," or else to renounce his prebendary.] |
| The wall at the Blakfreris. | The samyn day, my lord provest baillies and counsale forsaid ordanis the theasurer, Alexander Park, togidder with the maister of wark to pas and vesye the toun wallis fallin doun at the Blakfreris, and to caus reedify and mend the samyn, and the expenssis maid vpoun the samyn salbe allowit to thame in thair compttis; and siclike to close vp the durris of the waist land vpoun the west syde of Leyth Wynde. |
| Escheit wyne. | The prouest, baillies, and counsale disponis and gevis the seriandis to be equalye delt amangis thame the half pype of wyne quhilk pertenit to Daniel Somer and escheit for his inobedienttis and braiking of the statutis be selling of the said wyne aboue the price statute, etc.; and this said wyne disponit to the saidis seriandis in recompence of thair dentie of the schereffis gluflis dischargit at this present fair of Alhallomes. |

## 12 November 1557.

The samin day, it being requerit be me lord provest at the baillies and counsale forsaid that he for the request of my lord the erle of Glancearin and vtheris genttillmen of court mycht haue ane burgeschip to [*blank*]; to the quhilk the saidis baillies and counsale ansuret that thay wer sworne that thai suld nocht grant to the disponing of ony burgeschippis for ane yeir intocum except to men of fame honestie and sufficiante substance quhilkis had or schortlie suld hawe stob and staik within this towne and that man pay thair dewtie the tyme of thair admissioun, and thairfore prayit his lordship be nocht offendit with thame, to the quhilk he alswa condisendit, quhairvpone the dene of gild askit instrumenttis.

*Making of burgessis.*

## 23 November 1557.

The prouest baillies and ane pairt of the counsale, being convenit for resonyng vpoun the commoun effaris of this burgh, and because the hale nowmer of the counsale wer nocht present, the samyn ceissit at that tyme, and vnderstanding that conforme to the ordour of this burgh vpoun the ressonyng and concluding of onye mater of wecht the full nowmer of counsale sould be present, and that in defalt of thair convenyng on the dayis apoynttit the commoun materris war deferrit and oursene, to the greit hurt of the commoun weill, for remeid of the quhilk my said lord prouest and counsale foirsaid ordanys that Wedinsday and Friday oulklie be counsale dayis, baith before and eftir none, and that the hale counsale convene before none at the seising of the bell efter x houris and at ij efter none, and quha that faillis to pay xviij d. sa oft as the falc is to be put in ane box to be destribut at the plesour of the counsale.

*Counsale dayis, with the panys.*

## 26 November 1557.

The quhilk day, my lord Seytoun prouest, maister James Lyndesay, Alexander Achesoun, Eduard Litill, and Williame Lawsoun, ballies, James Carmichaell dene of gild, James Adamesoun thesaurar, Archibald Dowglas of Kynspindie, maister Jhone Prestoun, Alexander Park, William Ker,

*Burges bairnys.*

Burges
bairnys.

Dauid Forestar, maister Johne Spens, James Curle, and Robert Hendersoun of the counsall, being convenit within the Tolbuyth of this burgh,
and efter ressonyng vpoun the complaynt gevin in before thame be
William Fowlar, Alexander Vddert and vtheris, in name and behalf of the
haill young men burgessis sonnis of this burgh, makand mentioun that
thai wer hevely hurt in this last taxt of xij$^c$ lib, rasit for licence grantit
to the inhabitanttis of this burgh to remane and abyde at hame fra our
Souerane Ladeyis hoist and armye ordanit to convene vpoun Fawlay
Mure the [blank] day of [blank] lastbypast for the assault of Wark,
etc., in sa far as thai wer ordanit be the settaris of the said taxt to pay
ane pairt thairof expres contrar to the landabill ws and obseruit priuelegis grantit and obseruit to burges sonis nocht mareit, as at mair lenth is
contenit in thair said complaint; quhilk being considerit, as my lord
prouest baillies and counsall foresaid fand the samyn to be ane noveltye,
and to the gret hurt of thair barnis, and expres contrar to the actis
statutis and priuilegis grantit and obseruit to burges barnis past memour
of man as said is, concludis decernis all in ane voce that na burges sonn
within this burgh salbe haldin to pay taxt stent walk or waird in ony
tyme cumin, nocht haffing stob nor staik and being vnmareit, bot sall
bruke and joyse the priviIege of the actis maid in thair fauouris of before,
prouyding alwayis thai pay the sowmes to the quhilk thai wer sett in the
extent aboue wretin.

10 December 1557.

Precept, Regina.

The prouest baillies and counsale foresaidis ordanis James Adamsoun,
thesaurer, to furneis lay in and deliuir to the Quenis grace and hir seruitouris thre tunnis wyne, and to wair xx lib, vpoun walx to hir grace,
agane this Yuill nixt to cum.

15 December 1557.

For vnlawing of the absentis fra the mos-touris.

The prouest [bailies, dean of guild and councillors], being convenit,
fyndis delineris and ordanis that all and sindry personis quhilkis wer nocht
present with the prouest arrayit in thair best maner of armour the last
day of the parliament, conforme to the proclamatioun be sound of bell, that

alsueill thay quhilkis wer nocht rady before the calling of the rollis vpoun For vulawing
the Castellhill as thay quhilk laid away, salbe vnlawit onery persoun in fra the mos-
the pane of xviij s., vnforgevin, sa monye as ar abill. . . . . touris.

### 29 December 1557.

The quhilk day the bailies, dean of guild, assessor, conncillors, and Fortefeing of
deacons], being convenit in the tolbuith of this burgh to the effect the towne.
vndirwrittin, all with ane consent thinkis expedient and ordanis this
town to be fortit strenthit and the wallis thairof reparit in all places
of the samin eftir the devyis and sicht of the personis eftir following,
namit to that effect, that is to say :—maister Thomas M'Calyeane [and
nine others]; and for performing and fulfilling of the ordinances and
devyses of the foirsaidis personis, anent the forting and bigging of the
wallis foirsaidis, it is ordanit be the baillies assessour dene of gild counsall
and dekynnis forsaidis that ane generall taxatioun or stent be vpliftit of
all maner of landis and annualrentis within this burgh and wallis thairof,
viz., xij d. of ilk pund of yeirlie maill and annuall of the samin, and for
setting and rentalling thairof hes nominat the personis efter specifeitt to
that effect, viz.: [eight persons for each of the north-west, north-east,
south-east, and south-west quarters.]

### 19 January 1557.

The quhilk day, being convenit within the ovir counsale hous, the President.
provest baillies counsale and hale dekynnis of craftis, my said lord provest
desyring thame to call to thair remembrance his haistye departing towert
the pairttis of France as ane of the lordis ordanit to pas thair for completing of our Souerane Ladeis mariage, and how necessar it wes for thame
and commoun weill of this burgh to haue ane honest and qualefeit man to
be thair president induring the tyme of his absence, and presentlie to name
certane honest men of this burgh and vtheris as thay thocht expedient to
the nowmer of viij or xij personis, and amangis thame as vse hes bene to
voit and elect ane to haue the said office as said is, at quhais desyre and
vpoun consideratioun foresaid diuers personis being put in wryt and thair
names being red to my said lord provest baillies and counsale and dekynnis

President.  foresaid, all in ane voce names vottis and electis Robert Maitland of Leithingtoun to be thair president induring the tyme of the said prouestis absence and forther induring the said counsalis will.

### 21 January 1557.

Magdalene brig.  It being menit to the prouest baillies and counsall of this burgh of Edinburgh be Joseph Rammage and George Notman, masonis, that the Magdalene brig betwix and Mussilburgh is dekeyit and at the falling down, and for support and help of the samin desyrit ane day throw the town for obtening of almous and guid ded of honest men, quhilk desyir my said lord prouest baillies and counsall thocht ressonable and for the commoun weill, and heirfor grantis and gevis licence to the saidis personis to cheis quhat day thai pleis quhat personis thai may haif for obtening of the said almous, provyding alwayis the almous obtenit be presentit to the saidis prouest baillies and counsall and cautionn fund that the samin salbe bestowit vpoun the said brig and na vtherwyis.

### 9 February 1557.

Wauchlott.  My lordis presidenttis and counsale foresaidis ordanis James Adamsoun thesaurer to deliuer and pay to John Wauchlott officer and chirurgeane the sowme of thre pundis for curing and mending of James Hendersonis leg in the townys seruice at the taiking of Ramsay ane theif quha wes slane in the taiking, etc.

Clayth mercat.  The quhilk day, the forsaidis president baillies counsall and dekynnis forsaid, convenit in the counsalhous, anent the supplicationn gevin in be the awneris of diners and sindric landis and tenementis liand within this burgh be west the tolbuith thairof, and the drapperis of lynning clayth, cottane, quhite, gray, and all vtheris within sex quarteris breid, inhabitouris of diners of the saidis landis liand as saidis, [which supplication refers to the act of the council confirmed by King James III., on 3d October 1477 (Vol. I., p. 34), ordaining the clothmarket to be held "betwix Libertownis Wynd heid and the traveis bewest the tolbuith," and to the change introduced by the act dated 24th April 1555 (Vol. II., p. 214,) when, at the "solistatioun and persuasioun of diuers nychtbouris remanand be eist the said tolbuith," the market was appointed Clayth mercat. to be held "betuix the Nether Bow and Freir Wynd,"] be ressoun quhairof the said mercate wes haldin in that pairt sensyne, and the saidis compleneris nocht sufferit to hald the samin be west the said tolbuith in the pairt befoir expremit, nochtwithstanding the ordinance act and privelege foirsaid maid in thair favouris with the confirmatioun following thairupoun, contenand diuers panis contrair the brekaris thairof, to thair grite dampnage and skayth, that hes maid grite biggingis in the foirsaidis pairtis bewest the said tolbuith for respect and commoditie of the said mercate thair to be haldin, and of the saidis drapperis and inhabitouris foirsaidis that hes preparit thame thairto and maid thair inhabitationes within the saidis boundis for the samin respect, and als contrair the commoun weill of the said burgh, gevand occasioun thairby that ane grite pairt of the inhabitouris thairof to remoif furth of the samin and remane in the Cannogaitt and to mak biggingis within thai pairtis and to leif this town vnbiggit, as at mair lenth is contenit in the said supplicatioun gevin in thairupoun, the richtis ressones and allegationes of bayth the saidis pairtiis comperand in the counsalhous of this burgh, the saidis presidentis baillies counsale and dekynnis foirsaid decernis and ordanis the said clayth merkat to be restoirit and brocht vpe agane abone the tolbuthe of this burgh, thair to be vsit and haldin in the samyn place quhairintill it was of befoir vpone all merkat dayis vsit and wount according to the foirsaidis aulde statutis and ordinancis confermit thairvpone, as said is, and ay and quhill the samyn [be re]ducit and all parteis callit thairto havand enteressis, and [als] dischargis the new act foirsaid maid for moving and [halding] of the said merkat be eist the towbuithe and de[cernis the] effect thairof to ceis and expyre in all tyme cuming.

### 11 *February* 1557.

My lordis presidentis baillies and counsall decernis and ordanis Mow, candyl-Thomas Mow, candilmaker, and Elezabeth Nudry his spous, to abstene maker. desist and ceis in all tyme cuming fra all melting of ony crakkingis of talloun within thair bak hous or ony vthir houssis liand in William

| | |
|---|---|
| Mow, candylmakar. | Huchesonis clos sa lang as maister Henrie Sinclair dene of Glasgow, president of oure Souerane Ladeis counsall and sessioun, remanis within this burgh, for avoyding of the corrupt and vnhalsum air cumand thairthrow to my said lord presidentis hous, and that in respect of the saidis personis consentis gevin to the premissis: and gif thai failye thairintill to pay to the commoun guid of this burgh for the first falt xl s. with the escheting of the stuff; for the nixt, banissing of the toun but fauouris. |
| Markett of skynnis. | The presidentis baillies haill counsall and dekynnis foirsaidis, all with ane consent, ordanis the merkett of hydis and skynnis in tymes cuming to be brocht doun frome the place abone the tolbuith quhair it presentlie remanis, and be sett and haldin beneth the salt trone, betuix Walter Scottis close and Nudreis Wynd on bayth sydis, induring the townis will allanerlie, and that for guid caussis considerationis and motives moving thaim thairto at this instant tyme, and that officeris put this present act to executioun with all diligens. |

6 March 1557.

| | |
|---|---|
| Lindesay, Makdougall. | My lordis presidentis baillies and counsale forsaid ordanis maister James Lindesay baillie, and Sir William M'Dougall maister of werk, to contract and aggre with the lyme men of Conslaud for furnessing of lyme to the wallis of the toun, and thay to be the price makaris thairof allanerlie. |
| Precept, Lytstar. | My lordis presidenttis baillies and counsale foresaid ordanis James Adamsoun, thesaurer, to deliuer to Dauid Lytstar in Leyth xl s., for pulder and bullet furnist be him at thair command to certane artailye quhilk thay sould haue bocht fra him and shott to assay the saymn. |

16 April 1558.

| | |
|---|---|
| For paying of extent. | The president baillies and counsale forsaid ordanis in all tymes cuming, quhen ony taxtis stenttis or otheris portabill chargis sall happin to cum vpoun this burgh, that all maner of personis that hanttis vsis or exersis the libertie and priviclege of merchandis or fre burgessis of the same, that is to say the venting of wyne or onye other kynd of merchandice, quhat- |

sumcner stait thai be, men of law scribe or other priueliegit persoun, For paying of nochtwithstanding thair saidis priueliegis, in all tymes cuming thay stent extent. scait lott and beir chargis walk and waird with the saidis merchandis sa lang as thai vse thair libertie or onye pairt thairof.

9 *May* 1558.

The presidenttis baillies counsale and dekynnis, with ane greit nowmer Concerning of merchandis craftismen and vtheris of the commvnite of this burgh, the superiour defence of the being convenit within the tolbuth of the same, quhair it wes proponit to burgh. thame be maister Thomas M'Calyeane, president, the present apperance of weris and invasioun of inimeis, and how that this said burgh wes desolait of ane superiour of jugement knawledge and habilite to haue the charge caire and reull of the samyn in case of invasioun as said is, quhairfor he according to his dewitie towert this said burgh and fauour he bair to the commoun weill of the samyn exhortit thame amang the nobillis and greit baronys of this realme to nominat certane and put the samyn in wryt, and to pas to the Quenis grace and lordis of Secreit Counsale desyring hir grace to gyf to thame ane of the saidis nobill men to haue the charge our thame and thair said toun, vnto the tyme of the returne of my lord Seytoun, prouest, now in the pairttis of France; quhilk propositioun being hard be the vther president baillies counsale dekynnis burgessis craftismen and ane pairt of the commvnite as said is thay all in ane voce thocht the saymn gude, and ordanit James Carmychell dene of gild, maister Jhonn Spens baillie, James Adamsoun thesaurer, maister Jhonn Prestoun, James Young cutler, David Kynloch baxter, Robert Hendersoun barbour, and Alexander Guthre commoun clerk, to pas to the abbay to the Quenys grace Marye Quene Dowrear Regent of this realme, and lordis of secreit counsale being thair and gyf in the supplicatioun of the quhilk the tenour followis: Madame, the presidenttis baillies counsale and commonite of this burgh of Edinburgh maist humlie exhorttis your grace and lordis of secreit counsale to haue remembrance of oure complaynt gevin in to yow of before and, conforme to the desyre of the samyn, grant ws ane of the nobill men quhais names followis to haue the cure and charge our ws and our said toun vnto the returne of my lord Seytoun our prouest, etc.; and your grace's ansuer. The names of the nobill men :—My Lord erle Boith-

EXTRACTS FROM THE RECORDS       [1558.

*Concerning the superiour defence of the burgh.*

uell, my lord erle of Mortoun, my lord erle of Glencarne, the lord Erskyn, the lord Sempill and the lord Ruthven. With the quhilk writing conforme to the said ordinance the personis aboue writtin deput to pas thairwith past to the abbay and deliuerit the samyn to the Quenys Grace and lordis of secreit counsale foirsaid.

11 *May* 1558.

*Concerning extentouris.*

The presidenttis, maister James Lindesay, maister Jhonn Spens, William Lausonn baillies, James Adamsoun thesaurer, maister Jhonne Prestoun, Alexander Barronn, William Kar, James Curle of the counsale, ordanis that in all tymes cuming quhen it sallhappin ony extenttis to be laid vpoun this burgh that the extentouris sall be taxt and thair extent sett be the baillies and counsale and nocht be thame selfis as vse hes bene, for eschewing of mwrmur of the pepill; and siclike that Andro Murray of Blakbaronye, Jhonn Carkettill of Fynglen, Thomas Kantt of Sanct Gelys Grange and vtheris gentill men heritouris within this burgh that vssis na marchandice nor exchange within the samyn be mair gentillie handillit in tymes cuming nor thay haue bene of before, and to that effect ordanis thame to be alsua taxt be the said counsale and nocht be the extentouris for the caus foresaid.

21 *May* 1558.

*Gunnaris.*

The presidenttis baillies dene of gild and haile counsale, with auise of the maist pairt of the dekynnis and certane vtheris honest nychtbouris of of this burgh, fyndis necessar that certane gunneris men of experience be hyrit for handling graithing and shutting of the townyis monitionn in case of invasionn, and to that effect hes presentlie hyrit Robert Caldour and William Kelle gunneris for thre monethis, thair begynning to be vpoun Sounday xxij day of Maii instant, and euerye ane of thame to haue monethlie v li. to be payit be the thesaurer of this burgh, and Gilbert Balfour sonertie for the said Calder, and Gilbert Balfour to be maister of the townys artailye.

*Close futtis.*

The presidenttis baillies and counsale foresaid fyndis gude and necessar that all the close futtis on layth syddis of the Hie Streit of this

burgh be closyt and bigit vp with stane and lyme or vtherwayis sufficient Close futtis.
be the occupearis of the landis within the samyn vpoun the expenssis of
the heritouris in case of invasioun of inimeis, and the wynde futtis onle to
be oppin, quhilk the forsaidis ordanis to be done.

The foresaidis ordanis James Adamsoun, thesaurer, to big ane but of But, port.
fale at James Bassendennis hous aboue the Nether Bow quhair the samyn
wes of before, vpoun the townys expenssis, and siclike to big vp the eist
port of the Cougait callit Sanct Marye port vpoun the townys expensses
quhilk salbe allowit to him; and siclike ordanis the said James to caus
mak tua hundreth small creillis for be[ring] of eird, and to by half hundreth
schod schullis with tua dosane matokis, quhilk sall alsua be allowit to
him, and put the samin in the monitioun hous of the toun.

The presidenttis baillies and counsale foresaid ordanis proclamatioun [Preparations
to be maid through the toun chairgeing all inhabitanttis of this burgh to the burgh.]
convene before thame the morne at thre houris efter none, thair to declair
how monye men euerye man will sustene for defence of this burgh in case
of invasioun, with certificatioun and thay failye to convene at the hour
appoynttit to the effect foresaid that the counsale will extent and set
euerye man according to thair knawlege, and siclike ordanis that euerye
honest man within burgh haue ane schod schule spaid and mattok within
his hous to be in radynes in case the gude toun haue ado.

The presidenttis baillies and counsale ordanis maister Jhonn Spens Villa.
baillie, Dauid Forster and Gilbert Balfoure of counsale, and Alexander
Guthre commoun clerk, to await continuallie vpoun the Quenys grace
and lordis of secreit counsale in the ablay vpoun the answer of the gude
townys desyre twiching ane greit man to haue the steir reull and gouernance of the toun vnto the returne of my lord Seytoun provost.

The presidenttis baillies and counsale foresaid ordainis James Adam- Artailye.
soun, thesaurer, to by fra Dauid Bell in Leyth vj cutthrottis with thair
chalmeris and calmes, and to pay to the said Dauid xiiij s. for euerye stane
wecht of the samyn.

27 *May* 1558.

The townys evidenttis.

The presidenttis baillies counsale and dekynnis, beand convenit in the tolbuith of this burgh, is content granttis consenttis and als commandis James Carmychaell dene of gyld, James Adamsoun thesaurar of this burgh and James Barroun burges, that gif it salhappin our ald inemyis of Ingland to cum fordwart for persute of this toun, to convoy and transport the haill evidenttis and wryttingis now beand in the thesaurar hous of this burgh to the castell and to put the samyn in the thesaurar hous of the said castell thair to remane in sure keping ; and siclike ordanis the said dene of gyld to haif the reliquis syluer chandlaris with the rest of the sylner wark capis and ornamentis of the kirk of Sanct Geill to the said thesaurar hous of the castell thair to be kepit in lyke maner, quhairupoun the said James Carmichaell dene of gild askit instrumentis.

Craftis.

The saidis presidentis baillies and counsale ordanis the officiaris to pas and charge the dekynis of ilk craft to consult and awys with the remanent of the fremen of his occupatioun to se quhat nomer of men thai may be furnising thame self for resistance of our ald inemeis of Ingland in cais thai persew this burgh, and that euery dekyn be himself gif in the nomer that thai may be in roll to the baillies and counsall vpoun Thurisday nixtocum, to the effect that thai may knaw quhat the haill toun may do.

30 *May* 1558.

Or Inance for defence of the town.

The presidenttis baillies and counsale ordanis proclamatioun to be maid at the mercat croce of this burgh, in our Soucrane Ladeis name and thairis, commandand and chargeand all and sindry the inhabitanttis of this burgh, merchanttis craftismen and all vtheris occupearis and induellaris within the samyn, that in case this burgh happin to be invadit with inimeis, nane of thame tak vpoun hand to remove or pas furth of the samyn the tyme of the invasioun, bot remane thairintill weill and sufficientlie furnist with all maner of armour and wappinnis according to thair power for defence of this said burgh, certefeing all and sindry the personis foresaid that gyf ony of thame absenttis thame selffis or beis away the samin tyme thair landis and guddis salbe escheit and confiscat disponit and deltt to the wyllis and bairnys of thame that salhappin to *Ordnance for defence of the town.* remane quhilkis beis hurt mutilat or slane in the defence of this said burgh, and the vtheris personis fremen quhilkis hes na landis nor guddis, and absent tis thame selffis as said is, to be dischargit thair fredome and banyst this toun for evir; and this to be done without ony fauour, efter the jugement and discretioun of the provest presidentis and baillies for the tyme.

### 5 June 1558.

It is statute and ordanit be the presidentis baillies counsale and hale *Anent the hyring of thair seruandis.* dekynnis that na maner of persoun, burges craftisman nor vther inhabiter within this burgh, contract or hyre ane vther mannis seruand now in tyme of weyr, bot that euerye man to be haldin to ansuer for his awin seruand and haue him sufficientlie prouidit for defence of this burgh in case the samyn be invadyt be our auld inimeis, certefeing him that hyris or gevis wage to his nychtbouris seruand as said is the said wage salbe tynt to the gever tane and applyit to the commoun proffit of this burgh, and the seruand that passis fra his maister pvnist in his persoun and be compellit to enter agane to his said maister and serue him and nane vtheris during all tyme he is detbound till do the samyn.

The presidenttis baillies dekynnis and counsale foirsaid, for the [Men to be furnished for defence of the town.] commoun weill and defence of this burgh in case of invasioun as said is, ordanis all nychtbouris merchanttis craftismen and vtheris to be convenit within the tolbuth of the samyn, and thair be thair awin avise counsale and consent to heir and se euerye ane of thame to be set to samonye men as his substance may sustene, weill prouidit in armour and wappynnis, for the defence of this burgh in case of invasioun, [and] to be waigit and sustenyt be thame to serue vnder captanes as salbe chosin be the presidenttis baillies and counsale [and that] induring the said invasioun or langer as salbe necessarie.

The samyn day, the merchanttis of this burgh beand convenit as said [Men to be furnished by merchants.] is, of thair awin fre willis, consenttis euerye man to furnys the nowmer following, weill prouidit in armour and wappinnis, and ma gyf neid beis, induring the tyme foresaid: [Here follows the roll of names, the numbers being

[Men to be furnished by merchants.] for the north-west quarter, two hundred and nineteen men; for the south-east quarter one hundred and ninety-five; for the south-west quarter, three hundred and twenty-two—in all, seven hundred and thirty-six men.]

10 *June* 1558.

Dekyn of the masounis. The saidis president baillies and counsale ordanis Dauid Grahame dekyn of the masounis, of his awyn consent, to gif in the roll of the maisteris and habill men seruandis of the said craft on Wednisday nixtocum, vnder the pane of wardyn.

[Skinner craft.] The president baillies and counsale sittand in judgement, haifand considderatioun of the havie complaint maid to thame be the brethir and maisteris of the skynnar craft anent the gret skayth thai incur throu vnfremen that cumis furth of Sanct Johnstoun and otheris partis, that daylie vsis to vent and sell thair pursis gluflis panttis and otheris maid wark pertening to the said craft, nocht onlie in fuill grossis bot alssua in smallis, daylie and oppinlie vpon the Quenis streit of this burgh, quhilk thai aucht nocht to do bot on Monunday and the tyme of proclamit fairis, vsurpand thairthrow als gret priuelegis as thai that ar fremen, quhairby [ar] put to sic preiudice that thai are nocht abill to taxt stent [walk and waird] without remeid be put thairto; thairfoir ordanis the ofliciaris of this burgh to pas and discharge all vnfremen, vsand to vent or sell sic wark pertening to the said craft, that nane of thame tak vpoun hand fra Monunday nixtocum furth to sell the same bot vpoun the merket day vsit and wont, that is to say Monunday, or in proclamit fairis, vnder the pane of eschaet-ing, [and they to find surety to comply with this act]; and for the second falt, or sa oft as thai failye efter the fynding of the said soucrte, his soucrte to be pynist at the townis will, and the saidis purssis gluflis panttis or otheris maid wark fund selland be thame to be eschaet and applyit to the commoun wirkis of the burgh.

[Men to be furnished by crafts.] The quhilk day the craftis of this burgh being convenit within the tolbuyth of this burgh, of thair awin fre willis [consentis] euerye man to furneis the number following weill prouydit men and waippinis, and ma gif neid beis, induring the tyme forsaid: [Here follows a roll of the names, of

which the following is an abstract:—Skinners, 42 masters, 21 servants, together [Men to be
63; Furriers, 9; Websters, 13 masters, 13 servants, together 26; Tailors, 81 "free- furnished by
men," 72 servants, "the names of thame in merchant houssis and vp and doun the crafts.]
in hole and Lore," 25, together 178; Bonnet-makers, 14 masters, 39 servants,
together 53; Barbers, 25; Hammermen, 66 masters, 85 servants, together 151;
Goldsmiths, 14 masters, 6 servants, together 20; Walkers, masters and servants'
within town, 24, outwith the West Port, 19, together 43; Baxters, 45 masters,
55 servants, together 100; Cordiners, 19; "summa of the hale nowmer of the
maisteris and seruandis abill men of craftis for defence of the toun," 717.]

### 17 *June* 1558.

The indwellaris of Leyth may on na wayis buy woll hyde claith skin [Divers privi-
salmound wyne walx victuellis, or ony maner of stapill gudis, fra unfre- legeis obtenit
men in the countrie, bot all sic merchandice sould first cum and be pre- Edinburgh
sentit to the burgh of Edinburgh, and thairefter sould be bocht fra the aganis Leyth.
fremen thairof. Item, the indwellaris, nor na uther unfremen, may pack
and peill the saidis gudis in the town of Leyth, quhilk is ane unfre town,
nor yit in ony uther place within the fredome of Edinburgh, bot all sic
merchandice and gudis aucht and sould be brocht to the said burgh, as
principall stapill thairof, and thair to pack and peill the samin, and pay
thair customis and dewteis thairfor as efferis.

### 23 *June* 1558.

The presidenttis baillies and counsale, efter consideratioun and avise- [Bonnet-
ment with the complaynt gevin in before thaim be the dekyn and brother makers.]
of the bonet makaris, makand mentioun that the outlandis men of Sanct
Jonistoun and vtheris vnfremen vpoun all dayis in commoun pas throuch
this toun with thair bonettis and commounlie and oppinlie sauld the samyn
to all our soueranis lieges, to thair greit hurt and contrair to the privelegis
granttit to thame in thair gyft vnder the seill of caus of this gude toun, as
at mair lenth is contenit in thair said complaynt, the saidis presidenttis
ballies and counsale foresaid having regaird to thair said letter of gyft
granttit to the said craft, the privelegis and liberteis contenit in the
samyn, togidder with the greit charges sustenit be thame in stent-

[Bonnet-makers.]

ing and wairding, statutis and ordanis that it sall nocht be lesum to na outland man nor vtheris vnfremen to sell thair bonettis within this toun vpon the Hie Gait, nor vpoun crames vtouth buthis, bot vpon merkat dayis [vsit and wount] and fre fairis . . .

1558.

Queen's mariage.

The presidenttis ballies and counsale ordanis James Adamsoun thesaurer to delyuer to William Adamsoun for his travell takin in the play maid at the tryumphe of our Souerane Ladyis mariage the sowm of foure lib.; . . . to Walter Bynning, painter, for his panting and all his lawbouris takin be him in the tryumphe maid at our Souerane Ladyis mariage the sowm of xxv merkis; to William Lauder the sowm of aucht lib., by the fourtie schillingis quhilkis he hes ellis ressauit for his travell and lawbour tane vpone him in setting furth of the play maid at our Souerane Ladyis mariage; . . . to all the wrychtis quhilkis wrocht the play grayth in the play maid at the tryumphe of our Souerane Ladyis mariage for thair tymmer and workmanschip the sowm of fyve lib, four s. nyne d. . . . to Patrik Dorane for his travell takin on him for making of certane claythis agane the tryumphe of our Souerane Ladyis mariage the sowm of four lib. . . . to Adam Smyth, takkisman of Andro Mowbrayis yarde the sowm of vj s. viij d. for the dampnage and skayth sustenit be him in tramping down of his gers of the said yard be the convoy and remanent playeris the tyme of the trumphe.

15 December 1558.

Precept, Regina.

The prouest baillies and counsale ordanis maister James Lindesay, thesaurer, to waill thre twn of the best wyne may be gottin for money, togidder with xx li. worth of walx; and caus the samyn be propynit to the Quenys grace aganis this Yule.

29 December 1558.

Cowgait cālsay.

The prouest baillies counsale and dekynnis fynddis that the commoun and hie passege of the Cowgait and commoun calsay of the samyn salbe rasyt and laid and biggit of new vpoun the equale expenssis

of the heritouris of the landis vpoun bayth the syddis of the said gait, lyke  Cowgait
as the samyn is begvn, fra the Freir Wynde to Merlyeonis Wynde; and  calsay.
to the effect that the samyn may be the mair haistye diligence, ordanis the
copye of this present act to be gevin to euerye ane of the four baillies, and
thay to caus put the samyn to executioun with all deligence, and to tak
attendance and gyf speciall commannd and charge to the heritouris of the
saidis landis that nane of thame tak vpoun hand to set furth the conductis
of thair closettis furth of thair syd wallis or gavillis of the saidis landis
towert the calsay or hie streit, vnder the pane of pvnissing of thair
personis and guddis at the counsallis will quha dois in the contrair.

### 7 January 1558-9.

[Of this date the provost, bailies, council, and deacons gave a "beddrelschip" of  Hospital of St.
the hospitall of Sanct Marie Wynd" to Agnes Storie.]  Mary's Wynd.

The prouest baillies and counsall ordanis Jhone Charteris, eldar, dene  Jowallis.
of gild, to ressaue the jowallis vnderwrittin fra Schir Henrye Bonche
sacristane of thair kirk of Sanct Geill now hafar of the same, and to keip
thame be himself and his deputis that he will ansuer for, that the samyn
salbe furtheumand to the toun quhen thai think expedient, and to serue
the nychtbouris thairof as vse is, and that the said dene of gild tak
souertie of his said depute of honest responsibill nychtbouris of this burgh
for his lawte and suir keping of the saidis jowallis, and that thai wey and
keip the pais vnder specifyit, becaus vpon the sextene day of December
last bypast thay war weyit in presens of the counsall in the tolbuith of
this burgh be James Mosman, goldsmyth, of the wecht particularle as eftir
followis, and at the ische of his office the said counsall ordanis the said
dene of gild to deliuer the same of the wecht efter following to the counsall, that thai may be delinerit and weyit in lyk maner to his successouris,
dene of gild for the tyme, to the effect forsaid, viz., the relict and arme of
Sanct Geill with the bane and paper, with ane ring set with ane dyamant
on the litill fingar of the said arme, and fourte perle and sevinteine stanis,
all weyand fiyve pund thre vnce and ane half; the syluer croce by the
fute, weyand sex pund foure vnce and ane half; item, the fute of this croce

28   EXTRACTS FROM THE RECORDS   [1558-9.

Jowallis.  fillit with pik and other mettall within the same to cause it stand, weyand ten pund nyne vnce; tua crowattis, weyand tuentye tua vnce; ane challece with the patene of syluer, weyand threttie tua vnce and ane half, qubairof the spvne weyis half ane vnce; tua chandlaris of syluer, weyand sevin pund four vnce; tua grettar chandlaris of syluer, baith weyand aucht pund thretteine vnce; tua sensairis, weyand togidder thre pund fyvetene vnce; ane ship for insence, sex vnce.

### 3 *February* 1558-9.

Precept, prouest.  The qubilk day, Alexander Barroun, Danid Forster, maister Jhonn Spens and James Curle, baillies, James Carmychaell, James Adamsoun, William Lausoun, Thomas Thomsoun, William Aikman, William Patersoun, Andro Sclater and James Young of the counsale, maister Thomas Makealycane assessour, togidder with the hale dekynnis of goldsmythis, massonis, wrychtis, barbouris, baxtaris, walkaris, bonetmakaris, being convenyt in the counsale hous of this burgh, and having consideratioun of the gude and thankfull seruice done be my Lord Seytoun prouest, for the commoun weill and priueleges of this burgh, and that his lordship is presentlie to mak the triumphe and banket to the Quenys grace in honorabill maner, ordanis maister James Lindesay, thesaurer, thankfullie to content deliuer and pay to James Barroun, merchand, the somme of ane hundreth crownis of the sone for taffateis silkis and vtheris necessaris furnyst be him at the command of my said lord prouest to the convoy of the said banket, and that the samyn be payit at Beltane nixt to cum, but onye delay, off the first and radeast of thair fermes of the said terme.

### 3 *February* 1558-9.

Moscrop.  The baillies and counsall, haifand considderatioun of the gude and thankfull seruice done to thame at all tymes be maister Jhone Moscrop aduocat, granttis and giffis licence to the said maister Jhone to vent and haif wyne in his awyn houss for serving of his taible, and nocht to be taxat stentit nor haldin on the portabill chargis of this burgh for that caus in ony tyme cuming, dischargeand the taxteris, extentouris, present and to cum, of all taxting and extenting of him thairfore; providing

allwayis the said maister Jhone continew in guid mynd towert this burgh  Moscrop.
in the common effairis thairof, and accept and tak vpoun him the office of
procuratore fiscall of this toun, to persew and defend thair caussis befoir
quhatsumeuer judge, vpoun the townis expenssis.

### 12 *February* 1558-9.

[Of this date the council ordained that wine should not be sold dearer than  Wine.
twelvepence per pint.]

In presens of the baillies and certane of the counsale, comperit Charllis  Regina.
Sanguilleir, Flemyng, and producit the wryting vnderwrittin, of the quhilk  Licence to Charllis San-
the tenour followis, and desyrit thair ansuer of the samyn: Regina. We  guilleir.
for certane ressonable caussis moving ws be thir presenttis gevis licence
to Charllis Sanguilleir merchand in Flandaris to lois his guddis furth of
his schippis now being in the port of Leyth, and to seller the samyn in
the said toun of Leyth, and to sell the samyn to fre men as he thinkis
expedient, and to ladyn his said schip agane with all lesum merchandice,
providing alwayis he offer his saidis guddis fyrst to the burgh of Edinburgh, dischargeing heirfor the prouest baillies counsale and communite of
the said burgh to mak onye stop or impedyment to the said Charllis in losing
sellaring of his said guddis and laiding of the said schip agane with lesum
merchandice, or to mak ony arrestment vpoun him or his guddis thairfor,
and of thair offices in that pairt, he payand customes and dewities vsit and
wont. Subscriuit with our hand at Edinburgh the aucht day of Fabruer
1558. *Sequitur subscriptio*, MARIE, etc. To the quhilk it wes ansuerit be
the counsale foresaid that thay wald gyf thair ansuer to the Quenis grace.

### 13 *February* 1558-9.

Richert Douglas masour. intymeit the Quenys graces writing to my  Regina.
lord Seytoun prouest and the four baillies, of the quhilk the tenour
followis: Apud Edinburgh, xiij° Februarii anno, etc. lviij°: Forsamekill as
it is vnderstand to the Quenys grace that the prouest baillies and counsale
of the burgh of Edinbnrgh hes wardit within the tolbuith thairof Charles
Sangler, Fleming, and withhaldis him thairin, thairfoir, and for certane

| | |
|---|---|
| Regina. | motivis moving hir hienes, ordanis ane messinger pas incontinent eftir the sycht heirof and charge the said provest baillies and counsale of the said burgh that thai incontinent put the said Charles to libertie and fredome furth of thair waird, and deliuer him to the said messour to be enterit before hir grace, vnder the pane of tresoun. *Sequitur subscriptio*, MARIE R. |

### 14 *February* 1558-9.

| | |
|---|---|
| Regina. | REGINA. Provest baillies and counsale of Edinburgh: Forsamekle as it is our plessour that Charles Sanguiller, Fleming, be sufferit to vse and dispone vpon his gudis laitlie brocht in be him as he sall think best, quhairfoir we requeist yow that ye mak him na impediment in vsing selling or disponing thairvpon, nor in ladyng of his schip with lesum merchandice and departing, quhilk we promyt yow sall nocht be in preiudice of your rychtis or priuelegis grantit to yow tuiching your fredome; and this on na way ye leif vndone, as ye will ansuer to ws vpone your vtermaist charge. At Edinburgh the xiiij day of Februarii, anno 1558. |

### 8 *March* 1558-9.

| | |
|---|---|
| Jowallis. | Item, vpon the 8 day of Merche 1558 yeris, in the ravestre of the kirk, in presens of the counsall afoir specifyit, the eucharist wes weyit contenand of wecht all syluer ourgilt, with four bellis of gold hingand thairat, half ane stane and tua vnce wecht; haif hingand aboue ane hart set with perle, ane litill blew bell of gold, ane litill jasmint, ane sapheir, ane agat, tua perlis, tua stanis and othir tua fyne stanis, and hingand laych ane lytill hart of gold, ane mekill croce with thre perle, image of our Lady, ane litill croce with thre perle; quhilkis all is contenit within the said eucharist; ane round eucharist of syluer, weyand tuentye thre vnce; item, the cresum stok, weyand xxxix vnce and ane quarter. |

### 24 *March* 1558-9.

| | |
|---|---|
| Certane persones chosin for awaiting vpone the materis betuix the town and Leyth. | The provest [bailies, assessors, councillors, treasurer, and deacons,] haveand consideratioun that the maist pairt of thair priuilegis quhilkis ar grantit to thame be our Soueraine Lord and Ladyis maist noble progenitouris anent thair fredome within the toun and schoir of Leyth, and of |

bying of the guddis inbrocht be strangearis thairto, ar hable tak les Certane personis chosin
effect for non awaiting thairvpone, all with ane voce ordanis Edward for awaiting
Litill, Daniel Somer and Thomas Ridpethe, coniunctlie and seuerallie, to vpone the
await vpone the selling and disponying of all guddis inbrocht at the said materis betuix the town and
schoir, and that na inhabitant of the said town pak nor peill thairin, with Leyth.
power to thame to caus all actis and decreitis maid and sett furthe for
the libertie of this burgh vpone the said toun of Leyth to be putt to dew
execution in all poyntis efter the forme and tenour thairof, and gif any
maner of persone ather fre or vnfre contravene the saidis statutis or ony
pairt thairof, to call follow and persew the contraueneris of the samyn befoir
ony juge competent; quhilkis personis hes acceptit the said office vpone
thame, and ar sworne be thair grit aithis the halie ewangelistis tweehit to
minister leilliclie and trewlie thairintill for the weill of this burgh ay and
quhill thai be dischargit thairof be the gude tonne, for the quhilkis
caussis the provest baillies counsall and dekinnis forsaidis grantis to the
saidis personis the thrid pairt of all and syndrie sowmes of money to be
obtenit and recouerit be thame vpone all and syndre contraweneris of the
saidis statutis, to be equallie devidit amang thame, in recompence of
thair lawbouris.

### 12 April 1559.

[Of this date the bailies council and deacons of crafts granted to James Chaplainries in St. Giles Kirk.
Marioribanks, scribe, the service and chaiplainry founded at the high altar by
umquhile Robert Vans; and to John Scott, chaplain, at the request of Andrew Mansion, wright, the service and chaiplainry founded at St Ninians' altar in St Giles
kirk by umquhile Andrew Mowbray, both vacant by decease of Sir Alexander
Cunningham. Marioribanks renounced the half of his yearly pension of ten pounds
granted to him on 30th March 1542, and Mansion renounced the yearly pension of
ten merks he had of the good town.]

### 20 April 1559.

The ballies [assessors, councillors, and deacons of crafts], and als ane Seytoun proueat, Barroun,
greite pairt of the communitie of the said burgh being present, comperit Guthre.
Alexander Barroun baillie, and Alexander Guthre commoun clerk of this

Seytoun pro-
uest, Barroun,
Guthre.

burgh, and presentit to the ballies counsaill dekinnis and communtie foirsaid thair supplicatioun, makand mentioun that quhair vpone the xix day of
this instant monethe of Apryle at nyne houris at evin George lord Seetoun
provest of this burgh, for quhat caus thai knew nocht, chargeit thaim to
enter in warde within the tolbuyth of the said burgh, thair to remane
induring his lordships will, quhilk charge thai at the tyme obeyit, and
according thairto enterit in warde within the said tollmyth and hes remanit thair continewallie sensyne, and that thai vnderstand thaim to be
wardit wranguslie for nane offence, and throw thair wairding the commoun
effairis of this burgh [are] diferrit and hynderit to thair greit sklander
and appeirand dekey of the commoun weill thairof, desyrand thairfoir the
ballies counsaill dekinnis and communitie foirsaid to requeist my lord provest to compeir befoir thaim incontinent thairefter to heir coguitioun
takin in the said complaynt, and to heir and se thaim fred and putt to
libertie, or ellis to allege ane ressonable caus in the contrair, with certificatioun and his lordship falyeit the ballies counsaill dekinnis and communitie forsaid wald provyde sic remeid thairto as mycht stand with
equitie and ressoun, as at mair lenthe is contenit in the said supplicatioun
gevin in thairvpone: Quhilk being red, considderit, and the ballies counsaill
etc. being riplie awisit thairwith, ordanit the saidis Danid Forrester and
James Curle ballies, the said Thomas Thomsoun of the counsaill, and the
said maister Robert Creichtoun ane of the assessouris, and the said James
Mure dekin of the hammermen, to pas and requyre my lord provest to
compeir befor thaim incontinent thairefter, to heir coguitioun takin in the
said mater conforme to the desyre of the saidis compleneris, with certificatioun contenit in the said supplicatioun, as in the directioun maid on the
bak thairof at mair lenthe is contenit; quhilkis personis accepttit the said
charge vpone thaim, and conforme thairto past to my lord provest, and
maid intimatioun to his lordschip of thair said directioun, quhilkis being
returnit and in enterit agane the said Mr Robert Creichtoun, in name
behalf and at commande of the saidis Danidis Forrester, James Curll,
Thomas Thomsonu, and James Mure, his collegis declarit that thai had
past to my lord provest, and schawin to his lordschip the charge and
directioun gevin to thaim be the ballies counsaill dekinnis and communitie

foirsaid, desyrand his lordship to compeir befor thaim to heir tryall and *Seytoun pro-*
cognitioun takin in the said complant, or ellis gif his lordship pleisit nocht, *uest Barroun*
or mycht nocht be present at that tyme, to sclaw and declair to thaim *Guthre.*
the caus of the warding of the saidis Alexander Barroun and Alexander
Guthrie, to the effect that the samyn mycht be dismissit with expeditioun, in respect that the personis wardit wer necessar memberis of the
court for administratioun of iustice and performing of the necessar effaris
of the toun; quha ansuerit to thame that his lordship wald nocht compeir
for that caus, nor wald nocht cum in ressonyng with thaim thairin, but
that he had put the saidis personis in warde for certane caussis knawin
to his lordship, and wald nocht consent that thai wer fred quhill his lordschip wer farther awisit. The ballies counsaill dekinnis and communitie
foirsaid with thair assessouris foirsaidis, haveand consideratioun of the
said complaynt and answer maid be my lord provest thairto, and als have-
and respect to the personis of the saidis Alexander Barroun and Alexander Guthre, and thairwith being ryplie awisit, the ballies counsaill
assessouris dekinnis and communitie forsaid all in ane voce ordanis the
saidis Alexander Barroun and Alexander Guthrie to be fred relevit and
putt to libertie furthe of thair said warde, thai and ilkane of thaim
fyndand cawtioun to ansuer to sic poyntis as sall be layid to thair
chargeis be my lord provest vpone sex houris warnyug, ilke persone vnder
the pane of ane hundreth poundis; and Dauid Symer is becumin
cawtioun for the said Alexander Guthreis entreis, and Frances Tennend
for the said Alexander Barroun to ansuer as said is, ilk persone vnder
the panis forsaidis, and thairvpone the saidis compleneris askit instrumentis.

### 22 April 1559.

The quhilk day, Alexander Barroun, maister John Spens and James *Message by*
Curle baillies, sittand in jugement, comperyt Robert Fyndour wrycht and *Lord Seytoun*
schew thir wordis following: Schiris baillies, my lord provest he send me *to the bailies.*
furth of Seytoun and hes biddin me say to yow that he commandis yow
all thre to tak Adam Diksoun, seruand to Thomas Thomsoun, ipoticar,
and vther twa quhais names I knaw nocht, bot I belief thay ar Thomas

E

## 34  EXTRACTS FROM THE RECORDS  [1559.

*Message by Lord Seytoun to the bailies.*

Thomsonys sonnys, and put thame all thre in the irnys, thair to remane quhill his lordschipis returnyng to this toun, and bad me forther say gyf ye dyd nocht the samyn with deligence, that he sould put yow thre in irnys, to remane thairintill at his plesour. And the said Robert Fyndour being demandit of the saidis baillies gyf he had ony commissioun in wryt fra my said lord prouest towert the premissis, answerit he had na forther commissioun nor command be toung; and in lik maner being demandit quhairfor the saidis personis sould be put in irnys, said he knew nocht; and siclike being demandit be the saidis baillies of the names of the vther tway that sould be put in irnys with the said Diksoun, and quhilk of Thomas Thomsonys [sonys] thai war becaus he had monye, said he knew na forther nor he had said of before: Quhairuponn the saidis baillies askit instrumentis and actis of court, and protestit for remeid.

### 26 April 1559.

*Complaint of Adam Diksoun, prisoner.*

The quhilk day Alexander Barroun baillie, [the dean of guild, treasurer and council,] being convenit in the tolbuth of this burgh, within the counsale hous of the samyn, tuiching the complaynt gevin in before thame be Adam Diksoun presoner, desyring him to be put at libertie vpoun cautioun vnder quhat sowmes thair wysdomes plesit to enter, and answer at the instance of quhatsumevir pairtye, and quhat day and place thai wald appoynt, quhilk desyre thay thocht resonabill and conforme to the ordour cuir obseruit within this burgh, and in speciall to the inhabitanttis and nychtbouris of the samyn nocht committand hie and odious crymes; and thairfor all in ane voce fyndis concludis and decernys the said Adam Diksoun to be put to libertie, cautioun beand found in maner abone writtin: Quairuponn the said Adam askit instrumentis and actis of court. Allan Diksoun, burges, becumes cautioun and souertie for the entre of Adam Diksoun. . . . .

### 28 April 1559.

*Leyth, villa.*

The provost [bailies, dean of guild, treasurer, assessors, council and deacons of crafts] convenit in the counsaill hous, efter consideratioun had of the Quenis grace writting schawin and producit to thame be my lord provest, direct to the provest ballies counsaill and communitie of this burgh, makand mentioun that hir grace was informit that thai had callit or wer to call certane induellairis of the toun of Leyth for certane auld actionis and querellis being betwix thame; and hir grace, desyrand the induellairis of Layth the said townis to be at vnitie and quietnes, requeistit the provest ballies counsaill and communitie of the said burgh to supereeid the calling of the saidis actionis vnto hir graces returnyng to the said burgh, as thai wald ansuer to hir grace and do acceptable gratitude in that behalf, as the said writting bure: quhilk being red, considderit, and the provest ballies counsaill and dekynnis with thair assessouris foirsaidis being thairwith awisit, ordanis all actionis being betwix thame and the induelleris of Leyth to ceis quhill the Quenis grace returnyng, and inhibitioun to be maid to Edward Litill, Daniel Somer and Thomas Ridpethe, deputt be thame to persew the saidis actionis, to desist and ceis fra farther persewing thairof vnto the tyme thai ressauit farther directioun fra the counsaill thairto; providing allwayis that becaus the induellaris of Leyth quhilkis ar summond at the townis instance to ansuer in the saidis actionis hes obtenit chairgeis of the lordis of counsaill chargeing all and syndrie the procuratouris, or als money of thame as the saidis induellairis of Leyth thinkis expedient to defend in the saidis actionis vpone thair ressonable expenssis, that the geving of the saidis procuratouris and chargeis of the lordis obtenit thairvpon be callit and tak effect nochtwithstanding the said delay grantit as said is, providing allwayis that the samyn be nocht preindiciall to thair saidis actionis. *Leyth, villa.*

The provest ballies counsaill and dekinnis forsaidis sittand in jugement, compeirit maister James Lyndsay thesaurer, and presentit ane supplicatioun makand mentioun that quhair be the said office of thesaurerie, quhairin he servit this instant yeir, it become him to augment the commoun rentaill of this burgh be quhatsumever honest way he mycht, and it was nocht vnknawin to thame that thair was ane waist place be eist the butterege on the eist syde of the northe kirk durre quhilk mycht be ane sufficient and meitt roume to iij choppis, quhilkis wald gif yerlie to the gude toun the sowme of xx merkis yerlie proffeit in cais the samyn wer *Thesaurer, villa.*

Thesaurer, villa.

biggit to the kirk gavill with tymer, nocht passand farther furthe nor the breid of the saidis butteraigis, quhilk wald mak the said passage equall and of ane breid and mair honest, speciallie becaus the said wast place servit for nathing bot collecting of filthe, desyrand thame to ressoun thairin anent thair ansuer. Quhilk supplicatioun being red, vnderstand, and thairwith being riplie awisit, and the provest ballies assessouris counsall and dekinnis foirsaidis being seuerallie requirit vpone thair voittis, my lord provest, the saidis assessouris, Michell Gilbert dekin of the goldsmythis, and Danid Schang of the wrychtis, votit that the saidis choppis mycht be lesumlie biggit conforme to the said desyre, providing that thay pas nocht farther furthe nor the buttergeis; and all the rest in the contrair; and thairvpone James Adamsoun askit instrumentis.

### 10 May 1559.

Stent of Innerkeithing.

The prowest baillies and counsall ordainis maister James Lyndesay thesaurer to intromet and tak wp the first and secund termes stentis of Innerkeithing, and the secund terme of Kingorn, and to releif the baillies thairwith of xxxiij li. xj s. quhilk thai want of thair quarteris and is restand to the laird of Coldainknowis of the secund terme.

### 14 May 1559.

Regina, villa.

In presens of Alexander Barroun baillie, the maist pairt of the counsaill and ane greit pairt of the communitie, my lord provest presentit the Quenis grace writting direct to the provest and ballies of this burgh of the tenour following:—Provest and ballies of Edinburgh we greit yow weill: We traist it be nocht vnknawin to yow the greit mysreull laitlie maid within the burgh of Perthe, be certane seditious and evill gevin personnis, quha hes spulyeit and distroyit the religious places of the samyn, and fering that sum rasche and insolent people sall attempt to do the semblable in vtheris townis gif remeid be nocht haistelie providit, hes thocht expedient to mak yow warnyng herof in tyme: quhairfoir we charge yow that ye fra thyne furthe gif gude heid and attendence that na sic vproir nor seditioun rys within your toun, bot that the religious places be surelie kepit, and gude ordour observit as accordis, certefeying yow gif ony mysreull happinnis hereftir in sic behalfis that we sall nocht faill to lay the deid and wyt thairof to your charge. At Strineling the xiiij day of Maii 1559. *Sic subscribitur*, la bien vra, MARIA, R. Quhilk writing being red in presens of the baillie counsall and communitie foirsaid, my lord provest desyrit thair ansner thairof, quha ansuerit that thai wald do thair diligence and power to keip gude ordour in the toun, and to sauff the samyn fra all sic seditioun and trubill efter thair possibillite, conforme to the will and myud of the said writing, and the communitie anent the provisioun of the maner of defens of the religious places referrit thame to the counsaill, and thairvpon my lord provest askit instrumentis, and ordanit the counsaill to convene efter none to tak ordour thairintill. [Regina, villa.]

### 20 May 1559.

The ballies counsall and dekynnis, conforme to the Quenis grace wreting of before, findis necessar that the townis artelye be brocht furth of thair mvnitioun hows, and be laid vpone sic partis of the town as the prouest and ballies sall think expedient, and that for the handilling of the samyn that thair be feit vj gunnaris, qualefeit at the sicht of the said prouest and ballies, and sic wagis to be gevin to thame and thai to be hyrit for sic space as the saidis prouest and ballies sall think expedient; and siclyke for the mair apperand obedience of the Quenis grace will, and of the contentis of hir hienes said wreting, ordanis ane nichtlie wache to be set efter the aduys of the said lord prouest, induring sic space and contening sic nomer as he sall think expedient; and ordanis the ballies to gif the coppye of thair quarter rollis to the prouest to that effect. [Anent the keping of the town.]

The prouest ballies and counsall and dekinnis foresaidis grantis and gevis to Jonet Guthre the bedralship in the hospitall of Saint Marye Wynde now vacand in thair handis be deceis of Jonet Thomesoun. [Guthrie, bedrall.]

### 24 May 1559.

The prouest [bailies, dean of guild, councillors and deacons,] being convenit within the tolbuth for ressonyng vpoun the impresonyng [Prouest Seytoun.]

Prouest
Seytoun.

and warding of Dauid Forster baillie, fyrst in the castell of Edinburgh be the said prouest, and thaireftir be letteris purchest be his lordship at the Quenys grace in the Castell of Dunbar, quhilk thai allegeit to be to the greit hurt of thair libertie and contrair his lordships dentie beand thair prouest as said is, to the quhilk it wes ansuerit be my said lord prouest that he commandit nocht the said Dauid to the said castell of Edinburgh, as prouest, bot be virteu of ane greitar office and power committit to him be the Quenys grace at this present; and as tuiching his warding in Dunber the samyn wes be the Quenys grace writing for crymes committit aganis hir hienes, and na could nocht justlie be imput to him any falt in his said office of prouestrye in that case, in respect the said Dauidis warding and impresonment wes for crymes committit aganis the Quenys grace as said is, and be hir hienes speciall writing and command, to the quhilkis all personis within this realme war subiect; and heirupoun his lordship askit instrumentis. It being alsua alleget that gyf my said lord prouest providit nocht remeid haistelye for the said Dauid Forsteris releif furth of the said castell of Dunbar the samyn mycht be occatioun of vpror and insurrectioun of the commoun pepill of this burgh, to the greit hurt of the commoun weill of the samyn, and eftir his lordship had demandit the apperance of the said vpror, na ansuer being gevin, declarit and offerit himself with his kyn freindis and that wald do for him radye for resisting of the samyn, and heirupoun askit instrumentis.

The baillies, counsale, assessour, dene of gyld and dekynnis forsaid, all in ane voce conoludis and thinkis gude that my said lord prouest wryte effectnislie to the Quenys grace for the said Dauid Forsteris releif, and effectuislie requeistit his lordship till do the samyn, to the quhilk requeist his lordship glaidlie consenttit, and promyst to wryte in maist effectuus maner at thair desyre, and thocht gude that tua of the counsale war send with the said writing, and forther to heir the Quenys grace gude mynd towert this gude toun for the faythfull seruice done be thame to hir hienes at this tyme, to the effect the samyn may be reportit to thame agane and to gyf thame the better occatioun to serue in times cuming, quhilk the baillies counsale and dekynnis foresaid thocht alsua neidfull and ordanyt

James Adamsoun of the counsale and Dauid Kynloeht dekyn of the Prouest baxstaris to depairt the morne with the said writing to the Quenys grace, Seytoun. and to report hir hienes ansuer of the samyn to thame as said is.

### 26 May 1559.

The quhilk day, maister Jhonn Spens baillie [the dean of guild and Decanus gilde. nine members] of the counsale, efter ressonyng with the said dene of gyld tuiching the libertye and privelege of fre burgessis occupeit be vnfremen, fyndis that in the said dene of gyldis defalt the saidis fre burgesses ar hauelie hurt and the commoun proflit ouresene, in sa fer as he sufferis bayth merchanttis and craftismen to greit nowmer within this burgh to occupye the libertye of fre merchanttis they beand na burgessis, and for remeid heirof in tymes cuming ordanis the said dene of gyld with ane baillie and clerk and membris of court to fence and set gyld courttis for calling of the saidis vnfremen bayth merchanttis and craftismen and ordour putting to thame in tymes cuming; and for his help heirintill ordanis the baillies to gyf to him the copye of thair stent rollis to the effect the vnfremen occupyaris of merchandice may be first callit and ordour put to thame; and siclike the dekynnis of all craftis to gyf him alsua the names off all personis occupearis of thair saidis craftis to the effect foresaid; and ordanis the officiaris to pas at the command of the said dene of gyld fence and arreist all personis quhais names he sall gyf thame iu bill at quhat tymes he commandis thame, vnder the pane of tynsale of thair offices; and appoynttis to the said dene of gyld all the Wednisdayis and Frydayis following for halding of the saidis courttis quhill ordour be taikin in the premissis as said is.

### 28 May 1559.

The prouest baillies counsale dekynnis and ane greit pairt of the com- Regina. munitie being convenit within the Tolbuth, at the desyre of my said lord prouest, his lordship produeit the Quenys grace writing, of the quhilk the tenour followis, and desyrit the samyn to be registrat :—Counsale of Edinburgh we greit yow weill. Forsamekle as we vnderstand be ane writing of our

| | |
|---|---|
| Regina. | cousing the lord Seytonis your pronest the gude will and mynd ye beyr to ws in assisting to him at this troublous tyme in setting fordwert of oure seruice, quhairof we thank yow hartlie, praying yow to continew thairintill as ye and ilkane of yow sall fynd ws willing for defence of your liberteis of your said toun, or in ony vther case as ye sall happin till haue ado with ws, as we fynd yow applyabill in setting fordwert of oure seruice at this time, and sa fair ye weill. At Striuiling the xxvj of Maii 1559. *Sequitur subscriptio*, MARIE. R. |

3 *June* 1559.

| | |
|---|---|
| Stewinstoun in the townis will. | In presens of my lord provest, maister Jhone Spens baillie and James Barroun of the counsall, Mathow Stewinstoun sernand to Alexander Bruce barbour being accusit for casting of stanis at the Blak and Gray Freiris wyndowis the last nycht that he was vpon the waiche, grantit and confessit the samin and submittit him in the provest and baillies will for the samin, and the said Alexander Bruce his maister become oblist vnder the pane of ij$^e$ lib. for entre of the said Mathow within the tolbuyth or quhat tyme he be requerit. |

14 *June* 1559.

| | |
|---|---|
| Protestatio decani gilde. | The baillies and counsale being convenit, Jhone Charteris dene of gild being present, thay all in ane voce requirit the said Jhone Charteris to rasaue and tak in suir keping the jowallis ornamentis and silner werk of the hye alter to be suirlie kepit be him now in this trublous tyme, to the quhilk answerit the said Jhone Charteris that he was agit, seyklie, haveand na bodye with him in his hows bot his wyf and serning weming, and in cace the samin wer inuadit the saidis gudis being thairintill he wer nocht habill to resist, and forther he wes nocht responsabill for the awaill of thame, quhairfor he dissasentit expresse to thair desyre or ony ordinance maid to that effect of before, and refusit alluterlie to have ony forther intromissioun charge or keping of the saidis jowallis ornamentis and silner work otherwyis nor the dene of gildis his predicessouris had of before, that |

is to say to remane in lokfast hmes within the rawestre, and to be reddy  Protestatio
to serue at tymes convenient, and heirvpone askyt instrumentis. decani gilde.

### 16 June 1559.

Maister Jhone Spens baillie, Jhone Charteris dene of gild, James  Anent keiping
Barroun, William Lawsoun, William Patersoun, Andro Sklaittar, William of the toun.
Aikman and James Young of the counsale findis gude and necessar that
all the portis of the towne be lokit day and nycht, the West Port and
Nether Bow onlie except, and that thair be sett at euery ane of thay portis
xij habill men with halbartis all the day, for stopping of tumult pley or
cumaris quhilkis may happin betuix pairteis and keping of guid ordour
within this burgh, and siclyke other xxiiij habill men to walk all the nycht
within the toun on the streittis for keping of gude ordour; and this ordour
to pas quarterlie throwcht the towne induring sic tyme as my lord provest
baillies and counsall foresaid sall think neidfull and expedient, and the
said maister Jhone Spens to list samonye of his quarter as is aboue
expremit the morne nixt, and fra hyne furth euery baillie to do the samin
induring as said is.

The baillies and counsall foresaid ordanis maister James Lindesay Sanct Geill.
thesawrar to rasaue fra Dauid Somer burges of this burgh the commissioun
impetrat at the instance of the gude towne in the court of Rome aganis
Jhone archiebischope of Sanctandrois for non vpputting of Sanct Geill,
and to delyuer to the said Dauid the sowme of x crounis of the sone in compleit payment of the expenssis maid vpone the impetratting of the said
commissioun.

### 21 June 1559.

The provest ballies and counsale gewis and disponis to Cuthbert Bedrellschip.
Dik, walker, the bedderelschip of Sanct Paulis werk vacand be deceis of
vmquhile. . . .

Grantis and faithfullie promittis to Richard Henrisoun, baxter, the
next beidmanschip vacand.

F

| | |
|---|---|
| Precept, Gowane, Symsoun, Home. | The provest baillies and counsale ordanis Jhonn Charteris dene of gyld to content and pay to Patrik Govane belman, Johnne Symsoun and Thomas Home keparis and walkaris of Sanct Geillis kirk sen Witsounday ewin last bipast, nychtlie twa s.; and siclik ilk nycht alsmekill in times cuming salang as it salbe thocht neidfull that thai sall walk and keip the samin. |
| Precept, Dow. | [The treasurer ordained " to deliuer to Jacques Dow and his souis ane croun of the sone for thair labouris in playing of the sweis this last wapinschawin."] |
| Anent the calsay. | The baillies counsall and dekynnis foirsaid ordanis Michell, the France calsay makar, to be send for to Dumbar for mending of the commone calsayis of this burgh, and to the effect he sall haue the better occasioun to remane within the samyn ordanis ane yeirlie fe of sex merkis to be grantit and gevin to him for all the dayis of his life, prouiding alwayis that he remane apoun the commoun werkis and depairt nocht furth of the toun without licence of the prouest or ane of the baillies for the tyme; nochtwithstanding the said fe he to be payit for his lanbouris as the maister of wark and he for the tyme sall aggre. |
| Anent davis throuch the toun. | The baillies counsall and dekynnis forsaid, vnderstanding that the granting of dayis throuch the toun to pure folkis hes bene the occasioun of drawing of mony strang beggeris to the burgh in hoip of obtening of sic almes, and that alsua the samin hes done gret hinder to the auld faillit burgessis and craftis men of this burgh for quhais support the samin wes onlie devisit, for remeid thairof statutis and ordanis that na dayis be grantit in tymes cuming to ony maner of persoun throw the toun for getting of almes fra this day furth, bot onlie but faill burgessis merchandis and craftismen or sic vtheris as hes spendit thair youth in honest maner within this burgh. |

27 June 1559.

| | |
|---|---|
| Jowallis and vestiamentis. | The baillies and counsaill vnderwrittin consentit and grantit all in ane voce that the personis vnder specifyit ressauit in custode the jowallis and vestiamentis vnder writtin, to be furtheumand and delinerit be thame quhen thai suld be requirit thairto be the counsall, quhilkis personis |

ressauit the same and promist to do thair vter deligence for keping *Jowallis and vestiamentis.*
thairof. The names of the counsaill and baillies: Alexander Barroun, James Curll and Mr John Spens baillies, Mr Thomas M'Calzeane assessour, Jhone Charterhous dene of gild, Mr James Lyndesay thesaurar, James Broun, Thomas Thomsoun, Williame Patersoun, William Lawsoun, James Young, Andro Sclater of the dekynnis, Alexander Sawche tailyeour, Thomas Jaksoun masoun, James Cranstoun dekyn of the hammermen, Richart Hendersoun dekyn of the fleshcouris, Mychael Gilbert dekyn of the goldsmythis, Robert Huntroddis dekyn of the cordinaris, Peter Turnet dekyn of the skynneris, Hew Canne dekyn of the furrouris, with the rest of the dekynnis.

The names of the honest men quha ressauit this yeir in keping :— *Deliuerance of* 
*In primis*, to James Barroun merchand, the ewcharcist ; item, maister *the jowallis and vestiamentis*
Thomas M'Calyeane, the arme of Sanct Geill ; James Young, the tua maist *afoir the*
chandlaris of syluer ; Michaell Gilbert, tua lytill chandlar of sylwer ; Jhone *cuming of the congregatioun.*
Charterhous dene of gild, the mekill croce with the fute ; Alexander Guthrie, ane challice with the patene and spyne ; Thomas Thomsoun, tua crowattis with the cresum stoke ; James Carmychaell, tua censuris and the schipp ; Alexander Barroun baillie, the round ewcharist ; quhilk haill jowallis ar of the wecht specifyit in the act maid the sevint day of Januar, the yeir of God 1558 yeris, and insert in the same buke.

The names of thame that ressauit the vestiamentis of the kirk :—
*In primis*, to maister James Lyndesay the sacrament clayth with Saint Gelis cloke of welwote droppit with gold, with the pendicle of reid crammesye welwote, alias callit the waill ; item, to maister Jhone Spens baillie, ane paill of reid saten with ane kaip of clayth of gold ; item, to James Curll, vestiament dekyn subdekyn preistheid and kaip, with the ornamenttis compleittand the haill stand all of clayth of gold ; item, ressauit be Williame Lawsoun merchand, ane westiament dekyn and subdekyn of grene dalmes with the pertinentis begareit with strypis of gold ; item, to Alexander Sawche dekyn of the tailycouris, tua frontellis ane of blak welwot and ane other of reid welwote ; item, ressauit be James Cranstoun, preist dekyn and subdekyn of quhite dalmes ; item, be Thomas

44    EXTRACTS FROM THE RECORDS    [1559.

Deliuerance of the jowallis and vestimentis afoir the cuming of the congregatioun.

Jaksoun dekyn of the masounis, ane chesobell of reid welwote myxt with clayth of gold with the pertinentis; item, delinerit to Rychart Hendersoun dekyn of the flesheouris, the mort stand contenand thre capis dekyn and subdekyn and preistheid, with the orpheis of blak welwote and graith pertenand thairto ; item, ressauit be Robert Huntroddis dekyn of the cordineris, a haill stand of blew welwote contenand thre capis dekyn subdekyn and preist with the pertinents; item, to Hew Canne dekyn of the furrouris, tua twneclis of quhite dalmes, ane blew chesobell of welwote with the pertinentis, ane chesobell of tanny welwote; item, to Andro Sclater, vestment dekyn and subdekyn of clayth of gold alias callit Daime Lauderis stande; item, ressauit be Peter Turnet dekyn of the skynneris, vestment dekyn and subdekyn of clayth of sylner and blew welwote with the frontell; to John Charterhous eldar, dene of gild, the [*blank*] candilstykis of tyn of the hie altar, with the arres wark of the same altar; to Patrik Govane belman, the vale afoir the hie altar of lyning clayth with the pulpet clayth.

29 *June* 1559.

Commissioun gevin to certane direct to the congregatioun.

The quhilk day, maister Thomas Makcalzeane assessour, [bailies, dean of guild, conncillors and deacons,] being convenit in the tolbuyth, and efter lang ressoning vpone the cuming of the congregatioun to this burgh, fyndis gude that certane honest men be send to meit thame at Linlithgow, to quhome commissioun salbe gevin to trait and commoun with thame for vphald of the ruiffis of the religious placcis and kyrkis within this burgh and for sawying of the stallis bakis of aulteris and otheris tymmer werk within the saidis kyrkis, and siclyke to desyre of thame to obserne and keip gude ordour within the said burgh at their cuming to the samin, and forder to labour at thair handis be all menis ressonable for the commoun weill of the samin, and vnto this effect constitutis and nominatis James Barroun, Alexander Guthrie, Andro Sklaitter, Thomas Thomsoun, James Young, Michaell Gilbert and Archibald Dowar, and ordanis speciall commissioun to be maid and geiffin to thame vnder the seill of caus of this burgh to the effect foresaid, for approving of thair weillis consenttis and speciall directioun of the saidis personis in the premissis, subscrywit be the commoun clerk.

The baillies assessouris counsale and dekynnis foresaid fyndis gude **Anent keping of the kirk.** and necessar for keping of Sanct Gelys kirk and vphald of the stawis of the queyr thair he feyit and hyrit thre score men of weyr, and ordanis maister James Lindesay theasurer to fee thame, and to gyf to euery ane xxx d. on the day sa lang as he thinkis neidfull thay sall serue and walk for keiping of the said kirk and stallis, and the samyn salbe allowit to him in his compttis.

In presens of maister Jhone Spens and Dauid Forrestar baillies, and **Protestatio, Small.** in presens of the maist pairt of the counsall and haill dekyns, comperit George Small saidlar, and protestit for him self and in name and behalf of the rest of the brethir of the hambermen, that James Cranstoun powderar, presentlie dekyn of the said hambermen, that he suld nocht be haldin to be thair deikyn ony langer, in respect that he refusit to serue his God and obedience to his prynce.

### 12 July 1559.

[The bailies and council] fyndis necessar that the stawis of the queyr **Anent the stawis.** be tane and put in the nether tolbuth for the mair sure keiping of thame, and ordanis the samyn to be careit thair with deligence, and Jhone Charterhouse dene of gild to pay the warkmen for thair laubouris in doun-taking and careing of the samyin.

The baillies and counsale foresaid ordanis maister James Lindesay **Precept, wark-men.** thesaurer to aggre with the warkmen quhilkis at thair command had vpbigit the sloppis at the Blakfreris and satifye thame for thair laubouris, and siclike to satifye Adam Purves wrycht for mending agane of the Gray-freir port.

Maister Jhone Spens, Dauid Forrestar and James Curle, baillies of **Propositioun of the lordis of the congregatioun.** the burgh of Edinburgh, James Carmychaell, James Barroun, William Lawsoun, Andro Sklatter, Thomas Thomesonu and James Young of the counsall of the said burgh, maister James Lindesay thesawrar, with ane certane of the deikynnis and ane gryt pairt of the commvnite of the samin, being convenit within thair tolbuyth for ressonning vpone the caussis of

Propositioun of the lordis of the congregatioun. their commoun weill, comperit before thame ane nowbill and mychtie lord Patrik lord Ruthwen, Jhone Sandelandis of Calder youngar, dirrect frome the lordis of the congregatioun to the baillies counsall and commvnite foresaid, and desyrit of thame to be harde to declair sic thingis as wes gevin thame in commissioun be the saidis lordis, off the quhilk the tennour followis : Beluflit brethering, we think ye ar nocht ignorant quhat hes movit my lordis of this present congregatioun to convene within this burgh at this tyme, and in cais ye be thair lordshippis be quhome we ar direct to yow hes gevin ws ane speciale charge and command to declair and oppoyn to yow the samin, that is to mak it knowin to yow and euery ane of yow that they pretend na sic thing as the commoun brute is twiching the inobediance of the prynce or vsurping of hiear powaris, bot that thai ar onlie convenit for the awanciement and furthsetting of Godis glore according to the trew and pure ewangell, and thairwith enir mening ye dow obediance of the princes to be manteinit be thame thair bodye and gudis at thair vter powaris, requering alswa the samin of yow and that ye will adione yow with thame vnfenyeit as thay sall with yow to the furthsetting of Godis trew worde and dew obediance of the prynce as said is, and that ye will heir plainlie and in all tymes cuming tak vpone yow the manteinance and defence of the samin, and swa money of yow as will glaidlie consent heirto to bynd and obleis yow be vphalding of your handis and to send thame your names in writt.

29 *July* 1559.

Anent the Quenis grace and brether of the congregatioun. In presens of the provest ballies ane pairt of the counsall dekynnis and ane greit number of the communite, compeirit the nobel and mychty lordis, viz., James duke of Chattelerault, erle of Arran, etc., erle Huntlie etc., and Johne lord Erskein, and declairit that anent the appointment maid betwix thame as commissaris for our Souerane Lady Quene Marie drowriar and regent of this realme and the lordis of the congregatioun the [*blank*] day of Julii instant, it was appontit and commvnit thairin that the toun of Edinburgh sould without compulsioun vs and cheis quhat religioun and maner thairof thai pleisit to the tent day of Januar nixt to cum, swa that euery man may hawe fredome of his conscience

vnto the said day, for satefeing of the quhilk artikle it was the quenis Anent the
grace will that the inhabitantis of this burgh wer convenit and euery ane Quenis grace
to be examinit quhat religioun he wald be of, and that religioun to be of the congre-
mantenead to the said day that the greitast number consentit to, and gatioun.
desyrit the communite present quhither thai wald voit seuerallie or
remitt the samyn to the voitis of the provest ballies counsaill and
dekynnis as hes been vsit in ordour taking of ciuill caussis befoir; and
thairefter compeirit Adame Foullertoun, for himself and in name and
behalf of the haill brether of the congregatioun within this toun, being
personallie present, and presentit to the saidis lordis the supplicatioun
eftir following, and the samyn being red and considderit be thame
desyrit the said supplicatioun to be insert in thir lukis, of the quhilk
the tenour followis: My lordis, vnto your lordschippis humlie menis and
schawis the faythfull bretherine of the congregatioun within Edinburgh,
induelleris thairof, that quhair as we ar informit your lordschippis ar heir
couvenit of mynd and purpois to tak euery mannis voit quhat religioun
he will be of, and quhair the ministratioun thairof sall be vsit, and we for
our pairtis knawand the religioun quhilk we hawe presentlie to be of God
and conforme to his word, and on the vther pairt knawand the mes and
the papis haill religioun to be without the word of God, altogither superstitious damnable idolatrie and of the devill, can nocht consent for oure
pairtis that Goddis treuthe and that oure religioun now establischit conforme to his worde sall be subiect to voiting of men, as gif the maist pairt
of men allowit it nocht it sould be rejectit, for it is na new thing bot mair
nor notoir that fra the beginnyng of the world to this day and evin
now in all controyis tounis and citeis the maist pairt of men hes ouer bene
aganis God and his treuthe, at the leist hes nocht planlie embraced the
samyn. Secoundlie, anent the place we say that in the appointment maid
betwix youre lordschippis and the lordis of the congregatioun it is in
speciall providit that oure prechouris sall nocht be molestit nor trubblit
nor yit thair ministerie, nor that the said congregatioun sall nocht be
trublit in thair guddis bodyis landis or possessionis quhatsumeuer vnto
the tent day of Januar, bot swa it is that we the congregatioun of this
toun, the tyme of the making of the said appointment lang of befor and

48     EXTRACTS OF THE RECORDS     [1559.

Anent the  
Quenis grace  
and brether of  
the congrega-  
tioun.

continewallie sensyne, wer in possessioun, lykas we ar yit, of the hie kirk of this toun callit Sanct Geillis kirk, haveand our commoun prayeris preching of the word and the ministratioun of the sacramentis and haill vther ministerie thairintill but interruptioun, and thairfoir aucht and sould to possess the samyn vnto the said day but ony voting controuersie and trubbill, and swa can na way consent to submitt that to voting quhilk the saidis lordis lefit vs possest in ; and swa in effect your lordschippis of your honouris can nocht suffer vs to be trubblit in oure maner of religioun nor yit in the place of ministratioun thairof quhilk we peciabillie posses, mekle les trubbhill vs youreselfis be compelling of vs vpone the thingis quhilkis we hawe ellis but controuersie as said is, without ye will planlie contravene the said appontment ; beseikand your lordschippis that ye will hawe regarde to the said appontment and to your awin honouris, and seing that we can na way consent to ony voting in the caissis foirsaidis, except we will by the appontment ellis maid mak new transactioun or be oure awin consent putt tha thingis in dowt quhilkis be the said appont- ment ar to vs fre, and in respect that we can on na wys do the samyn without the saidis lordis of congregatioun wer heir present to consent thairto, that youre lordschippis will manteine and defend, at the leist nocht trubbill nor suffer vs to be trubblit in, oure maner of religioun and place of ministratioun quhilk we now possess and possest the tyme of the making of the said appontment, protesting heir in your presens befoir God gif ye do in the contrair and submitt the samyn to voiting, the voting of the wikkit, (as for vs we aucht nocht nor can nocht consent thairto nor voit thairintill) that ye do vs plane wrang and iniurie and planlie contra- uenis your said appontment besyde the opponyng of yourselfis to God and his treuthe, quhilk we surelie and stedfastlie beleif he will nocht leiff sudanlie vnreuengit ; and your lordschippis ansuer humlie we beseik. Quhilk supplicatioun being oppinlie red the saidis lordis declarit that thai wald compell na man to do by his conscience, nor do ony thing that mycht contravene the said appontment, and thairvpone askit instrumentis.

Protestatio,  
prepositi.

The quhilk day, in presens of the ballies counsaill dekynnis and com- munitie foirsaid, my lord provest declarit that all the commoun questionis and canssis of this burgh wer in tymes past referrit to the decisioun of the counsaill, as for the merchantis and dekinnis as for thair craftis respectiue, and in cais the mater proponit be the lordis contenit in the act aboue writtin come to voting desyrit the said auld ordour to be obseruit thairin, protestand awayis incais nouationn wer inbrocht and that the haill communitie votit thairin, that the samyn wer nocht inputt to him, and that he wer nocht accusit be the authoritie as negligent in his office thairanent. *Protestatio prepositi.*

2 *August* 1559.

The baillies and counsaill, haueand consideratioun that thair is ane commoun passaige and gait throw the slop in the Blakfreir yarde dik at the eist end of the blockhous, and that syndrie personis in tyme of nycht and vtheris tymes passis and repassis thairthrow, ordanis maister James Lyndsay thesaurer to vpbig and reperall the said slop conforme in work to the toun wall nixt adaicent thairto, and to mend and reparrell all places ruynois and apperand to decay with all hoillis of the said freir dyk. *Anent the toun wall.*

[The bailies ordained the treasurer and two or three of the council to inspect the ports and consider if they " be faultes or neidis reformation," and to report to the bailies and council. *Keping of the portis.*

The bailies accepted the charge of the keys of the ports as follows :—James Curll, the Nether Bow and Water Yett ports; John Spens, the Kirk of Feild and Cowgait ports; Alexander Barroun, the Greyfreir port; and Dauid Forrester, the West port; "and euery ane of thame to ressaue the keyis at evin in dew tyme, and to deliuer the samyn at morne as thai sall think gude and tyme sall requyre."]

The baillies and counsaill ordanis maister James Lyndsay thesaurer to content and pay to Alane Purves the sowme of xxx s., for his lawbouris takin in awaiting vpone the kirk the tyme that the congregatioun was in this toun, and doun taking of the stallis; and syklyk ordanis him to content and pay to Robert Drummond and Alexander Cuke ilk ane of thame xx s. for thair lawbouris takin thairin. *Precept, Purves, Cuke, Drummond.*

4 *August* 1559.

The baillies and counsall foirsaid ordanis maister James Lindesay to *Prebendaris.*

Prebendaris. mak thankfull payment to Sir Walter Haliburtoun, Sir James Craufurd, Sir George Manderstoun, Sir Johne Keir, Sir William Johnnstoun, Sir James Abircrumby, and the vtheris prebendairis of Sanct Geillis queir, to quhom the gude toun is detbund for ony annuell or dewitie, of all annuellis and dewiteis awin to thame in tymes bigane.

Mending of the portis. [The bailies and council having referred to two bailies and the treasurer "anentis the mending beiting and reparaling of the portis, now auld and failyeit," and they having reported that they "fand the cistor cheik of the Grayfreir port with the wickit thairof and the haill Kirk of Feild port failyeit; thairfor ordanis the samin to be biggit of new, with tua new barris vpoun the heid of Sanct Marie port."]

Anentis beggaris. The baillies and counsall foirsaidis, havand consideratioun of the gret multitude and dailie confluance of maisterfull strang beggerris to this burgh, and that the almes quhairon the native beggerris of this burgh borne and remanand within the samin aucht to be sustenit for the maist pairt is bestowit vpoun thame, ordanis all actis of parliament of oure Soueraue Lady and hir maist nobill progenitouris, with all actis statutis and ordinances the prouest baillies and counsall of this burgh maid and set furth for stanching of sturdy beggeris, to be put to executioun in all poyntis efter the forme and tennour thairof; and ordanis Adam Foulartoun with vtheris fiftene honest and vnsuspect personis quhilkis he sall elect thairto to be distributit, foure in every quarter, for furthseiking the saidis sturdye beggerris and expelling of thame furth of this toun; and ordanis ane baillie to assist and concur with thame thairin gif he beis requirit, and to thair execution the saidis baillies and counsall hes interponit and interponis thair auctorite.

14 August 1559.

Anent the wache. The quhilk day, maister Johne Spens baillie, [the treasurer, councillors and deacons], for certane ressonable caussis moving thame, and for eschewing of trubbill and incommoditie within the toun in tyme of nycht, fyndis that the nychtbouris of this toun sall wache successiue nychtlie to the number of xxiiij personis, viz., vj thairof to remane at the

Netherbow, sex at the Blakfreiris, iiij at the Lochend, twa at ilkane of the Cowgait, Kirk of Feild and Grayfreir portis; and this to stand induring the counsaillis will. And gif ony persone being warnit to the said wache be the officeris and comperis nocht that the said officer poynd him for the sowme of ij s. and for ane vther to wache on his expenssis. *Anent the wache.*

### 18 August 1559.

["The bedderrellschip vacand in Sanct Marie Wynd be deceis of Dame Fairulie" given to the "relict to vmquhile Johnne Pynkertoun."] *Bedderell-schip.*

[The treasurer ordered to pay "to Thomas Hall jewillour the sowme of thre lib. in recompance of the coillis furneist be him to the lordis of the cessioun frome Pensche to Witsounday last, and of the candill furneist be him to the wache befor this present day."] *Precept, Hall.*

The ballies assessores counsale and dekynnis foirsaid, efter considera- tioun of the hawy complaint of the puir and misterfull borne beggaris of this burgh, quhilk wer maisterfullie oppressit be maisterfull and strang beggaris of vther partis resortand to the said burgh, takand frome thame thair almes quhairvpoun thai suld leve, throuche the quhilkis thai wer in poynt of tynsale, for the quhilkis caussis and vtheris moving thame con- cerning the commone weill of this burgh, the support of the native impo- tent and faillit and misterfull pepill of the samin, ordanis officeris to pas throw all the partis and quarteris of this toun, charge and warne the in- habitantis and honest houshalderis of the samin to couuene before thame this eftir nowne, and sic vther tymes as salbe appointed, to se ordour takin for repelling of the saidis landwert beggaris furth of the said burgh, and prouisioun to be maid for sustening of oure awin pure in tymes cuming, conforme to the actis of parliament and statutis of this burgh maid to the samin effect of befoir. *Anent beggaris.* *Anent the puir.*

### 4 September 1559.

The bailies [and council] ordanis maister James Lindesay thesaurar to vpbig and reparell the Muse Well now fallin doun, als substantiuslie *Anentis the wellis.*

Anentis the Wellis.

and honestlie as the samin wes befoir the doun falling thairof; and als ordanis the said thesaurar to payment the brayis of the Stok Well and Sanct Michaellis Well with substantius flaggis.

Skyn merkatt.

The baillies and counsaill foirsaid ratefeis and apprevis the act maid of befoir for doun taking of the skyn merkatt fra the place quhair the samyn wes vsit to be had to the Freir Wynd heid, and fra thyne furthe to the Nether Bow, and ordanis the samyn to indure efter the tenour of the said act, and the samyn to be putt to executioun in all poyntis, and all personis havand skynnis to sell to keip merkat in the place foirsaid, vnder the pane of escheitting of the samin.

14 *September* 1559.

Lords of session.

[The dean of guild ordained to pay the "sowme of xx s. for ringing of the bell for couuenyng of the lordis of the sessioun at aucht houris, this yeir last bypast."]

Counsall, Regina.

The ballies [and counceil] ordanis the answer maid to the Quenis writting (send to thaim the xxviij day of August last bypast) and subscrivit be ane pairt of the counsaill, to be distroyit.

20 *September* 1559.

Prefectus, Spens, Barroun.

In presens of the ballies dene of gild thesaurer haill counsaill and assessouris, except William Aikman and Andro Sklater furthe of the realme and maister Robert Crechtoun ane of the assessouris absent, the provest, be vertew of ane charge committit to him as he alledgit be the Quenis grace and lordis of secreit counsaill, chargit maister Johne Spens baillie and James Barroun ane of the counsaill to pas incontinent to the saidis lordis to answer to thame of sic thingis as thai had to lay to thair charge, and thairvpone askit instrumentis. And the saidis personis ansuerit that thai wald obey the said command als sone as the new counsaill wer chosin for the quhilk thai wer convenit, and desyrit allwayis to sie the said charge in writt gif be ony had, and thairvpone askit instrumentis.

In presens of the ballies dene of gild counsaill thesaurer and assess- *Prefectus,* ouris foirsaidis, my lord provest desyrit thame to proceid in electioun of *Barroun,* the new counsaill be the votis of thame that wer present efter the auld *Lien* ordour; and Edward Litill James Barroun and James Adamsone of the counsaill alledgit that afoir ony electioun thair aucht certane personis to be chosin to voit for the present tyme in place of thame that wer absent, conforme to the consuetude vsit continewallie thairintill, and the provest dissasentit aluterlie thairto and declairit that gif thai electit ony personis to voit for the saidis absentis, he wald depairt and be na member of the said electioun.

The samyn day, compeirit William Brysone maisour and be vertew of *Regina, ballini.* ane charge direct to him in writt subscrivit be our Soueranis hand chargit the counsaill to present thameselfis incontinent befoir the Quenis grace for sic thingis as hir grace had to do with thame, and the ballies and counsaill foirsaid ansuerit that thai wald obey, and thairvpone askit instrumentis.

The provest ballies dene of gild thesaurer and counsaill with the *Provest, coun-* assessouris, except befoir exceptit, being convenit agane within the *saill.* counsaillhous betwix foure and fyve houris efter none for electioun of the new counsaill, my lord provest declarit that he was to pas to the Quenis [grace] for addressing of certane hir graces bissynes committit to his charge and thairfoir mycht nocht remane at the said electioun, quhairfoir his lordschip ratefeit and approvit all thingis done or to be done be the saidis personis or the maist pairt of thame in the said mater.

The ballies counsaill dene of gild thesaurer and assessouris foir- *Hoip, Wat-* saidis fyndis be ane act maid the [*blank*] day of September 1554 it is *sone, of the* statut and ordanit that quhen ony persone ar absent of the counsaill *counsaill* quhen thair voitis ar requirit that it sall be lesum to thame that ar present to cheis vtheris in thair places to voit for that tyme, and thairfoir all with ane voce electit maister James Watsoun and Edward Hoip in place of Andro Sklater and William Aikman of the counsaill now absent

| | |
|---|---|
| Uoip, Watsone, of the counsaill. | and Alexander Guthre in place of maister Robert Crechtoun ane of the assessouris absent alswa, quhilkis wer sworne in presens foirsaid to gif thair best counsaill as thai sould be requirit ay and quhill thai wer dischargit thairof. |
| Villa, artifices. | In presens foirsaid, Robert Fynder dekin of the wrychtis, Thomas Jaksone of the masonis, Robert Meid of the wobstaris, Johne Auldinstoun of the bakstaris, Peter Turnett of the skynneris, Hew Canney of the furrouris, Richart Henrisone of the fleschouris, James Stirk of the walkeris, James Lansoun for Johne Welche dekin of the bonat makeris, James Cranstoun of the hammermen, Alexander Sanchie of the talyouris, Robert Huntrodis of the cordineris, and Patrik Lyndsay of the barbouris presentit the Quenis grace writing efter following, and alledgit that be vertew thairof, and of the gift of the restitutioun of thair craftis to thair priuelegis vnder the Quenis grace greit seill produceit with the said writting, thai aucht to voit particularlie in electioun of the said counsaill, and thairfoir protestit that nane wer chosin without thair votis tane thairintill, at the leist that thai wer nocht hald to obey the statutis and ordenances to be sett furthe be thame, of the quhilk writing the tenour followis :—Oure Soueranis Lord and Lady, vnderstanding that the craftismen of burrowis within thair realme of Scotland ar reponit to all priuilegeis fredomes and jurisdictioun vsit and occupyit be thame within burgh in thair maist noble progenitouris dayis, and in speciall to the chesing of thair dekynnis yeirlie at the tymes limite thairto for conseruatioun of guid ordour amang thamesellis, quhilkis dekynnis aucht and suld haue priuilege als weill in voting, particularlie in electing and chesing of all lytis quhilkis ar to be chosin to bruke offices within burgh at the feist of Michaelmes, sic as provest ballies counsale dene of gild thesaurer seriandis and all kynd of officeris within the samin, as in voting chesing and electing vpone the principall officeriis foirsaid; and albeit the saidis dekynnis of Edinburgh, sen thair restitutioun to the saidis liberteis be the space of thre yeiris syne or thairby, hes yeirlie the tyme of the electing of the new counsale offerit thame in reddines to vote in electing thairof, newirtheles the provest ballies and counsale of the said burgh refusit to ressawe thair wote thairunto nocht- |

OF THE BURGH OF EDINBURGH.

withstanding the liberteis grantit to thame thairvpone, in hie contemp- Villa, artifices tioun of thair auctoritie and expres aganis justice; chargeing heirfoir the saidis provest baillies and counsale foirsaid, now present and to cum, to suffir the saidis dekynnis and cuirilkane of thame particularlie be thameselfis to woit in electing and chesing of the counsale lytis and all vther officeris aboue specifiit in all tymes cuming, conforme to the priuilegeis grantit to thame thairvpoun, quhilkis priuilegeis be thir presentis we ratifie apprewis and ampleflis in all poyntis, and speciallie in the chesing of the counsall and lytis foirsaid, vnder the pane of dissobedience of our auctoritie and all charge and punisment that may follow thairvpone. Subscriuit be our said Soueranis darrest moder, at Halyrnidhous the [blank] day of September 1559. Sic subscribitur: MARIE R. The saidis dekynnis being removit and incallit againe, and the saidis ballies and counsale with thair assessouris foirsaidis being ryple awysit vpone the said writting and priuilegis mentionat thairin, findis that the saidis dekynnis suld haue na wote in the electioun of the new counsall in respect of the said writting as the samin is consavit, becaus it is relative to the said gift quhilk contenis allanerlie the restitutioun and repositioun of the saidis dekynnis to thair priuilegis fredomis and liberteis quhairof thai wer demudit be the act of parliament maid in the moneth of [June] the yeir of God j$^m$ v$^c$ l and [v] yeiris, and that thai wer in vse of befoir the making of the said act, and that it is of veritie that the dekynnis of craftis hes hade in na tymes bypast vote in electioun of the new counsale nor electioun of lytis but onlie in electioun of officeris; and thairvpone maister James Lyndesay theasurer askit instrumentis.

The baillies and counsale commandit and chargit [the deacons of crafts] and ilk ane of thame to remove thameselfis incontinent furth of the counsalehous, and to suffer the electioun of the counsaill for this yeir to cum to tak effect eftir the consuetude continewalle observit in tymis past, vnder the pane of dissobedience; and the saidis personis and euerilk ane of thame being seuerale reqnyrit gif thai wald obey the said charge or nocht ansuerit euerie ane seueralie that thai wald nocht remove thame selfis nor suffir the said electioun to tak effect without thai wotit particu-

Villa, artifices. Iarlie thairintill, and maister James Lyndesay thesaurer protestit for the townis actioun aganis the saidis dissobeyaris.

[The deacons of crafts] protestit that insafer as thai hade power grantit to thame be the Quenis grace to wote in electioun of the new counsale, and be vertew thairof remanit in the counsall hous nochtwithstanding that thai wer commandit be the baillies and counsale to remove thame furth thairof, that thai incurit na panis of dissobedience thairfoir.

22 September 1559.

Artifices, lytis.
The qubilk day, in presens of the prouest ballies and counsaill, being convenit for electioun of the lyttis to bruke offices within this burgh this yeir to cum, compeirit [the deacons of crafts] and desyrit to be admittit to voit in the said electioun in respect of the priuilegis grantit to thame be the Quenis grace thairvpone, and producit the xx day of September instant, and desyrit the saidis prouest ballies and counsaill answer thairvpone. The saidis dekynnis being furthe of courte removit and incallit agane, and the saidis prouest ballies and counsaill being with thair assessouris riplie awisit vpone the said allegiance, fyndis that the saidis dekynnis aucht to haue na voit in the said electioun in respect of the Quenis grace writing producit be thame and registrat in thir bukis the said xx day of September instant, as the samyn is consauit, in respect of the answer gevin thairto the said day and for the caussis contenit thairin, and the saidis dekynnis askit instrumentis that the prouest ballies and counsaill disobeyit the charge contenit in the said writing as thai alledgit, and protestit that thair disobedience wer nocht prejudiciall to thair prinileges and liberteis contenit in the said charge, and declarit that thai wald obey na officeris to be chosin for this yeir to cum in cais thai be nocht present at the electioun of thame, and thairvpone askit instrumentis.

Followis the tennour of the Quenis grace writting direct to the prouest baillies and counsaill of this burgh for electing and chesing of officeris:—
REGINA. Prouest baillies and counsall of Edinburgh, we greit you weill: Forsamekle as we for certain caussis moving vs hes thocht neidfull that

ye at this present feist of Michaelmes elect and cheis sic personis, honest *Artificers, lytis.*
merchandmen of your awin burgh, to be vponn your counsale and beir other
hiear offices abone you for this yeir intocum, qnhais names we sall send to
yow be sum speciall sernand of our awin or other wyis declair to sum of
yow be our awin monthe, quhilkis personis we pray yow effectuonslie, as ye
will do vs singulair plesour and report our speciall thankis, that ye elect
and admit to be vponn your counsale and beir your other offices for this
yeir intocum as said is, promitting be this present that the samin sall
nocht be hurtfull preparatiwe nor preiudiciall to your privilegiis nor auld
liberteis in tymes cunning be this present. Subscriuit with our hand at
our palyce of Halyruidhous, the xxij day of September 1559. *Sic subscribibatur:* MARIE R.

### 26 *September* 1559.

[The treasurer ordained to pay to "William Thomsone, quhisler, the soume of *Precept* vj s. viij d., for his labouris in playing vpone the quhissall at the wache be the space *Thomsone.* of ij nychts in the monethe of Julij last bipast."]

### 30 *September* 1559.

[The treasurer ordained "to thik the southe syde of the towlbuyth with new *Thesaurer,* sklait and mak the samyn watter tycht."] *villa.*

The ballies and counsaill foirsaidis, for eschewing of danger appeirand *Anent the* to cum, ordanit the townis evidentis of grit awaill to be putt away furthe *townis evidentis.* of the toun, and anent the away putting thairof referrit thame to the saidis James Carmichell, Edward Litill, Johne Charteris dene of gild, maister Thomas Makcalyean and James Young, and for away putting thairof ordainis the dene of gild to caus mak ane litill substantious coffer and furneis the expenssis of the carying thairof, providing allwayis that the inuentar of the saidis evidentis to be away putt be tane, and that the saidis persons be sworne for conceling of the place quhair the samyn sall be putt in keping.

The foirsaidis ballies and counsaill ordanis maister James Lyndsay *Thesaurer,* thesaurer, with James Young, James Curll and William Lausoun, to fie six *villa.*

| | |
|---|---|
| Thesaurer, villa. | gunneris, weill qualefeit men and of gude practik, for ane monethe nixttocum, for handeling of the townis artalyearie gif neid be, and ordainis the said thesaurer to vpputt iiij cuttbrottis vpon platforme aboue the revestery. |
| Anent the keiping of the portis. | The bailies and counsaill foirsaid ordanis the West Port, Nether Bow and Kirk of Feild port, ilkane of thame to be keipit be twa officeris. . . . Ordanis ane candill to be putt at the Nether Bow, thair to remane euery nycht induring the tyme of wynter. |

6 October 1559.

| | |
|---|---|
| Anent the evidentis. | [The bailies and council ratified the acts of 30th September as to putting away the town's evidents, ordained Alexander Barroun to assist the persons therein named, "and declaris that the saidis personis sall nocht be callit for the saidis evidentis incais thai be tynt, thai doand that dew diligence in keiping thairof becaus thair lautie is apprevit to the toun thairanent and experimentit befoirtyme." The persons appointed to take charge of the evidents "protestit insafar as thai wer reddy to performe the chargeis laid to thame in the said act . . . and the delay thairof come nocht of thame, that quhatt happinnit vpone the saidis evidentis thai wer nocht haldin to ansuer thairfor."] |

14 October 1559.

| | |
|---|---|
| Anent the artailyerie. | The provest bailies counsaill and maist part of the dekinnis ordanis the haill artalyerie of the toun, with the chahoeris puder and bullattis, to be had to the castell to be keipit thair quhill the toun think expedient to bring furthe the samyn, and ordanis maister James Lyndsay thesaurer to tak Danid Rowanis handwritt of the ressait thairof; and John lord Erskin captane of the said castell hes promittit faythfullie to maister Johne Prestoun baillie and the said maister James Lyndsay, in name and behalf of the saidis provest bailies and counsaill, to delyuer the saidis artalyerie chahueris puder and bullattis quheneuer he beis requirit thairto. |

27 October 1559.

| | |
|---|---|
| Extent of ij<sup>m</sup> merkis. | Archibald Douglas of Kinspindie provest, [bailies, councillors, and deacons of crafts,] being oftymes warnit to the mater efter speecefit, hes |

grantit to the lordis of the congregatioun, presentlie assembled within this burgh, ane extent of twa thowsand merkis to be vpliftit of the nychtbouris of this burgh, merchantis and craftismen, for rasing of men of weir; and hes nominat the personis vnderwrittin to extent the saidis nychtbouris merchandis in the said extent euery ane conforme to thair habilite and substance: [here follow the names of nine persons.]

Extent of ij^m merkis.

### 29 October 1559.

The provest ballies and counsaill ordanis maister Richart Strang to pas to maister Thomas Makcalyeane assessour quhair he can convene him, and desyre the said maister Thomas to send doun his pairt of the extent of ij^m merkis grantit be the toun to the lordis of the congregatioun for rasing of men of weir, extending to the sowme of x li., and to desyre the said maister Thomas to delyver to the said maister Richart Sanct Gelis [arm] quhilk he hes now in keiping, to be laid in plege of money to be auanced of the said extent, or ellis to len samekle vpone the said arme and hald the samyn in pledge thairof, and gif he delyueris the said arme to ressave the said maister Richartis acquittance thairof, and the provest ballies and counsaill oblissis thame and thair successouris to releif and keip him skaythles thairof as efferis.

Maister Thomas Makcalyeane.

William Lyndsay, in name of maister James Lyndsay, at the command of the provest ballies and counsaill presentit Dauid Rowannis ressait of the artalyerie pulder and bullat subscrivit be Dauid Rowan, and protestit the said maister James wes free thairof.

Lyndsay, villa.

### 13 November 1559.

The provest ballies and counsaill, fyndand that the siluer werk of the kirk vestementis and vtheris ornamentis delyuerit in keiping to syndrie personis burgessis of this burgh for feir of the lordis of the congregatioun vpone the [xxviij] day of Junii last bypast, as the act maid thairvpone of the dait foirsaid proportis, may now be saiflie delyuerit and putt in places quhair thai hawe vsit to be keipit of befoir, thairfoir ordanis the officiaris to pas and charge all and syndrie the saidis personis that

Anent the kirk geir.

| | |
|---|---|
| Anent the kirk geir. | thai and ilkane of thame for thair awin pairtis present the syluer werk jewellis vestementis and ornamentis, delyuerit in keiping to thame efter the tenour of the said act, to the prouest ballies and counsaill within thre dayis nixt efter thai be chargit thairto, as thai and ilkane of thame will ausuer to thame thairvpone. |

21 *November* 1559.

| | |
|---|---|
| Anent the pitte customes. | The prouest [ballies and council] fyndand that the pitte customes of this burgh with the trone at the Over [Bow], gyf thai remanit in the thesaureris handis as it was devisit vpon the x day of Nouember instant at the rouping thairof, could nocht be gatherit but multitude of servandis and grit expens, and for vther considerationis moving thame, hes sett the saidis customes with the trone at the Over Bow to Jhone Weir for this yeir to cum, for the sowme of thre hundreth merkis to be payit quarterlie. |
| Protestationes prepositi et Lyndesay. | In presens of the prouest ballies and counsaill foirsaid, maister James Lyndsay protestit that gyf the vestementis of the kirk laid in keiping to him incurrit ony danger in thair hamebringing to this toun he wer nocht haldin to ausuer thairfoir bot that the toun bure the awenture thairof, and my lord provest protestit that the said maister James wer haldin to delyuer the saidis vestementis in the sam place he ressauit thame. |

12 *December* 1559.

| | |
|---|---|
| Regina, prepositus, Sarlabus. | The ballies and counsaill ordanis Alexander Park thesaurer to propyne the Quenis grace with thre tvn wyne of best that can be had, togither with xx li. worthe waxt, and my lord provest with ane tvn wyne and that the samyn be conveyit to Setoun vpon the townis expenssis, and siklyke to propyne Monsieur Sarlabus with j half tvn wyne. |
| Curll, Huntrodis, cordiules. | James Curll, at command of the ballies and counsaill, delyuerit to thame the preist, dekin, subdekin, caip, abbas, and the rest, compleitand the haill stand of clayth of gold delyuerit to him in keiping the [xxviij] day of Junii last bipast ; and syklyk Robert Huntrodis cordenar delyuerit the vestement, dekin, subdekin, [*blank*] caipis of blew veluott scarmit with gold laid in keping to him the said day ; and the ballies and counsaill |

foirsaid ordanit the saidis vestementis to be imputt in the chartour hous to be kepit thair quhill thai awys farther.   *Curlle, Huntrodis, consules.*

24 *December* 1559.

The ballies and counsaill ordanis ane wache of xxiiij men to be sett daylie and nychtlie for keping of the toun and awating vpon the portis in sic ordour as the ballies sall think expedient, and that at the nycht wache the nychbouris being warnit convene thame selfis or send ane hable man for thame, and that in the day wache the nychbouris convene thame selfis in proper persone gyf thai be nocht furthe of the toun, vnder the pane of warding of thair personis, and thairefter to be punishit at the counsaillis will.   *Anent the wache.*

10 *January* 1559-60.

[Acts passed as to bread, malt, and ale, in terms similar to those in October of previous years. The fourpence loaf baked by baxters within burgh to weigh twenty-two ounces, and that baked by outland baxters four ounces more. Malt to be sold not dearer than nine firlots for £3, 10s.; and ale not dearer than 3½d. the pint.   *Ratificatione of certane statutis.*

The provost, bailies and council also ratified the acts made in 1558 " anent the moill merkatt, talloun, candill, myddingis on the hie gait, vagaboundis, regratouris, assisis, and burgessis of this burgh to resort within the samyn, and ordanis thame to be proclamit of new."]

[The bailies and council having considered a supplication by the farmer of the " wyld awenturis" for the year to Martinmas 1559 " desyring ane pairt of the fermes thairof to be rebaitit to him, be ressoun of the gritt trubbils that rais within this realme and closing of the port of Leyth that na schippis mycht resort thairto for ane lang tyme," ordained him to make complete payment in respect he "tuke the saidis customes with all awenture."]   *Wilsoun, villa, thesaurer.*

The ballies and counsall ordanis that na maner persone berand office or publict government within the toun, nor being vpone the counsaill, depairt furthe of this burgh and remane thairfra the space of foure dayis without speciall licence grantit and gevin him thairto.   *Anent the officeris and counsaill.*

## 19 *January* 1559-60.

[Provost's house.]

The [bailies and counsell,] vnderstanding be report of maister William Setoun, seruitour to my lord provest, that his lordschip desyrit to be ludgit in maister Thomas Makcalyeonis hous, and that the said maister Thomas was willing to luitt his said ludgeing for maill, ordanit the said ludgeing to be maid voyd that my lord provest may enter thairto quhen his lordschip thinkis expedient, and the bailies and counsall sall caus the said maister Thomas be payit of samekle maill as James Adamsoun hes ressauit or is to ressave for his ludgeing quhairin my lord provest now remanis, efter the rate of the tyme that he sall remane in the said ludgeing; and efter the making of the ordenance foirsaid compeirit the said maister Thomas and protestit for remeid and nullitie of the said ordenance gevin but ony ordour of proces without calling and aganis him that was nocht subiect to thair jurisdictioun, and thairvpone askit instrumentis.

## 16 *February* 1559-60.

Prebendaris of the queir.

The bailies and counsall ordanis Alexander Park thesaurer to content and pay to Sir Walter Haliburtoun, Sir George Manderstoun and Sir William Johnestoun, prebendaris of the queir, the sowme of vij merkis for the Mertynmes payment last bipast of the annualrentis awing to thame be the toun, and siklyk to Sir James Crawfurde chaplane of the Rude loft the sowme of x s. for the said termes payment of his annualrent and vther x s. for the Lady mes sylner; and dischargis the thesaurer of ony mair payment to ony of the rest of the prebendaris becaus thai hawe nocht awatit vpone thair devyne service.

Fermoraris of the pitte customes.

[The bailies and council, considering that the farmers of the petty customs with the tron at the Over Bow, for the year to Martinmas 1559, " hes be the grit trubblis raisit in this realme in the said yere bene damnefeit in thair profleit of the saidis customes," remitted to them the sum of twenty merks].

## 16 *April* 1560.

Villa, decanus gilde.

Archibald Dowglas of Kinspinde provest, [the bailies, council and deacons of crafts.] ordanis James Barroun dene of gild to reparrall the kirk, to lay the throwchis thairof of new and sparge the samyn, mend the glasen wyndokis, and mak settis convenient.

[The provost, baillies and counsall] ordanis maister Johne Spens to administrat the office of balyerie in place of Adam Fullertoun baillie quhill his returnying furthe of Ingland. <sub>Villa, Spens.</sub>

### 30 April 1560.

The prouest baillies counsall and dekynnis, at the requeist desyre and will of the lordis of congregatioun, for furthsetting of this present interpryis dependand for expelling of the Franche men out of Leith to the gret commone weill of this realme, ordanis ane generall taxt of sextene hundreth pund tobe set commonlie vpoun the nychtbouris of this burgh, to be gevin for ane monethis waigis to foure hundreth men of weir, and ordanis the samin tobe collectit with all deligence and delinerit to the capitanis nominat to haue the gouernance of the said men of weir, and thair acquittances tobe sufficient discharge to the baillies collectouris and deliueraris of the samin. <sub>Extent of xvj<sup>c</sup> li.</sub>

### 1 May 1560.

[The treasurer ordained to pay "iij li. x s. for sand lyme and workmanschip at the vpbigging of the yettis of the Trinitie Colledge and mending of the sloppis thairof," and "xxxij s. for bigging vpe of certane sloppis at the Trinitie College in the monethe of October lastbipast."] <sub>Trinitie College.</sub>

### 4 May 1560.

The treasurer ordained to pay to "John and Moreis Dowis the sowme of xxviij s. for playing vpone the swesche and quhissill befoir the nychbouris of this burgh twa dayis quhen thai wer in armorie."] <sub>Army.</sub>

### 6 May 1560.

[John Hammyltoun, for refusing, on being ordered by a bailie, to go to "warde" for non payment of his extent, ordained "to cum in presens of the precher, efter the sermon on Sounday nixttocum, and thair declair his falt and ask the baill peple forgifnes for the sklander."] <sub>Hammyltoun, bulliuis.</sub>

### 8 May 1560.

The provest ballies and counsall ordanis Alexander Park thesaurer to delyuer to Johne Carnis the sowme of xl li. for furnesching of thair minister Johne Knox in his honshold, and becaus the said Johne Knox <sub>Anent the precher.</sub>

| | |
|---|---|
| Anent the precher. | hes bene furnesit vpone Dauid Forresteris expenssis sen his cuming to this toun be the space of xv dayis lastbipast, ordanis the said Johne Carnis to ressave the said Dauid comptis and mak him payment of the sowmes debursit be him on the first end of the sowme of xl li. to be delyuerit to him. |
| Thesaurer, villa. | The provest ballies and counsaill inhibit and dischargit Alexander Park thesaurer, personallie present, of payment of ony pentionis or dewiteis awand furthe of the commoun gude to ony kirkis kirkmen or vtheris that seruit in sic service of befoir, certefeing the said thesaurer gif he do the samyn he sall gett na allowance thairof. |
| Anent the doun taking of the Marie Bell. | The provest ballies and counsall, vnderstanding that the kirk mycht be servit be thre bellis, ane rung to the prayeris, ane vther for serving of the knok, and the thrid to be the common bell, ordanis James Barroun dene of gild to tak doun the ferd bell callit the Marie bell and to kepe the samyn quhill he ressave further directioun fra the counsall. |

10 May 1560.

| | |
|---|---|
| Gilbert, villa, extent. | [The provost bailies and council] haveand consideratioun that thair man be money delyuerit in haist to the lordis of secreit counsall, and that the extent grantit for obteyning of the samyn can nocht be sa haistelie inbrocht, thairfoir hes borrowit and ressauit fra Michell Gilbert goldsmyth the sowme of foure scoir poundis : . . . . and the syluer chandeleris lyand in keping to the said Michell in the monethe of Junii last bipast to remane with him as plege. |

15 May 1560.

| | |
|---|---|
| Cowgait port, John Knox lodgeing. | [The treasurer ordained to pay " xx s. for making of the keyis of the Cowgait port, and for ane lok to Johne Knox ludgeing."] |

26 May 1560.

| | |
|---|---|
| Waching of the prisaneris in the tolbuith. | The provest baillies and counsall ordanis euerye baillie quhais quartar wachis that that nycht of his wache he caus four of his quarter to walk within the tolbuith of this burgh for wacheing of the prisaneris thairinto nychtlie, at the desyre and wryting of the lordis of secreit counsel, quha being |

## OF THE BURGH OF EDINBURGH.

present wes content to do the samyn, and ordanitt he baillie being present to mak the wache this nycht becaus it fell him to wache, quhilk he acceptit. *Waching of the prisaneris in the tolbuith.*

[The provost, bailies, council and deacons of crafts] ordanis and consenttis that the bell callit the Marie bell, and the brasyn pillaris of the kirk of Sanct Geill, sall be intromettit with be James Barroun dene of gild, and that all intromettouris thairwith deliuer to him the samyn to be maid in artalyere for the townis vse as he sall think maist expedient to quhome thai refer quhat pecis it salbe maid into, and gif it may nocht gudlie be maid in artalyere in this cuntre thai licence him to send the samyn to Flanderis to be maid or coft thair, and the gud toun sal beir the aventure thairof. *Making of the bell and brasyn pillaris in monitioun.*

The provest ballies and counsaill ordanis inhibitioun to be till all personis heretouris of landis within this burgh detbound to kirkmen for ony dewtie, that thai ansuer na farther quhill generall ordour be tane thairanent. *Anent annualis awand to kirkmen.*

1 *June* 1560.

[The treasurer ordained " to delyuer to Johne Carnis the sowme of xx li. for furnesing of Johne Willok, precher."] *Precept Carnis.*

10 *June* 1560.

The provest ballies counsaill and ane pairt of the dekines of craftis, haveing consideratioun of the grit number of idolatreris quhoremaisteris and harlottis daylie resortand within this burgh, provokand the indignatioun of God vpone the samyn ofttymes furtheschawin be the prechouris, ordanis ane proclamatioun to be maid in dew forme and ample that all sic personis cum in presens of the minister or the elderis to gif testimonie of thair conuersioun for the saidis abusis respectiue betwix and Sonday at none nixttocum, or falyeing thairof the saidis idolatreris to be diffamit be setting thame vpone the merkatt croce thair to remane for the space of vj houris for thair first falt, carying of the saidis bordelaris houremaisteris and harlottis throw the toun in ane carte for thair first falt, birnying of bayth the kyndis of the saidis personis on the cheik for the secound falt, and banisching the toun, and for the thrid falt to be punischit to the deid. *Anent idolatreris houremaisteris and harlottis.*

12 *June* 1560.

Anent the stanis of the freiris.

The provest ballies and counsaill ordanis proclamatioun to be maid that na maner [of] persoun putt hand in the stanis of the kirkis of the freris latlie cassin down, and the stanis that ar tane away befoir to remane vnder arrestment to be furthecumand to the commoun werkis.

19 *June* 1560.

Anent the tolbuyth, schule, and clerkis chalmer.

The prowest, baillies, dene of gyld, thesaurare, [council and deacons of crafts], haifand considderatioun of the gret inquietatioun that thai haif had in tymes past within the tolbuith of this burgh for laik of rowme to minister justice and to do thair other effaris at all sic tymes quhen the sessioun did sit, or quhen other courttis and convocationis war in the samyn, and alssua considdering the skant of prisoun houssis and incommoditie of thair clerkis chalmer, and for inhalding of the yeirlie maill of the samyn and other gret sowmes of money debursit be thame for thair scole, haifling mair commodius place and sic rowmes within thair kirk as may be ane fair tolbuithe for serving of the toun in thair effairis, and of all other necessar rowmes vpoun the west pairt of thair said kirk, and siclyke vpoun the est pairt of the samyn ane other convenient rowme for ane scole to thair barinis, besyde sufficient rowme for the preiching and ministratioun of the sacramentis; thairfoir, and for divers otheris ressonable caussis moving thame, all in ane voce concludis decernis and ordanis James Barroun dene of gilde with all deligence to repair and big wp ane stane wall, viz., ane parpall wall of [*blank*] fute thyk, beginand [at] the southe kirk dur callit the kirk yarde dur and streicht northe to the northe kirk dur at the Stynkand Styll for the said towbuyth; and vpone the eist end of the said kirk ane vther parpall wall of the sam thiknes. beginnand at the eist cheik of the kirk dur at our Lady steppis, and swa in langis the breid of the said kirk be just lyne to the southe sydwall of the samyn for thair schule; and that the said James furnesche big and sett vp all thingis necessar for the said schole, towbuyth, prisoun hous, clerkis chalmer and all vtheris necessaris within the samyn.

The provest baillies and counsale and deiknys foresaid ordanis Wellis, Alexander Park, thesaurer, with all deligence possibill to put to warkmen calsayis, for mending of the brokin calsayis, biggin of the Mwse well, dichting of the new well, flaging and mending of the calsayis before thame, and alsua for mending of the hale brokin calsayis of this toun. And to this effect ordanis the said Alexander to hyre ane maister of wark vpoun the townys expensis, and efter the completing of the wellis and calsayis ordanis him with like deligence to caus big the wall langis the college yairdis fra the Northt Loch to Leyth Wynde, and siclike langis Leyth Wynde to the biggit land at the heid of the samyn vpoun the west syde thairof.

The provest baillies and counsale and dekynnis foresaidis ordanis Kyrk. James Barroun, dene of gild, to mak snittis, fwrmes and stullis of the radeast of the tymmer convenient thairfor lyand within the volt vnder the tolbuith for the peple to syt vpoun the tyme of the sermoun and prayarris within the kirk, and all vther thingis till do as salbe thocht gude for decoring of the said kirk.

The provest baillies and counsale with the dekynnis forsaid ordanis Thesaurer, Alexander Park, thesaurer, to caus mend the lokis on the eist port of the villa. Cowgait [and] mak new keyis, becaus the ald keyis can nocht be gottin sen the Franchemennis last being in the toun. And ordanis the said port to be oppin at certane tymes of day for lattin furth of the filth in tha pairttis; alsua to contract with sum honest sure man for keiping of the said port.

It being havelie menyt to the provest baillies counsale and dekynnis Anent the foresaidis be the pure beidmen of Sanct Paullis Wark, thay in the defalt of hospitall of Sanct Paulis Sir William Makdougall thair collectour, quha presentlie keipit hinnself Wark. within the castell, they could na wayis have thair annuellis and dewiteis, in defalt quhairof thay war constrenit to beg, and thairfor desyrit thair lordschippis that thay wald deput and gyf to thame William Stewert ane of thair clerkis deput to be thair collectour in tymes cuming, quhilk desyre the provest baillies counsale and deikynnis foresaid, as patronis to the

Anent the hospitall of Sanct Paulis Wark.

saidis beidmen, and having the disposition of thair plaissis and offices, nominatis makis constitutis and ordanis the said William Stewert collectour generale of all and sindrye the annuellis mailles and dewiteis pertenyng to the said beidmen, with command to all and sindrye within thair jurisdictioun to ansuer and obey him thairof, to be furthenmand to the vtilite and proffit of the said beidmen, and the said William to haue thairfor all feis and dewiteis that onye vtheris collectouris had for the samyn in onye tyme past.

26 *June* 1560.

Precept, Carnis.

[The treasurer ordanued to " pay Johne Carnis the sowme of thre scoir poundis for furnesing of the ministeris."]

12 *July* 1560.

Anent James Nycolsoun and Jhone Jhonstoun, factoreis.

The foirsaid provest ballies and counsall ordanis names and constitutis the four ballies and James Barroun to aggre commoun and appoint with Jhone Jhonstoun and James Nycolsoun, wryteris, anent thair factoreis maid to thame be the lordis of counsall of the annuallis malis and dewiteis quhilkis pertenit to the freris and Magdalene landis, or ony other landis or annuall rentis within the fredome of this burgh, and as thai sall appoint thairanent the saidis provest counsall and dekynnis sall stand thairat.

Irne roddis and shaikles.

[The treasurer ordained to pay " foure pund xiij s. iiij d. for tua irne roddis with xij irne shaikles vpoun thame, weyand vij stane twelf pund and ane half, quhilkis ar deliuerit to Thomas Hall javelour."]

19 *July* 1560.

Bread, ale, flesh.

[The fourpence loaf of bread baked by baxters within burgh to weigh fifteen ounces, and that baked by baxters without burgh to weigh nineteen ounces. Ale not to be sold dearer than fourpence a pint. Best mutton to be sold for 8 s., and the second for 6 s.]

Beggaris.

It is statute that na beggaris be tholit within this burgh bot thay that ar borne within the samyn, vpbrocht, or of lang tyme hes bene trafficcearis within the samyn, and that nane of thame be sufferit to beg except thay be ald crukit lamit and debilitat be gret seiknes quhilkis may nocht laubour

nor wyrk for thair lewyng, and gif ony other be at this present within  Beggaris.
this burgh that thai depesche thame of the samyn betuix and the morne
at none nixtocum, vndir the pane of byrning of the cheik and banesyng of
the toun for euer; and that nane of the porteris of this burgh suffer ony
outland beggar to haif interes within the samyn, vnder the pane of extreme
pvnisment of thame in thair personis and depriuatioun of thame in thair
offices.

Item, it is statute that all vagaboundis fydlaris pyparis minstrallis,  Fydlaris,
and otheris without maisteris, nocht haifing houssis within this toun nor  vagaboundis.
sum honest shift to vphald thame self with, that thay depairt furth of the
samyn betuix and the morne at none, vnder the pane of byrning of the
cheik and banesyng of the toun as said is; [and] that the keparis of the
porttis mak impediment to thame to enter within the samyn, vnder the
pane foirsaid.

### 23 July 1560.

The prowest baillies and counsall and dekynnis of craftis namit con-  Anent the
stitute and chesit thir personis vnder speciffit, that is to say [three persons  wallis of Leyth.
for each of the north-west, north-east, south-west, and south-east quarters]
to taxt the hale nychtbouris of this burgh efter thair conscience and
knawlage to sa mony men as thai may gudlie perfurneis efter thair landis
gudis and substance, for douncasting and demolesyng of wallis and fortres
of Leythe, begynning at Sanct Anthonis Port and passing westwart to the
Walter of Leythe, for making of the blokhous and curting equall to the
ground, and to enter thairto the morn be v houris, conforme to the chairgis
gevin to the saidis prowest baillies and counsall be the counsall of Scotland
and subscriuit be thair handis, quhairof the tenour followis:—Apud Edinburgh ij° July 1560. Forsamekle as it is notourlie knawyn how hurtfull
the fortificatioun of Leyth hes bene to this haill realme, and in speciall to
thair rowmes nyxt adiacent thairvnto, and how preiudiciall this samyn
salbe to the libertie of this haill cuntre in cais strangearis sall at ony tyme
heirefter intruse thameselffis thairin, for thir and siclyke consideracionis,
the counsall hes thocht expedient and chargis the prowest baillies
and counsall of Edinburgh to tak ordour with the toun and communite of

Anent the
wallis of
Leyth.

the samyn and caus and compell thame to appoint ane sufficient noumer to cast doun and dimolishe the southe pairt of the said toun, begynnand at Sanct Anthonis port and passing westwart to the Walter of Leithe making the blokhous and courtene equall with the ground, and that thai enter to the said wark vpoun Wedinsday nixcunnis be fyve houris in the mornyng, and to continow and perseweir in the samyn to the accomplishment of the said doun casting, conforme to the thing abone writtin. *Et sic subscribitur:* James, James Hamiltoun, Mortoun, James Stewart.

1 *August* 1560.

Silver wark.

[The provost bailies council and deacons of crafts] decernis and concludis that the silver wark perteunyng to the gude toun vsit in Sanct Gelis Kirk in tymes past, bayth gilt and vngilt, be with all deligence sauld or cunyet, and the money thairof to be waryt vpoun the commoun warkis, and in speciall vpoun the reparatioun and decoring of the kirk conforme to the ordinance maid the xix day of [Junii] last, and siclike ordanis the hale vestimenttis kaipis and vther kirk grayth in lik maner to be sauld and bestowit vpoun the said kirk wark, quhilk beand compleit the superplus to be deliuerit to Alexander Park, or the vther thesaurer for the tyme, to be waryt vpoun the wallis, commoun warkis of the toun, or for redemyng of the townys landis being in wedsett, as the counsale sall think maist expedient. And for mair haistye expeditioun and completing of the said kirk wark ordanis the personis quhilkis hes the said silner wark and kirk grayth in keiping to be warnyt vpoun [*blank*] nyxt to produce the samyn before the counsale, and to be deliuerit to James Barroun dene of gild and Alexander Park thesaurer, to be sauld or cunyet be thair avise, and the money thairof to be intromettit with be the said dene of gild and applyit as said is, and he to render compt of the samyn.

Anent the
articulis to be
given in
perliament.

The prouest baillies counsale and dekynnis foresaid, efter the reding of the articules to be gevin in in this present perliament concerning the manteinance of the libertie of merchanttis and craftismen, and siclyke concernyng the reformatioun and reparatioun of the kirkis, edefeing of hospitallis vniuersiteis collegis and scolis, and all sic vther thingis, as at mair lenth is contenit in the saidis articulis red in thair presens as said is, all in ane voce granttis and apprevis the samin to be inventit and devisit conforme and aggreing with Goddis trew ordinance for the manteinance of the trew religioun, as alsua for the commoun weill of the hale estait of merchanttis and fre craftismen, and for presenting and explanyng of the samyn in this present perliament hes nominat constitute and ordanit Archibald Douglas of Kinspindie provest, James Barroun, maister Richert Strang and Dauid Forster, thair commissaris in this perliament, and ordanis commissioun to be gevin to thame in ample and dew forme vnder thair commoun seill subscriuit be the commoun clerk for thame and in thair names as vse is.

*Anent the articulis to be given in perliament.*

The samyn day, as concernyng the complaynt gevin in and producit before the provest baillies counsale and dekynnis foresaid be James Norvell dekyn of the tailyeoris, bering in effect that the traves close rowme or sait biggit and maid be command of James Barroun, dene of gild, at Sanct Annys alter, sumtyme callit the tailyeouris alter, aucht and sould be removit and the dekyn and brether of the tailyeour craft permyttit to big thair saittis thair, to be vsit be thame and thair said craft at all sermonis and vther tymes convenient and nane vtheris, conforme to thair auld possessioun ; to the quhilk it wes ansuerit, and for plane ordinance be the provest baillies counsale and dekynnis before writin declarit, that in respect of the godlie ordour now taikin in religioun all title and clame to altaris and sic vther superstitious pretenssis ar and sould be abolischit, and na forther word nor clame thairof to be in tymes cuming, bot as it is commandit be Goddis mast haly word that brotherlie amyte be amangis ws joynit in his congregatioun, the nobelite provest baillies counsale eldares and dekynnis being first placit, the honest merchanttis and honest craftismen to place and set thameselflis togidder as loving brether and freindis in that and all vther places of the kirk vacand at all tymes neidfull, prouiding alwayis that nowther the prentissis or seruandis of merchanttis or craftismen or vther commoun peple tak vpoun thame the places or rowmes of the saidis merchanttis and fre craftismen ; and this present act and ordinance to tak effect without alteratioun in tymes cuming.

*Dekynnis.*

| | |
|---|---|
| Toun wallis. | The prouest baillies and counsale foresaid, with the avise of the saidis dekynnis, ordanis Alexander Park thesaurer to begin to the biging of the toun wallis langis college dike and Leyth Wynde vpoun Monunday nixt, conforme to the ordinance maid of before. |
| Anent vnfremen. | The samyn day, efter the complaynt gevin in be James Barroun dene of gild that thair wes divers personis within this toun quhilkis occupeit the libertie of fre merchanttis and fre craftismen, being na fre burgessis, to the greit hurt of merchanttis craftismen and commoun weill of this burgh gyf remeid war nocht providit, vpoun consideratioun of the samyn complaynt, the prouest baillies counsale and dekynnis foresaid commandis and ordanis the said James Barroun dene of gild and Dauid Somer baillie, takand with thame sic nowmer of officeris as thay sall think gude, to pas throuch the toun and diligentlie serche and seik the vnfremen occuperis of the liberteis of merchanttis, caus and compell [thame] to becum fre, vtherwise to put thame in ward quhill cautioun be found that thay sall desist in all tymes cuming; and for the vnfremen occuperis of craftis ordanis the dekynnis foresaid to gyf vp the names of the hale maisteris of craftis to the said dene of gyld that sic ordour may be taikin with thame tuiching thair fredome as with the vtheris abone writtin for the commoun weill as said is, providing that gif ony of the saidis craftismen hes occupeit the libertie of fre burges be lang tyme and is nocht able at this tyme to satifye according to the present vse, or vtherwise may nocht be povertie, sic personis to be considerit be the prouest ballies and counsale and vsit according to thair power. |

16 *August* 1560.

| | |
|---|---|
| Precept, Carnis. | [The treasurer ordained "to delyuer to Johne Carnis the sowme of fyue li. for furnessing of the minister."] |
| Constable deputt, villa. | The provest ballies and counsaill forsaid, efter consideratioun and rype awysment with the complaynt gevin in be the haill communitie of the nychtbouris of this burgh, and vtheris our Soueranis leidgis resortand with victuallis and vtheris guddis thairto, vpone William Henrisoun constable |

deputt, makand mentioun that quhair the said William had be the haill space of xv dayis last bipast had be himself and vtheris in his name vsit extortioun of custome at the portis of this burgh, alledgeand the samyn to perteue to him as his perliament fie, quharthrow all personis resortand with thair guddis and speciallie with victuallis to this burgh now in this tyme of perliament wer compellit to pay dowbill custome, viz., bayth to the toun and to the said constable deputt, by ony richt or titill gevin to him thairvpone but onlie be vsurpatioun and extorsioun forsaid, as at mair lenthe is contenit in the said complaynt ; the said William being personallie present, as lawfullie warnit to ansuer to the said complant, the provest ballies and counsaill forsaidis findis the said William to hawe done wrang in asking and craving of ony dewtie fra our Soueranis leidgis inwith or besyde the portis of this burgh, and thairfor ordanis him to desist and ceis fra all farther vsurpatioun of the said extorsioun or asking of ony dewitie at the saidis portis or about the samyn in all tyme cunning, becaus the said William Henrisoun being personallie present and inquirit gif he had ony rycht or titill quhairthrow he mycht lefullie vse the said exactioun vpone our saidis Soueranis leidges schew na titill thairvpone, as wes clerlie vnderstand to the provest ballies and counsaill forsaid, and the said William protestit for remeid of law and that the said decreit wer nocht prejudiciall to the priuiledge of his office. <sup>Constable deputt, villa.</sup>

*Memorandum.*—Thair is ane act of parliament of Kyng James the Secund, ca. sexagesimo septimo, that aggreis with this act aboue writtin ; and siclik in Kyng James the Thrid, ca xlj ; and siclik in Kyng James the Secund, ca lxxxvj<sup>to</sup>.

The provest ballies and counsaill forsaidis findis that William Henrisoun constabill deputt ancht hald na courte within the libertie of this burgh except with ane baillie and clerk of the toun, and thairfor ordanis the said William, personsallie present, to desist and ceis fra halding of ony courtis within this burgh bot in maner forsaid, with certificatioun and he failye thai will provide sic remeid thairto as thai may of law, and the said William Henrisoun protestit for remeid.

K

21 *August* 1560.

Anent the downcasting of the wallis of Leyth.

[The bailies and council] fyndis, for the mair haistie expeditioun in the doun casting of the wallis and filling of the trinches at Leyth, that euerye baillie sall charge and tak with him thre or foure honest men of his quarter, sic as sall pleis him to name, to beir him cumpanye and be ourscaris and maisteris of wark to the warkmen at the said trinches, and to remane with him and at the said wark fra morne to evin the day that fallis to his quarter, and the said personis warnyt, taikand laubour as said is, to be dischargit for the day of thair laubouris of ane man expenssis, and gyf onye of thame being requyrit as said is comperis nocht, to be poyndit for the vnlaw of xviij s., without fauouris, for thair dissobedience, and this ordour to be obseruit quhill the said wark at Leyth be compleitlie endit.

Hendersoun, counstable.

William Hendersoun constable, of his fre will oblist him that fra this furth he sall in na tyme cuming hald ony court within the fredome and libertie of Edinburgh without the concurrance of ane baillie and clerk of the samyn, nor attech poynde or arreist within the saidis boundis without ane officer of the toun adionit to his officer; and to this effect the prouest baillies and counsale commandis and ordanis thair officiaris, present and to cum, to concur with the said Williames officer in all lauchfull poynding summonyng or arreisting, vpoun the ressonable expenssis of the pairtye; and siclik commandis ane of thair clerkis to be rady at all his courttis within the bowndis foresaid for seruing of him and nane vther clerk bot ane of thairis as said is.

24 *August* 1560.

Precept tabroneris.

[The treasurer ordainned to pay to " the sax tabroneris that playit thre sindrie dayis at the parliament quhen the toun wes in armour, the sowm of xl s."]

30 *August* 1560.

Delyuerance of certane jowallis.

In presens of [the provost bailies and deacons of crafts], Alexander Guthre, commoun clerk of this burgh, delyuerit to James Barroun, dene of gild, the chalice patene and spvne weyand xxxij vnce and ane half; and the relict callit the arme of Sanct Geill, in presens foirsaid, wes delyuerit to the said dene of gild be maister Thomas Makcalyeane; and siklyk Thomas Thomsoun, apothecair, delyuerit to the said dene of gild the chresom stok and twa crowattis of sylucr: and siklyk the said James Barroun presentit the greit eucharist with the goldin werk and stanis, and of the wecht contenit in the act maid the sevint day of Januar the yeire of God j^m v^c and fyftie aucht yeris,[1] and the foure goldein bellis with twa croces. ane greit and ane vther small, with ane lytill hart, weyit in presens foirsaid, extendit to foure vnce ane half and ane vnicorne weicht of gold, and siklike the pece of gold that held the breid within the ewcharist, ane litill blew bell of gold, ane litill hart with twa perles, and four sindrie stanis sett with gold, with the litill ring and dyamont thairvpone that wes vpone the said arme, weyit in the haill to ane vnce foure vnicorne wecht; and siklyk maister James Lyndsay delyuerit to the said dene of gild the sacrament clayth of gold with Sanct Gelis coatt and the litill pendekle of reid velnott that hang at his feit; quhilkis jowallis and ornamentis wer laid in keping to the personis respectiue foirsaidis the [xxvij] day of Junii the yere of God j^m v^c and fyftie nyne yeiris, and were delyuerit to the said dene of gild be ane act maid thairvpone the first day of August instant, and thairfor the provost ballies counsall and dekynnis forsaidis, for thame selfis and thair successouris, dischargit the saidis personis and ilk ane of thame of the saidis jowellis respectiue for now and euer.

Delyuerance of certane jowallis.

[The bailies and council] ordanis Alexander Park, thesaurer, to delyuer to Johne Willok xx^ti crownis of the sone, for recompans of the greit travell sustenit be him this haill yere bigane in preching and ministering of the sacramentis within this burgh; and ordanis ane number of the counsaill to thank him of his greit benevolence for the greit trawaill forsaid.

Villa, Willok.

It is statut and ordanit that in all tyme cuming, quhen euer it sall happin ony burgesses or gild brether to be maid, that thai ressave with thair tikkatt of burgeschip or gildre the forme of thair aithe that thai mak at thair creatioun fra the clerkis, vpone thair expenssis.

Anent burgessis and gild brether.

---
[1] See act, dated 8th March 1558-9, antea, p. 30.

*4 September* 1560.

Villa, Durie.

The ballies and counsaill, haveing consideratioun that, for the eis of Johne Knox minister, Johne Durie talyeour removit him furth of the ludgeing occupyit be the abbot of Drumfermeling to the effect the said minister mycht enter thairto, ordanis Alexander Park thesaurer to content and pay to the said John Durie the sowme of viij merkis, and the samyn sall be allowit, etc.; and als the saidis ballies and counsaill faithfullie promittis that how sone thai may provide the said minister ane vther ludgeing, to enter the said Johne to the possessioun thairof.

Barroun, Symmer, Pennecuke.

The ballies counsaill and dekynnis of craftis assolycis and decernis quyte Dauid Somer, baillie, and James Barroun, dene of gild, fra the complaynt gevin in vpone thame be maister Johne Pennecuke, persoun of that ilk, contenand in effect the saidis personis to hawe sclanderit and iniurit him, sayand it wer weill worthy he wer harlitt throw the toun at ane hors taill; and that in respect of the narration of bayth the saidis parties aggreing togidder. Fyndis that maister Johne Pennecuke hes done wrang in missaying of Dauid Symer, baillie, vpone Monunday last bipast, in execution of his office, sayand: Thow leis lyk ane fals knayff, as the said maister Johne confessit. [He is ordained to find surety for appearance to "vnderly sic pvnischment as thai sall inioyne to him."]

Barroun, villa, jowelles.

In presens of the ballies and counsaill, Alexander Barroun delyuerit to James Barroun, dene of gild, the round enchareist of sylver laid in keping to him in the moneth of Junii 1559.

*5 September* 1560.

Pennecuke, villa.

Comperit maister Johne Pennecuke, persoun of that ilk, and referrit him to the discretioun of the counsaill anent the offence done be him to Dauid Somer vpone Monunday last bipast, and for breking of the warde, and vthers trubblis rasit be him within the toun vpoun Wedinsday last bipast, and William Ra and Thomas Ewing ar becumin cantioneris and sourcties for the entre of the said maister within xxiiij houris efter the cuming of the abbot of Hallirudhous to this toun gif thay be requyrit thairto, vnder Penneeuke, the pane of j$^m$ merkis, and that he sall committ na trubill in the mene villa. tyme within the toun, vnder the said pane.

The provest bailies and counsaill ordanis the personis quhilkis hes in Syluer wark. keiping ony of the sylner werk of the toun yet vndelyuerit to present the samyn to the counsaill vpone Fryday next to cum, vnder the pane of warding of thair personis.

The prowest baillies counsall and dekynnis beand convenit in the tol- Manteinance buith of this burgh, and efter lang ressonyng vpoun the lait deforcementis of officiaris. and inobedience of the bailies and officiaris of this burgh and occasioun thairof, findis that the particular hatrent of sum of the subjectis and inhabitantis of the said burgh inemeis to all gude ordour, as alssua the inobedience and ignorance of otheris nocht regarding nor having in remembrance the commoun weill of the samyn thair bound dewitie and aith maid in manteinyng of the saidis officiaris and commoun weill foirsaid, quhilkis personis at all sic tymes as thay haif sene or hard the saidis officiaris dissobeyit and deforsit in executioun of thair officis hes nocht ryssyn nor cumyng fordwart to thair fortefecatioun, bot hes withdrawyn thame selflis and otheris be thair persuatioun and exampill within thair buthis and houssis, and sua left the saidis officiaris desolait of all support vpoun the danger and perall of thair lyflis, to the gret schame and sclander of the magistraittis and haill pepill inhabitaris of this burgh, and to the grit discurageing of men of honeste and judgement to accept office burding or charge within the said burgh, and inlykwys to the incurageing of euery lycht persoun and outlandis man to ga fordwart in thair inequietie and contemptioun to the manifest ourethraw of the saidis magistratis the commoun weill of the said burgh and vter distructioun of the samyn gif haistye remeid be nocht prouidit : Quhairfoir the prowest baillies counsall and dekynnis foirsaidis, willing the manteinance and defence of thair toun the magistratis liberteis and commoun weill of the samyn, ordanis that proclamatioun be maid at all neidfull pairtis of this burgh, sua that nane sall alledge nor pretend ignorance thairof, chargeing

Manteinance of officiaris.

all maner of personis induellland within the said burgh, als weill merchand craftis men as vtheris quhatsumener, that quhen it salhappin thame to heir so or haif knawlege of ony maner of besynes or twmult within the said toun, be sound of the commoun bell, publict clamour, conventioun, or otherwys, concernyng the disobedience of officiaris, stopping of tulyeis, suddand debaittis, and stancheing of wrangis within the samyn burgh, that thai, without exceptioun of tyme or persoun, cum fordwart in feir of weir with all possibill deligence to the saidis officiaris for fortefeing and manteinyng of thame in the caussis abone writtin ; certefeing all and syndrye the inhabitantis of this said burgh, but exceptioun of personis as said is, quhilk sall happin to withraw and absent thame selfis at ony sic tymes as is abone expremit, that for the first falt thay sall pay to the commoun warkis of the said burgh the sowme of fyve pund vnforgevin ; the second falt, doubling of the said vnlaw and tynsaill of thair fredome for yeir and day ; the thrid and last falt, banesing of the toun tynsall of all libertie and fredome of the samyn for euer ; and to this effect ordanis the actis and ordinancis maid for haifing of lang wappinnis in foir houssis and buthis be of new proclamit, and that the officiaris and visitouris chosyn for sersing of the saidis lmithis and foirhoussis pas vpoun Wedinsday nyxt to serche and vesie the samyn, and quhair thai fynd the saidis wappinnis nocht to be present to putt he panis contenit in the saidis ordinance to executioun, but favour as said is.

Irne hous.

[The treasurer ordained, "with all diligence possebill, to loft and flure the ovir irne hous, and to put in greit stanchcouris of irne in all the wyndois of the ovir tolbuith."

Silver wark.

Persons having "ony of the siluer werk ornamentis or jowellis of the kirk" ordered to deliver them on Monday next.

*6th September* 1560.

James Carmychell, by special command of the provost, bailies, council, and deacons, delivered to James Barroun, dean of guild, " the tua siluer sensouris with the schip of siluer quhilkis he had in keping of the gude toun, of the samyn wecht and fassoun as he resauit thaim."

The last dean of guild delivered to the dean for the present year, "the greit Silver wark. siluer croce with the fute quhilk he had in keiping, of the samyn wecht and fassioun as he resauit it."

"The cressouud stok being brokin, in presens of the prouest baillies counsale and dekynnis forsaid, thair wes within the samyn ane lowmpe of tre holkit for the oyle, weyand sextene vnce, quhilk James Barroun desyrit to be deducit of the first wecht of siluer, quhilk wes thocht ressonable."

Mychael Gilbert, goldsmith, delivered to James Barroun, dean of guild, "the tua litill chandlaris of siluer pertenying to the gude toun quhilk he had in keiping, weyand sevin pund thre vnce and ane half vnce wecht."]

The prouest baillies counsale and dekynnis foresaid ordanis to warne Haley Blude. the maisteris of the Hally Blude, and siclik the maister of Sanct Anthonis, St Anthony. vpoun Wedinsday nixt to answer to sic thingis as thay haue ado with thame.

9 *September* 1560.

The baillies counsale and dekynnis being convenit, and efter ressonyng Restalrig. vpoun the contemptioun committit be the laird of Restalrig vpoun Sounday last aganis the gude toun, fyndis gude sen thay haue put handis in him, and havand him presentlie in thair warde, that he be surelie keipit in the laych counsale hous, all the durris makand passage thairto to be doubill lokit and strenthit, and that fyve of the officeris remane with him dailie and nychtlie quhill thay be forther avisit.

It is statute and ordanit be the baillies counsale and communitie for- Proclamatioun said that proclamatioun be maid at the mercat croce in maner following: for idyll men. —Item, forsamekle as it is manifestlie knawin to the prouest and baillies of this burgh that this toun is charget and oureladin with brokin men of weyr and vtheris idill men desolait of maisteris, tending to mak thair residence and remanyng within the samyn, to the greit apperand danger of the commoun weill gyf thay be sufferrit and nocht suddanlie expellit, quhairfor it is to be commandit and chargit in our Soueraue Lord and

80                EXTRACTS FROM THE RECORDS                [1560.

Proclamatioun  Ladeis name, and in name and behalf of my lord provest and baillies of
for idyll men. this burgh, that all idill men, hable of persoun, being desolait of maisteris
or craft or vther verteous industrie, depesche thame of this toun within
v houris nixt heirefter, vnder the pane of deid; and siclike that na
inhabitane of the samyn, hostler nor vther, loge fortife sustene or menteine
thaim fra the said houre furth, vnder the pane of ten pundis to be applyit
to the commoun warkis, and forther to be pvnissit in thair personis as fos-
teraris and nurisseris of iniquite, with all rigour.

10 *September* 1560.

Restalrig.      [The bailies council and deacons of crafts] ordanis that ane sure
wache be maid of the maist abill men of the toun for sure keiping of the
laird of Restalrig quhill sufficient souertie and cautioun be found that the
tounschip and communite salbe skaythles of him and all that he may latt,
viz., xviij abill and weill geryt men to wache nychtlie within and about the
tolbuith euerye nycht, and sex siclik on the day, and that the baillie of
the quarter be present at the resaving and setting of the said wache and
be haldin to ansuer for thame quhome he resauis.

Item, it is ordanit be the baillies and counsale foresaid that deligent
inquisitioun be maid throuch all the toun for the laird of Restalrigis con-
cubyne, and that incontinent efter scho be apprehendit scho be carttit
throuch the toun and banischit the samyn, vnder the panys contenit in
the proclamatioun maid for hurris; and that the samyn ordour be obseruit
tuiching all hurris within the said toun, conforme to the said proclamatioun, as the saidis baillies will ansuer vpoun thair offices.

11 *September* 1560.

Restalrig.      [The bailies council and deacons of crafts] ordanis the laird of Restalrigis writing, send to the baillies vpoun Sounday last, to be registrat,
of the quhilk the tenour followis: Baillies of Edinburgh. I lat yow wyt
that ye haue ane puir fallow of myne in your keiping in your tolbuth,
quhairfor I desyre him to be lattin furth, vtherwise I salbe evin with yow
or Mertymes. Nocht ellis quhill oure meting quhilk I sall fynd ane vther

rowme to meit in nor the calsay of Edinburgh. *Sequitur subscriptio:* Restalrig. ROBERT LOGANE. And efter the subscriptioun ; Gyf this present beis nocht answerit I sall put yow in als gude ane tolbuth.

The baillies counsale and dekynnis foresaid, efter aduisment with the said writing, vpoun consideratioun of the [dread] of the said laird of Restalrig and his wikit companye, fyndis that be aventour thame selflis and the commoun pepill of this burgh salbe in danger of thair lyflis gif the said laird eschaipe the waird and at onye tyme be thair maisteris, and in thair conscience deponis that he may be justlie feryt of bodylie harme towert the communite quhair he may be thair maister as said is, and thairfor ordanis him to be keipit in suir warde quhill sufficient cautioun be found, vnder the pane of ten thousand pundis, that thay salbe harmeles and skaythles of him and all that he may lat.

The baillies and counsale ordanis Alexander Park, thesaurer, to deliuer to Stevin Storie the price of thre bollis of quheit as the samyn wes sauld in the yeir of God j$^m$ v$^e$ lix yeirs, in the quhilk the said Stevin wes dampnagit the said yeir in his corne landis quhilk he had in associatioun of the Blackfreris be bigging of the toun wall and makand of ane plane passage throuch the said land bayth to man and hors to the said wall, as maister James Lyndesay than maister of wark to the toun be his ayth declaryt.

The saurer Park, Story.

16 *September* 1560.

[The provost, bailies, and deacons of crafts ordained " the ovir turnepike dur of the laich counsale hous, quhair the laird of Restalrig is, to be bigit vp with stane and lyme ;" and also ordered " the wache to be 'maid stranger within the tolbuth sa lang as the laird of Restalrig remanis thairintill, viz., xxx able weill furnyst men for the nycht wache, and xv for the day wache."]

Tolbuth, wache, Restalrig.

The provest baillies counsale and dekynnis foresaid, having sure knaulege that the multitude of pepill quhilkis wes lattin in and resortit to the laird of Restalrig movit him sum tymes by the way, etc., thairfor and [for] vther caussis moving thame ordains that fra this furth thair sall

Restalrig.

82    EXTRACTS FROM THE RECORDS    [1560.

Restalrig.    nane remane with the said laird sa lang as he is in thair tolbuth allanerlie bot tua boyis, and he and thay bayth to want wappinnis ; and siclike that na maner of persoun be lattin in to him bot men of honour and jugement quha salbe knawin to feir God and of mynd to gyf him gude counsale for his weill, and thay alsua to haue na wappinnis.

The prouest baillies and counsale ordanis the officiaris to be payit dalie wages quhilkis hes keipit the laird of Restalrig or salbe commandit to keip him. viz., ilk day iij s.

Johnestoun,    The prouest baillies counsale and dekynnis foresaid be generale voit
flescheouris.   fyndis that Jhonn Jhonnstoun, flescheour, salbe admyttit and resauit freman to the said craft, and that in respect he wes first prentice, is now burges, and offerris all dewiteis to the said craft that of consuetude may be cravit, and thairfor ordanis Jhonn Sandersoun dekyn of the said craft, than present, to caus him be resauit and admyttit to the said craft as fre broder and to haue all princleges thairof fra this furth that to ane fre broder pertenis.

*20 September 1560.*

Proclamatioun    The provest ballies counsaill and dekynns of craftis ordanis publica-
for idolataris.  toun to be maid of the act of parliament lattie set furthe vpone blasphe-meris of the name of God, abuseris of the sacramentis and manteneris of idolatrie, to the effect that na persoun pretend ignorance thairof, of the quhilk act the tenour followis : Forsamekle as Almychty God be his maist trew and blessed [word] hes declarit the reuerence and honour quhilk sould be gevin to him, and be his sone Jhesus Christ hes alswa declarit the trew vse of the Sacramentis, willing the samyn to be vsit according to his will and word, be the quhilk it is notoir and perfythe knawn that the sacramentis of baptisme and of the bodie and blude of Jesus Christ hes bene in all tymes bipast corruptit be the papisticall kirk and be thair ministeris, and presentlie, nochtwithstanding the reformatioun albredelie maid according to Goddis word, nochttheles thair is sum of the samyn papis kirk that stubburnelie perseueris in thair idolatrie, sayand messis and

baptisand conforme to the papis kirk, prophand thairthrow the sacra- Proclamatioun
mentis foirsaidis, in quyett and secreit places, regardand thairthrow for idolataris
nowther God nor his word ; Thairfoir it is statut and ordanit in this
present parliament that na maner persoun nor personis in ony tyme
cuming administrat ony of the sacramentis secreitlie or ony vther maner
way bot thai that ar admittit and heveand power to that effect, nor say
mes, nor yet heir mes, nor be present thairat, vnder the pane of confiscatioun
of all thair guiddis and pvnising of thair bodyis at the discretioun of the
judge within quhais jurisdictioun the personis happinnis to be apprehendit
for the first falt, banesing of the realme for the secound falt, and justefeing
to the deid for the thrid falt; and ordanis all scherefis, stewartis, ballies
and thair deputtis, provestis and ballies of borrowis, and vtheris judges
quhatsumeuer within this realme to tak diligent sute and inquisitioun
within thair boundis quhair ony sic vsurpit muster messaying or thai that
beis present at the doing thairof, ratefeand and apprevand the samyn, and
tak and apprehend thame to the effect that the panis abone writtin may
be execut vpone thame.

The provest ballies and counsaill ordanis the heretouris and occupyaris Nether Kirk-
of the landis lyand on the west syde of the Nether Kirk yarde to stik vpe yarde.
or stanchel the windokis and durris of the saidis landis, swa that na
bestiall hawe entres to the said kirk yarde, nor na filthe be laid vpone the
samyn, and this to be done within iiij dayis nixt efter thai be chargit,
vnder the pane of warding of thair personis.

[The treasurer ordaned to pay " the sowme of xiij li. xiij s. for the hyre of thrie Precept.
furneist fedder beddis, furneist be the gude toun to certane Inglis men, be the space
of xiij oulkos and iiij dayis."]

### 26 September 1560.

It is statut and ordanit be the provest, ballies, counsaill and dekynnis Anent the
of crafttis that in all tyme cuming at the electioun of the new counsaill twa craftismen
the electaris thairof sall cheis the twa crafttismen, quhilkis sould be thair- vpone the
vpone, furthe of the sax personis to be presentit to thame be the dekynnis counsaill.

[1560.

Anent the chesing of the twa craftismen vpoune the counsaill.

of craftis, providing alwayis that gif the saidis electaris sall nocht think the saidis personis nor ony twa of thame to be presentit sufficient meit nor hable to be vpone the counsall, the saidis dekynnis sall present vther sax personis in ane vther tikkatt to the saidis electaris, and fra thyne furthe vther sax in cais tha be nocht satefeit, ay and quhill the saidis ij crafttismen of the counsaill be electit.

## 14 October 1560.

Bread, malt, ale.

[Of bread baked by baxters within burgh the fourpenny loaf to weigh eighteen ounces, and that baked by baxters without burgh to weigh twenty-two ounces. Malt to be sold not dearer than nine firlots for £3, 10s. Ale not to be dearer than fourpence the pint.]

Browsteris.

It is statute and ordanit that na maner of persoun brew within this burgh bot fremen, fremennis wyffis, wedowis and relictis of fremen.

Pultre.

The best cuppill of ewnyngis quhyte quhill Yule to be sald for iij s., the other pair secundar for ij s. iiij d.; and efter Yule quhill Fastrans ewyn the best cuppill ewnyngis for iiij s., the otheris for ij s. the cuppill; the pair of pertrikis, iij s.; the pair of pluwaris, xviij d.; the pair of wydcokkis, xviij d.; the blak kok and gray hen, the pece xvj d.; the cuppill muir hennis, xx d.; the quhape, xij d.; the wyld gwis, iiij s.; the wyld duke, xvj d.; the tame duke, xij d.; the tame gwis, ij s.; and the best ij s. vj d.; the cuppill of pudyeanis, quyk and otherwys nocht to be sald, viij d.; the best capoun, ij. s.; the other secunder, xx d.; the pultre, xij d.

Candle, hay, wine.

[Candles to be sold at 10d. the pound the "rag week," and 8d. the "hard week"; hay, 10d. the stone; best oats, 12d. the peck; the second, 10d.; "Burdeous wyne," 14d. the pint; and "Sherand wyne," 12 d. the pint.]

Corne Merket.

Item, that all maner of personis resortand to this burgh with hors corne to be sald place and set doun the samyn at the fute of the Ower Bow; and that thai sall nocht stryk vp nane of thair ladis afoir ix houris be strykyn, and than to sell the samyn to fre nychtbouris, fre staiblaris and sic otheris as vsis the samyn to thair awyn proper gudis, and nocht to be regraittit agane.

The saidis ballies and hale counsall ordanis the dene of gild, maister  Anent the
James Watsoun, to caus the hale stanis of the Black and Gray Freris  stanis of the
places, now instantlie intromettit with be ony personis and as yit beand  freris places.
furth of wark, and in speciale the stanis quhilk Jhone Slowane, Robert
Dalglesche, Thomas Heslope and Walter Bynning hes in thair possessioun,
and all otheris lows stanis aboute the said placis, be brocht with all deligence and transportit fra thair warkis and placis forsaidis to the kirkyaird
of this burgh for bigging of the dikkis of the samyn and otheris warkis
quhilk thai ar preparand within thair said kirk, and als to caus certane men
cast doun the rest of the said placis yet standand and to intromet with
the stanis thairof, and the samyn be brocht to the said kirk yaird to be
put in wark, and this to be done with deligence possabill becaus the saidis
stanis ar all stollyn away and intromettit with be diuers personis incontrair
thair proclamationis maid thairanent of befoir.

### 20 October 1560.

[The dean of guild ordained to sell and dispone to Adam Foullertoun, "the bell  The Mary bell.
callit the Marye bell, with the hale brasin pillaris and vther brasin wark quhilk he
hes that pertenit to the kirk," Foullertoun having "biddin maist thairfor efter the
samyn wes roupit diuers tymes throuch the toun."]

Katharene Haitlie the spouse of [blank] Williamesoun obleist hirself [Minister.,
to compeir befoir the counsall on Fryday nyxtocum to answer to sic
thingis as salbe laid to hir charge, and in speciall for sclandering of the
minister.

### 30 October 1560.

It is statut and ordanit that in all tyme cuming the halie day callit  Anent the
the Sabbaothe day or day of rest commonlie callit be Sounday be in all  keping of the
tyme cuming kepit commonly be all maner personis, induelleris of this  halie day.
burgh or resortand within the samyn, swa that nane, of quhat estait that
ener thai be of, mak merkatt or merchandice, oppin buthe durris, or exerce
ony kynd of warldlie operatioun thairin, bot that vpone the said day all
personis be astrictit to be present at the ordenarie sermonis alsweill efter
none as befoir none, and that fra the last jow of the bell to the saidis

86                EXTRACTS FROM THE RECORDS            [1560.

Anent the keping of the halie day.

sermouis to the finall end thairfoir thair be nather meit nor drynk sauld in oppin tavernes or hostillareis, bot that induring the said tyme thai be closit; and siklyk that the flesche merkatt vsit to be vpone the Sounday be now and in all tyme cuming vpone the Setterday, and that the merkatt of bestiall at the Hous of the Mure quhilk hes bene in tymes past on the Sonday be in all tyme cuming on the Thursday, that sufficient provisioun of flesche may be had aganis the said Setterday affixt and assignit to the said merkatt of flesche, vnder the pane of pvnisment of the personis that sall happin [to] contraveue the premissis or ony poynt thairof at the counsaillis will.

Blasflemirs of Goddis name.

Item, it is statute and ordanit that na maner persoun within this burgh tak vpone hand to bane, sweir, tak in vane or blasfleme the name of God in ony wys, vnder the pane of setting of thame in the irne brankis, thair to remane during the judges will.

Wemen tavernouris.

Item, becaus in tymes bipast the iniquitie of wemen taverneris within this burgh hes bene ane greit occasioun of huredome within this burgh, swa that it apperis ane bordall to be in euery taverne, thairfor that all ventaris of wyne that may provide thame of wemen taverneris do the samyn betuix and Mertymes nixt herefter, certefeing thame that gif thair be ony filthines committit be the saidis wemen taverneris thai sall be haldin to pay to the commoun werkis the sowne of x li. except thai delyner the offender in the ballies handis to be pvnisit according to the lawis sa sone as the offence cumis to thair knawledge.

Anent the dewtie of wyne that pertenit to the fraternite of St Anthone.

Item, it is statut and ordanit that the dewitie of wyne, viz., ane quart of euery tvn, vsit of befoir to be gadderit to the behuff [of] the fraternitie of St Anthone be in tyme cuming collectit and gadderit for administratioun to be maid thairof to the pure, and that the samyn with the rest of the commoun gude be yerlic roupit vpone Mertymes evin.

Sundry acts.

[Acts passed, in terms similiar to those of previous years, relative to selling of goods by regraters, punishing of vagabonds, removal of "fulye and myddingis" from the street, attendance of all persons when warned to attend assizes or inquests, setting goods for sale on boards on the street, booth doors or common passages, removal of stranger beggars, merchants and others having weapons ready in their booths or dwelling-houses, selling of goods by foreign merchants, and weighing and paying custom on goods arriving at Leith.] — Sundry acts

 Item, it is statut and ordanit be the provest ballies and counsall of this burgh that, consideryng thair is dyners and money syndry personis maid burgesses and fremen within this burgh quhilkis dwellis nocht within the samyne nor yit nother scattis lottis extentis walkis nor wardis nor yit beris na portable charges within this burgh siclik as thai aucht to do, and as other nychtbouris and fremen of this burgh dois, incontrair the ald statutis maid thairvpoun, heirfor the saidis pronest ballies and counsall declaris and makis intimatioun be oppin proclamatioun that all maner of personis quhilkis ar burgesses maid and fremen of this burgh that thai cum and remane within the samyne, and hald thair stob and staik thairintill, with certificatioun that and thai cum nocht within fourtie dayis and mak thair dwelling place within this said burgh, and fulfill the pointis foirsaid, that thay sall bruk na maner of fredome within the samyne, conforme to the saidis ald statutis maid thairvpoun. — Burgesses.

 The provest ballies and counsaill ordanis James Barroun to content and pay to Johne Knox the sowme of sax scoir poundis of the reddiest money of the townis being in his handis, and siklyk the sowme of xx. li. for irne and fyre werk furnesit and maid to his hous. — Precept, Knox.

 The provest ballies and counsaill, in consideratioun that Robert Drummond, gild seriand, is subject to await continewallie vpone the counsaill for warnyng of thame to the affaris of the town at all tymes neidfull, and siklyk to await vpone the minister eldaris and dekynnis at all thair assembleis and conventionis for the caussis of the kirk, and that the said Robert hes of the commoun gyde bot oulie fyftie s., and he wes sustenit in tyme of the papisticall kirk be vther wages he had thairof, thairfor the provest ballies and counsaill ordanis the said Robert to hawe yerlie for his fie the sowme of xij merkis; . . . providing that the — Drummond, villa, gild officer.

88    EXTRACTS FROM THE RECORDS    [1560.

Drummond, villa, gild officer.

said Robert await continewallie vpone the sermounis for keping of the kirk quyett, and to fulfill and observe the remanent poyntis abone writtin.

15 *November* 1560.

Park, villa, prouest, counsall.

The baillies and counsall ordanis Alexander Park, last thesaurer, to pay to my lord prowest the thre rois nobillis quhilkis he suld haif had on Merty mes ewyn for the setting of the commoun gude in anno j$^m$ v$^c$ and fiftie nine yeris, and to pay the new counsall thair fees.

Netherbow.

The prowest ballies and counsall ordanis the but at the Nether Bow to be cryit fre to be tane away be quhasumener that pleissis, and the dene of gild or thesaurar to intromet with the tymmar thairof, and to charge thame thairwith in thair comptis.

16 *November* 1560.

The bigging of the wall at the Northe Louche syde.

It is appointit and fynalle aggreit and concordit betuix the prowest ballies and counsall of the burgh foirsaid on that ane pairt and Murdo Walker masoun on that other pairt, in maner forme and effect as efter followis, that is to say, the said Murdo sall, God willyng, himself with fyve layaris and sa mony barromen and servandis as is neidful enter on Monunday nixtocum to the bigging of thair wall and hous now foundit at the Northe Louche syde foranent the Trinitie College and yairdis thairof, and sall big the samyn conforme to the thiknes and breid of wallis ellis foundit vnto the bartesing, viz., [*blank*] of breid; and als the said Murdo vpoun his expenssis sall tak doun the hale ruinows wallis and ald houssis pertening to the colledge, and caus carye the stanis thairof and materiallis the wall, and sall furnes vpoun his expenssis all warkmanschip and barromen with all other necessairis as efferis for bigging and reperalling of the said wall and that pertenis to the craft of masounrie, except sand lyme and sa monye stanis as the said wall and hous sall myster, by and attour the stanis being in the forsaid ruinous houssis of the collage, quhilk the foirsaid Murdo is bound to tak doun vpoun his expenssis, and cause carye thame as said is, and this to be endit with all possable deligens. For doing of the quhilk the saidis prowest baillies and counsall sall content pay and deliuer to the said Murdo Walker the sowme of foure pund ten schillingis for ilk rude bigging of the said wark contenand the thiknes and breid of the wall ellis foundit as said is, and fourtye schillingis for ilk rude of the battallrice to be payit imediatlie efter the bigging of the rude be the thesaurar James Lowrie ; and the said Murdo sall big the said hous with sic esiamentis, and after the maner as salbe appointit to him be the said thesaurar or vthers quhilk salbe appointit thairto be the guid toun. *The bigging of the wall at the Northe Louche syde*

### 20 November 1560.

The prowest ballies and counsall ordanis the prowest, with certane honest men accumpaneit, to pas to the Hous of the Myre the morn for putting of ordour to the merket as efteris. *House of Muir*

[" Burdeous or Sherand wyne " not to be sold dearer than 1s. 4d, the pint.] *Wine.*

The prowest baillies and counsall ordanis the dene of gild, maister James Watsoun, to pas throuch this burgh and to se quhat personis ar sellaris of stapill gudis, sic as velwottis, sylkis, fyne clayth or otheris siclyke costlie waris, and to discharge thame to sell or vse ony trafficet thairof without thay be bayth burges and gyld ; and gif thay do, efter thay be wairnit and requirit thairto be him, that he steik vp thair buithe durris and intromet with the keyis thairof vnto [the tyme] they cum and mak thame self gyld nochtwithstanding thai be fre burgessis ellis. *Dene of gyld, burgessis.*

### 22 November 1560.

The baillies and counsale, being convenit in the ovir counsale hous of the tolbuth of this burgh, comperit William Harlay, dekyn of the Hammyrmen, and certane vther craftismen, and desyrit the decreit and scentence gevin aganis Jhone Sandersoun deikin of the fleschouris decernyng him to be cairttit throuch the toun and thairefter banischit the samyn for his manifest adulterie committit with Margaret Lyell, to be continewit quhill the morne, quhilk the prouest baillies and counsale foresaid granttit, and thairupoun the said William askit instrumentis. *Sandersoun, craftis.*

23 *November* 1560.

Craftis.

The prouest baillies and counsale being convenit in the place abone writtin, comperit the hale dekynnis of craftis and being informyt of the decreit and sentence pronouncit agaims the said Jhonn Sandersoun, fleschour, and executioun to follow thairupoun, and thair ayde being requyrit thairto, all in ane voce disassenttit that ony sic executioun sould follow vpoun him be the said ordinance, and that on na wayis thay wald appreve the samyn nor na sic extreme lawis vpoun honest craftismen, nocht withstanding it was allegit that thay, at leist the maist pairt of thame, had be speciall voit of before consenttit to the maiking of the said statute vpoun adulteraris contening the foresaid pane, as at lenth is contenit in the samyn statute of the dait the [x] day of [June] the yeir of God j$^m$ v$^c$ [lx].

The samyn day, Adam Purves wrycht, and James Frissell saidler, requyrit of the baillies, Dauid Somer, Adam Foullertoun, and the said counsale, to freith and put to libertie the said Jhonn Sandersoun fleschour, and to be enterit agane quhat tyme he sould be requyrit vnder quhat panis thay plesit, quhilk the baillies and counsale foresaid refusit in respect thay had pronyst na executioun sould follow vpoun him quhill Wedinsday nixt, and for vther caussis moving thame, quhilk in the said counsale was concludit in the presens of the said hale deikynnis, and heirupoun the said Frissell and Purvis askit instrumentis.

The samyn day, the saidis prouest baillies and hale counsale ordanis the baillies and maist pairt of the counsale to pas to my lord dukis lugeing, to the lordis of secreit counsale being thair convenit, and schew be way of complaynt the contempt and inobedience committit be the craftismen quha had be way of deid and be force takin the said Jhonn Sandersoun fleschour furthe of warde, and to desyre the help and support of the saidis lordis for remeid.

28 *November* 1560.

Obligatioun of the craftis.

The prouest baillies and counsale being convenit in the tolbuth, comperit William Raa cutler for the smythis, James Norvell deikin of the tailyeouris, Jhonn Inglis dekin of the masonis, Jhonn Cvnynghame dekin of the wriehtis, Robert Hendersonn dekin of the barbouris, Thomas Hog dekin of the cordineris, Hercules Methven dekin of the baxstaris, Robert Hendersonn for the fleschouris, Mychaell Gilbert dekin of the goldsmythis, How Canny dekin of the furrouris, [blank] Lausonn dekin of the bonet makaris, [blank] dekin of the wobstaris, [blank] dekin of the walkaris, Dauid Kinloch baxster, James Young cutler, [blank] Mow candylmakar, Jhonn Gilbert goldsmyth, William Brokas smyth, for thame self and in name and behalf of the hale craftis of this burgh, and in humill maner presentit the suplicatioun vnder writtin, exhorting my lord prouest to caus the samyn be red and thairefter registrat in the counsale buke in witnessing of thair offerris and obedience, faythfullie promyssing be vphalding of thair handis in the presens of God the juges and counsale thair present, for thaimseltis and the hale craftis, to fulfill and abide at the said supplicatioun and all ponttis thairintill contenit, off the quhilk the tenor follois:—To yow my lord prouest baillies and counsale maist humlie menis the dekynnis maisteris and principale brethering of the craftis within this burgh heir presentlie convenit, nocht onelie for purging thame selffis and declaring of their innocencie tuiching the lait inobedience inventit and rasit be wikit memberis, alsweill inimeis to ws as to your lordschippis, bot alsua to requeist yow, and in the name of the Lord God maist eirnistlie to desyre yow, that for the cryme and offence of the wikit the innocent be nocht be yow nor your procurement prosecutit and trublit, and as ye tender the obedience of the Almychti and willis the intres and establisching of your common weill, that broderlie amyte may be had amangis ws, all hatrent and gruge set on syde, quhilk in the presens of the Lord oure God with all humilite we maist effectuislie desyre, promissing frome this furth, be our selffis and all oure quhome we haue or sall happin to haue power or charge, all faithfull dew obedience fortificatioun and manteinance to yow as to oure lauchfull magistratis; and to the effect that the amyte and broderlielufe quhilk we requyre of yow to be amangis ws may appeir in the eis of all pepill to be groundit and haif procedit according to the will and wourd of the eternall God, and it may be knawyn that the maist godlie wourd dalie preichit amangis ws sall

*Obligatioun of the craftis.*

Obligatioun of the craftis.   nocht be all fruitles, lat ws all togidder with vnfeinyeit harttis and myndis frelie emit all offences past, and frome the boddomis of our harttis call vpoun our God that his and his wikit memberis quhilkis hes rowsit at this our lait variance may be expellit and rutit out frome amangis ws to thair vter confusioun, and that it may be knawyn amangis the godlie that in this toun it hes plesit the Almychti to place and establische sic ane kirk quhilk be his omnipotent power, in despyte of Sathan, sall so be joynit in sic godlie ametie that the samyn salbe mirrour and exampill to all the rest of this realme ; and sua in the name of God lat ws pas all togidder to my lordis of secreit counsall and with all gud harttis and mynd laubour and procur the libertie of our brother presentlie in the castell, that the mowthis of the wikkit may be stoppit, and that it may [be] knawyn that it is nocht the blude of our saidis brethering as thai ymagyn that ye desyre, and als to otheris wikkit memberis quhilkis ar fugetive and hes takyn vpoun thame the occasioun and begyning of this lait besynes and twmult that it may be als knawyn to you that the samyn wes done by our consent and adwys, we promeis heir in the presens of God that with all our harttis and poweris we sall fortefie concur and assist yow in the persowing of thame to the vtermaist throuche all pairtis of this realme. Thir offeris we maist humlie beseik you to accept, and the spirit of God be amang you and move your harttis with pietie towert ws and your brethering quhom we tak to record we craif the samyn of you with all humilitie as of our lawfull magistratis to quhome we promes all dew obedience and manteinance at our vter power ; and your answer.   Quhilk being red it wes demandit of the dekynnis and brether forsaid be the commoun clerk, haifing command of the said prowest ballies and counsall, gif thai wald abyde be the said supplicatioun ratifie and approve the samyn and all heiddis thairintill contenit, quha all in ane voce be vpholding of thair handis and renewing of thair ayth, calling God to witnes, that sua thai wald do, and neuir to cum in the contrair, and humlie requeistit the said prowest baillies and counsall to command the said clerk to register the said supplicatioun for the mair sure witnessing of thair said promeis, etc., And further requirit answer.

The samyn day, the prowest baillies and counsale, for caussis moving

thame, continewis thair answer to the said supplicatioun quhill Wednisday **Obligatioun of the craftis.**
nyxtocum.

The samyn day, the prowest baillies and counsall dekynnis and maisteris of craftis befoir writtin, ordanis letteris to be impetrat for summonyng of Jhone Rynd powderar, Jhone Sandersoum flesheour, Walter Wycht cutlar, and James Fraser saidlair, to vnderly the law for the lait conspiracie inventit and manteinit be thame aganis the judgis, promes and to do faithfullie all in ane voce to persew the saidis letteris to the extremitie, and vpoun this the said craftismennis grant and promeis the said prowest askit instrumentis; and the said prowest and counsall oblissis thame to releif the saidis baillies of all panis as souerteis for agane bringing to the justice clerk of the saidis letteris dulie execute and indorsit, and the saidis baillies askit instrumentis.

### 6 December 1560.

The baillies haill counsale and dekynnis, togidder with maister James M'Gill clerk of register, maister Jhone Ballandene justice clerk, and the laird of Dwn and laird of Pittarrow, being convenit, the saidis dekynnis all in ane voce humlie requeistit the saidis ballies and counsall to laubour for thair brethering in the castell at the handis of my lord dukis grace and lordis of secreit counsall, promissand as of before all humill and faithfull obedience in tymes cuming according to thair promeis contenit in thair supplicatioun presentit to the prowest baillies and counsall foirsaid, registrat in this buke at thair request the xxviij day of November last, for the mair sure testificatioun of thair saidis promissis and to remane for thair accusatioun in cais thay pass fra ony point of the samyn in tymes cuming or the other actis following, and willis the said supplicatioun togidder with the proclamatioun following to be publishit on Monunday next at xj houris befoir none in presens of the haill pepill, quhair thai promis to gif thair presens, and be vphalding of thair handis in Goddis presens and the said pepill to sweir to abyde at the contentis of the said supplicatioun and proclamatioun, and all pointtis thairintill contenit. Followis the proclamatioun: Forsamekill as it is thocht neidfull and expedient

Obligatioun of the craftis.

for satefeing of the godlie, as alssua for stopping of the mouthis of the wikit quhilkis hes rewsit at the lait variance and inobedience within this burgh begun sterit vp and set furth aganis the magistratis of the samyn, be the procurment laubouris and fortefecatioun of certane wikit personis quhilkis shortlie ar to be callit and accusit thairfoir, and to mak patent that the selander and wikit judgement rasit vpoun the dekynnis and principall maisteris of craftis, at the leist the maist pairt of thame, concerning the said inobedience, is rather be the wikit inventit nor of the saidis dekynnis and maisteris desire, as to the saidis magistrattis is notourlie knawin be deligent inquisitioun and sure tryall, besydis the saidis dekynnis and maisteris awyn purgatioun be thair ayth faithfullie sworne, quha in the presens of God, the saidis magistratis, the haill counsall of this burgh and diuers nobill men lordis of the secreit counsall, hes declarit thame selflis innocent of the said twmult and inobedience art and pairt thairof, and that thai neuir myndit nor willis to mynde the lyke, bot with all humilitie hes submittit and in tymes cuming will submit thame to thair lawfull magistrattis present and to cum, viz., the prowest ballies and officiaris of this burgh, with all dew obedience and manteinance of quhatsumener lawis or statutis be thame deuisit and set furth for the commoun weill, pvncsing of trespassouris, or otheris gude caussis quhatsumener, as alssua thair forteficatioun manteinance and assistance be thameselflis and all other quhome thai haif or salhappin to haif charge or cure, in the persewing of all sic with thair assisteris as wikkitlie hes offendit and contempnit, or sall happin to offend contempne or dissobay the said magistrattis and officiaris in tyme cuming; lykeas the saidis dekynnis maisteris and principall honest men of craftis heir presentlie conuenit for apprewing of the premissis and satifying of all as be thame hes takyn ony selander or of thair ewill judgement as said is, etc. Followis the supplicatioun :— To you my lord prowest, etc.:—This supplicatioun writtin on the leif befoir, quhilkis beand red and proclamit at the mercat croce of this burgh, the ix day of December instant, the saidis dekynnis and maisteris heir present vpheld thair handis, in presens of God and the haill pepill, as wes befoir promisit, to abyde at all and sundrie the premisses in the said supplicatioun and proclamatioun contenit.

OF THE BURGH OF EDINBURGH.

It is statute and ordanit be the prouest baillies counsale and dekynnis, [Dissobedi-
in prosens of the men of gude before writtin, that quhatsumeuir persoun ence.]
in ony tyme cuming, merchant craftisman or vther within this burgh, that
salhappin to dissobey the maiestratis and officeris of the samyn, contempt
and ganestand the lawis and statutis thairoff, that bayth thay thair
fauoraris mantenaris and assistaris salbe pvnist in thair personis and
guddis according to the lawis, and forther tyne thair fredome for euir.

Item, becaus in tymes past quhen ony craftisman war callit to the [Craftsmen
lawis be ony pairtye, or for braiking of the statutis of this burgh, the haile called to the
craftis war wont to convene with the pairtye callit for fortefeing of him, for laws.]
remeid heirof it is statut and ordanit that na sic conventionis be in tymes
cuming vnder the pane of tynsale of thair fredomes that convenis in
maner foresaid, and forther to be pvnist at the will of the saidis maiestratis in thair guddis, without prejudice of the act of parliament.

Item, becaus it is surelie vnderstand be the prouest baillies counsale [Craftsmen's
and dekynnis forsaid that certane young fallowis, craftismennis sernandis servants to be
of this burgh, war the principale fortifearis and furthsettaris of this lait punished.]
tvmult, and as yit continewis in thair proude and wikit speiking, for remeid
heirof it is statute and ordanit that the principalis of thame be callit and
accusit at particuler dyettis before the prouest and baillies foresaid, and sa
monye as beis conviet to be pvnist to the rigour in exemple of vtheris.

The proucst baillies [and council] ordanis the capis vestmentis and Vestementis.
ornamentis of the kirk now being in the thesaurer hous or ellis quhair
within this burgh, vndisponit, be delinerit to Maister James Watsoun dene
of gild, to be sauld and disponit be him, and the money thairof to be
applyit to the warkis of the kirk.

[The dean of guild of the past, ordained to deliver to the dean of the present, Kirk.
year, "the money restand in his handis pertenying to the toun vpliftit be him the
last yeir of his office for reperaling of the kirk instantlie."]

| | |
|---|---|
| Extent jⁿ merkis | The prouest baillies and counsale foresaid names thir personis vnderwrittin to be extentouris of this present taxt of ane thousand merkis rasit vpoun this toun, as thair pairt of the extent granttit for furnessing of the ambassadouris in France and Ingland, and ordanis the saidis extentouris to convene the morne at viij houris for taxting of the nychbouris vnder the pane of warding; Arthure Granger, [and eleven others.] |
| Paullis bell. | The prouest baillies and counsale ordanis maister James Watsoun to caus hing vp the bell of Sanct Paullis Wark for conveuing of the pepill to prayerris at the houris appoynttit. |
| Anent the burgessis and baillies. | The prowest, James Lowrie thesaurer, James Barroun, Jhone Adamsoun, James Adamsoun, Williame Aikman, Thomas Thomsoun, and Alexander Hoip of the counsall, haifland considderatioun of the gret hurt and skaith sustenit be the fremen, merchandis craftismen and nychtbouris of this burgh, be vnfremen traffecteris within the samyn, namis and constitutis maister Richert Glen, maister Jhone Spens, Daniel Somer and Adam Fullartoun, ballies, to command and charge all nychtbouris and induellaris of the samyn, merchand or craftismen or ony otheris that vsis ony traffect within the said burgh and is nocht fre burges or gild, and hes substance to do the samyn, that thai mak thame sall fre with possable deligens, and gif thai refuis to compell thame be imprisoning of thair personis or other wayis as thai sall think maist gude, and siclik to compell all sic as ar onlie burges and ventaris of wyne walx welwottis sylkis or fyne clathis to mak thame gild or ellis desist fra all selling of sic merchandice, vnder the panis foirsaidis. |
| Wallis. | And als names the saidis baillies to get in the rest of the xij d. of the pund grantit for ligging of the wallis and restand vnpayit. |

20 *December* 1560.

| | |
|---|---|
| Anent the deliuerance of the halie blude claithis and jowallis. | The prouest ballies and counsall ordanis Jhone Dougall merchand, being personallie present, to compeir befoir thame on Wedinsday cum aucht |

dayis and bring with him the haill westimentis and jowallis pertening to the Haly Blude alter and mak deliuerance thairof to the saidis prowest ballies and counsall.

*Anent the deliuerance of the halie blu'e clathis and jowallis.*

The saidis prowest ballies and counsall ordanis James Lowrie thesaurer, being personallie present, to enter on Monunday nyxtocum xx pyoneris to the doun casting of the dyk and fows biggit be the Franchemen betuix thair bulwark of Leith and [blank] hous, foranent the northe pairt of the Kingis wark, vpoun thair fredome, and to continew the samyn quhill the samyn be cassin doun.

*Douncasting of the dik and fous foranent Jhone Dalmahoy.*

The prowest ballies and counsall ordanis James Barroun to content and pay to Jhone Knox, minister, the sowme of fyftie pund money of this realme for the second termes payment, of the reddiest money that the said James hes in his handis of the gud townis.

*Precept, Barroun, Knox.*

### 26 December 1560.

The baillies and counsale foirsaid, vnderstanding that be the resort of pepill and barnys to the kirk, the bynkis and saittis ar fylit be the saidis bairnyis and vtheris vngodlie pepill, and for eschewing thairof and sic vther ingodlynes as hes bene vsit in the said kirk be wikit pepill as said is, ordanis that the durris of the said kirk be lokit and keipit close all the day throuch, the appoyntit tymes of preiching and prayeris allanerlie except.

*Kyrk.*

### 3 January 1560.

The baillies and counsall ordanis maister James Watsoun dene of gyld to ressaue sic nychtbouris of this burgh as is knawyn, or salbe thocht be the said counsall or ballies, nocht of puissance to pay thair haill burges or gyldschipps in hand, actit for the half of thair dewitie, and to ressaue reddy payment of the other half. And als that he aduerteis the counsall or he begyn to ony new wark in the kirk or other pairt, and to tak thair awys anent the furthsetting thairof.

*Anent the payment of burges and gyldschippis.*

N

| | |
|---|---|
| Quariouris. | The baillies ordanis Andro Lyndesay, javellour, to rander agane the warklomes tane fra the quariouris for douncasting of the Freris, and thai obleis thame selflis nouir to be fund doing the lyk vnder the pane of the wanting of thair rycht hand, quhilkis ar Alexander Reid, Andro Reid, Hew Reid, James Galbrayth, with otheris thair complices to the nomer of xvj men. |
| Precept, Barroun, Carnis. | The baillies and counsall ordanis James Barroun to deliuer to Jhone Cairnis the sowme of fourtye pund money for his expenssis maid and seruice in tymes bigane, and to be maid quhill the feist of Fastrenis ewyn nyxtocum, and that of the reddiest of the money quhilk he restis awand to the guid toun. |

15 *January* 1560.

| | |
|---|---|
| Schole maile. | [The treasurer "to pay to Maister Alexander Mauchane the sowme of viij li. for the Mertymes termes male last bipast of the grammer scule."] |

17 *January* 1560.

| | |
|---|---|
| Dowgall villa. | [Johne Dowgall, elder, merchant, being charged to give up the jewels and ornaments in his keeping pertaining to the "Halie Blude aulter," delivered to the bailies and council "ane syluer challice with ane syluer croce that stude vpone the aulter, all weyit to thre scoire fyftene vnces syluer."] |

4 *February* 1560.

| | |
|---|---|
| Corsbe. | The provest baillies and counsale ordanis Dauid Corsbe to produce before thame vpoun Friday nixt the siluer chelleis and vtheris ornamentis of the Halie Blude altare quhilk he hes in keping, vnder the pane of warding. |
| Precept, Provost. | [The treasurer ordained the sum of two hundred merks to be paid to "Archibald Dowglas, provest, in consideratioun of his seruice and large expenssis in the tounis effaris."] |
| Beidmen. | The provest baillies and counsale ordanis Luce Wilsoun, thesaurare, to pay to the beidmen of St Andros hospitale the soume of fyve poundis as for thair pensioun of the Mertymes last bipast. |

In presence of the provest baillies and counsale foirsaid, Michael Bre, Calsay makar. Frencheman, calsay makar, bindis and obleissis him that incontinent heirefter he, togidder with his sone and samony sernandis as he may get, sall enter to the making and mending of the tovnis calsayis, and begin at sic place as pleissis thame to appoint him, continualie to remane and laubour thairat without taking vpoun him of ony vther menis laubouris, quhill the haill calsayis of the toun be compleitlie endit and mendit or quhill he be dischargeit be thame, and sall furneis stane sand and all maner of thingis necessar for the said work vpoun his awin expenssis; for the quhilk caus Luce Wilsoun, thesaurar, sall pay to him ouklie on Setterday at evin for ilk rude of new work the soume of xlviij s., and for ilk rude of auld work xxxviij s.; and the rudis to be met be Alexander Pery, Jhonne Wilsoun or James Edmund, and the said Michell grantis him to hane ressauit at thir presentis iij lib. in pairt of payment of the said work.

### 7 *February* 1560.

The prouest baillies and counsale foresaid ordanis maister James Kirk Wark. Watsoun, dene of gild, with all deligence to begyn and compleit the stane gavill ordanit of before at the west end of Sanct Gelis Kirk within the west gavill of the samyn, conforme to the said ordinance; and sielike to proceid in the vther necessar warkis within the said kirk.

The prouest baillies and counsale foresaid ordanis Louke Wilsoun, Toun wallis. thesaurer, with all diligence possebill to by lyme and sand and all vther necessaris for the completing of the toun wall at the Blakfreris, and to proceid and go fordwert with the samyn as it salbe appoynttit be the counsale.

### 12 *February* 1560.

[The dean of guild ordained to pay to "Johne Knox, minister, the sowme of Precept, Knox fyftie poundis for supporting of his chargeis;" and the treasurer to pay "Robert Mowbray, heretour of the hous occupyit be Johne Knox," ten merks, as the duty thereof to the preceding Martinmas, "and fra thinefurth to pay him termelie according to fyftie merkis in the yeir sa lang as the samyne sall be occupyit be him."]

100        EXTRACTS FROM THE RECORDS        [1560.

## 19 *February* 1560.

**Thesaurer, toun wark.**  The prouest baillies and counsale ordanis Louke Wilsoun, thesaurer, with deligence to put to workmen to the doun taking of the Blackfreir wallis and dikis, and gadder in all stanys of the samyn intromettit with be quhatsumevir persoun, and big the toun wall thairwith, and oblissis thame and thair successouris to releif and keip him skaythles thairof in all tymes cuming at all handis quhome efferis.

## 21 *February* 1560.

**Dene gyld, Corsbye.**  In presens of the baillies and hale counsale, Dauid Corsby burges of Edinburgh, presentit and deliuerit to maister James Watsoun, dene of gild, at thair command, conforme to thair ordinance of before, ane siluer challice, our gilt, weyand twenty vnces and half ane vnce wecht, quhilk pertenit to the Haly Blude alter, gevin to him in keiping be the maisteris and brether thairof.

**Charge, dene gyld, Sauchie.**  The baillies and counsale foresaid ordanis the dene of gild to call Alexander Sauchye, tailyeour, for the thre bras pillaris quhilkis he hes confessit him to haue of Sant Anthonis Ile, and ordanis the said dene of gyld to be chargit with the samyn in his compttis, and siclike with the hale vther pillaris and bellis resauit be him.

## 5 *March* 1560.

**Foullertoun, dene gild, charge.**  Maister James Watsoun dene of gild, being demandit quhat money he had resauit fra Adam Foullertoun, baillie, for the bellis and brasin pillaris of the kirk, confessit him to haue resauit fra the said baillie the sowme of tuelf score of pundis, and the said baillie askit instrumentis.

## 12 *March* 1560.

**Toun wall, Blakfreris.**  The prouest baillies and counsale ordanis Luk Wilsoun, thesaurer, with all diligence possible, to caus begyn and big the town wall at the Blak freirs, quhair the samyne wes left be maister James Lyndsey, and tak doun and intromett with the rest of the stanis and wallis of the Blak freris kirk and yardis, and siclik to seik throuch all the towne quhair ony

of the stanis of the said freirs ar caryeit, and caus bring the samyne agane  Toun wall,
to the said towne wark, and with the saidis haill stanyis big vp the said  Blakfreris.
wall.

The ballies and counsall ordanis Louk Wilsonn, thesaurer, to deliuer  Franche
to Andro Williamsonn, wrycht, the sowme of xj s. vj d. for his harbouris in  ambassadour
doun taking and vpsetting of certane beddis and vther necessar besynes,
in maister Jhone Robertsonis hous preparit for the Franche ambassatour.

The ballies and counsall ordanis Louk Wilsonn thesaurer to deliuer
for four elnis and ane quarter of swttis grene bocht to be ane covering to
the Franche ambassatouris buird, the sowme of iij li. iiij s. ix d.

2-4 *March* 1560.

Forsamekill as it is nocht vuknawin that, be the brute of the preistis  Proclamationn,
monkis freris and vtheris of that vngodlie sort and that opinioun, it wes  preistis, freris.
doung in the ciris of all pepill of this realme, and speciallie of the inhabitantis of this burgh, that albeit thai war willing to heir the trew worde
preicheit thai durst nocht resorte to this burgh for feir of pvnisment, and
sua be croweltie war debarrit and haldin abak frome hering of the sermonnis
now publeist; for remeid heirof, and satefeing of all faithfull, frie licence
wes gevin to all preistis monkis freris chanuonis nunnis and vtheris of
thair sorte sectis and opinioun, frelie without impediment or ony kynde of
iniurie, to resorte to the saidis sermonis, and thair place appointit, and all
vtheris forbiddin to occupy the same, and siklike of all sic thingis as thai
war iu dowte of the samyn to be opinit to thame be word or writ as thai
suld think maist gude, and albeit the sort foirsaid hes be the space of thre
monethis past had libertie and fredome as said is, na signe nor apperance
is or can be found of thair amendment, bot rather hes done and dailie dois
that may ly in thame to hald the sempill pepill in blindnes and errour,
ganging maist bisselie, as is surelie knawin to vse, the magistratis
of this burgh, [into] all the pairtis of the said toun, sawing thair
vngodlie opinionis and detestable [workis.] Quharefore sen trew it is
that, be the infallable word of the eternale and [trew] God, we ar commandit to rute owte from the middis of ws oure toun and commoun weill
the wikit and vngodlie, and in speciale quhen the workis of the samin

Proclamatioun, preistis, freris.

dois appeir to the hurte thairof, as we will eschew the wrath and indignatioun threitnit vpoun ws gif we do nocht oure dewitie, for pureging of our said toun of sic vngodlie peple thair errouris and detestabill workis, I command and charge in our Soverane Ladeis name, and in name and behalf of the lordis of secreit counsale, provest and bailles of this burgh, that within xlviij houreis nixt heirefter all preistis monkis freris channonis nunnis and vtheris of the vngodlie sectis and opinionis, quhilkis heirtofore hes joisit the priuilege and liberte abone writtin, and hes nocht gevin thair repentence of thair formar iniquiteis and opinionis, as alssua all mes sayaris and mes mauteinaris, huremongaris, adulteraris and fornicatouris, deposche thame of this toun fredome liberte bonndis and suberbbis thairof, and that thai nothir hant resorte nor frequent sa lang as thai remane abstinat; yitt nocht withstanding the said toun being anis purgeit of thame, quhen it sall pleis the Almychttie to move thair hartis to acknawlege thair ignorance, and to crave to be hard and ressauit in the fallowschip of the faithfull, vpoun apperance of thair repentence, efter obtening of the saidis provest and baillies licence, thai sall nocht be refusit nor denyit, sua that it salbe knawin to all peple that we the saidis provest baillies and counsale and haill faithfull within this burgh thristis na thing mare than thair godlie conversioun and repentence. And this to all quhome it efferis we mak knawin and requiris yow witnes. Quhilk proclamatioun being red in presens of the saidis provest baillies counsale and dekynnis of craftis, the saidis dekynnis approvit the same and thocht the same maist ressonable to be allowit and put to executioun, and all in ane voce ordanis the samyn to be proclamyt at the mercat croce, and the execution to follow vpoun the contempnaris.

The pure.

The provest, baillies, dene of gild, thesaurare, [counceil, assessors and deacons of crafts,] all in ane voce grantis and consentis that the ordour takin for the sustenyng of the pure, that is to say, that all maner of man induellaris within this burgh, baith merchandis and craftismen, quhilkis refussis to gif onlklie almous be compellit be the saidis provest baillies and counsale, with avise of the saidis dekynnis, to gif of thair gudis for the caus foirsaid according to thair power and substance, and gif neid be the reddiest gudis of the refusar to be poindit and distrinyeit thairfore.

[The council ordanit the decreet aganist the fleshers, for payment of thair mails *Fleschouris* and duties, to be put in force, and appointed "the Blakfreir kirk yarde for the saidis flescheouris thair to [sett] and place thair flesch stokkis, and to be dischargeit of [the flesh] marcat that now is, and to flit and remove thair flesche stokkis thairfra vnder all hiest pane and charge."]

### 2 April 1561.

The ballies and counsall ordanis to convene the dekynnis on Fryday *The pure.* nyxt, and to desyre and haif thair awys and counsall to the furthsetting of certane statutis devisit for ordoring of the towne, the pure of the samyne, in compleitting of certane gude warkis ellis begowne and nocht endit in the said towne.

James Barroun deliuerit, in presens of the counsall, the pece of clayth *Vestments.* of gold with Sanct Gelis coit ressauit be him in keping; . . . . . . Andro Sclattar deliuerit the vestment dekyne and subdekyne of clayth of gold quhilk he had in keping; . . . . Thomas Jaksoun, massoun, deliuerit the chesobell of red welnott myxt with gold, with the pertinentis thairof.

The ballies and counsall, haifing consideratioun of the pure within this *The pure.* burgh, and movit of petie according to thair bunding dewtie towart thame, hes thocht gude that certane honest men of this towne, merchandis and craftismen, be chosin furth to the nvmer of thre personis within ewery quartar to pas to the hussis and buthis of euery gud and godly nychtbor and requyre of thame thair almos and support to the said pure, and samekle as beis gottin to be distributit to thame euery Setterday eftirnone be the eldaris and dekynnis sworne thairto, and compt to be maid of the money collectit, befoir the minister ballies eldaris and dekynnis euery moneth anis, be the saidis collectouris and dispositouris, and this ordour to be obseruit for the said pure quhill it sall pleis God that better be prouidit; and thir collectouris following to indure for the first quartar of yeir, begynnand the said second of Apryle, that is to say :—[Here follow names.]

## 5 April 1561.

[Vestment.] Williame Lausoun, in presens of the ballies dene of gyld and counsall, presentit and deliuerit the westment dekyne and subdekyne of grene dalmes with the pertinentis, quhilk he had in keping.

Precept, Knox. [The bailies and council] ordanis maister James Watsoun, dene of gild, to deliuer and pay to the minister, Jhone Knox, the sowme of fyftie pundis as for the compleit payment [for a quarter.]

Vestmentis. The ballies and counsall ordanis the vestmentis and kirk geir to be gadderit in and sauld with diligence; and of the reddiest money thairof the fyfty pund debursit and deliuerit be maister James Watsoun to Jhone Knox to be refundit and payit to him agane.

Flescheouris. [Proclamation to be made forbidding any freeman of the flesher craft to sell their flesh "in ony vther place within this burgh bot at the overend of the Tolbuith passand vpwart to the over Bow ; and that na vnfreman sell ony flesche bot in the Vinell and passage lyand on the sowthe pairt of the Cowgait passand fra the commoun calsay of the Bow to the place of the Blakfreris."]

## 9 April 1561.

Propositiouns of the dekynnis for the fleschouris. [Referring to a previous act of the council as to the removing of the fleshers from the fleshmarket, Robert Henrisoun, on behalf of the deacons of crafts, alleged " that in sa far as the saidis fleschouris wer removit by the avise and consent of the dekynnis, [thay had been] evill done to, forsamekle as in tymes past in transporting of all merkettis or placeing of thame the saidis dekynnis consenttis and voittis wer requyrit, as is notour be the speciall actis maid vpoun the transporting of the clayth merket, in the yeiris of God j ᵐ vᶜ lv and lvij yeris," and therefore any act as to removal of the fleshmarket passed without consent of the deacons was contrary to their privileges ; " quhairfor he in name foresaid desyrit it to be votit of new concernyng the changing of the merket and thair voittis hard thairintill." The deacons thereupon ratified and approved " the ordinance and decreit laitlie set furth and pronounceit aganis the flescheouris," "for the commoun weill."

Decreit aganis Flescheouris. The provost bailies and council, knowing the disobedience of the fleshers in refusing to pay their mails and duties or to remove from the fleshmarket, decerned them to remove, "and to place thair said stokis and hald merket at the west pairt and end of the tolbuth stair quhair the landis merket stude of before."]

The prouest baillies counsale and [hale dekynnis], vnderstanding the place quhair the victuell merkettis is presentlie haldin, viz., vpoun the Hie Streit aboue the tolbuth, to be na convenient place in respect of the thrang of merkettis haldin thair, and for vtheris diuers caussis moving thame concernyng the commoun weill, findis gude and all in ane voce decernis concludis and granttis the said victuell merket be changit and transporttit to the biggit place quhair the flesche merket is presentlie haldin sa sone as ane convenient vther place may be gottin bocht and bigit for the saidis fleschouris. [Victuell merkett.

The prouest baillies counsale and dekynnis, efter aduisement, findis that the yaird and biggit land liand at the fute of the flesche merket pertenyng heretablie to Jouet Wycht and Dauid Levingstoun hir spous sallbe the maist meit and convenient place for ane flesche merket. [The council agree to take steps for acquiring the property.] [Levingstonis yard.

### 23 April 1561.

[Sums resting of the extent granted for bigging of the town walls to be gathered in and to be delivered "to Dauid Somer, baillie, to be wairrit vpoun the bigging of the wallis in Leyth Wynde."] [Leyth Wynde.

The articulis following proponit to the prouest baillies counsale and dekynnis for the commoun and commoun policie of this burgh, quhilk thay ordane to be registrat:— [Articles proposed to the council.]

Item, in the first, it is thocht gude that the renttis annuellis and vtheris emolimentis quhilkis of before war payit furth of landis and tenementis within this burgh to papistis, preistis, feris, monkis, nonis, and vtheris of that wikit sort, for manteinyng of idolatrie and vane superstitioun, seing it hes plesit the Almychti to oppin the eis of all pepill and to gyf thame the knaulege of sic vane abussis, thairfor that the saidis renttis [Rents and annuals payable to papists.]

[Rents and annuals payable to papists.]

and emolimentis be applyit to mair proffitable and godlie vssis, sic as for sustenyng of the trew ministerris of Goddis word, founding and biging of hospitalis for the pure and collegis for leirnyng and vpbring of the youth, and sic vther godlie warkis.

[Deceased's goods.]

Item, becaus it apertenis to the maiestratis as commandit of God to defend and procure the caussis of the wedow and peple, heirfor, that ane ordinance be maid for the ayd and support of pupillis and infanttis quha ar destitute be inlaik of thair parenttis, that the just inventure being takin be ane of the juges, with the clerk, of the haile guddis quhilkis pertenit to the deid, thairefter the samyn to be registrat in the townis bukeis to be furthcummand to the vtelite of the bairnys, and sufficient cautioun to be taikin of the tutour curatour or intromettouris thairwith for the samyn and avale thairof to the bairnys weill as said is, and iiij d. to be granttit of euerye pound of the dedis pairt to the support and vphald of the misterfull and puir.

[Duty on wine.]

Item, quhair of before, in the tyme of ignorance and blindnes, thair wes ane choppin of wyne granttit and gevin for the mantenyng the wikitnes and idolatrie of Sanct Anthonis Ile, of the tvn of wyne, that now of euery tvn of wyne thair be vpliftit be the dene of gild present and to cum xij d. allanerlie, to be put in ane box and disponit for sustenyng of the pure and fallit brethering marchanttis and craftismen of this burgh.

[Burial place.]

Item, becaus it is thocht gude that thair be na buriell within the kirk, and that the kirk yard is nocht of sufficient rowme for bureing of the deid, and for eschewing of the savour and inconuenientis that may follow thairupoun in the heit of somer, it wald be prouidit that ane buriall place be maid farer fra the myddis of the toun, sic as in the Gray Freir yaird, and the samyn biggit and maid close.

[Games.]

Item, for exercing and vsing of the youth in honest and neidfull gammys at lauchfull tymes, thair wald be maid in sum convenient place diuers pairris of buttis for hand bow corse bowe and culvering.

[Swearers and blasphemers.]

Item, that the name of God may be had in sic reuerence as in his awin maist blissit scriptouris is commandit, and for eschewing of the curse and plaigis hinging our the heidis of all townis cuntreis cieteis and peple quhair the samyn his blissit name is contempuit and blasphemyt, ane [Swearers and ordoure wald be establischit for pvnischeing of all proud vane and blasphemers.] vngodllie aithis and sueraris thairof without fauouris.

Item, siclik ordoure wald be taiken for compelling of the stubburne [Prayers and and abstinat inimeis to the treuth to cum to the prayerris and preiching preaching.] of the worde of God.

Quhilkis articules being red in presens of the prouest baillies and dekynnis, it wes concludit that euery dekin sould haue ane copye thairof to be schewin to his craft and ansuer reporttit the nixt counsale day.

The prouest baillies counsale and dekynnis ordanis Louke Wilsoun, Artalye. thesaurer, and certane of the counsale to pas to my lord Arskin, capitane of the castell, and in the name of the said prouest baillies counsale and hale communitie ask and reassaue fra him the townys artailye pulder bullet, and all vther thing thairto pertenyng, quhilk he ressauit in keiping the first tyme of the cuming of the congregatioun to this burgh, and gyf he refussis to report his ansuer the nixt counsale day.

The prouest baillies and counsale, vnderstanding that the prentissis Proclamatioun and seruandis of merchanttis and craftismen and vtheris within this burgh anent prentissis. ar of mynd vpoun Sounday nixt to mak convocatioun and assemblie efter the auld wikit maner of Robene Hude, nocht regarding the pvnisment thretnit in Goddis word vpoun the braikaris of the Saboth, nor having feir of the temporale pvnischment content in our Soueraine actis vpoun the vsurparris of sic vane pastymes, quhairfor they all in ane voce, as cairfull fadderis our their commontie, and for eschewing of the pvnismentis and dangerris aboue written, ordanis ane proclamatioun to be maid at the foure principale pairttis of this burgh, in our Soueraine Ladeis and thair names, dischargeing all sic conventionis and assemblais within this burgh and boundis of the samyn, and of all bering of armour, wappinnis, striking of suesche, sounding of trumpet, bering of baner standert or ansenye, or like instrument, for sic vane besynes, certefeing the maister quhais seruand sall happin to be found cumand in the contrair heirof that he sall tyne his

108    EXTRACTS FROM THE RECORDS    [1561.

Proclamatioun anent prentissis.
fredome of this burgh for euir, the seruand prentise or vther apprehendit or notat to tyne the armour and abulyement apprehendit with him and banist the toun for euer; the lenneris of armour wappinnis and abulyement to be reput and haldin as manteinaris of the wikit inemeis to all gude ordour, and thairfor pvnist in thair personis and guddis at the will of the said prouest baillies and counsale: and siclik that na assemblay nor convocatioun be found within this burgh with armour and wappinnis of the inhabitantis of the samyn, nor of the tounis adiacent, bot euerye man to gang and behaif him self in honest and sempill maner without multitude or gaddering, vnder the said pane of warding and pwnisment at the saidis jugis will.

Dewtie of wyne.
Item, the samyn day, the prouest baillies and counsale foresaid, vpoun consideratioun of the maist godlie articule proponit for collecting of xij d. of euerye tvn of wyne for sustenyng of the misterfull and faillit brethering, all in ane voce consenttis and approvis the samyn, and ordanis proclamatioun to be maid dischargeing the auld dewite granttit for mantenyng the wikitnes of Sanct Anthonis Ile and all confrareis bandis and premissis thairof, vnder all hieast panys and charge.

24 April 1561.

Levingstonis yarde.
In presens of [the bailies and council], comperit Dauid Levingstoun and offerit his yaird and landis diuisit for the flesche merket for the sowme of ane thousand pundis and to mak the gude toun sure thairof for the said sowme, and Dauid Somer baillie at command and in name of the prouest baillies counsale and communite offerit him thairfor the sowme of vij$^c$ merkis qubilk the said Dauid Levingstoun refusit, quhairfor the baillies and counsale foresaid constitute and nominat the personys following to be comprisaris of the saidis landis and yard, and ordanis thair aithis to be taikin for just comprysing according to the ordour in sic caissis within burgh and conforme to the ordinance maid of before, and the said Dauid Levingstoun dissasentit and protestit for remeid in caise thai procedit in comprising and askit instrumentis.

The samyn day, the baillies and counsale foresaid desyrit the said Levingstonis
Dauid Levingstoun to cheis for his pairt tua honest men and thay vther yardu.
tua for the pairt of thame, and the commonytie with ane discreit ourman
to pas vpoun the comprising of the saidis landis and yairdis, to be sworne
to comprise according to the just avale, and thay in lik maner sworne to
abide at thair delineranee, quhilk the said Levingstoun refusit, and instrumentis being taiken thairof be the said Dauid Somer baillie in maner
forsaid, ordanis as of befoire to proceid in comprising according to the
ordour abone writton.

The names of the comprisaris: [here follow twelve names.]

The prouest baillies and counsale ordanis Louk Wilsoun, thesaurer, to Carnys.
deliuer to Johnne Carnys the sowme of ten pundis to ane compt of his
dewtie for his seruice.

### 25 *April* 1561.

The prouest baillies and counsale, efter the forme tenour and desyre Testamentis.
of the secund article befoir writin, and according to thair bundin dewtie
towert the fatherles and desolait youth, statutis and ordanis that fra this
furth all testamentis that salhappin to be maid within this burgh of craftisman merchant or vther inhabitant quhatsumeuir be presentit and delinerit
to the vesitouris chosin for the yeir and to the commoun clerk of the
burgh to be registrat in the townis bukeis, to be furthcummand to the
bairnys and freindis of the depairtit and vtheris havand rycht thairto,
and gyf it happinnis ony to depairt vutestit that incontinent the saidis
vesitouris pas to the houssis buthis and vtheris places quhair the guddis
and geir of the depairtit sall happin to be, requyre and call for the narrest
and vnsuspect freindis gyf thay may be, and failyeing of the saidis freindis
that they put in writ and mak just inventour off all guddis quhilk thai
may apprehend out of lokfast lvmes, and seill and lok the saidis lokfast
lvmes, and gif neid be tak the keyis of the samin with thame, and be thair
avise it be aggreit be the narrest freindis thai sall nocht be opinit for
the weill of the bairnis and vthiris haifand rycht and iust intromettouris

Testamentis. thairwith as of befoir togidder with diuisioun according to the ordour, and gif it beis fundin gude that the gudeis and geir be rowpit to the iust avale sauld and disponit to the weill of the saidis bairnis and vthiris haifand richt as said is the saidis visitouris tobe settaris thairof, thai being sworne thairto. This inventure to be registrat in the tovnis bukis tobe gevin furth to all parteis haifand richt, vnder the subscriptioun of the commoun clerk. And the saidis visitouris, as thai will answer in the presens of God, without respect of gude proffet hatrent or affectioun, tak diligent labour and care that the will of the deid in the testamentis maid be fulfillit and obseruit, and this present ordour takin for the bairnis and (*blank*) of thaim that deis vntestit inlikmaner be thame be obseruit and at thair power set furth, and gif neid be the provest and baillies to assist thame, and yeirlie as the visitouris salbe chosin thair aith of faithfull administratioun to be taikin.

Buriall. The provest baillies and counsale ordanis maister James Watsoun, dene of gild, with all diligence, with certane of the counsale depute thairto, to pas and vesie the Grayfreir dykis and yardeis of this burgh, beig vp and mend the same quhair thai ar ruinous and falty, and to mak ane sufficient stark yet for owtchalding of beistis; quhilk place is appointit be the said counsale in all tymes cuming to be the place of buriale as the place maist apt and conuenient thairto.

Dewtie of wyne. The provest baillies and counsale, according to the desyre of the thrid article before writtin, findis gude that xij d. of euery tvn of wyne that salhappin tobe ventit within this burgh be collectit and takin vp be the dene of gild and put in ane close box, to be disponit and gevin be the avise of the said provest baillies and counsale to the support of pure misterfull falit brethirne, merchandis and craftismen onlie, nychtbouris of this burgh and nane vtheris, and for the sure knawledge heirof that the viij workmen of Leith togidder with Jhonne Pinkertoun, gild officiar, and the workmen of the trone of this burgh be send for and cawsit gif thair aithis for making of trew and sure inuenture of all wynis that cumis to the burgh, and to gif vp the names of the byaris and sellaris togidder with the quantitie of the tvnnis of wyne to the said dene of gild. *Dewtie of wyne.*

The prouest baillies and counsale, vnderstanding that in the tyme of blindnes and mysknawlege of the trewth thair wes be consent of the nychtbouris of this burgh ane confrarie and bruderheid of ventaris of wyne quhilkis payit of euerye puntioun wyne ane choppoun to Sanct Authonis alter for sustenyng of idolatrie and wikitnes, and sen at this present it hes plesit the Almychti to oppin the eis of all pepill, sua that it is knawin that all sic confrareis baudis and promissis, inventit be the vngodlie sort of papistis for filling of thair belleis, ar contrair to the will and glorye of God, thairfor ordanis proclamatioun to be maid at all pairttis of this burgh neidfull, dischargeing the confrarie of Sanct Authonis, the Hally Blude, and all vther confrareis quhatsumeuir quhilk hes bene heirtofore in tyme of ignorance, and all sic dewiteis as wes gevin thairto according to the statutis maid heiranent, to be vptaikin and applyit to the pure, vnder all hieast pane that to the offender may be imput at the will and plesour of the juges present and to cum. *Discharge of confrareis.*

### 10 May 1561.

The baillies and counsale ordanis the proclamatioun following to be proclamyt and publischit at the mercat croce of this burgh, the schore of Leyth and vther places neidfull, off the quhilk the tenour followis:—Sen it hes plesit the Almychti, of his omnipotent mercye and gudenes, to oppin the lycht of his worde and mak patent to ws, the professouris of his maist hally gospell, our dewtie towert our nychtbouris, and in speciall towert the innocent laying to oure charge, to deill with euerye cristeane broder and nychtbour as we oure selflis wald be delt withall; and hering that laitlie thair is arryvit certane prissis, apprehendit vpoun sic ground as God knawis alwayis, to the apperance of the godlie sic guddis as may nocht be bocht or sauld be ony faythfull with saif conscience, quhairfor I command and charge in oure Souerane Ladeis name, and in name and bebalf of my *Proclamatioun anent prisses.*

Proclamatioun ancnt prisses.

lord prouest and baillies of this burgh, that na maner of persoun, merchant, craftisman nor vther occupear nor induellar within the samyn or boundis thairof, intromet blok by or sell ony of the saidis prisses or guddis being thairintill, nor be participant of the bloking bying or selling thairof, vnder the pane of tinsale of thair fredomes for euir and pvnischement of thair personis without fauouris at the juges will.

Ordinance for the insurrectioun of the prentisses.

The baillies and counsale, togidder with Andro Elphinstoun dekin of the furrouris, Jhonn Robesoun dekin of the smythis, Patrik Schang dekin of the wrychtis, Robert Hog dekyn of the cordineris, James Norvell dekin of the tailyeouris, Hercules Methuen dekin of the baxsteris, Jhonn Loch dekin of the skynnerris, Robert Hendersonn dekin of the barbouris, Murdo [Walker] for the masonis, being convenit within the tolbuth of this burgh, maister Jhonn Spens, baillie, declarit and schew how that yisterday eftirnone, being the Saboth of the Lord, the craftismennis seruandis and prentisses enterit at the Nether Bow with displayit baner in armour and wappinnis and passit throuch the toun to the Castill Hill, nochtwithstanding thay war chargit be the said baillie in our Soueranis name and in name and behalf of the prouest [and] baillies of this burgh; and siclike the samyn nycht, betuix viij and ix houris at evin, enterit in the samyn maner returnyt to the Nether Port and keipit the samyn at thair plesour, in manifest contempt of oure Soueranis autorite and magistratis of this burgh and thair proclamatione set furth in the contrair, quhairfor the said maister Jhonne Spens, for himself the remanent baillies and hale counsale, havand thair speciall command thairto, askit of the saidis dekynnis gyf thay fand that the personis foresaidis had contravenit the proclamatioun and ordinance maid the thrid day of Apprile with all thair consenttis, and gyf thay had done wrang and deseruit pvnischment for dissobeying of the officeris yisterday and keiping of the porttis and commanding the baillies to pas of the stretis, mannesing thame with wappinnis; quhilkis dekynnis, all in ane voce, declarit the samyn to be expres wrang and inobedience deserning extreme pvnischment to the exemple of vtheris, and promist faithfullie to the saidis juges thair assistance in apprehending and pvnisching of the saidis contempnaris quhat tyme thay sould be requyrit, and heirupoun the *Ordinance for* said baillie in name foresaid askit instrumentis. *the insurrection of the prentissses.*

It is statut and ordanit be the baillies and counsale that the dekynnis *For convening of the* of craftis convene thair hale maisteris this eftirnone and requyre of thame *craftis.* quhat will be thair pairt in pvnischeing the offendaris before writtin, and to report thair ansuer the morne before none.

### 13 *May* 1561.

The baillies and counsale being convenit, comperit the dekynnis of the *The answer* goldsmythis, barboris, skynnaris, tailyeouris, smythis, wrychtis, cordineris, *the craftis.* furrouris, masonis, bonetmakaris, wobstaris, bakstaris and fleschouris, and takand the burding vpoun thame for the hale maisteris of craftis, and desyrit that Robert Hendersoun, dekin of the barbouris, and Mychaell Gilbert, dekyn of the goldsymthis, mycht be hard to report thair and the hale maisteris ansueris, to quhome thay haue gevin full commissioun, and oblissis thame to abide at thair sayingis, quhilk wes acceptit and granttit, and be the saidis Hendersoun reporttit as followis, that is to say, that the hale maisteris and dekynnis, according to thair bonndin dewtie, faythfullie promyttis thair assistance fortificatioun and manteinance to the proest baillies and counsale in the serching and apprehending of the craftismennis seruandis and vtheris quhilkis vpoun Somday last committit the inobedience abone writtin, and sall be rady to ryse and convene quhen thay ar requyrit, and to fortifie the saidis provest and baillies in the executioun of justice vpoun thame, alwayis exhorting the saidis juges, sen thai had sufficient power and autorite to execute and pvnise the offenssis committit within thame, that thai wald seik na hiear powerris in this caus and tak the pvnischment and executioun in thayr awin handis, and to be mercyfull to sa monye of the saidis offendaris as wer penitent.

### 14 *May* 1561.

The hale counsale, being convenit, and vnderstanding that the craftis *To tak the* childer had trublit and molestit diuers nychtbouris in thair passeg to *prentissis.*

P

To tak the prentissis.

Leyth, ordanis the baillies with all deligence, with sic nowmer of nychtbouris as thay sall think gude to haue with thame for thair fortificatioun, and pas tak and apprehend the saidis craftis childer quhairevnir thay may be gottin and put thaim within warde within the tolbuth quhyll forther ordour be taikin for thair pvnischement.

21 *May* 1561.

Ordinance for seruing of the jugeis.

The prouest, baillies, [council, and deacons of crafts,] being convenit in the tolbuth, and vnderstanding that the nobelite of this realme ar to convene at this present perliament with greit cumpaneis, and hering of sum variance amangis sum of the said nobelite, for stopping of trublis, ordanis that thre score able men hagbuttaris be listit and put in wages for half ane moneth to await at all tymes of the day and nycht vpoun the prouestis and baillies, and thair wages to be payit of the radeast of the commoun gude, and the samyn to be cikit to the nixt extent that sall be set within this burgh and refoundit to the thesaurer; and siclik ordanis the snidis dekynnis to aduertice the maisteris and sernandis of thair craftis to be in radynes to cum to the said prouest and baillies at the sound of the commoun bell, trumpet or tabroun, in armour and wappinnis, in case of trublis as said is, and that the saidis baillies be thame selflis and ofliceris pas throuch all buthis of merchanttis and craftismen and vther places neidfull and warne and se the occupiaris thairof be sufficientlie prouidit in armour and lang wappinnis according to the auld ordinances, and to be in radynes as said is.

23 *May* 1561.

Sir Jhonne Wilsoun.

The baillies and counsale grauttis and gevis licence to Jhonn alias Sir Jhonne Wilsonn, sumtyme chaplane of Sanct Katherinis alter within Sanct Gelis Kirk within this burgh, to dispone and set in few, with thair conseuttis, to qulatsumeuir persoun he pleissis, all and sundrye landis within this burgh pertenyng to the said alterege, and ordanis onye ane of the baillies, in name and behalf of the prouest baillies and counsale, as lauchfull patronis to the said alterege, to pas with the said Jhonn Wilsonn

and gif the said sesing, without preiudice of the viij merkis yeirlie ground Sir Jhonne
annuell quhilk thay haue annixt to thair commoun gude of the tenement Wilsoun.
of land liand in the Cowgate. . . . .

27 *May* 1561.

The baillies and counsale ordanis the kaipis, vestimentis, ornamentis Alter grayth.
and alter grayth, quhilk pertenit to Sanct Gelys alter presentlie in handis,
or sa fer as may be gottin in, to be deliuerit to Dauid Somer, baillie, and to
James Barroun, and thay to dispone the samyn to the maist avantage.

The baillies and counsale ordinis Louke Wilsoun, thesaurer, to Precept, capi-
propyne in thair names to my lord Arskin, capitane of the castell of tane castell.
Edinburgh, ane tvn of the best wyne, quhite wyne and claret, can be
gottin.

30 *May* 1561.

Maister Alexander Skyne, aduocate, being callit and accusit for taking Skene.
and ressaning of the diabolicall idoll callit the preistis sacrament at
Pasche last, in the contempt of the religioun and the glorie of God now
establischeed, and expres contrar to the actis of parliament incurrand
thairthrow the panys thairintill contenit, confessit the ressaning of the
said sacrament efter the auld maner, bot nocht in contempt as wes allegit
nor yit within thair jurisdictioun; vpoun this his confessioun Dauid Somer,
baillie, askit instrumentis, and the remanent judges ordanit the said
maister Alexander to pas in ward within the tolbuith, thair to remane
vpoun his awin expenssis quhill farther ordour be taking for the offence
abone writting.

The ballies and haill counsall ordanis maister James Watsoun, dene Precept, Knox
of gyld, incontinent to deliuer to Jhone Knox, minister, the sowme of fyftie
pundis as for his quartar payment.

The baillies and counsale, yit as of before, ordanis maister Robert Artailye.
Glen, James Barroun, Eduard Hope, Alexander Guthre, to pas and require
thair artailyerie fra the capitane of the castell, and to reporte his ansuer.

11 *June* 1561.

*Wardling of prentisses.*

The baillies and counsale, vnderstanding the mysrewle of the craftis childer in the Over Tolbuith in frie warde, quhilkis war apprehendit for the lait insurrection, ordanis thame to be put in fast irnis, thair to remane quhill cautionn be fonnd, vnder greit panis, for keping of gude ordour induring thair tyme of the said warde, that thai sall nocht eschew furth of the same induring the said provest and baillies will and quhill forder ordour be takin with thame anent thair offence.

*Artailye, Barroun, Killoch.*

It being requirit of the provest baillies and counsale, James Barroun and the vthiris direct for requiring of the tovnis artailyerie fra the capitane of the castell qnhy the samyn wes nocht deliuerit to thame, James Barronn ansuerand that it wes said to him be the laird of Drvmquhassill that Dauid Kinloch, baxster, had said to him and Alexander Erskene that he thocht nocht gude the artailye suld be deliuerit to them that sutit the same without it war requireit be the haill commvnitie, and that it mycht be applyit to better vse in the castell nor in the toun, and comnsalit thame to keip still the samyn; and the said Kinloch, being callit and accuseit heirof, askit instrumentis of the said Baronis reporte, and denyit that he had spokin to the said laird of Drvmquhassill to send the said artailye, bot being forder inquireit be his aith that he had spokin the said Alexander Erskine anent the said artailye, confessit that vpoun [*blank*] lastbipast, he being gangand abone the tollbuith, Alexander Erskene callit vpoun him and said to him that certane of the baillies and counsale had cumit to the castell requiring the tovnis artailyerie, and askit of him quhat his counsale wes thairanent, and the said Dauid said: This is my opinioun, sen trew it is that the castell of Edinburgh in tyme of bissines hes bene worth to the toune j^m lib, be haifing of the haill gudeis of the toun in thair keping, and the same wes randerit and na man wantit worth a penny, quharefore he concludeit that thai suld nocht pairt with the artailye for it wald be als weill keipit thair as better geir is, and thir war the onlie wordis that he said and nocht ellis; vpoun the quhilkis wordis Dauid Somer, baillie, askit instrumentis; and the remanent baillies and counsale commandit the said

Dauid in warde quhill forder tryall war tane of his stopping of the said Artailye, Barroun Killoch.
artailyerie to be deliuerit to the toun agane.

### 16 June 1561.

At the desyre and requeist of maister William Skene, the prouest Skene, aduocat.
baillies and counsale ordanis maister Alexander Skene, aduocat, to be put
to libertie furth of warde to the x day of Julii nixt, prouiding that in the
mene tyme he behaif himself godlie and honestlie within this burgh and to
all nychtbouris of the samyn, and resort and keip the sermounttis and
prayerris, and to communicat with the minister and vtheris godlie leruyt
men for resoluing of his douttis in relegioun, and in speciall tuiching his
openioun of the idoll the preistis sacrament; and vpoun the said x day, gyf
it sall pleis the Almychti betuix and than to gyf him forther knaulege in
the treuth, to cum before the kirk to gyf his penitence and confessioun of
his former inniquitie, failling heirof to remove him self and hale familie of
this burgh and boundis thairof, and to hawe na enteris thairintill sa lang as
thay remane wikit, vnder the panys contenit in the actis of parliament
statutis and proclamationis of this burgh maid and proclamyt aganis
papistis idolataris and mes mongaris; and this present ordinance beand
red to the said maister Alexander Skene that he sould pretend na ignorance
gyf he war apprehendit within this burgh or boundis thairof efter the
said x day, ordanis to gif him the copye of the samyn vpone his expenssis
gif it be requyrit.

The samyn day, ordanis Sir George Strauchane, preist, to depesche of Strauchane, preist.
this toun and boundis thairof within xij houris nixt heirefter, and that he
be nocht found thairintill quhyll thay be surelie certefiit of his publict
repentance of his papistrie and former iniquite, vnder the panis contenit
in the proclamationis.

The prouest, remanent baillies and counsale, ordanis Dauid Somer and Prentisses.
maister Jhonne Spens, baillies, to pas to the Justice Clerk and requyre his
lordship to set ane justice court vpoun Wedinsday nixt for accusing the
personis apprehendit and in warde for rasing of the tvmult within this

Prentisses.

burgh vpoun Sounday the [xi] day of Maij last, and the said baillies to caus mak thair dittay and deliuer the samyn to the said Justice Clerk.

11 *July* 1561.

Succharis.

The baillies and counsale ordanis the succhis to be tane fra the succhouris quhilkis playit before the craftis childer, failing to put thame in the irnys quhill the samyn be deliuerit.

Craftis childer.

The baillies and counsale ordanis ane cumpayne of xxiiij haghuttaris to be lystit to pas furth of the toun with the said prouest and baillies and sic nychtbouris as they pleis charge, for apprehending of the craftis childer being at the horne.

18 *July* 1561.

Moresoun, tailyeour.

In presens of the baillies and counsale William Moresoun, tailyeour, being callit and accusit for suffering of George Durye, callit lord of obedience, and [*blank*] Cok, his seruandis, to pas furth with armour and wappinnis, and for resset and manteinance of thame, contrair the [ordinance and proclamation of 24th April, and having confessed] the said William is decernit to tyne his fredome and libertie, and to remane in ward within the tolbuith quhill the keyis of his buth be deliuerit to the baillies foresaid.

25 *July* 1561.

Barroun dischargit.

Patrik Barroun, seriand, depriuit and dischargit of his office . . . for lowping furth at ane of the wyndokis of the laich tolbuith the tyme the prouest baillies and counsale wes assegit thairin be the craftis childer.

Arrane.

The prouest baillies and counsale fyndis gude that certane of the counsale pas to my lord erle of Arrane, and in the gude townys name requeist his lordship to send for his garde of men of armes, and to suffer thame to remane within the toun to await vpoun the prouest, vpoun the townys charges, for repressing of the wikit, vnto the convenyng of the lordis of counsale.

### 30 July 1561.

Ordanis James Barroun to furnis and pay to my lord of Arrannis gaird thair dalie wages sa lang as it salbe thocht neidfull thay sall serue, to euery ane of thame on the day fyve s.  *Barroun.*

### 13 August 1561.

The prouest baillies and counsale ordanis Louke Wilsoun, thesaurer, thankfullie to content and pay to James Barroun the sowme of sevin score thre pundis v s., debursit and payit be him to my lord of Arrannis gaird.  *Barroun.*

### 22 August 1561.

[The bailies ordered to be paid the sum of twenty pounds each for their labours, " in getting in of diuers greit sowmes to the commoun gude be causing of merchanttis and vtheris of this burgh becum fre burgessis and gild."]  *Baillies.*

### 25 August 1561.

[The bailies and council.] vpoun consideratioun of the gude seruice done be Jhonne Flemyng the xxj day of August instant to my lord prouest baillies and honest nychtbouris within the tolbuth the tyme thai wer assegit thairintill, quhair the said Johne wes hurt in the heid with ane culvering. ordanis [the dean of guild to deliuer to him the duty of a burgess-ship extending to five pounds.]  *Flemyng.*

### 26 August 1561.

The prouest baillies and counsale and dekynnis findis gude that, for the plesour of our Soucrane and obtenyng of hir hienes fauouris, thair be ane honorable banquet maid to the princes hir graces cousingis vpoun Sonday nixt, and siclike with all deligence the triumphe to be maid of hir graces entre within this toun; and for furnessing and payment heirof willis ane generale taxt to be rasit of the hale toun, and thairfor requyris the saidis dekynnis answer and consent to the said taxt, quha desyrit licence to convene thair craftis and to report thair answer the morne.  *Banquett.*

27 *August* 1561.

Counsale, craftis.

The provest, baillies, [council and deacons of crafts], being all togidder convenit in the counselhous, Archibald Douglas, provest, requirit of the saidis dekynnis thair ansueris concernyng the banquet and triumphe. [The deacon desired Thomas Ewyne, goldsmith, to be heard for them, and this being agreed to] the said Thomas Ewyne, in name foresaid, ansuerand as said is that rather or the Quenys grace be propynit at this tyme with ony propyne be ane taxt quhilk sall engender mwrmur, that rather the propyne be nocht gevin, and thairfor granttis nocht to the taxt; bot rather quhat salbe debursit vpoun the banquet triumphe or propyne be tane and vpliftit of the radeast of the commoun gude, and gyf the commoun guide will nocht serue fyndis that the commoun mylnis or borrow landis sould be set in takis, fore male, or analiit to thame that will gyf maist thairfor, at leist to the avale of xxiiij$^c$ merkis, and quhatevner the charges of the said banquet triumphe or propyne will extend to aboue the said xxiiij$^c$ merkis consenttis ane taxt be set thairfor, and gif it war v$^m$ merkis for the Quenys grace honour the craftis sall pay thair pairt thairof, and vtherwayis thay will grant to na taxt.

Protestatio, Kynloch.

Danid Kinloch, dekyn of the baxstaris, desyris the commoun mylnis to be sett in assedatioun to the craftis for certane yeris vpoun sic sowmes as thay culd agre, and thay sall furnys the hale charges of the triumphe banquet and propyne, and vtherwise granttis to na taxt.

Counsale, craftis.

The provest, baillies, dene of gild, thesaurer and counsale foresaid, fyndis it salbe voittit quhidder the saidis charges salbe vpliftit be taxt or be seting or annalcing of the commoun mylnis and commoun landis, and requyris the saidis dekynnis affirmative or negatiue to gyf thair votis, quhilk thay refusit vtherwise nor according to thair protestatioun of before; and the said provest baillies counsale and vtheris aboue writtin being monyast in nowmer fyndis the samyn sould be votit, quhais votis being requyrit according to the commoun ordour, all in ane voce consenttis and willis ane generale stent to be maid vpoun all nychtbouris, occupiaris within this burgh, merchanttis craftis and vtheris, and sa sone as the Counsale, comptis of the said banquet triumphe and propyne may be gottin in craftis. according to the samyn the said extent to be sett with deligence, and the saidis dekynnis votis being requyrit as saidis dissasentis as of before; and the said Thomas Ewyne, procuratour foresaid, protestit that insafer as the saidis dekynnis consenttit nocht to the said extent that thay sould nocht be haldin nor compellit to pay onye pairt, becaus as he alleget na extent nor taxt within this burgh mycht be rasit by the awise of the craftis.

The provest baillies and counsale ordanis Louke Wilsoun, thesaurer, Thesaurer, with all diligence possible, to mak preparatioun for the banquet and banquet, tryumph triumphe.

### 28 August 1561.

The provest baillies and counsale ordanis Louke Wilsoun, thesaurer, to Lyverayis, deliuer to euery ane of the tuelf seriandis, the javillour, and gild seriandis, officeris. als mekle Franche blak as wilbe euery ane of thame ane coit, als mekle blak stemmyng as wilbe euery ane of thame ane pair of hois, and euery ane of thame ane blak bonet agane the tyme of the triumphe. [Also] to Schang. furnes and deliuer to Patrik Schang, wrycht, and Walter Bynning tymmer, canves, and all vther necessaris convenient for the triumphis and fairssis [at] the over trone, tolbuth, croce, salt tron, and Nether Bow.

The provest baillies and counsale ordanis Alexander Guthre commoun Weluot clerk, Louke Wilsoun thesaurer, Maister James Watsoun dene of gild, gownys. James Barroun, James Adamsoun, Alexander Park, James Jhonestoun of Kellobank, James Stevinsoun, Andro Stevinsoun and Alexander Achesoun, euery ane of thame, to haue and mak ane goun of fyne blak weluot syde to thair fut lynit with pane weluot, ane coit of blak weluot, ane doublet of crammosyne satyne, with weluot bonet and hois efferand thairto; and thir tuelf to beyre the pale abone the Quenys grace heid, and nane vtheris; and all the vther nychtbouris that salbe sene vpoun the gait to haue syde gownys of fyne Franche blak sychtit with pane weluot, coittis of weluot, and doublettis of sating, and euerye man to gang in his dew and gude ordour; and the seriandis to ordour the calsay and to mak rowme for the

Q

| | |
|---|---|
| Weluot gownys | nobelitie and nychtbouris foresaid; and siclike that the young men of the toun devise for thame selffis sum brawf abulyement of taffate or vther silk and mak the convoy before the cairt triumphant. |
| Wilsone, Adamsone, Park. | The provest baillies and counsale ordanis Louke Wilsoun, thesaurer, James Adamsoun and Alexander Park to pas to my lord erle of Mortoun and the laird of Lethingtoun, mak end and aggre with thame for thair cop burddis to be propynit to the Quenys grace, and to be actit and cum gude for the prices and payment thairof to be payit at sic dayis as thay can agre, and the said provest baillies and counsale oblissis thame to releif thame thairof. |

29 *August* 1561.

| | |
|---|---|
| Proclamatioun. | It is statut and ordanit be the provest baillies and counsale that proclamatioun be maid throuch the toun be sound of bell, chargeing all maner of personis that hes furnist onye thing to the banquet and triumphe that thay produce and gyf in thair comptis the morne anys on the day before the counsale, and ordanis the said counsale to be auditouris thairof and to allow and dissalow as thay sall think gude in thair conscience. |

3 *September* 1561.

| | |
|---|---|
| Extent of xxviij li. | The provest baillies and counsale, efter avisement with the lairge and greit sowmes contenit in the comptis debursit vpoun the banquet, triumphe, and propyne to the Quenys grace, quhilk will extend to the sowme of iiij$^m$ merkis or thairby, ordanis, conforme to the ordinance maid of befoir, that ane generall extent be set and lyftit of all the nychtbouris of this burgh, bayth merchant and craftisman, to the quantite of the said sowme of iiij$^m$ merkis, and with all deligence to be collectit and debursit for the releif of the creditouris, furnissaris of the necessaris of the said banquet triumphe and propyne. |

24 *September* 1561.

| | |
|---|---|
| Counsale, craftis. | The provest baillies and counsale, being convenit within the tolbuth for electing of the new counsale according to the ordour, comperit |

Thomas Ewyne, dekin of the goldsmythis, and presentit the personys *Counsale,* following, and desyrit tua of thame to be chosen vpoun the counsale *craftis.* for the yeir to cum, viz., Mychaell Gilbert goldsmyth, Peter Turnet skynner, Thomas Jaksoun masoun, Nycholc Purves smyth, Danid Schang wrycht, and [blank], and desyrit tua of thame to be chosin vpoun the counsale for the yeir to cum, quhilk being red and sene, the prouest baillies and counsale foresaid desyrit the said Thomas Ewyne to gyf thame vther sex in tiket, according to the tenour of the act maid the xxvj day of September the yeir of God j^m v^c lx yeris, quhilk the said Thomas refusit, allegeand him to haue na vther command of the dekynnis to present ony vtheris bot tha sex allanerlic, and that in sa fer as thay wer honest men thay nowther aucht nor sould be refusit, nochtwithstanding ony act maid in the contrair; and Danid Somer baillie, in name of the prouest baillies and counsale foresaid, protestit that in sa fer as the said Thomas wes requyrit and refusit according to the said act that it mycht be lesum to the said counsale to cheis quhome thay plesit of the saidis craftis; and Thomas Ewyne in the contrair, and in case thay refusit tua of the sex foresaid, dissasentit to ony vtheris, and protestit for remeid.

*26 September* 1561.

The prouest baillies and counsale, vpoun consideratioun of the *Carnys.* necessar and godlie seruice dalie done be Jhonne Carnys, actour of the mornyng prayeris, ordanis the collectouris of the taxt to deliuer to the said Jhonne Carnys the sowme of thre score of pundis, in recompence and compleit payment of his seruice of all tymes bigane vnto the feist of Mychaelmes nixt; and ordanis the collectouris of the annuellis appoyntit for the ministeris of the kirk to refound the said thre score of pundis agane to the saidis collectouris of the taxt, and forther in tyme cuming appoynttis yeirlie to the said Jhonne Carnys the sowme of ane hundreth merkis in the yeir of the radeast of the saidis annuellis, to be payit to him termelie as vse is, begynnand at the said feist of Mychaelmes and to indure induring thair willis.

Ewyne.

In presens of the proueist baillies counsale and assassouris, being convenit in the tolbuth for chesing of the litis, comperit Thomas Ewyne, with
the maist pairt of the dekynnis, and desyrit Jhonne Weyr, pewderar, quha
was chosin vpoun the counsale yesterday, to be removit in sa fer as he
wes nocht ane of the vj presentit be thame, and tua of the said vj to be
resauit as vse wes as he allegit, and the said proueist baillies and counsale
desyrit the said Thomas to schaw ony act or consuetude quhair the saidis
craftis war in vse of presentting of onye names vtherwise nor is contenit
in the act aboue writtin and thay sould be hard, quha ansuerit he had na
actis presentlie bot belevit he sould get sum, and the said counsale being
avisit gevis for ansuer: The said Jhonne Weyr being sworne resauit and
admittit, and being ane man of honestie jugement and gude fame, thay
could nocht remove him for this yeir, and the said Ewyne protestit for
remeid.

The samyn day, the said Thomas Ewyne presenttit ane act of parliament of King James the Thrid, togidder with the copye of ane writing
contenyng certane princlegis grantit to the craftis of this burgh be the
Quene Regent, be vertew of the quhilk he allegit the said dekynnis of
craftis aucht to haue thair voit in chesing of all lytis to offices, and desyrit
thame to be admittit to that effect, and thair ansuer thairupoun; and the
said proueist baillies counsale and assasouris, efter avisement with the
said writtis, fyndis na forther princlegis granttit to thame forther nor
princlege to voit in electing of seriandis allanerlie, and can grant thame
na forther princlege concernyng the litis, and the said Ewyne protestit as
of before.

Protestatio, Ewyne, assassouris.

The said Thomas Ewyne, in name of the hale dekynnis, desyrit the
proueist baillies and counsale foresaid to remove the thre assassouris quha
as he allegit sould nocht be hard to gyf ony voit in chesing of the lytis;
and the said proueist baillies and counsale, vnderstanding that thair predecessouris officiaris of this burgh hes thocht expedient diuers yeris
bigane that sic qualifeit men war present, nocht onlie at chesing of officeris

bot alsua in all vther effaris conceernyng the commoun weill of this burgh thair counsale and voit had thairintill, and fyndis thame sa necessar in respect of the premisses that thay can na way grant to thair removing, and the said Ewyne protestit for remeid and that in case the saidis assassouris votit at this present thair votys sould nocht preinge the saidis craftis in thair princlegis quhairintill thay war havelie hurt be admitting of the said assassouris to voit as he allegit.

<small>Protestatio Ewyne, assassouris.</small>

### 2 October 1561.

The prouest baillies counsale and hale dekynnis, persaving the preistis, monkis, freris, and vtheris of the wikit rable of the antechrist the paip, to resort to this toun, incontrair the tenour of the proclamatioun maid in the contrair, thairfor ordanis the said proclamatioun to be proclamyt of new, chargeing all monkis, freris, preistis, nonnys, adulteraris, fornicatouris, and all sic filthy personis, to remove thameselflis of this toun and boundis thairof within xxiiij houris, vnder the pane of carting throuch the toun, byrning on the cheik, and banessing the samyn for euir.

<small>Proclamatio</small>

### 5 October 1561.

In presens of the baillies and counsale, comperit William Bryse, masour, and presenttit the Quenys grace writing, of the qubilk the tenour followis :—REGINA. We, vnderstanding that the prouest and baillies of the burgh of Edinburgh vpoun Friday last bipast, the feird day of October instant, set furth publict proclamatioun at the merket croce of oure said burgh, expres contrair our commandment, nocht makand ws princ thairto, nor seikand to knaw oure plesour in sic behalflis, thairfor we ordane and will commandis and charges the counsale and communite of oure said burgh to convene incontinent within the tolbuth of our said burgh and deprine the prouest and baillies quha presentlie beris office thairin of all forther bering of office for this instant yeir, and to cheis vther qualifeit personis in thair rowme, as thay will answer to ws thairupoun. *Sequitur subscriptio:* MARIA.

<small>Regina.</small>

8 *October* 1561.

[Provost and baillies dischargeit.]

The counsale and dekynnis, being convenit within the tolbuth of this burgh, and at the command of our Soueranis writing before writtin, dischargit Archibald Douglas prouest, Dauid Forster, Robert Kar, Alexander Home and Allane Dikesoun baillies, ar dischargit of thair offices, and in thair places maister Thomas Makcalycane prouest, James Thomsoun, Jhonne Adamsoun, maister Jhonn Marioribankis, Alexander Achesoun, baillies, electit and chosin be moniest votis, for the yeir to cum.

Protestatio, Symer.

Dauid Somer, in name and behalf of the counsale and communite of this burgh, protestit this depriuationn, as alsua the new electionn of the officeris abone writtin, be nocht preiudiciall to the fredome and libertie of this burgh and auld ordour of the samyn granttit be our Soueranis maist noble progenitouris in electing and chesing of officeris, nor stand nocht for preparatiue in tymes cuming by the plesour of the prince.

Dekynnis.

David Kinloch dekin of the baxtaris, for himself and the maist pairt of the remanent dekynnis, protestit that in sa fer as thay dissasentit to the electing of the said prouest maister Thomas Makcalycane, because thay could nocht get the assessouris remouit of voting as thay allegit, that thay be nocht haldin to obey the said prouest, nor that it be nocht imput for fault to thame in case thay complenit to the Quenys maiestie.

Thomas Ewyne

Thomas Ewyne, dekin of the goldsmythis, askit instrumentis that according to the Quenys grace writing he had consenttit to the electing of ane new prouest, and that his conscience movit him to gyf his voit to maister Thomas Makcalycane as maist qualefeit amangis the names quhilkis he hard red, and gyf the Quenys grace had send ony names in speciall that he wald haue obeyit hir graces will.

[Persons proposed by Queen for provost.]

The samyn day, the prouest and baillies foresaid being electit and chosin, Neill Layng, writer, producit ane tiket direct to the counsale be the laird of Lethingtoun, secreter, as he allegit, contenyng the names of the

Lord Seytoun, Alexander Arskin and the laird of Craigmyller, schewing it was the Quenys grace mynd that ane of thay thre sould be chosing provest, quhilk being producit before the said counsale, all in ane voce, in respect this tiket contenit bot thre names without ony subscriptioun, and that thay had electit thair officeris before the presentting of the said tiket, according to our Soueranys writing of before, thocht gude to pas to hir grace incontinent and declair quhat thay had done allrady, and quhat hir grace wald forther command thame tuiching the saidis names, in case the officeris ellis chosin plesit nocht hir grace, that thay wald obey. [Persons proposed by Queen for Provost.]

David Kinloch, dekyn of the baxteris, askit instrumentis that he wald obey the Quenys grace mynd towert the thre names in the tiket before writtin; and Thomas Hog, cordiner, askit instrumentis that he wald do as the gudeman Dauid Kinloch dyd.

Dauid Somer, in name and behalf of the prouest baillies and counsale, becaus it apperit that diuers of the dekynnis and vtheris grudgit at the electing of the officeris, and thairfor that the hale names quhilkis woittit with the saidis officeris be registrat, quhais names followis: maister Clement Litill, maister Richert Strang, and Alexander Guthre for ane assasour and dene of gild; Dauid Somer, Adam Fonllertoun, maister Robert Glen, James Adamsonn for maister Jhonn Spens, James Barroun for the prouest, maister James Watsoun, Louke Wilsoun, maister Jhonn Marioribankis, James Jhonnstoun, Robert Cynynghame, James Adamsoun for the thesaurer, Mychaell Gilbert for himself and Jhonn Weyr of the counsale, Thomas Ewyne dekin of the goldsmythis and Robert Hendersonn dekin of the barboris. [Votis for the prouest.]

22 *October* 1561.

[Alexander Achesoun having been elected a bailie and called upon to accept office, was fined in the sum of forty pounds " becaus he hes refusit to accept his said office and comperit nocht this day, being lauchfullie warnyt to that effect." From other entries it is found that Achesoun subsequently accepted office.] [Achesoun, charge, thesaurer.]

5 *November* 1561.

Baxsterris, candle.
[The fourpence loaf to weigh eighteen ounces three and a half quarters. The pound of candles to be sold, the " rag weik " at tenpence, and the " hard weik " for ninepence.]

Ane studye to the minister.
[The dean of guild ordained " with all deligence to mak ane warme studye of daillis to the minister, Jhonne Knox, within his lugeing abone the hall of the samyn, with lychtis and wyndokis thairto and all vther necessaris."]

8 *November* 1561.

Jok, belman.
The provest baillies and counsale, vnderstanding the nychtlie wages quhilk wes gevin for walking of the kirk to be sumpteous, quhairfor thay will this ordour be taikin anent the keiping of the said kirk, that is that Jok Symsoun sall nychtlie walk the said kirk with his doggis as he did of before, and ansuer for the wyndokis and all vther graith of the kirk, sowpe and hald the samyn clene, ring the x houris bell, and do all vther service quhilk he did of before, and sall haue thairfor yeirlie induring the counsallis will the sowme of tuelf merkis allanerlie.

Precept, Carnys.
The provest baillies and counsale ordanis Patrik Barroun to content and pay to Jhonne Carnis, redar of the commoun prayaris, the somme of fourty poundis of the reddiest money he hes in his hand pertenying to the toun; . . . and that vnto ane compt to be maid betuix the said Jhonne and the gude toun anent his fie appointit to him.

21 *November* 1561.

Ordour for the markattis, baillies.
The provest baillies and counsale ordanis this ordour to be obseruit in all tymes cuming tuiching the merketis, in the first, that euerye baillie his oulk about sit in jugement vpoun the commoun caussis, examyng of witnes and avysing of processis, and the vther thre baillies to await vpoun the merkettis, the trying of the baxsteris, browsteris, maltmen, fleshchouris, regratouris, and vtheris enormiteis within the toun, and puting of remeid thairto.

25 *November* 1561.

[The provost bailies and council, in consequence of John Preston, treasurer, being unable to attend to his duties from ill health, elected Lowk Wilsoun treasurer for the year to come, the deacons of crafts protesting that they would not consent to the election unless the assessors were discharged from voting in election of officers or in other common affairs.]

Wilsoun, thesaurer.

26 *November* 1561.

[The provost bailies and council ordered " Grissell Simpill Lady Stanehous, adulterer, to remoif hir self furth of this toun betuix and Monunday nixt, vnder the panys contenit in the proclamatioun set furth aganis adulteraris."]

Lady Stanhous.

27 *November* 1561.

[Lord Morton and the laird of Lethington, having obtained letters against the council for payment of the sums advanced for the " banquet copburde and triumph," it was ordained that, for payment of these and other sums due, an extent should be set for one half thereof, and the remainder to be raised by letting the common mills for the year to come.]

[Banquet and triumph.] Common mills.

31 *December* 1561.

The prouest baillies and counsale, vnderstanding that the minister, Jhonne Knox, is reqnyrit be the hale kirk to pas in the parttis of Angus and Mernys for electing of ane superintendent thair, to the quhilk thay thame selffis hes granttit, thairfor ordanis Alexander Guthre, dene of gild, to pas in cumpanye with him for furnessing of the said ministerris charges, and to deburse and pay the samyn of the radeast of the townis guddis in his handis, quhilk salbe allowit in his compttis, and forther to haist the said minister hame that the kirk heir be nocht desolait.

Minister, gyld.

30 *January* 1561-2.

[In an action at the instance of the owner of a ship in Kinghorn and the bailies of that town against certain indwellers in Leith, for the " wrangus spoliatioun fra the saidis awnaris of ane irne gvn " furth of the ship while lying in the port of Leith, it was alleged on behalf of the defenders, that the provost bailies and council

Kingorne, Leith.

Kingorne, Leith.

could not be lawful judges against them, "becaus the haill toun of Leith hes lang of before tane lanborrowis of the haill toun of Edinburgh, and that the toun of Kingorne is ane pairte and pendicle of this toun, beris charges and stentis thairwith." The council repelled the allegations and ordered further process to be taken.]

### 10 *February* 1561-2.

Regina Tolbuth.

Williame Brysoun masour presentit and delinerit to the prouest baillies and counsale oure Souerane Ladeis writing, of the quhilk the tenour followis, and desyrit ansuer to be gevin to oure said Souerane and lordis of secreit counsale the morne be tua efter none. *Sequitur:* Apud Edinburgh sexto Februarii anno lxi°. The Quenis Maiestie, vnderstanding that the tolbuith of the burgh of Edinburgh is ruinous and abill haistelie to dekay and fall doun, quhilk wilbe werray dampnabill and skaithfull to the pepill duelland thairaboutt and repairand towert the samin, nocht onlie in destructioun of thair houssis bot als greit slauchter gif sindrie personis happin and chance thairthrow, without haistye remeid be prouidit thairin; thairfor hir hienes ordanis ane masour to pas and charge the prouest baillies and counsale of the said burgh of Edinburgh to cans put warkmen to the taking doun of the said tolbuth, for doun taiking thairof with all possable diligence for the caussis foirsaid, as thai will ansuer to hir hienes thairupoun at hir vter charge, and in the menetyme that thai pronide sufficient hous and rowmes reparit as efferis for the lordis of the sessioun, justice and sheref, for ministering of justice to the lieges of the realme. *Sequitur subscriptio:* MARIE, R. Quhilk writing being red, and, efter avisement thairwith, the samyn delinerit to the prouest to be alsua schewin to the dekynnis and vtheris nychtbouris.

### 11 *February* 1561-2.

Banquet, wallis, extent.

[The provost, bailies, council and deacons of crafts, for payment of the expenses of the banquet and triumph, agreed to roup the mills for the year from Martinmas 1562 to Martinmas 1563; and consented that a general extent of one thousand pounds should "be set and vpliftit of all nychtbouris of this burgh with all diligence for biging of the wallis of the samyn." It was agreed to discharge the extents "set and maid of before for ony of the caussis foresaid."]

[The provost bailies and council ordained Peter Turnet, skinner, to be received in the council in place of John Weyr, "powderer," he having been elected "at Mychaelmas last by the auld ordour and nocht gevin in tiket be the dekynnis;" "and sicklike at the electing of the nixt seriandis the saidis dekynnis be requyrit to gyf thair consent thairto."] *Turnet, in the counsale, Dekynnis.*

### 24 *February* 1561-2.

[The provost bailies council and deacons of crafts,] all in ane voce, consenttis and ordanis that the tolbuth of this burgh be tane doun vpoun bayth sides safer as salbe neidfull, and to that effect nominatis and makis Danid Somer maister of thair warkis, and ordanis him to begin vpoun Monunday nixt to the doun taikin of the sclaittis and rufe thairof, and forther to proceid as neid sall requyre, and siclike ordanis the baillies with all deligence to deliuer to the said maister of wark the sowme of sex hundreth merkis of the first and radeast of the taxt for paying of the warkmen lauborarisat the said tolbuth, and at the vther tolbuth to be maid in the west end of the kirk for the lordis of sessioun, and gyf the tymmer of the auld tolbuth will serue to the wark of the said new tolbuth the said maister of wark to aply the samyn as will serue. *Tolbuyth, maister wark, Somer.*

### 8 *April* 1562.

The counsale ordainit Freir Blak to be haldin in warde within the tolbuith of Edinburgh for sic crimes committit be him, quhairof thai sall certifie the Quenys grace, quhill thai send writing to hir grace, my lord James and the Secreter, certefeing thame of the same, togidder with the copie of his awin bill writtin be him to be send furth of the realme, contenying the secretis thairof and vtheris fals reportis. *Freir Blak.*

The counsale, vnderstanding the tedious and hauie lauboris sustenit be thair minister, Johnne Knox, in preiching thris in the oulk and twis on the Sounday, ordanis with ane consent to solist and persuade maister Johnne Craig, presentlie minister of the Canongait, to accept vpoun him the half chargeis of the preiching in the said kirk of Edinburgh, for sic gude deid as thai can aggre on. *Craig, minister.*

The counsale, vnderstanding the greit corruptioun of the youth be maister William Robertsoun, maister of the grammar scole, being ane obstinat *Scolemaister.*

Scolemaister. papeist, ordanis tender writingis to be directit fra the said counsale to my lord James exhorting his lordschip to labour at my lorde Robertis hand for granting ane gift of the office of the maisterschip to sic ane leirnit and qualifeit man as thai can find maist abill thairfore, to the effect thai may remove the said maister William fra the office foirsaid, and for vphalding and susteining of the said maister and doctouris, as alsua of the regentis of ane college to be beigit within this burgh, and for beiging of hospitellis, that it be labourit with the Quenis grace it mycht pleis hir grace to dispone and grant to the toun the place yairdis and annuellis of the freris and altarageis of the kirk.

[Slander against John Knox.]
Niniane M'Creehane, cuke to Timothie Cancour, granttit and confest he said yisterday on the hie gait: Loving to God, my lord Arrane and my lord Boitlmile ar aggreit now; Knox quarter is run, he is skurgeit throw the toun; with sic vther injurious wordis, quharfore, as ane raillar and sklanderer, wes ordanit to be skurgeit within the tolbuith, and thairefter to be brankit, and in case he euir committit the like iniurie in tyme cuming aganis the minister actit himself of his awin consent to be skurgeit throw this toun and baneist the same for euir.

### 11 *April* 1562.

Wine. [Wine to be sold at the price of xiij d. and xij d. the pynt.]

Wobsterris. The prouest baillies and counsale foresaid ordanis proclamationn to be maid with sound of bell throuch all the parttis of the toun neidfull, certefeing thame that vpoun the suspecioun and evill brute rasit vpoun the wobsteris of thair vnjust deling with all sic as hes ado with thair craft, it is appoynttit that betuix and Monunday nixt the saidis wobsteris set vp their lymes in ane wolt preparit for thame in the rufe of Sanct Gelis Kirk, and thair to wyrk for tryell of thair said wark quhair certane honest sworne men, merchanttis and craftismen, sall be deput to await vpoun thame, and thairfor that the saidis nychtbouris bring thair wark to the said wolt and na vther place quhill the said tryell be tane, ilk persoun that sall do in the contrair to be poyndit for the vnlaw of xviij s. vnforgevin.

[Katherine Ewyne, who had been divorced from her sponse, Jhonn Westoun, "for manifest adulterye committit with freir Jhonne Blak, to be keipit in sure waird quhill forther ordour be taikin tuiching adulteraris."]  *Freir Blak.*

James Bannatyne writer, depute to the justice clerk, presentit our Soueranis writing to the prouest and baillies foresaid, and desyrit the samyn to be obeyit according to our said Soueranis mynd thairintill contenit, and to be registrat, quhairof the tenour followis: Prouest baillies and counsale of Edinburgh. It is oure will, and we charge yow, that incontinent efter the sicht heirof, ye deliuer freir Jhonne Blak to the capitane constabill and keiparis of our castell of Edinburgh, till be keipit thairintill surelie vnto sic tyme as we haue ordanyt for the triell of his offences before our Justice generale or his deputtis, and this on na wayis ye leif vndone, as ye will ansuer to ws thairuponn. At Sanctandrois the xj of Aprile 1562. *Sequitur subscriptio:* MARIE, R. *The Quenys writing tueching Freir Blak.*

In presens of the prouest baillies and counsale forsaid, maister William Robertoun, maister of the hie scule, being chargit to produce before thame all sic priuelege or rycht as he had granttit to him be the abbottis of Hallyrudhous or ony vtherris for the said scule and teiching of the bairnys, thairfor producit than presentlie ane gyft granttit be abbot Carnecors to vmquhile Sir Jhonn Allane, and allegit he could cum be na vther at this present, and that his awin gyft wes furth of this toun with his bukis and vtheris his guddis be the space of tua yeris past and could nocht get it schortlie, and the said prouest baillies and counsale ordanit him to produce before thame this day aucht dayis his awin proper gyft, with certificatioun and he failyeit thay wald discharge him of his said masterschipe, and put sum vther mair qualifeit in his place. *Maister of scule.*

The prouest baillies and counsale, being informyt that the lordis of sessioun war of mynde to rais the sait and remowe to Sanctandrois in defalt of ane hous heir, [ordained the] maister of wark with all deligence possebill to end furth the hous in the west end of the kirk ordanit for the saidis lordis. *Maister of wark.*

30 *April* 1562.

Discharge, Robene Hude.
The same day, wes presentit to the provest baillies counsale and dekynnis of craftis oure Soueranc Ladeis charge vnder hir grace signet, subscriuit with hir hand, for the making of the proclamatioun vnder specifeit, of the quhilk charge and proclamatioun the tennour followis : Provest baillies counsale and dekynnis of craft of oure burgh of Edinburgh, it is notour vnto yow that be oure act of parliament it is statute and commandit that na Robene Hudis nor Litil Jhoneis suld be chosin within oure realme, nochttheles as we ar informeit ye intend to elect and cheis personis to beir sic offices this Maii approcheand, incontrair the tennour of oure said act, quha vnder colour of Robene Hudis play purpoissis to rais seditione and tumult within our said burgh, for perturbatioun of the commoun tranquilitie quhairin oure gude subjectis ar desyrous to leif ; quhairfore it is oure will, and we charge yow, that on na wys ye permit nor suffer this yeir ony sic as Robene Hude or Litil Jhonne to be chosin, nor that ony vther vnleissum gammis be vseit within oure said burgh quhilk may disquiet the communitie thairof as ye will ansuer to ws vpoun youre vternmest perell and charge in that behalf. Subscriuit with our hand, at Sanctandros, the xx of Aprile and of our regnne the xx<sup>d</sup> yeir. Followis the proclamatioun maid thairefter : Quhairfore I command and charge in our said Soueranis name, and in name and behalf of my lorde provest baillies and counsale of this burgh, that na maner of persoun of quhat estait sa euir thai be, merchant craftisman or vther, tak vpoun hand to attempt or tak vpoun thaime ony sic office or power as Robene Hude, Litil Jhonne, Abbat of Vnressoun or the like office, vnder quhatsumeuir pretense or colour, to mak convocatioun or beir armour, contrar the tennour and mynde of the actis of parliament and this our Soueranis charge, as thai will ansuer vpoun thair vternmest dainger and perell for breking of the saidis actis and dissobeying of this hir maiesteis writing as said is.

3 *May* 1562.

Electing of dekynnis.
[Jhonne Robesoun, deacon of the hammermen, complained to the council and deacons of crafts that, upon 30th April, William Brokas and others " to the nowmer of xl personis or thairby, assemblit, convenit thame selflis at the Burro Loch of this

burgh" and chose William Brokas to be deacon for the year to come, " expres contrar our Soucrane Lordis actis of perliament, the fredome and priuilege granttit to ws in our scill of caus bering that na maner of conventioun of craftis salbe without the avise and consent and speciall command of the dekin for the tyme." The whole craft was convened on 3d May, being the ordinary day of election, " be the ordour forsaid" to choose a deacon, "nochtheles the saidis personis with thair complices foresaidis vpoun the said thrid day electit and chosit the said William Brokas thair dekyn, and maid thair aithis to obey him and nane vtheris for the yeir in to cum neuir ane of the honest nor godlie of oure craft being present." After hearing the complaint, William Brokas was discharged of the office of deacon, and the craft ordered " to obey and acknauleg Jamies Young thair dekyn for the yeir in to cum becaus he wes lauchfullie chosen be the honest men efter thair auld ordour."]

### 22 May 1562.

The provest baillies and counsale, haifing respect to the contempt of discipline presentlie execute within this burgh vpoun fornicatouris, for suppressing of the said vice, quhilk daylie for laik of pvnesing mair and mair increscis, ordanis maister Robert Glen, maister Jhonne Spens, Adame Fowlertoun, to pas incontinent sycht and consider ane place maist apt and abill thairto in the North Loch for dowkeing of the saidis fornicatouris thairin, being ane pillie, and the same being fund ordanis the thesaurar, Luce Wilsoun, to repare red and dres the said hole with all diligence to the effect foirsaid.

*For pvnissing of fornicatouris.*

### 10 June 1562.

Comperit maister William Robertoun and maister Edmound Hay his prolocutour, and produceit his defenssis dilatouris declinatouris and peremptouris in writ aganis the clame intentit contrar him be maister Jhonne Moscrop, procuratour fiscale for the toun of Edinburgh, for removeing of him fra the teiching and instructing of the youth thairof, and assignis to him Fryday nixttocum to answer thairto *partibus citatis*.

*Schoolmaster.*

### 19 June 1562.

The provest baillies counsale [and deacons of crafts,] efter lang ressonyng vpoun the necessite of ministeris, fyndis that thair salbe ane

*Electing of Ministeris.*

| | |
|---|---|
| Electing of ministeris. | vther minister electit be the prouest baillies and counsale dekynnis and eldaris of this burgh, and adionit to Jhonn Knox minister, and for sustenyng of thame bayth, togidder with Jhonn Cairnys reder, ordanis the baillies, eueryane within his awin quarter, to convene the merchanttis and requyre of eueryane of thame quhat thay will quarterlie gyf for the caus foresaid; and siclike the saidis dekynnis to couvene thair craftis, and report thair ansuerris vpoun Wednisday nixt. |

24 June 1562.

| | |
|---|---|
| Ministeris dekynnis of craftis. | In presens of the prouest baillies and counsale, comperit [the deacons of the smiths, tailors, wrights, masons, websters and bonnet makers,] and the remanent dekynnis of craftis, and thair ansner being requyirit quhat euerye craft wald gyf in the yeir for sustenyng of the ministeris within this toun, it wes ansnerit be the dekynnis particularlie nominat as is aboue wryttin:—Gyf my lord prouest baillies and counsale foresaid wald appoynt ane speciall sowme in the yeir for the saidis ministeris, thay with thair crafftis wald glaidlie consent for thair pairttis to gyf according to the fyft pairt of the hale, efter the ordour of all taxtis past; and the remanent dekynnis quhais names ar nocht specifeit allegit thay had nocht gottin sufficient ansuer of thair brethering, and thairfor desyrit to be super-cedit quhill Wednisday nixt, quhilk day the prouest baillies and counsale assignis to all the hale dekynnis to report better answer but forder delay. |
| Precept, Rynde. | The prouest baillies and counsale, foreseing that at this present wappinschawin thair wer apperand danger of tvmult gyf the townys standert wer sufferit to remane in the handis of Jhonn Rynde pewderer, thairfor ordanis Alexander Guthre, dene of gyld, to lauboure at the said Jhonis handis for the said standert, and gyf the samyn may be gottin fra him that Louk Wilsoun, thesaurer, at the command of the said Alexander, deliuer to the said Jhonne the sowme of x li. |
| Regina. Tuiching seditioun. | The Quenys graces writing for stancheing of tvmult, quhairof the tenour followis and direct: To oure welbelouittis the prouest baillies and counsale of Edinburgh. The Quenis grace, vnderstanding that thair is certane seditious personis within the toun of Edinburgh, quhilk for thair particulariteis will nocht be content to leif in quyetnes, according to |

the ordour and lawis of this realme, heirtofor statute for stanching  Regina.
of tvmult seditioun and rebellioun within burgh, bot will atempt, Tuiching sedi-
be way of ambitioun and partiale avirice, to seik novelteis and vther-  tioun.
wayis, quhilk may desolue the lufe and vnioun that aucht to be amang
the inhabitanttis and burgessess of the said burgh, thairfor hir Maiestie,
havand the cair and thocht that becumis ane Princes Souerane to haue
vpoun thair subiectis, ordanis the prouest baillies and counsale of the said
burgh to mak deligent serche and inquisitioun gyf thair be ony within
thair jurisdictioun that ar apperand to attempt or to be auctouris of
seditioun tvmult or rebellioun within burgh, or gyf thair be onye sic way
inventtit set fordwert or to be set furth quhilk may mak onye ovirture of
seditioun or tvmult, that thay with all deligence and dexterite stanche,
suppres and impeid the samyn be all pvnitioun dew, and all vtheris menis
possibill, sua that hir Maiestie may knaw that hir Maiestie hes worthye
officeris and reullaris now presentlie within the said burgh, quhilkis baith
can and will keip and caus be kepit gude reule within the boundis com-
mitit vnto thame, certefeing the saidis prouest baillies and counsale that
and thay be found negligent and remis in the executioun of the premissis,
or that thair happin heirefter onye truble sedetioun rebellioun or tumult
within the said burgh, hir grace will justlie think that she may imput the
wyte of all the inconvenienttis heirefter to follow vnto thame, and according to thair deseruingis pvnis thame with all rigour, as, vpon the vther
pairt, in cace hir saidis officeris be thair deligence and behavour procure the
commoun peax and gude reull within thair burgh, hir Maiestie will recog-
noce thame as hir faythfull seruitouris and recompence thame thairfor
accordinglie. *Sic subscribitur:* MARIE, R. Quhilk writing being red in
presens of the prouest baillies and counsale and dekynnis, thay ordane the
samyn to be pvblischit and registrat and the principale to be keipit.

The prouest baillies and counsale ordanis the idole Sanct Geyll to be Standdert,
cuttit furth of the townys standert and the thrissill put in place thairof, idoll Geyll.
and that the thesaurer furnis taffate to the samyn.

The samyn day, the prouest and counsale ordanis the baillies to con- Ministerris.
vene the hale merchanttis of this burgh and vtheris by the craftismen,

s

| | |
|---|---|
| Ministerris. | and put in wryt quhat euery man will frelie gyf for sustenyng of the ministeris, and to report vpoun Wedinsday nixt. |
| Commissioneris. | The prouest baillies and counsale constitutis and nominatis James Barroun, Edwerd Houpe and James Young cutler, commissioneris for this burgh to compeir and be present at all tymes neidfull with the kirk, presentlie convenit within this said burgh, and for this hale toun to ressoun and aggrie with thame in all godlie caussis concernyng relegioun. |

### 28 June 1562.

| | |
|---|---|
| Lord Ogilvye, Jhonne Gordoun. | The prouest, baillies, dene of gild, thesaurer [and council,] with the maist pairt of the dekynnis, decernis Jhonne Gordoun of Fynlater to be kepit in waird within the counsalhous of this burgh, thair to be kepit be xij men dalie and nychtlie vpoun his awin expenssis quhill it be knawin quhat cumis of my lord Ogilvy; hurt be him vpoun Setterday last, and that in respect of the aith of Robert Hendersoun, cherurgeane, quha declarit the thre principale membris of the said lordis rycht arme to be cuttit, quhilkis ar the ciphalik, the basilik and the greit arteir, and gyf he bledis agane the samyn wilbe his deid; and forther deponis that the said Jhonn Gordonis sernandis quhilkis ar hurt ar nocht in danger of thair lyfis. |
| Fynlater. | The samyn day, the prouest baillies and dekynnis foresaid ordanis maister James Ogilvy of Balfoure and James Ogilvy of Fynlater, maister houshald to oure Souerane, to be keipit in ward in the Ouir counsale hous, siclike, vpoun thair awin expens quhill forther be knawin of the Quenys Maiesteis mynde; and ordanis Robert Trowop to be direct away with deligence, with ane writing to the Quenys grace declaring the maner of the discorde betuix the lord Ogilvy and Jhonne Gordoun, togidder with the waiknes of our presoun, and to desyre hir Maiestie to relief ws of the presoneris abone wryttin. |

### 29 June 1562.

| | |
|---|---|
| The Quenis writing. | Richert Trowpe, massour, presentit the Quenys Maiesties writing, of the quhilk the tenour followis: Traist freindis we greit yow weill. We haue |

resauit your letter fra this berer, quhairby we vnderstand the variance that The Quenis
of lait hes happinit betuix the lord Ogilvy and Jhonne Gordoun, and as we writing.
haue found your proceding and handling of that mater werray gude sua
will we thank yow hartlye of your deligence done in apprehending of the
personis trublaris of your toun, for albeit the party be greit, as ye wryte,
yit nevirtheles sall thair greitnes nor respect of thair kinrent stay ws to
exeeut justice as accordis, and seing thay ar to warne thair freindis on
ather syde ye sall nocht neid to haue ony feir thairof becaus oure broder
of Mar is to be thair quha will declair yow quhat fortificatioun ye sall
haue in that behalf. In the menetyme caus the better watche and deligence be maid for the suretie of your wairde, quhairin ye sall do ws
acceptable sernice. Subscriuit with our hand, at Strineling, the xxviij
day of Junii 1562, MARIE R.

30 *June* 1562.

The provest baillies and counsale sittand in iugement, be sentence Maister seole.
interlocutour repellis the first, secound, thrid and ferde of the defenssis
proponit be maister Williame Robertsonn, pretendit maister of the hie
scole of Edinburgh as thai ar proponit and consauit aganis the clame
intentit contrair him be maister Jhonne Moscrop, procuratour to the said
burgh, in respect of the said clame and ansueris maid to the saidis
defenssis, and admittis the lift and sext exceptionis to the said maister
Williameis probatioun to be prouin be him coniunctim as salbe appointit,
reseruand alwis to the said maister Johnne Moscrop his defenssis quhilkis
may result to him be inspectioun of the said maister Williameis gift
mentionat in his said lift exceptioun in pena quhairof the said maister
Williame lauchfullie warnit to this day be Jhonne Roger, officer, to haue
harde interlocutour gevin and pronouncit and comperit nocht, and
ordanis the said maister Williame to be warnit of new to compeir on
Tyisday nixttocum for taking of ane day for preifing of the saidis exceptionis quhen the saidis provest baillies and counsale sall prescrive to
him the maner of the said probatioun; the said maister Johnne Moscrop
warnit *apud acta*.

3 *July* 1562.

Cordinaris.

[To prevent the "darth and exhorbitand prices of buittis, schone, and all vther sic thingis as pertenit to the occupatioun of cordiner craft," proclamation made "discharging all maner of regratouris, cowperris and foirstalleris of reid and barkit ledder," and that none be sold except by the owners and labourers of the same, and not to be "hurdit, hyd and kepit within close houssis, for vphalding of darth, bot to be presentit to oppin market hale and togidder at lauchfull tyme of day."]

15 *July* 1562.

Extent j^m li.

The provest bailies and counsale [with the deacons of crafts,] being convenit within the new tolbuth of this burgh, and efter ressonyng, and declaratioun maid to thame be my said lord provest how that the wark of the said new tolbuth wes ceissit and left of in defalt of money to pay the warkmen, quhairat the Quenys Maiestie wald be offendit, becaus hir hienes had commandit the samyn to be endit with all deligence; and siclike gyf the said tolbuth war nocht rady be Mertymes nixt the sait of the sessioun wald be movit to sum vther toun, quhilk sould be na litill harme to the commoun weill of this burgh; vpoun the quhilkis considerationis, and becaus thair wes na money to be gottin of the commoun gude, becaus the samyn wes analiit for tua yeris to cum, he thocht gude that ane extent of ane thousand pundis sould be lyftit of all nychtbouris to the biging of the said wark. [which proposition was agreed to and an extent granted accordingly.]

17 *July* 1562.

Off sic as sall bruke offices within this burgh and nane vtheris.

The provest baillies [council and deacons of crafts,] being convenit within the tolbuth, and efter lang ressonyng vpoun the monye trublis and variances chanceit within this burgh thir tua yeris past amangis the inhabitanttis of the samyn, nocht onlie to the contempt of God, oure Soverane and the lauchfull Maiestratis of this burgh, bot alsua to the greit apperand distructioun of thame selffis and hale commoun weill of the

samyn, and that as yit thair remanys within this said burgh certane wikit Off sic as sall
besy and seditious personis menying no les nor the like insurrectioun and bruke offices
inobedience gyf remeid be nocht fundin in tyme, and knawing the onlie within this
occatioun thairof to be and to haue bene for the want of gude and godlie burgh and
officeris, nocht having the trew feir of God in thair harttis nor detfull nane vtheris.
regaird to thair conscience and commoun weill foresaid, all in ane voce, votis,
granttis, consenttis, statutis and ordanis that fra this furth thair sall nane
bruke office within this burgh of provest, baillies, dene of gild, thesaurer, coun-
salour, dekyn of craft, nor vther office, bot sic as hes adionit thame to the
trew kirk of God and congregatioun, and hes commvnicat with bayth sacramentis, and hes submittit thameselffis vnder discipline, and gyf ony vther
beis chosin, nocht onlie sic to be deprivit bot the electerris and chesaris of
thame with thame selffis to be pvnissit with rigour as manifest contempnaris of all gude and godlie ordour; and this act to be obseruit in all
tymes cumming without the preiudice of the officeris and dekynnis presentlie
in office for this instant yeir, and to this effect that the dekynnis of craftis
set ane peremptour day for chesing of thair dekynnis, and that vponn
that day the hale dekynnis be chosin and nane vther, vnder the pane
foresaid.

[*Note.*—In the original record the foregoing act is delete, in terms of the
following resolution written at its commencement :—" xxvij Januarii 1563. [The
bailies council and deacons of crafts,] ordanis the act efter following to be deleit
at the Quenis Maiesteis command and for eschewing of hir anger."]

## 22 *July* 1562.

The provest baillies and counsale sittand in iugement, in the [Robertsoun,
terme assignit to maister William Robertsoun, pretendit maister of the hie maister of
scole of Edinburgh, to preif the last twa exceptionis admittit to be provin High School.]
this day be him coniunctim proponit aganis the clame intentit contrar
him be maister Jhonne Moscrop, procuratour for the toun, as suld be
prescriuet be the saidis provest, baillies, and counsale, comperit the
said maister Williame, and for probatioun of the saidis exceptionis
producit ane gift maid to him be the abbat of Halierudehous, with consent

[Robertsoun, maister of High School.] of the abbay of Camskynneth his coadiutour et administratour, subscriveit with the said abbat of Halierudehous hand and seillit with the cheptour seill thairof, of the dait the tent day of Januar, the yeir of God j$^m$ v$^c$ xlvj yeris, and als producit ane tikat contening the names underwrittin, viz., Lord Provand, maister Ednard Henresoun, maister Alexander Sym, maister Jhonne Marioribankis, baillie, maister Alexander Skene, maister Thomas Craig, Alexander Chaip, merchand, James, James, Carmichell, James Harlaw writer, Patrik Govane belman, Patrik Kene, Robert Craig, Alexander Bruce, barbour, maister Henrie Blakwod, maister Jhonne Scherp Jhonne Sinclare, Jhonne Ker, James Richie, Cul. Strang, Williame Broun, Jho, M'Calyeane, Fra. Adamsonn, to preif the rest of the saidis exceptionis ; and the iuges assignis to the said maister Jhonne Moscrop, Setterday nixttocum to produce his obiectionis aganis the said letter of gift *partibus citatis*.

Maister Jhonne Moscrop allegeit that na witnes suld be ressauit vpoun that parte of the said maister Williamis exceptiounis anent his qualificatioun, quhair he offeris to preif the negatiue of the affirmatiue contenit in the said maister Jhonneis claime, viz., that he is qualifeit in grammer, greik and latene, etc., because the probatioun thairof, according to the tennor of the last act and pronunceing of the interlocutour, suld be prescriueit and appointit to him be the provest baillies and counsale, viz., that the said maister William suld gyf demonstratioun of his sciences and artis, being examinat be sic cunning and leirnit men as thai can find maist abill thairto, and the said maister William allegeit in the contrar and disassentit to all vther examinatioun nor be the witnes aboue writtin.

The iuges findis that the probatioun and tryale of that pairt of the said allegeance proponit be the said maister William tuiching his habilitie and qualificatioun aucht and sould ressaue vther ordour tryale and probatioun nor be particular witnes, as vther commoun allegeanceis requiris, and as the said maister William desireis, viz., be demonstratioun of his science eruditioun and knawledge, being examinat be cunning and leirnit men of vnderstanding, in sic sciences ordour and maneris as ar requeseit to be in ane man of sic place of doctrine as the said maister Williame pretendis, and thairfore assignis to the said maister William to compeir before the provest baillies and counsale on Fryday nixtocum, betuix ij and iij houreis [Robertsoun, efternone, in the over tolbuith of this burgh, new beigit, and thair to master of High School.] ressaue vse and leid tryale and probatioun of his said qualificatioun and eruditioun be demonstratioun and ostentioun of his science, and knawledge, being thairanent examinat and requireit as ordour is, in presence of the saidis provest baillies and counsale, be thir personis vnderwrittin, viz., the superintendent of Lothiane, maister Johnne Craig, minister of Halierudehous, maister George Hay, maister George Baquhannane, maister James Panter, maister Jhonne Hendersoun, maister Clement Litill, maister James Kinpont, maister Dauid Colles, maister Alexander Sym, or the maist pairt, or ane sufficient nummer of thame, quha than war nemmit and appointit in presence of the said maister Williame, with certificatioun gyf he comperit nocht the tyme aboue writtin to the effect foirsaid, the said exceptioun anent his qualificatioun suld be haldin as vnprovin. The said maister Jhonne and maister William warnit heirof *apud acta*.

Maister William Robertsoun protestit for remeid of law and reductioun of the interlocutour aboue writtin and alluterlie disassentit thairto.

Maister Johnne Moscrop askit instrumentis that maister William Robertsoun refuseit to gyf demonstratioun of his knawledge, being examinit be the leirnit men aboue writtin, and, in case he comperit nocht on Fryday nixttocum the tyme and place appointit, protestit he be repute thairefter na apt nor erudite persoun for sic office and place of doctrine as he pretendis, and siclike for circumduction of the terme.

## 24 *July* 1562.

The provest baillies and counsale, in the tolbuith, comperit maister Jhonne Moscrop, as in the terme assignit to maister Williame Robertsoun to gif demonstratioun and ostentioun of his qualificatioun, being examinat be the cunning and leirnit men appointit in his awin presence in ingcment the xxij of Julii lastbipast, and protestit that insafer as this day wes assignit to the said maister William to gif demonstratioun of his erudition and knawlege be examinatioun of the leirnit men heir present, for probatioun of his exceptioun as towart his qualificatioun specifiit thairin, and that the said cunning men war heir present according to the desire of the

[Robertsoun, master of High School.] terme, reddy to examine him vpoun [his qualificatioun.] his said exceptioun anent the qualificatioun be haldin and repute as vnprovin according to the certificatioun contenit in the last act.

The samyn day, maister Edmound Hay protestit that be the confessioun of the said maister Jhonne that the desire of this terme is onlie vpoun the probatioun of his qualificatioun, qnhilk is ane pairt of his exceptioun, that thair be na forder done as this day sen the desire of the terme requireit na forder as this day.

The jugeis circumduces the exceptioun proponit be maister William Roberttoun anent the probatioun of his qualificatioun this day vpoun his manifest contempt and contumelie warnit to this day *apud acta* to the effect foirsaid and comperit nocht, and thairfore admittit the said maister Jhonne Moscropis protestatioun aganis him.

### 25 *July* 1562.

The provest baillies and counsale, sittand in iugement, comperit maister Jhonne Moscrop and producit his allegeit obiectionis into writ aganis the pretendit gift producit be maister William Roberttoun, for probatioun of ane pairt of his exceptionis admittit to his probatioun, and ordanis the said maister William Roberttoun tobe warnit agane Tyisday nixttocum to gif in ansueris in writ to the saidis obiectionis, the said maister Jhonne warnit *apud acta*.

### 6 *August* 1562.

[Mr William Robertson having produced answers "in writ" to the objections against his gift, the judges assigned Saturday next to give sentence.]

### 11 *August* 1562.

The baillies sittand in iugement, be sentence interlocutour, efter avisement with thair assessouris, repellis the haill ansueris of maister William Robertsoun maid to the obiectionis gevin in aganis his gift of scholemaisterschip be maister Jhonne Moscrop in the actioun and caus persewit aganis him be the said maister Jhonne and admittis the said maister Jhonne to preif the minoritie of the abbat of Halierudhous [Robertsoun, specifiit in the first of his saidis obiectionis, viz., the said abbat to haue master of High School.] bene within the aige of xiiij yeris the tyme of the granting of the said gift to the said maister William and that in respect of the contentis of the said gift, and for probatioun thairof assignis to him Furisday nixttocum.

### 17 August 1562.

The tounys supplicatioun to the Quenys Maiestie for the freris Freris. places :—Madame, vnto your grace humilie menis and schewis we your seruitouris, the prouest baillies counsale and communitie of the burgh of Edinburgh, that quhair for laik of prouisioun to support thame quhilkis ar in deid puir, that thair miserabill estait being vnder the handis of God and veseit be him be seiknes aige and vtherwis, the nummer of sturdy beggerris daylie increscis in sic sorte that thai quhilkis baith of the law of God and nature aucht tobe helpit ar nocht vnknawin fra thame quhilkis of all ressoun and equitie suld be compellit to travell for thair leifing and sustentatioun, being stark and potent of body that way to laubour, and nocht onlie ar the sturdy beggerris thairthrow fosterit bot als in thair beggerrie begettis childrene quhilkis fra thair youth ar brocht vp beggand, makand thair begging quhairby thai presentlie leif, and ar withdrawin fra laubour to leif idillie tobe ane craft, sua that gif remeid be nocht had thairto the policie salbe havelie hurte and the ponir alwys contempnit and neglectit ; and siklike it is nocht vnknawin to your hienes that the commoun ordour quhairby men attenis to serue the commoun weill of thair cuntre ennis be letteris loirning and scienceis, quhilkis can nocht be obtenit bot be leirning at sculis, quhilkis for the maist parte dois in all partis decay, sua that na regarde is had thairto and the youth thairthrow brocht to sic barborous ignorance that lamentablie it is tobe regratit; the remeid of baith the quhilkis we doute nocht bot be the erecting of hospitalis to sustene the pure, planting of sculis to bring vp the youth, quhairto is nocht onlie requireit places and rowmes bot als ressonabill livingis and stipendis, quhilkis for inhabilitie and pouirtie of the burrowis can nocht be thame be performit ; and your hienes vnderstanding that [to] oure said toun resortis ma ponir than to ony vthir of this realme, and

| | |
|---|---|
| Freris. | als that oure youth is of sic nummer that pietie it war, seing God at this tyme gevis sic pregnant moynis the same suld perveis, and thairfore with supporte of youre grace we mynd na thing mair than to erect hospitalis and ressonable seulis within our said toun, quhairin the puir quhilkis ar indeid puir may be sustenit and the youth nuresit and brocht vp in letteris, sua that ressonabill levingis war provideit thairto, quhilkis at na tyme before culd better be done nor now quhen laudis and annuellis within our said toun pertening to preistis freiris and vtheris ar cumin in your hienes handis, with the quhilkis we doute nocht bot youre grace, bering sic fauour to letteris and science and supporte of the ponir, will partlie bestow to the effect foirsaid; heirfore we beseik your guid grace haif consideratioun heirof, and seing that ye ar myndit that letteris and science incresce within youre realme, and that the ponir quhais clamour ascendis to the hevin be sustenit, that youre grace will grant and dispone to ws the situatioun quhair the Blakfreiris war, togidder with thair yairdis to beig ane hospitale vpoun for the ponir, and als caus sume dres be maid that we may hane the place kirk chalmeris and houssis of the Kirk of Field to big ane seule, we satifiand ressonablie thairfore, and als that your grace will gif and dispone to ws, for sustening of the hospitale and seule foirsaid, the annuellis of chaplainreis and freris being presentlie in your graces handis and the remanent of the samen thai sall pertene to youre grace; and becaus our said toun is populous, and the multitude thairof greit, that your hienes will gif to ws the yairdis of the Grayfreiris and situatioun thairof, being sumquhat distant fra oure toun, to mak ane buriale place of to burie and eird the personis deceissand thairin, sua that thairthrow the air within oure said toun may be the mair pure and clene, and we doute nocht bot your grace sall schortlie se the power within our said toun be sa supportit, the youth sa brocht vp in letteris, that the posteriteis to cum sall haif greit comforte thairof to the prais of youre hienes in all tymes cuming; and your answer humelie we beseik. |
| Regina. | Followis the deliuerance vpoun the bak of the said supplicatioun, subserniit be the Quenys Maiestie :—Apud Striniling xvij° Augusti anno |

1562. The Quenys Maiestie appoyntis the Grayfreir yaird within writtin to be ane buriall place to the personis deceissand within the burgh of Edinburgh, sua that the samyn salbe ane buriall place, and it salbe lesum to burye the deid of the said toun thairin; and hir grace promisses quhen ouir sufficient prouisioun is maid for biging of the hospitale and scule within writtin hir grace sall prouide ane rowme convenient thairfor and sall support that the samyn may be dotyt to be interteneit in tyme cuming. *Sic subscribitur*: MARIE, R.  *Regina.*

### 27 August 1562.

The prouest baillies and counsale, in consideratioun of the heirschep committit vpoun Alexander Weland, lorymer, be the Franschemen the tyme of thair raig within this burgh vpoun the peple of God, and for his gude seruice done to the gude toun in all tymes bigane and to cum, granttis and gevis to the said Alexander ane gildschip fre, and ordanis the dene of gyld to ressaue him gratis.  *Weland.*

The prouest baillies and hale counsale ordanis Louk Wilsoun, thesaurer, with all deligence possable, to big vp the toun wallis at the Blakfreris and mend the sloppis thairintill, and begyn vpoun Monunday nixt.  *Thesaurer, toun wallis.*

Rowye Gairduer, fleschour, actit himself of his awin consent that the hale cornys sawin be him vpoun the ground of the eist yarde of the Grayfreris salbe furtheumand to the gude toun, according to the quantite being vpoun the said ground, arreistit be thair officeris yesterday, and failling of the said cornys the avale thairof.  *Gardner, fleschour, Freir yardis.*

The prouest baillies and counsale ordanis Edwerd, alias Sir Edwerd, Hendersoun to tak cure and charge ovir the warkis of the toun at Sanct Gelys Kirk yaird, the Blak and Gray freris, and ordanis to gyve him ij s. on the day for his lauboris induring thair willis.  *Hendersoun, maister wark.*

The prouest baillies and counsale foresaid ordanis Alexander Guthre, dene of gild, to big vp the Gray freir dikis fra the fore entres to the greit  *Dene gyld, Freir yairde.*

Dene gyld,
Freir yairde.

yairde, according to the ground of the auld fore wall, and siclik to caus mak ane new dur to the said fore entres.

## 18 September 1562.

Bonet makaris.

[Complaint made by the bonnet-makers that "diuers craftismen, sic as fleschouris, wrychtis, sclateris, cordineris, and diuers vtheris within this burgh, had tystit and drawin fra thame thair seruandis and prentissis, vnfre personis, and caussis thame wyrk and laubour vnder thame the wark pertenyng to thair craft." The provost bailies counsel and deacons agreed that the bonnet-makers should be protected in their privileges and liberties; "bot in case it plesit the gudenes of God to gyf the gyft to strangearis or vtheris resortand to this toun to lanbour and invent vpoun prikis ane mair perfyte and fyner fassoun of hois slevis gluflis, and siclike as they thameseffis seruandis nor prentisses could nocht do nor hes nocht done at ony tyme befor this, that in sic caissis the saidis personis sall nocht be stoppit nor the gyftis of God smorit; prouiding alwayis that nowther thay nor nane vtheris salbe seruit be thair seruandis or prentissis, vnfre personis, quhilk hes had thair begynning vnder the said dekin and masterris;" and further, that their servants and prentices should be discharged from working with other unfreemen.]

## 25 September 1562.

Regina,
Douglas.

The prouest, dene of gild, thesaurer, [old and new councils, and assessors,] being convenit in the tolbuth according to the auld ordour, comperit Archibald Dowglas of Kilspindie and produceit the Quenis Maiesteis writing, off the quhilk the tennour followis, and vpoun the productioun thairof askit instrumentis, requireing also the said provest baillies and counsalis answeris to the samin: *Sequitur litera:* Provest, baillies, counsale and deikins of our burgh of Edinburgh, we greit yow weill. Forsamekill as oure louit Archibald Dowglas of Kinspindie wes provest of oure said burgh of before, quha knawis how to rewle youre said toun, haifand experience thairof, and to do ws seruice thairin, and is abill and meit to brouke the said office this nixt yeir, oure will is heirfore and we charge yow that ye mak the said Archibald ane cf the lytis to be chosin provest to yow at Michaelmes nixttocum, and than that ye elect and cheis him to be youre prouest the said yeir, conforme to youre ordour obseruit in sic caissis. This ye do, for oure will and mynde is that the samin be done. Subscriueit with oure hand, at Cowper in Angus, the xxj day of

August and of our regnne the twenty yeir. *Sic subscribitur:* MARIE. And Regina, efter auisement with the said writing the provest baillies counsale and Douglas. assessouris foirsaidis, all in ane voce, continuit thair ansuer quhill the day viij dayis.

### 3 October 1562.

The quhilk day, maister Thomas Makcalyeane of Cliftounhall Decreit aganis provest, maister Jhonne Marioribankis and James Thomesoun, baillies of maister scole. the burgh of Edinburgh, sittand in ingement as ingeis ordineris to the persoun of maister Williame Robertsoun, haifand consent of Robert, commendatar of Halicrudehous, to cognosce in the actioun and caus persewit be maister Jhonne Moscrop, procuratour to the said burgh, aganis the said maister William, that quhair the said maister Jhonne Moscrop calling to remembrance the lovabill purpois of the maist eloquent and politik oratour and philosophour, Marcus Tullius Cicero, willing to haue Marcus his sone instructit in letteris and maneris, knawand the maist famous and literat philosophour, Cratippus, to be instructar of the youthheid in the maist fluresant cictic of Athens, send his sone to be auditour to the said Cratippus within the said cictic, baith for the heich authoritie of the reder and cictic foirsaid, off the quhilkis the ane mycht augment him with letteres and science and the vther with gude exemplis; and like as this burgh is the maist nobill and famous burgh and murrour of gude maneris and ciuilitie within this realme, sua the same aucht to haue the maist famois and literat pedagogis for instructing of the yowthheid of the samin, and to gif vtheris wis and nobill men occasioun, as had the said Cicero, to send their bairnis to be instructit thairin, to the greit inceresce of science and augmenting of the commoun weill thairof; and being surelie informit that the said maister Williame, be the space of xvij yeris syne or thairby, vnder pretense of ane pedagoge qualefeit in letteris and maneris, he haifand nane or litill eruditioun in grammer greik or latene, bot empty thairof, nocht onlie hes wranguslie and ignorantlie vsurpeit the office of schole maister within this burgh, like as he yit vsurpis, to the greit ignominie and detractioun of the fame of the samin burgh and detening of the tender youth bred within the samin committit to his cure in ignorance

Decreit aganis maister scole. of all letteris humane and diuine, bot als, schewand him self ane inimie to Godis worde and contemnar thairof, hes refusit and refussis to frequent the sermonis of the trew and sincere doctrine of God and to communicat in the tabill of the suppour of our Lorde, geifand evill exampill to the said tender youth to the greit apperand perditioun of thair sawlis, quhairthrow he is vnhabill to bronke the said office of schole maister *cum periculosum sit, vt in prouerbio habetur, ouem lupo committere, et eum quem puero preeceptorem adhibueris corruptorem experiri*, and thairfore the said maister Williame aucht to be declareit and decernit vnhabill to the said office, and decernit to be removeit thairfra, and compellit to desist and ceis fra all forder exerceing of that office, as at mair lenth is contenit in the clame gevin in be the said maister Jhonne Moscrop aganis the said maister William Robertsoun thairupoun: The richttis ressonis and allegationis of baith the saidis parteis harde vnderstande and considderit, and the saidis ingeis being avisit thairwith, togidder with the depositionis of diuers famois witnes ressauit suorne and admittit heirto, the said maister Jhonne Moscrop comperand personalie in iugement, and the said maister William Robertsoun being lauchfullie wairnit to this day be Alexander Cuke and George Gourlaw, officeris, oft tymes callit lauchfull tyme of day biddin and nocht comperit, the saidis provest and baillies, with avis of thair assessouris, findis the said maister William to be vnhabill to exerce the office of schole maister within the said burgh, and thairfore decernis him to remove him self fra exerceing of the said office and desist and ceis in all tymes cuming fra forder vseing and exerceing thairof, and dischargis him of all teiching and instructing of the youth within this burgh becaus . . . . . [Here follows a narrative of the previous proceedings and pleadings, the principal of which have already been given.]

6 October 1562.

Dowglas, dekynnis.
The provest, baillies, dene of gilde, thesaurar, counsale auld and new, aboue writtin, maister Jhonne Moscrop, maister Jhonne Scherp and Alexander King, assessouris, being convenit as the letter day appointit for lyting and electing of thair officiaris, comperit Archibald Dowglas and

desireit thair ansuer affirmatiue or negatiue to the Quenis writing, and Dowglas, desireit the samyn to be votit quhether thai wald obey the said writing or dekymis. nocht, and the commoun clerk to note eury manis vote as he wald ansuer to the Quenis grace .... and desireit the said writing to be red in presence of the haill deikins, and thai to be harde to vote according to the tennour of the said writing, quhilk being red the saidis deikins all in ane voce askit instrumentis that thai wald obey the samin in all pointis, and conforme thairto desireit that thai mycht be harde to vote alsweill in lyting as electing, and heirupoun desireit thair ansuer; quha being alssua removeit, the proveist, baillies, counsale and assessouris forsaidis findis and decernis the saidis deikins salhaue na vote in lyting, bot in electing allanerlie, nochtwithstanding the said writing, quhilk in the self is sufficient for thair ansuer.

[Maister Thomas Makcalycane having renounced the office of provestry, Alex- Makcalycane, ander Guthrie, dene of gild, [and five others] "desyreis the lytis to be chosin protestatio, according to the auld ordour, and Archibald Dowglas to be chosin prouest."] Guthrie, etc.

[The council continued their answer to the Queen's writing for fifteen days, till Council's they might have time to " ressoun with hir hienes concerning the contentis thairof."] ansuer.

### 21 October 1562.

[The council to convene every Wednesday and Friday, during the ringing of the Council con- bell from a quarter till half-past ten, under the penalty of one shilling and sixpence vening. to be paid to the poor; those absent from the meeting without reasonable cause to pay five shillings; and none to "depairt of the toun or oute of this realme to remane ony space, without licence obtenit be the said counsale."]

### 6 November 1562.

[James Thomesoun, one of the bailies of the past year, delivered to David Keys. Forrester, bailie, the key of the charter house and the key of the common seal; and Thomas M'Calycane, provost of last year, delivered the seal of cause to Archibald Douglas of Kinspindie, the present provost. The keys of the charter house and common seal, which were in the hands of the previous treasurer, were delivered to his successor, John Prestoun.]

| | |
|---|---|
| Adulteraris, fornicatouris. | The provest, baillies, counsale, assessouris, dene of gild and thesaurar, persaveing that the abhominabill viceis of adulterie and fornicatioun daylie increseit within this burgh for laik of pvnisment, thairfore ordanit the saidis baillies, as thai will ansuer in presence of thair God, and farder vpoun the executioun of thair office, that thai mak deligent tryale throw all the pairtis of the toun quhair ony fornicatour or adulterar may be apprehendit, man or woman, without exceptioun of persoun, to be takin and put fast in the irnehous, and thair to be fied be the space of ane moneth with breid and water allanerlie, and thairefter vpoun the sure tryale of thair offens to be baneist the toun for euir; and siklike the fornicatouris apprehendit in the vice or vtheris tryit be ordour, baith the man and the woman, to be skurgeit thair at the cairt ers and banist the toun ay and quhill sume sure apperance be harde to the kirk and magistratis of the amendiment of their lifeis; and this ordour to be obseruit within this burgh as it sall pleis the Almichtie to move the hartis of the hiear powertis to statute ane better law for the saidis crymeis. |

### 9 November 1562.

| | |
|---|---|
| Pasturing of the mure and lynkis. | [Proclamation to be made that "the pasturing and gers of thair commoun mure, togidder with thair haill linkis betuix St Nicholas Chapell and Weirdy Brow," are to be rouped on Monday next.] |

### 11 November 1562.

| | |
|---|---|
| For fleshe eting. | [Proclamation to be made charging the inhabitants that no "flesche be drest nor etyn in thair houssis vpoun Friday and Setterday fra this day furth," under the penalty of ten pounds.] |

### 12 November 1562.

| | |
|---|---|
| Grahame, baptism. | Jhonne Grahame, merchant of this burgh, beand direct fra the minister and eldaris to the prouest and baillies, to be inquyrit of the baptesing of his last barne, and gif it war found that the said barne wes nocht baptesit, to put remeid thairto be thair obseruit, quhairof the said Jhonne being requyrit be his aith declarit his last barne, being ane las, to be baptisit in |

his awin hous be ane preist of Glasgw callit Houstoun, eftir the papis  Grahame, maner, and his witnes to be Maister Edmond Hay, Margaret Ramsay the baptism. spous of maister James Lindesay, and Helene Jhonnstoun the spous of Andro Stevinsoun; and thairefter the said Helene Jhonnstoun being callit, and hir greit aith taikin, swore that the said barne was baptisit in the abbay, in the Quenys Maiesteis chapell, be hir hienes Franche preist. Siclike Margaret Ramsay, sworne, deponis conforme to Johnne Grahame.

[John Charteris, younger, confessed] that in the moneth of December  Charterris. last bipast his barne wes baptizit in the abbay, in the Quenys Maiesteis chapell, vpone ane hallyday before none.

### 18 November 1562.

[The provost bailies and council,] being informyt that certane inhabi-  Leith, tantis of Leyth on the yonde syde of the brig had vsurpit vpoun thame the assessors. liberte and jurisdictioun of this toun, be biging of houssis vpoun the commoun passages, losing and lading of guddis thair without paying of dewtie, etc., and being forthir informyt that thay had sterit vp my lord abbot of Hallirudehous, the Quenys Maiesteis broder, to manteue thame aganis the gude toun, and foirseing that thir caussis and diuers vtheris the townys actionis sall schortlie cum before the lordis of sessioun and mon be defending be men of law, quhairfore all in ane voce thay nominat and constitute maisteris Danid Borthuik, Thomas M'Calycane and Richert Strang thair assasouris and procuratouris induring thair willis, and ordanis the thesaurare [to pay them each ten pounds yearly.]

The council continewis Jhonne Young, writer, thair scribe, and ordanis  Young, scribe. him to serue in the towyns effaris towert the sessioun, the Quenis Maiestie and vtheris the townlys effaris efter the auld ordour, and to be rady at the thesaureris command to wryte and resaif informatioun of the townys aduocatis in the townys besynes, [he being paid his "auld pentioun of ten merkis."]

## 5 December 1562.

**Dene gyld, presone.** The provest, baillies, assasour and counsale forsaid, ordanis the dene of gild to prepair the hous quhair the wobsteris wrocht in the steple with all necessaris, to be ane pressoun hous for adulteraris and fornicatouris, and to mak the samyn sure and lokfast.

**Villa. tolbuth. Currour.** [The treasurer to pay to "maister William Currour, heritour of the landis quhair the now tolbuth is bigand, the sowme of fourtye pundis in pairt of payment of his ground rycht thairof."]

## 8 December 1562.

**Prices.** [Tallow not to be sold dearer than 13s. the stone; candle, the "rug weik" 1s. 1d., and the "harde weik" 1s. the pound; the fourpence loaf of bread, baked by baxters within the burgh, to weigh thirteen ounces, and that baked by baxters outwith the burgh, to weigh seventeen ounces; ale not to be sold dearer than fivepence the pint; stable keepers to sell their hay not dearer than tenpence the stone, the best oats for 1s. 4d., and the second for 1s. 2d. the peck.]

## 11 December 1562.

**Gyld, minister.** [The dean of guild ordered to pay £8, 18s. 8d. for "certane necessaris of the ministeris ludgeing, as the particuler compt beris."]

## 22 December 1562.

**Bedrellis.** [The treasurer "to pay the bedrellis of Sanct Mary Wynde, for thair Yule dewtie, x s."]

## 6 January 1562-3.

**Murray.** [A supplication presented by Andro Murray of Blackbaronye, bearing that when extents were raised for the proper affairs of the burgh he was taxed among the common merchants, though "ane gintillman having his leving to landwert and vsing na maner of trafiquye within this burgh," and desiring the council to discharge him of all extents in future, as other free barons, "vtherwise he wald discharge himself of all sic liberties as they mycht allege him to hane of thame, and fra this furth nowther tak laubouris travell nor thocht of thair efferis as he hes done in tymes bygane." The council found that the extenters had done wrong, and agreed to make compensation for past payments, and discharged all extents in future "except at sic tymes as quhen our Soueranys proclamatioun salbe generale vpoun all hir hienes lieges aganis Murray. hir inimeis and than to brake the benefice of this burgh becaus he is fre burges, or at sic vther tymes quhen the landis of this toun ar extentit for strenth and policie of the burgh and than to be extentit efter his rent within burgh."]

[The following prices ordered to be observed and kept :—" The pair of double soillit schone of the lairgest mesour, weill wrocht, sufficient wark and sufficient stuf, for iij s. viij d. ; the pair of single solyt schone, of the lairgest mesour and wark, ij s. viij d. ; the pair of fynest doubill solyt buttis for xxiiij s. ; the pair of singill soillit buttis, of the like mesour and wark, xx s. ; the pair of mulis, pantonis, brotekynnis, and all vther wark pertenyng to the cordiner craft, conforme to the prices abone writtin."] Proclamatioun cordinaris.

### 15 January 1562-3.

[The treasurer to pay to two bailies twenty-six shillings and thirty-two shillings, "debursit be thame vpoun Newyerday to the porteris at the Quenys vter yet." Precept, thesaurer.

Proclamation to be made that no "hydis be sellerit, saltat, nor sauld furth of this burgh, nor gadderit togidder in greit, bot be sauld commonlie in the merket fresche to the cordineris and barbaris." Hydis.

No resignation of the town's lands to be made, except "in presens of the prouest baillies and counsale, and thair precept vnder the seill of caus obtenit for the sesing geving."] Sesings of the townys landis.

### 22 January 1562-3.

The prouest baillies and counsale dischargit Anthone Frankdeveill, Johne Wemyss, Henry Lumesden, and Jonet Clerk and George Welsche of all occupeing or vsing of cherurgeanrie or barbour craft vnto the tyme thay wer admytit and maid fre with the said craft. Barbouris.

### 27 January 1562-3.

Apud Edinburgh, xxvij° Januarii, anno lxij°. The Quenis Maiestie ordanis the prouest and baillies of the burgh of Edinburgh to put the lait act and statut of counsale maid anent the selling of wynis within this realme to dew executioun in all poynttis efter the tenour thairof, within Regina. The Quenis Maiesteis ordinance vpoun wynis and vpoun the cordineris.

*Regina. The Quenis Maiesteis ordinance vpoun wynis and vpoun the cordineris.*

the boundis and fredome of the said burgh, and that thai on na wise suffer the saidis wynis to be sauld thairin in greit or small vpoun hiear prices nor is expremyt in the said act, vnder the pane of forfalting and tynsale of thair fredome ; and als that thay serch and seik deligentlie within the fredome of thair said burgh that euery cordiner and man exerceand that craft thairin haif sufficient ledder and vther stuf to wirk and laubour for furnessing of the Quenis Maiesteis lieges, vpoun the prices statut, be the said prouest and baillies within the said burgh thairanent ; and in case ony of the said craftismen be destitute thairof that the said prouest and baillies put thair said act to excentioun and depriue the braikairis thairof fra all vsing of the said craft and bruking of ony fredome within the said burgh in tyme cuming, vnder the pane foresaid. *Sic subscribitur :* MARIE, R.

[The provost bailies and council ordained proclamation to be made in terms of the foregoing ordinance, a copy of which was to be sent to the deacon of the cordiners. Wines were ordered to be sold not dearer than " viij d. the pynt of Burdeaux wyne and vj d. the pynt Rochell and vther wynis."]

### 5 *February* 1562-3.

*Ordinance for convenyng of dekynnis.*

The prouest baillies and counsale, in presens of the maist pairt of the hale dekynnis, decernis and ordanis thame and thair successouris in all tymes cuming, quhen it salhappin thame to be convenit be the saidis prouest and baillies within the tolbuth or vther plaissis neidfull, for ressonyng vpoun the commoun effaris quhairintill thair counsale and consent salbe neidfull, that incontinent, but delay, thay gyf thair jugement openioun and conclusioun, according to thair knawlege and conscience, becaus in tymes past thair delayis and avisementis with the multitudes of thair craftis hes bene the occasioun of tymultis and vproris, nocht onlie amangis thameselfis bot alsua of this hale toun to the greit inquyetatioun and truble of the samyn and hinder of the commoun effaris to the greit hurt of the commoun weill ; and quhat dekynnis that deferris and delayis, that he remane in waird vpoun his awin expenssis ay and quhill he deliuer and gyf his jugement according to his knawlege and conscience as said is ; and for his inobedience, sa oft as he refussis, to pay the vnlaw of xx s. to the commoun warkis, vnforgevin. *Ordinance for convenyng of dekynnis.*

### 6 *February* 1562-3.

The prouest, baillies, counsale and dekynnis, all in ane voce, ordanis ane writing to be maid in maist effecteous manor to maister James Quhite, Scottisman, in Londone, requeisting him with all deligence to addres him to this toun and to accept vpoun him the maistership of the hie grammer scole and teiching of the youth of this toun, and becaus thai ar surelie informyt [he] hes greit proffit be his scole in Londone, and that he is ane man of excellent lernyng bayth in Lating and Greik toung, thay all in ane voce ordanis ane yeirlie pentionn to be gevin to him of iiij$^{xx}$ li. of the radeast of thair commoun gude, besyde and abone the proflit that he sall haue of the bairnys and scule induring thair willis, and bindis and oblissis thame and thair successouris for thankfull payment thairof; and ordanis this promys to be contenit in the said writing; and the samyn to be send to the said maister James with Archibald Grahame now at his depairting to England with my lord secreter, and requeist the said Archibald maist ernistlie to persuaid the said maister James to addres him heir with deligence. *Quhyte, maister of scole.*

### 23 *February* 1562-3.

[The following writing presented and ordered] to be registrat and keipit for the townis releif: Prouest and baillies of oure burgh of Edinburgh. It is oure will and we charge yow that incontinent efter the sicht heirof ye freith releif and lat to libertie Patrik Mwrdoch, now being in your waird within the tolbuth of the said burgh, keipand this present for your warrand. Subscriuit with our hand, at Sanctandrois, the tuenty day Fabruer, the yeir of God j$^m$ v$^c$ lxij yeirs. *Sic subscribitur:* MARIE, R. *The Quenis grace writing, Murdoch.*

### 5 *March* 1562-3.

The prouest baillies [and council] ordanis maister Jhoune Prestoun, thesaurer, to deliuer to Agnes Simsoun, relict of vmquhile Williame *Symsoun, villa.*

158      EXTRACTS FROM THE RECORDS      [1562-3.

Symsoun, villa. Chepman, and Robert Norvell now hir spous, the soume of threttie pounndis for the stanis and beging of the chapell in the Nether Kirkyarde founndit by vmquhile Walter Chepman.

Precept, thes- The baillies and counsale ordanis maister Jhonne Prestoun, thesaurer,
aurer. to content and pay to my lorde prouest, for the expenssis of the banket preparit be him to the commissaris of borrowis, auchtene pounndis iij s. j d.

Maister wark. The prouest baillies and counsale ordanis Dauid Somer, maister of wark, to intromet with the stanis of the chapell in the Nether Kirkyaird and bestow the samyn vpoun the new tolbuith.

Pennycuke, The prouest baillies and counsale ordanis maister Jhonne Spens,
Kirk of Feild. baillie, Andro Murray of Blakbaronye and maister Jhonne Prestoun, thesaurer, to talk and commoun with the persoun of Pennycuke tuiching the Kirk of Feild and hale bigingis thairof, and report his answer to thame agane vpoun the nixt counsale day.

10 *March* 1562-3.

Kincaid, villa. [Of this date a supplication was presented to the council by the spouse of James Kincaid, representing that her late father, John Scott, had obtained from King James V. the gift of "the kyln and barn founndit be him vpoun the ground suntyme callit the Kingis Stabillis, liand contigue to your calsay and commoun passage to your mylnis, betuix the said calsay on the eist, the commoun well and entres to the barres vpoun the west, the castell and bank thairof vpoun the north, and certane landis of my said vmquhile taderris vpoun the south, quhilk kyll and barn, being sufficientlie bigit be my said vmquhile fader, Johnn Hammyltoun of Clidhisdale, prouest of this burgh for the tyme, with certane vther nychtbouris of this burgh, for quhat caus vnknawin to my fader, kist down the said kyll and barn." The supplicants now asked that a charter should be given to them by the council and they complied with the request, the property to be held in "fre burgage," and the owners paying to the town, a yearly feu-duty of 13s. 4d.]

11 *March* 1562-3.

Paullis wark. The prouest, bailies, counsale, and dekynnis granttis and disponis to Dauid Grahame, masoun, the beidmanschip in Sanct Paullis Wark, vacand be deceis of Dauid Young, furrour, with all emolimentis and

dewties thairof, and ordanis ane baillie and clerk to put him in possessioun Paullis wark.
be entering of him to the sell of the said vmquhile Dauid as vse is; [and
also] granttis to Jhonne Cuke, talyeour, the beidmanschip vacand in Sanct
Paullis Werk be the deces of Jhone Wilsoun.

*April 1563.*

[The treasurer ordained "to pay to the calsay makarris, for tua ruddis foure Calsay.
clnis calsay bigit fornent the cardinallis lugeing in the Cowgait, the sowme of iij li.
xvj s."]

23 *April 1563.*

The prouest, baillie, dene of gild, thesaurer, [council and deacons of Tuiching the
crafts,] efter avisement with the Quenys Maiesteis writing, bering that the inhabi-
thair is ane day of law sett to the laird of Drumquhassill and Jhonne tantis of this
Schaw, and diuers vtheris greit personis, quhilkis hes maid greit con- tyme of need.
ventioun of thair freindis aganis the said day, and hir Maieste, fering
trublis, commandis and charges the prouest and baillies to couvene the
hale nychtbouris for stancheing of trublis as said is, vnder all heast pane;
quhairfor the said prouest baillies and counsale ordanis in all tymes
cuming quhen sic or the like occasionis sall occure that the dene of gild
caus poynd and destrenye euerye merchant that conveynis nocht, beand
warnyt be officer, sound of tabroun, or vtherwise, for the vnlaw of
xviij s. but famour; and siclike that euerye dekyn gyf vp the name of the
absenttis of his craft, and the officeris to poynd thame for the said
vnlaw, and gyf the samyn to the said dekyn to be vsit at his plesour,
and this ordour to be obseruit in all tyme cuming.

The baillies and counsale, efter avisement with the supplicatioun gevin Patersoun,
in before thame be Jhonne Patersoun, dekin of the masonis, bering that he masoun.
had seruit trenlie and deligentlie at the wark of the new tolbuth to the ending
thairof, and that vtheris masonis nocht sa qualifeit as he had obtenit thair
burgesschippis fre for thair bounteth and reward, and thair desyrit thair
lordschippis to mak him thair fre gild broder for his bonteth, etc.; to the
quhilk it wes ansuerit that thay haue nocht bene in vse to grant ony
sic libertie or priuilege to men vnmariit, and thairfor quhen it sould happin
the said dekyn to haue ane lauchful wyfe and mariit according to the

Patersoun, masoun.
ordour of the kirk now present, vpon his gude behavour and seruice, he sould be considerit in this his desyre and satifeit to his plesour.

30 *April* 1563.

Clerks chalmer.
The prouest, baillies, counsale and dekynnis, vnderstanding that thir monye yeris past thay haue bene subiect to pay furth of thair commoun gude yeirlie the sowme of xx merkis or thairby for the maill of thair clerkis chalmer, quhilk may be haldin in in all tymes cuming gyf the auld reuestrye of Sanct Gelis Kirk war put in ordour and maid able thairfor, quhilk at this present is desolat waist and sernis for litill or na thing, heirfor vpoun respect to thair commoun weill, and for halding in of sic sowmes in all tymes cuming, as alsua that thay may haue ane certane hous of thair awin for suir keiping of thair evidentis bukis and vther commoun enidentis continuallie in the handis of thair clerkis, fra the quhilk hous thay nor thair clerk sall nocht be removable at the plesour of particuler personis as thay haue bene in tymes past, all in ane voce concludis decernis delineris and ordanis that Alexander Guthrie, dene of gild, with all deligence possebill caus prepair the said reuestrye, bayth laych and heich, in maist honest and sure maner, with all thingis necessar, and that the dur be maid in the eist gavill of the said reuestrie, and the expens debursit thairupoun be him salbe allowit in his comptttis; and ordanis Thomas Reidpeth and James Young of the counsale to be vesitouris of the wark of the said chalmer and to tak cure and charge in the ordoring thairof.

11 *May* 1563.

Stewert, heidman.
[The bailies council and deacons, considering the good service done to the town by Jhonn Stewert, wright, "and in respect of his povertie, having monye bairnys," consent that he should have the next vacant beidmanship in St Paul's Work.]

17 *May* 1563.

[Trial of Bishop of St Andrews and other kirk- men.]
The baillies and counsale ordanis that proclamatioun be maid, be sound of bell, warnyng all nychtbouris, bayth merchant and craftismen, to be vpoun the hie streit the morne be viij houris, in thair best array in

feyr of weir, for seruing of our Soueraue justice, and to remaue vpoun [Trial of the samyn hie streit vnto the end of the justice court set for the Bischop Bishop of St Andrews and of Sanctandrois and the vtheris kirkmen quhilkis ar to thole law for other kirksaying mes. men.]

### 11 June 1563.

The baillies, counsale and hale dekynnis, vnderstanding that this half Ministeris, yeir past thair hes bene na maner of provisionn maid nor support gevin to reder. Jhonn Craige minister and Jhonne Carnys reder, nowther tuiching thair sustentatioun nor vtherwise; quhairfor thay ordane the personis following to pas amangis the faythfull quhilkis hes communicat and requyre of thame thair support to the said minister and reder for ane quarter of yeir quhill it sall pleis God that better ordour may be obtenit, and quhat euerye man granttis to wryte with his name, and ordanis the commoun clerk to gyf vnto thame in roll the names of the saidis communicantis, and the saidis collectouris to present the saidis rollis to the counsale with the sowmes granttit as said is. [Here follow the names of three persons for each of the south-west, south-east, north-east, and north-west quarters.]

### 18 June 1563.

The baillies and counsale ordanis Andro Murray of Blakbaronye and Commissaris Jhonn Adamsoun to pas with the minister, Jhonne Knox, to the assemblay for the kirk. of the kirk to be haldin in Sanct Jonistoun the xxv of this instant moneth of Junii, and gyflis thame full commissioun and power to treit and conclude vpoun the caussis of the said kirk.

The baillies and counsale ordanis James Thomsoun, Nychole Vddert Hospitale. and James Young to be ourscarris and tak cure vpoun the wark of the hospitale at the Blakfreris for the moneth nixt, and siclike that Allane Dikesoun, baillie, maister Jhonne Prestoun, thesaurer, James Mosman, Gilbert Clench and Jhonn Inglis, masonis, to set furth ane patron contenyng the forme of the said hospitale, and to produce before the kirk and counsale thair openioun in diuers hedis and artikles concernyng the said forme.

x

Ministerris, Dundas.

In presens of the baillies and counsale, comperit Jhonne Gray scribe to the kirk, and presentit the supplicatioun following, in name of the haile kirk, bering that it wes laitlie cumin to thair knaulege, be the report of faythfull brethering, that within thir few dayis Ewfame Dundas, in the presens of ane multitude, had spokin diuers injurious and sclandarous wordis bayth of the doctrine and ministeris, and in speciall of Jhonne Knox, minister, sayand that within few dayis past the said Jhonne Knox wes apprehendit and tane furth of ane killogye with ane commoun hure, and that he had bene ane commoun harlot all his dayis; quhairfor it was maist humlie desyrit that the said Euphame mycht be callit and examinat vpoun the said supplicatioun, and gyf the wordis abone writtin spokin be hir mycht be knawin or tryit to be of veritie, that the said Jhonne Knox mycht be pvnist with all rigour without fauour; vtherwise to tak sic ordour with hir as mycht stand with the glory of God, and that sclander mycht be taikin frome His kirk, as at mair lenth is contenit in the said supplicatioun; quhilk beand red to the said Eufame, personalie present in jugement, scho denyit the samyn, and Friday the xxv day of Junii instant assignit to hir to heir and se witnes producit for preving of the allegeance abone expremyt, and scho is warnyt *apud acta*.

Tennand.

The baillies and counsale ordanis Dauid Forster, baillie, to seik and apprehend Frances Tennand and put him in waird quhill cautioun be found that he sall ausner before thaim for the injurious and sclandarous wordis spokin be him of the ministrie and doctrine, and that becaus he hes bene oft and diuers tymes requyrit heirto and refusit.

Kirk, Grahame.

Johnne Grahame, merchant, being callit before the baillies and counsale foirsaid and accusit of diuers iniurious and sclandarous wordis spokin be him in manteinance of the mes, and contrair the doctrine now preichit in the kirk of God, denyit the samyn, and oblist himself in all tymes cuming to keip mesour in his speiking and behavour, vnder the pane of the sale of his fredome and forther pvnisment as the jugis and counsale sould fynd gude.

## 21 *June* 1563.

It is appoyntit and endit betuis [the bailies council and deacons of crafts,] on that ane pairt, for the prouest bailies counsale and communitie, and [maister Johne] Pennycuke, persoun of that ilk and prouest of the Kirk of Feild, on the vther pairt, in maner following, that is to say, the said [maister Johne] Pennycuke sellis and disponis to the gude toun the hale bigging, sumtyme callit the Kirk of Feild, bayth auld and new, with kirk yaird, with lugeingis, biggingis, mansionis, yardis, annuellis and dewteis quhatsumeuir perteuit ony tyme of before to the prouest and prebendaris of the samyn; and forther sall obtene to the gud toun the gyft and few maid thairof to my lord Robert Stewert of Hallyrudhous, and sall get to thame the Quenys Maiesteis confirmatioun vpoun the samyn, and sall transfer in thame all rycht that he had or may haue to the said prouestrie sa fer as lyis within the wallis of the toun as said is, and quhat vther rycht or securite thay can diuise for thame selfis sall obtene and get the samyn at our said Soueranes handis or vtheris hauand onye rycht to the said benefice, bigingis, houssis, yardis, kirk yard, kirk annuellis and dewiteis within the toun as said is, and sall mak na conditioun contract nor appoyntment with any vther before the fulfilling of the premissis and obtenyng of the gyftis and confirmationis aboue expremyt: For the quhilk caus, sa sone as the premissis beis fulfillit for the pairt of the said persoun, before the deliuering of ony evidentis gyft or confirmatioun furth of his handis, he sall haue bund and oblist to him, in maist siker forme he can diuise, tua or thre of the maist substanteous of the said counsale, for gude and thankfull payment to be maid to him of the sowme of ane thousand pundis vsuall money of this realme, to be payit within tua yeris nixt efter thair ressait of the saidis gyftis, confirmatioun, and sic vther securiteis ressonable as sall be diuisit.

[Villa, Pennycuke, Kirk of Feild.]

[One thousand merks to be borrowed on security cf the common mills "for completing of the new tolbuth and paying of the rest of the maister of warkis compttis."] [New Tolbuth.]

25 June 1563.

Old Tolbuth. [The treasurer ordained, " with all deligence, to mend the rufe of the toure of the auld tolbuth and mak the samyn waltertycht."]

Minister, Dundas.
In the actioun and caus of sklander and iniurie persewit before the prouest baillies and counsale be maister Johnne Chalmer, procurator for Johnne Knox, minister of Edinburgh, aganis Effame Dundas, relict of vmquhile Alexander Adamesoun, comperit the said maister Johnne, procutour foirsaid, as at the terme assignit to him to preif aganis the said Effame *pro prima*, and producit Andro Sklater, Alexander Achesoun, Mawsie Galbraith, the spous of James Merchell, ane woman of gude fame and honestie; and the said Effame wes content that maister Johnne Prestoun, Robert Watsoun and Margarete Nicholl, spous [of] the said maister Jhonne, ane woman inlikmaner of gude fame, war ressauit witnes in the said caus thai being suorne thairto and purgeit of partiale counsale, and the saidis witnesis produceit war admittit suorne ressauit and purgit of partiale counsale in the said Effamis presence opponand na thing aganis thame. The said maister Jhonne, procuratour foirsaid, renunceit forder probatioun, and the iugeis ordanis the saidis parteis to be warnit *literatorie* to heir sentence gevin in the said actioun.

30 June 1563.

Dischargeing bonet makaris wyrking on the Hie Streit.
The prouest baillies and counsale, efter avisement with the complaynt produceit before thame be Eduerd Hvme and the remanent nychtbouris, inhabitaris of the landis pertenyng to James Rig of Carbarrie and Andro Murray of Blakbarony, lyand within this burgh vpoun the north syde of the Quenis hie streit of the samyn fornent the croce, . . . vpoun James Lawsoun, bonet makar and dekin of the said craft, bering that the said James, havand ane fore buth vpoun the forestair of the said land, causit his seruandis to wirk thair wollin coittis and bonettis vpoun the said stair, in sycht of the hale nobelitie and strangearris, being ane vile craft never occupeit in sic oppin places of before, nocht onlie to the detryment of the

policie and honestie of this burgh bot to the greit hurt of the said hale  Dischargeing
nychtbouris merchanttis nixt to the said buith, quhais hale merchandice  bonet makarris
with thameselffis and vtheris resortand to thair buthis ar sa fylit with the  wyrking on the
calk dust and flokis of the saidis coittis and bonettis, that force it salbe  Hie Streit.
to thame to leif thair saidis buthis desolait, to their greit dampnage, gyf
mair haistye remeid be nocht providit. Quhilk complaynt being considerit
as said is, the prouest baillies counsale and maist pairt of dekynnis, all in
ane voce, decernys and ordanis the said James Lawsoun to desist and
ceis fra all forther vsing of his occupatioun vpoun or in sycht of the hie
streit, and siclike of hinging furth of coittis or bonnettis oure the stair
of the said buth, bot that he and all vtheris of his craft vse thair said
occupatioun in thair houssis and out places as the samyn hes bene in all
tymes past, vnder the pane of xl s. sa oft as thay salbe apprehendit doing
in the contrair.

## 2 July 1563.

The prouest baillies and counsale ordanis Andro Craig [and four  Tuiching the
others,] with all deligence, vpoun [thair] awin expenssis, to cary away the  red in the
red laid be thame in the Blakfreir Kirk yaird, to the effect that wark of the  Blakfreris
hospitale may proceid without impedyment thairof; quhilkis failling,  yarde.
ordanis the maisteris of wark of the said hospitale to caus carye [the]
samyn away vpone thair expenssis, and actis to be gevin to officeris to
poynd thairfor.

## 4 July 1563.

[The provost, bailies and council ordained, "conform to thair auld ordinances,  Woll merket.
that na merkat nor bargane be maid of woll, hyde, skyn, butter, cheis, vpoun the
Sounday oppinlie nor priuatlie, vnder pane of confiscatioun to the gude townis
vse."]

## 6 July 1563.

The prouest baillies counsale and dekynnis aboue writtin, vpoun con-  Precept Hen-
sideratioun of the greit laubouris and expenssis maid be Robert Hendersoun,  dersone.
cherurgeane, at the command of thame and thair predecessouris, baillies,

Precept, Hendersone.

on diuers personis hurt within this toun, and in speciall vpoun ane deid woman rasit furth of the graif efter scho had lyin tua dayis in the samyin allegit to haue bene wyrreit, curing and mending of tua fals noteris quhais handis war striken of, dressing and mending of ane man and ane woman strikin throuch the bodeis with ane suerd be the Franchmen, ordanis mainister Jhonne Prestoun, thesaurer, to deliuer to the said Robert the sowne of tuentye merkis.

12 *July* 1563.

Calsay, conductis vnder the wall.

[The bailies and council resolved] incontinent to big the haile calsay fra the Gray Freris to the West Port and to mak the samyn (*blank*) futtis braider on ilk side, and to close the mouthis of all the oppin conductis quhilk cumis to the hie streit, and to charge the haile heritouris to mak gude and suflicient conductis within thair bigingis, sua that the hie passage be keipit clene, vnder the pane of x li, to be taikin of euerye ane that faillis, vnforgevin, and that this calsay be biggit vpoun the expenssis of the heritouris according to the ordour obseruit in the rest of the Cowgait.

23 *July* 1563.

Precept.

[The treasurer ordained to pay a hundred merks, being the rent of a "greit lugeing taikin be the gude toun at Witsounday 1562, at the command of the Quenys Maiestie, for seruing of the King of Swaithnis ambassadour."]

Villa, Norvell, Grenesyde.

In presens of the prouest [bailies, council and deacons of crafts,] comperit Robert Norwell burges of this burgh and producit the supplicatioun efter following :—To yow my lord prouest bailies counsale and dekynnis of this burgh of Edinburgh humlie menis and schewis your seruitour Robert Norwell, burges of the said burgh, that forsamekle as, having sure report of sum my freindis and companyeonis, familier seruitouris to my lord abbot of Hallirudhous, that the said abbot wes of mynd to dispone and set in fewferme to ane seruand of his, duelland within the Cannogait, strangear fra the commoun weill of this burgh, the kirk place kirk yard and croft of the Grenesyde, with the peice grene liand besouth the samyn to your playfeild, to be haldin of him and his successouris vpoun certane conditionis and for certane yeirlie proflit and seruice to be gevin and done to him  Villa, Norvell, and thame, and forseing the samyn to be hurtfull to your fredome and  Grenesyde. rycht quhilk I vnderstand ye haue to the bigingis and boundis foresaid, as alsua for eschewing of querrell and dissensioun that mycht follow thairupoun betuix the said lord abbot and your wisdomes gyf he had disponit the samyn in maner abone writtin, I, be greit laubour, nocht onelie of myself bot of vtheris greit courteours, my freindis and fauoraris, hes obtenit his gyft, vnder the commoun seill, of the said place, with sesing following thairupoun, as the samyn heir present to sclaw will testifie, and sen trew it is that past memor of man thair hes bene continuale debait and stryfe betuix your predecessouris and the abbottis of Hallirudhous past for the said boundis of Grenesyde, and that my lord abbot now present is bruder to oure Souerane and great in court and may be mair trubbilsum to yow nor vtheris in case ye wald mowe questioun to this his gyft and sesing quhilk I haue obtenit, quhairfor, and for eschewing of all trublis betuix him and yow, gif it be your plesour, seing the said place of Grenesyde as it presentlie standis is bot ane spelmea and den for thevis murderaris and filthie personis, to despone and gyf the samyn to me with the boundis forsaid in few ferme to be haldin of yow and your successouris I maist glaidlie desyre the samyn and sall gyf yow yeirlie proflit seruice and dewtie thairfor, and quhair the samyn wes of before bot ane den of idolatrie and abhominatioun I sall big fair houssis, yairdis, stankis, and gyf I may haue the myre to the samyn fair buttis and prik merkis for serning of the nychtbouris in honest and necessar pastyme within your awin boundis, in the quhilk boundis and houssis nocht onlie the nychtbouris bot all vtheris our Soueranis lieges, sa far as the samyn may serue, sall at all tymes neidfull be honestlie and weill seruit in bedding meit and drink, and sall forther gyf and transfer in your wisdomes my gyft and sessing obtenit of the said abbot, selyt and subscriuit, quhilk being done your wisdomes may be assurit to be fre of all trublis or pretence of rycht that the said abbot or his successouris had hes or may clame or haue to the said place of Grenesyde and boundis thairof. This maist humlie I desyre of your wisdomes, or vtherwise that I be nocht trublit in biging and possessing of the saidis boundis conforme to my said gyft obtenit of the said abbot; and your answer

Villa, Norvell, Grenesyde.  The prouest baillies counsale and dekynnis foirsaid, after avisement and lang ressonyng with the supplicatioun abone mentionat, fynding the samyn maist ressonable, and for eschewing of trublis in case my lord Robert of Hallyrudhous and thay happin to cum in question tuiching the bonndis abone mentionat, as alsua to bring the samyn fra the possession of the vngodlie vnto thair awin commoun proffit, and vther ressonable caussis moving thame, all in ane voce gevis granttis and disponis and to few ferme lattis to the said Robert Norvell, Agnes Sympsoun his spous, and thair airis, qnhilkis failing the said Roberttis airis, all and hale the kirk, kirk yard, houssis, bigingis and croft of the Grenesyde, hale and togidder, as the samyn wes occupeit be the freris of before, viz., to the myre on the eist, the commoun passege to the Leith on the west, the aikerris and landis pertenyng to the airis of Robert Carmychaell on the north and the grene be north the play feild hard to the dik of the said croft on the south, togidder with thair myre striking south and north with the east pairt of the play feild on the west, the rod and passege vnder Craigingalt on the eist and south pairttis, and the said myre sa fer as pertenit to thame of before on the north; and ordanis ane charter of fewferme with sesing to follow thairvpoun contening the claussis and conditiones following: [*First*, The yearly feu-duty to be six shillings and eightpence.] *Item*, The said Robert sall begin and big quhair the kirk and houssis now standis ane honest lugeing with hallis chalmeris sellaris and houssis necessar for serning of the Quenys leges. *Item*, The inhabitaris of the saidis houssis sal be of gude lyfe, of honest and godlie conversatioun, na dronkarttis, bordalaris, manteinaris of fylthye and vngodlie personis, na hurdaris nor resettaris of thevis, pyrattis, brigandis and tulyeouris. *Item*, Within the said space in the said myre salbe maid dry buttis and prik merkis, bonndit and fixit within the samyn, for serning of our Soueranis lieges to lauchfull pastyme, and sall vphald the samyn. *Item*, The said Robert sall nocht [dispone the lands without the consent of the council.] *Item*, [The possessors and occupiers of the lands] salbe subiect to the prouest and baillies of this burgh, thair lawis and statutis, as ony vther nychtbour duelland within the wallis of the toun. *Item*, [The gift and sasine obtained from the abbot to be renounced and delivered up to the council.]

### 15 August 1563.

The baillies and counsale ordanis maister Jhonne Spens, baillie, Villa, Leith. maister Jhonne Prestoun, thesaurer, and Nychole Vddert of the counsale to pas to the Quenys Maiestie, and to ressone with hir hienes tuiching the writing purchest be the men of Leyth anent the biging of thair new tolbuth.

### 27 August 1563.

The baillies and counsale ordanis maister Jhonne Prestoun, thesaurer, Villa, Brokas. to intromet with the cornys growand in the Blakfreir Yairdis sawin thair be William Brokas, smyth, sell and dispone the samyn, and deliuer the money thairof to the maister of wark of the hospitale, to be applyit vpoun the said wark, and oblissis thame to keip him skaythles thairof.

Williame Brocas, smyth, producit ane letter of tak maid to him be freir Barnarde Stewart, prior of the Blakfreris, with consent of the convent as he allegeit, of all and haill thair yarde callit Baquhannanis yarde, of the dait at Edinburgh the xvij of Merche 1558 yeris, to indure for the space of five yeris nixt thairefter, quhilk letter of tak Dauid Symmer offerit to impreif and the samyn to be fals and fenyeit be the subscriptionis thairof, and thairfore desyrit the samin to be kept in the ingeis handis.

[Ale to be sold for sixpence the pint, and the fourpence loaf to weigh Ale, bread. fifteen ounces.]

### 11 September 1563.

The baillies and counsale being informyt be directioun fra my lord Commissioners prouest that the Quenys Maiestie had appoyntit Setterday nixt, in to Struieling. Struieling, to the men of Leyth to ressoun vpoun the actioun depending betuix thame and the gude toun concernyng thair new tolbuth, thairfor thay all in ane voce appoynttis and ordanis maister Jhonn Spens, baillie, maister Jhone Prestoun, thesaurer, maister Jhone Marioribankis and Thomas Reidpeth, of the counsale, to pas to Struieling, and gevis thame full commissioun to ressoun in the said action.

Statute, malt, ale.

[Nine firlots ground malt to be sold not dearer than £1, 8s.; ale to be sold not dearer than fourpence the pint.]

18 *September* 1563.

Commissaris to Strinelling.

The baillies counsale assessouris and dekynnis, being informyt be the report of maister Jhonne Spens, baillie, and the vtheris quhilkis laitlie war direct to the Quenis Maiestie to Strineling, that hir hienes wes movit and angrye with the nychtbouris of this burgh, and that scho refusit to gyf thame speche, the caus vuknawin to thame, heirfor all in ane voce decernis and ordanis the personis following to ryde vpoun Monunday nixt to Strineling to hir grace, taiking with thame the townis billis of credence, to hir hienes and to my lordis of Murray and Lethingtoun, and forther gevis the saidis personis full commissioun to ressoun in all caissis with hir hienes in all sic caussis quhairwith scho may burdein the gude toun or nychtbouris, and sic vther thingis till do as for the commoun weill sall appeir.

26 *September* 1563.

Scottis irnis, Alexander.

The baillies and counsale, vnderstanding be the complaynt of Thomas Alexander, burges of this burgh, that he had obtenit ane decreit before thame aganis Jhonn Scott, prenter, extending to ix li., and that the said Jhonne had na vtheris guddis saifing his prenting irnis and letteris quhilk war in the townis handis, and without the samyn wer deliuerit to him he war nocht able to get payment of his said decreit, and thairfor desyrit thair lordschippis to deliuer him the saidis irnis and letteris for the canssis forsaid and he sould bind and obliss him, vnder the pane of xl li, that the saidis letteris and irnis sould neuir cum in the possessioun of the said Jhonn Scott nor be applyit to ony vngodlie wark as they haue bene of before, quhilk complaynt the baillies and counsale foresaid thocht ressonabill and ordanis the saidis letteris and irnis to be deliuerit to the officeris to be comprisit as vse is, and gyf the said Thomas offerit maist thairfor to be deliuerit to him, and the said Thomas oblissis him be thir presenttis to fulfill the premissis vnder the panis abone written.

OF THE BURGH OF EDINBURGH.

*Note.*—In the original the foregoing act is delete, and the following written on the margin :—" xxj Martii 1564. Thir irnis, at command of the baillies and counsale, delinerit to Thomas Bassenden, and the said Thomas oblist as Thomas Alexander, and forthair that thair sall nathing be print quhill the samyn be first schewin to the baillies and counsale and thair licence had and obtenit thairto, vnder the pane contenit in this present act." *Scottis irnis, Alexander.*

*2 October 1563.*

[In an action at the instance of the procurator-fiscal against David Wans, in Leith, for having " groundit ane wall of asler extending in lenth to tuentie elnis and in breid to sex elnis, be the space of sex elnis or thairby within the flude mark of the port and hevin" of Leith, "vpoun the west syde thairof . . . tending thairby to appropriat the samin to him and mak ane bulwork thairof and to spuilye" the provost bailies and community of Edinburgh of their possession of the port and haven of Leith, the provost and bailies decerned Wans to desist from building of the wall, and ordered that it should be demolished and taken down.] *Villa, Leith, Wans.*

[The dean of guild was ordained "to tak of the beir samekle fyne Frenche blak as will staik the samin, and to the vthir beir samekill groffer claith as will suffice for ane vther beir." The neighbours were ordained to pay " to Patie Govane for making of ilk grane xij d., and for careing of the beir to the hous of the deid vj d., as alssua for vertesing of the bretherne with the bell iiij d."] *Buriell, mort clayth. Belman.*

*8 October 1563.*

The baillies and counsale ordanis maisteris Richard Strang and Jhonne Moscrop and maister Jhonne Spens, baillie, to tak inspectioun of the persoun of Penneenkis euidentis of the prouestrie of the Kirk of Feild, and to mak sic vther euidentis to be exped at our Soueranis hand, the handis of the abbat of Halierudehous, and the said persoun, as sal be maist sure for the gude toun tuiching the alienatioun and dispositioun to thame of the said Kirk of Feild, houssis, begingis and yairdis thairof, and to produce the samin before the saidis prouest baillies and counsale, and this to be done with all diligence sua that the said persoun haue no forder caus to complene of delay. *Villa, Penneeuke.*

13 *October* 1563.

Tuiching the ordour of the counsalhous.
It is statute and ordanit that in all tymes cuming quhen it salhappin ony mater or questioun to be proponit the proponar to be harde without impediment to the end of his purpois, and thairefter that nane of the said counsale nor vtheris tak vpoun hand to speik or ressoun without leif impetrat of the ingeis than present, and that nane speik bot ane at anis vnder the pane of xij d.

Glen, Strang, Strineling.
The baillies and counsale ordanis maister Robert Glen, baillie, and maister Richard Strang, assessour, to ride to Strineling to ressoun with the Qnenis maiestie tuiching hir hienes writingis send to thame in fauouris of the baillies of Leith and Dauid Wans.

Benefices dispunit.
The baillies and counsale ordanis to convene the deikins on Fryday nixt for thair consent to be had anent the disponing of the beneficies vacand in thair hand be deceis of Sir Henry Mow, Sir William Gray and Sir Symoun Blyth.

15 *October* 1563.

Prestoun, townis letteris.
[The treasurer ordained, "with all deligence, to caus wryt the townis leterris in the foure formes quhilk thay haue obtenit aganis the inhabitantis of Leyth, in parchment, and get the samyn exped vnder the quarter seill."]

Villa, walter baillie.
[The water bailie of Leith and his successors ordained not to "mak thair remaning or duelling in tyme cuming within the said toun of Leith, nor that he or thai hald or fens ony courtis within the said toun of Leith without the assistence of ane of the baillies of this burgh the commoun clerk or ane of his deputtis with him."]

Vdwart, baillie, dischargeit.
Nicholl Vdward, bailie, discharged of his office and decerned in an unlaw of £20, "becaus he departit of the realme in his perticular besynes . . . without licence had or obtenit of the prouest baillies and counsale." The council resolved that another bailie should be elected; and ordained that no person bearing office should leave the town for twenty days without licence, under the penalty of £20, and that those leaving the realm should be also discharged of their office.

James, alias Sir James, Crawfurd, ordained to produce "the rentell of the Crawfurd, prebendariis, rentis and dewiteis quhilk pertenit to the queir." *preist, rentale, queir.*

[The council gave to John, alias Sir John, Lithgow, the beneficeis and prebendary Craigcruke. of Craigcruke, vacant by decease of Sir William Gray.]

### 5 November 1563.

[The bailies council and deacons of crafts] decernis and ordanis the *Doun casting* dikis, wallis and bigingis, veseit be thame vpoun Alhallow evin last, and *and reformyng* biggit vpon thair commontie be the laird of Haltonis tennentis of Broun- *the lawre.* feild, maister Archibald Grahame, Thomas Cant, and vtheris duelland vpoun thair said commontie, to be castin doun vpoun Thurisday nixt, and ordanis the saidis baillies to convene certane nychtbouris and to hyre certane pyonaris for doun casting of the samyn.

The prouest baillies counsale and dekynnis, vnderstanding that the *Choppis.* entres to the hie kirk be the stoppis callit our Ladie stoppis vpoun the south part thairof is commonlie almaist with filth, and the samin sa odious that the pepill ar compellit to leve the said passage, for rameid quhairof and vpoun respect of polacey for avoiding of the said filth, as alsua for the commoun proffeit [agreed that the space should be set for the erection of two shops thereon].

### 10 November 1563.

[The provost bailies and council] ordanis Alexander Guthrie, dene of *Precept, dene* gild, with all diligence possibill, to tak doun the saittis within the traveis *gild, stawis.* befoir the pulpat, and in the place thairof he caus big and set vp ane suit and dask in honest maner for the prouest baillies and counsale.

The prouest baillies and counsale foirsaid ordanis that fra this furth *Presone, adul-* all men that salbe apprehendit in adulterie or fornicatioun to be impresonet *teraris.* in the presoun hous abone the northwest kirk dur callit the proistis presoun, and thair to be fed apoun breid and watter induring thair willis.

Presone, adulteraris.  but preiudice of ferther pvneisment, and to wemen apprehendit be like wice efter the samin ordoure to be impresonit in the woltis abone the kirk beside the stepill induring thair willis as said is.

### 26 November 1563.

For sustenyng of the ministeris.  [The bailies council and deacons of craftis,] efter lang ressouyng and gude avisement taikin for sustenyng of the ministeris reder and vtheris officeris of the kirk, fyndis concludis and decernis that induring thair willis, or quhill it sall pleis God that better occasioun of releif sall be had, that of euerye fyre hous within this burgh, and of the inhabitaris and possessouris thairof, salbe vplift gadderit and inbrocht be the baillies and officeris present and to cum foure schillingis in the yeir yeirlie at Candylmes and Lammes, for sustenyng of the saidis ministeris redaris and officeris as said is; and for the first and begyning of ordour in this caus, ordanis the baillies of this present yeir to pas throuch thair quarteris and tak deligent inquisitioun of euery houshalder and fyr kendler within thair quarteris, put thair names and nwmer in roll and present the samyn befoir the prouest baillies counsale and dekynnis foresaid vpoun Wednisday nixt, to the effect that calculatioun may be maid and knawlege had quhat the laif will extend to; and this to be done with all diligence becaus the saidis ministeris and redaris wanttis thair stipend for the maist pairt of ane yeir past.

Greneside.  [A committee appointed "to pas and vesie the Greneside and boundis thairof, sa fer as Robert Norvell desiris, according to the directioun gevin to thame, and report thair answer on Wednisday nixt."]

Prestoun, Boyll, hospitale.  [The council discharged the treasurer of "xx s. maile restand awand the gude toun be Jhonne Boyll, keipar of the lyme, sand, and wark lwmes at the hospitale, in recompance of his seruice."]

### 1 December 1563.

Villa, Leyth.  The prouest baillies [and council,] vnderstanding that thay ar to be callit the morne before the Quenis Maiestie and lordis of secreit counsale, at the instance of the abbot of Hallirudhous, tuiching thair libertie of the port and havin of Leyth, and thairfor fyndis gude and ordanis that thair evidenttis concernyng the samyn be brocht furth of the charter hous, and the assassouris couvenit to consult thairupoun.

*Villa, Leyth.*

### 24 December 1563.

The provest baillies [and counceil] gevis and disponis to William Abercrummy, tavernar, burges and gildschip fre, at requeist of the abbot of Sanct Comeis Inche.

*Abircrummy, burges and gild.*

The provest baillies and counsale abone writtin statutis and ordanis that na burgesschip nor gildrie be gevin gratis for ane yeir to cum, vnder the pane of ten pound to be tane of the consentar and gevar, but favour.

*That na burges be maid for ane yeir gratis.*

The provest baillies and counsale befoir writtin, vnderstanding that the generale counsale of the kirk is to be haldin at this present within the tolbuith of this burgh and the nobilitie for that purpois convenit, and becaus thai hane sum materis to propone tuiching the glorie of God and thair commoun weill in the said conventioun, thai constitute and ordanit James Barroun, maister Clement Littill and maister Johne Merioribankis to compeir for thame to ressone and propone in thair caussis and sik vtheris as sall occur, and geifis thame full commissioun sa to do, and siclike ordanis Richart Trolhope and the gild officeris to wait on the keiping of the tolbuith dure induring the tyme of the said assemblie and conventioun, and that the deue of gild se thame furneist in candill fire and vther necessaris vpoun the tounnis expenssis.

*Conventioun of the kirk.*

### 29 December 1563.

The provest baillies and counsale ordanis Alexander Park, thesaurer, to by thre twn of the best wyne can be gottin in Leyth, togidder with xx li. worth of torches, to be propynit to the Quenis grace.

*Propine, Queen.*

### 7 January 1563-4.

The baillies and counsale ordanis Daniel Forster and James Adam-soune to deliuer to Jhonne Blakburne the sowme of iij$^{xx}$ li. of the radeast

*Tymmer, hospitale.*

Tymmer, hospitale.  money in thair handis collectit for biging of the hospitale, and for tymmer bocht to the said hospitale.

### 21 January 1563-4.

Precept, Carnys.  The baillies and counsale ordanis Dauid Forster and maister Jhonne Prestoun, collectouris for the ministeris, to deliuer to Jhonne Carnys, reder, the sowme of xl li. of the radeast money in thair handis.

### 16 February 1563-4.

Villa, Reidpeth.  The prouest baillies [and council] ordanis Thomas Reidpeth to deliuer of the radeast money [in] his handis, or that he salhappin to get for the biging of the hospitale, the sowme of xxxv li., to Jhonne Blakburne rest- and awand him of the tymmer resauit be the said Thomas for the said hospitale, and oblissis thame to satilie him thairof in case he haif nocht or gettis nocht in of the collectouris of the said hospitale the said sowme agane.

### 18 February 1563-4.

Feu-duty to a sister of the Senys.  The prouest baillies and counsale, efter the forme and tenour of the Quenis Maiesteis writing vnderwrittin, ordanis the tenenttis takismen and occupearis of the craft vnder written to mak gude and thankfull payment of the ferme thairof to Beatrix Blakater of the crop in the yeir of God j$^m$ v$^c$ lxiij yeris, extending to viij bollis quheit and sex bollis beir, and sic- like yeirlie and termelie in tyme cuming . . . . . REGINA. Prouest baillies and counsale of oure burgh of Edinburgh, we greit yow weill. Forsa- mekill as we ar informyt be oure louit oratrice, deme Cristeane Ballenden pryores of the Senys on the Borro Mwre besyde oure said burgh, that scho, with the consent and assent of the sisteris thairof, set to yow and your predecessouris tuenty yeiris syne or thairby ane litill croft of land liand within the wallis of oure said burgh at the Grayfreir port, in few ferme, for yeirlie payment to hir and the saidis sisteris for viij bollis quheit and vj bollis beir, and that ye and your predecessouris in all tymes bipast sen obtenyng of the said few hes maid thame thankfull payment and thair assignais of the samyn quhill this last crop of lxiij yeris, quhilk victuell is assignit be the said priores and hir sisteris foresaid to Beatrix Blacater, ane Feu-duty to a sister of the Senyis. of the sisteris thairof, for hir pairt of sustentatioun furth of the fruittis of the said place, quha as we ar surelie informyt hes bene ane of the nowmer of the said sisterris thir fourtye yeris syne or thairby, and that the samyn croft wes conquest be hir fadir and predecessouris and dotit be thame to the sustentatioun of the said Beatrix, for sustenyng of hir and the saidis sisteris, quha now ar sa strikin in aige that scho hes na vther moyin to wyn hir leving bot onlie to depende vpoun that small portioun assignit to hir as said is, thairfor it is owre will and we desyre yow rycht effectuislie to mak thankfull payment to the said Beatrix of the foresaidis viij bollis quheit and vj bollis beir for the yeir of God abone specifeit, and siclike yeirlie and termelie in tyme cuming according to the said pryores assignatioun and ay and quhill scho discharge the samyn, as ye will do ws singular plesour, sua that we haue na forther occatioun to write to yow in this behalf be thir presentis. Subscriuit with oure hande, at Edinburgh, the penult day of Februar the yeir of God j<sup>m</sup> v<sup>c</sup> lxiij yeris. MARIE, R.

### 22 *March* 1563-4.

[The council, "for eschewing of the manifest fraud vsit within this burgh be Ordinance for walkaris, wob-staris, and lyt-staris, and for clayth making. drawarris and fals culloris of clayth and ordour to be put thairintill in tyme cuming, conforme to the act of parliament maid be vmquhile oure Soucrane lord King James the Fift," ordained that no person "vse or lyt ony kynd of fals cullour, or draw clayth, ding, calk, creche, flaill or caird clayth;" and it was agreed that an inspector should be appointed, and other steps taken to ensure that the law was kept.]

### 28 *March* 1564.

The baillies counsale and dekynnis ordanis ane extent of j merkis to Extent, j<sup>m</sup> merkis. be rasyt vpoun the hale nychtbouris, quhairof for furnessing of the ambassadour to Denmark vij<sup>c</sup> merkis, the remanent to be applyit vpoun the new tolbuth and remanent warkis of the toun.

### 24 *April* 1564.

The baillies and remanent counsale befoir writtin ordanis James Ministeris. Barroun, James Adamsoun, maister Johne Prestoun, Eduard Hoipe, to pas

| | |
|---|---|
| Ministeris. | out throuch the quarteris of the toun amangis the faithfull and require of euery ane of thame quhat thai will frelie gif be yeir for sustening of the ministeris, and to report thair ansueris in writ vpoun the nixt counsale day. |

### 28 April 1564.

| | |
|---|---|
| Villa, Innerkeything. | The baillies and counsale foirsaid, efter awisement with the supplicatioun gevin in befoir thame be the nychtbouris of Innerkeithing, lamenting that in this last extent vpliftit for furnesing of the ambassadour towart Denmark thai wer set to the soume of tuentie merkis quhilk thai wer nocht abill to pay becaus of their greit pouertie and vtheris caussis thai had in hand towart thair hevin, desirit consideratioun, etc., as at mair lenth is contenit in thair complaint etc. The quhilk complaint the saidis baillies and counsale vnderstanding to be of veritie, in consideratioun as said is, without preiudice of that commoun ordour in tyme cuming, ordanis that the saidis nichtbouris sall pay bot onlie fouretene merkis in this present, and dischargeis the officiaris collectouris of the remanent sax merkis, without preiudice as said is. |

### 1 May 1564.

| | |
|---|---|
| Precept, thesaurer. | The baillies [and council] ordanis Alexander Park, thesaurer, to deliuer to maister Lwes, sumbeleir to the Quenis Maiestie, the soume of thre scoir fyftene poundis for thre tunis wynis furneist be him to the gude toun, quhilk wes propynit to hir hienes at Yule last, and mair to deliuer to the said maister Lewes, for his seruice and reasonabill price, als mekill fyne sating as wilbe him ane doublit. |

### 3 May 1564.

| | |
|---|---|
| Ministeris. | [The bailies and council] ordanis the haill communicantis to be conveuit befoir thame vpoun Fryday nixt, and first the northwest quartar, and sa furth quarterlie that it may be sene quhat euerie ane of thame will frelie grant for sustening of the ministeris, and euerie baillie to convene his awin quarter. |

## 11 *May* 1564.

The proucst baillies and counsale ordanis the supper to be maid in honorabill maner vpoun the tounis expenssis, efter the device of the laird of Quhittinghame, ambassatour, in his lugeing, to the king of Denmarkis ambassatour, being present in this toun.  *Banket.*

## 15 *May* 1564.

The baillies and counsale, efter inspectioun of the compt and particular expensis thairin contenit, debursit vpoun the banket maid to the King of Denmarkis ambassatour, quhilk the samin extendis to tuentie sax pound, quhilk soume thai ordane Alexander Park, thesaurer, to deliuer to Johne Douglas, servand to the laird of Quhittinghame.  *Precept.*

## 24 *May* 1564.

The proucst baillies and counsale ordanis Alexander Park, thesaurer, to deliuer of the best of the townis monitioun being within the castell the peces follow to the laird of Wittinghame, for sernving of him in his vayege, and to tak the said lairdis obligatioun vpoun the ressait thairof, viz., tua slangis with thre chalmeris, sex cuttbrottis double and singill with xij chalmeris, four lyn nalis, sex wegis, half ane barrell of pulder, certane bullettis, tua pair of calmes of bras, the ane for the slangis, the vther for the cuttbrottis; and siclike ordanis the said Alexander to resane the samyn agane at the said ambassadouris returne.  *Mwnitioun.*

## 31 *May* 1564.

[The bailies and council,] being conveuit in the counsale hous, comperit before thame the richt honorabill laird of Quhittinghame, ambassatour towart the King of Denmark, and declairit that for the honestie of the realme and for furthsetting of the caus quhilk he hes in hand towart the said king of Denmark, necesser it wer to him to be honestlie set furth with ane coupbuird of siluer, of the availl of ane thousand merkis, quhilk he sould obtene and borrow of sum freind sua that thai wald becumit bound and  *Copbuird, Quhittinghame, villa.*

Copburd, Quhitting-hame, villa.

obleist thairfor incace the samin perresit vpoun the seis or reft be greitar powar or vther wayis inlaikit be chance of fortoun, nocht of his sleuth nor be him disponit ony maner of way at his plesour or his awin commoditie, quhilk desire thai thocht reasonabill, providing the said laird wald obtene the Quenis Maiesteis charge chargeing the remaning burrowis to beir burding with thame and to be compellit thairto according to thair pairtis incace the samin inlaikit in maner abone writtin, and the said laird promeist faithfullie to obtene the samin; quhairfoir the saidis baillies and counsale bindis and oblissis thame, be thir presentis, and thair successouris, incace the said copburde of the availl of ane thousand merkis perreis be reft or inlaik be chance of fortoun, nocht in the said lairdis defalt, to releve and keip him skaythles safer as thai may be burdenit according to the ordour of taxtis, viz., to pay (*blank*) pairt thairof.

## 2 *June* 1564.

Bread.

[The fourpence loaf of bread baked by baxteris within burgh to weigh 18¾ ounces; fleshers to sell best "muttoun bouk" for sixteen shillings.]

Wynes.

[Of this date, one of a series of acts, passed with regard to the selling of wine, provided that there] be collectit of euerie pvucheoun of wyne wenttit within this burgh ane choppin, and the money to be put in ane lokit box haueing thre keyis, quhairof ane to the dene of gild and the vther tua to tua of the maisteris, and the said box to be in the keiping of ane of the saidis maisteris, and of the money thairintill compt and rakning to be maid aneis or twyis in the yeir, and to be disponitt at the sicht of the prouest, baillies, dene of gild, counsale, maisteris [appointed to attend to the selling of wine,] and ane pairt of the saidis brethering, for the support of the pure, payand of thair officeris feis, help of dekayit brethering fallin in pouertie be chance, or vtherwayis as sall be found gude for the commoun weill.

## 16 *June* 1564.

Regina, villa, Leith, tol-buth.

In presens of the baillies and counsale, comperit Walter Cant, in Leyth, and producit the Quenis Maiesteis charge vnderwrittin, of the quhilk the tenour followis: REGINA. Provest baillies and counsale of Edinburgh. Forsamekle as we haue send oure requeistis sindry tymes vnto yow to permyt oure inhabitantis of oure toun of Leyth to big and edifie oure hous of iustice within the samyn and hes resauit na ansuer of yow, and sua the wark is stayit and cessis in your defalt; quhairfor we charge yow that ye permyt oure saidis inhabitanttis of oure said toun of Leyth to big and edifie oure said hous of iustice within oure said toun of Leyth, and mak na stop nor impedyment to thame to do the samyn, for it is oure will that the samyn be biggit, and that ye desist fra forther molesting of thame in tyme cuming as ye will ansuer to ws thairupoun. Subscriuit with oure hand, at Hallyrudhous, the fift day of Marche the yeir of God j$^m$ v$^c$ thre score thre yeris. *Sic subscribitur:* MARIE R. Quhilk writing, being red, the baillies and counsale foresaid commandit to be registrat in this present buke, and the principale to be put in the charter hous with sic vther supplicationis and writingis as hes bene purchest be the inhabitantis of Leyth in this caus of thair tolbuth.

*Regina, villa, Leith, tolbuth.*

### 9 *July* 1564.

[Ale not to be sold dearer than three pence the pint; best mutton, 12 s., second mutton, 8 s.; the fourpence loaf to weigh 20 ounces].

*Ales, flesh, bread.*

[Sir Jhonn Beyr, chaplain, renounced his yearly annual of £5 payable out of the common good, and the treasurer was ordained to deliver to him the sum of £27, 10 s. in full of said annual].

*Villa, Sir Jhonn Beyr.*

### 15 *July* 1564.

[Nychole Scott charged to remove "his stanis liand at the fut of the Kirk Yaird close quhair the auld cole merket stude of before."]

*Villa, Scott.*

The baillies and counsale ordanis officeris to pull vp the lynt sawin be William Brokas in the hospitale yairdis and dispone the samyn to thair awin vtilite, and forther to put the said Brokas in waird for his contempt.

*Villa, Brokas.*

The baillies and counsale ordanis officiaris, with ane of the baillies and clerk, to pas to Leyth this efter none and caus proclame the Quenis

*Proclamatioun, schippis.*

Proclama-
tioun, schippis.

Maiesteis letteris set furth for ordoring of the schippis laitlie cumin furth of Danskin suspectit of the pest, and to caus sa monye of the merchanttis and marinaris thairof as ar cumin on land to reteir to thair schippis, conforme to the saidis letteris.

### 2 August 1564.

Park, havin.

The baillies and counsale ordanis Alexander Park, thesaurer, with all posseble deligence, to caus clenge the havin of Leyth of the greit stanis brocht doun be the last greit spait, with certificatioun and he failye that the dampnege quhilk the schippis sall sustene be the saidis stanis salbe laid to his charge and he halden to recompance the samyn.

### 9 August 1564.

Villa, Penne-
cuke.

The baillies and counsale foresaid, togidder with [the deacons of crafts,] vnderstanding that the persoun of Pennycuke is takand doun the stane wark of the Kirk of Feild, and is of mynd to dispone and sell the samyn, quhilk thay fynd maist necessar to be bocht be the gude toun, owther for the hospitall or for ane vninersite to be maid in the said Kirk of Feild, quhairfor thai ordane maister Thomas Makcalyeane, assasour, [and five others] to convene appoynt aggre and mak finall end with the said persoun tuiching the haill stanis, stane wark of the auld and new kirkis, manssis, houssis, bigging, yairdis, kirkyaird, and all vther thingis concerning or pertening to the said persoun, be vertew of his prouestrie and be few, as alsua the donatioun of beneficis and prebendareis, and all vther thingis quhilk pertenit to the said prouestrie that he will or may sell to thame in the name of the gude toun, the securitie thairof to devise mak and put in forme, sowmes of money thairfoir in name foirsaid to promeis and gif.

### 11 August 1564.

Wache.

The prouest baillies and counsale ordanis ane stark wache of [blank] men, substantioun and able, to be set at Newhaven and peir and schoir of Leyth, bayth nycht and day, for keiping of the pepill suspect of the pest within thair schippis, and that nane sall resort to thame quhill forther Wache. ordour be taikin and thay haue [the] Quenis Maiesteis mynd in the contrair, and the said wache to begin this nycht at vj houris at evin be maister Robert Glen, baillie of the northwest quarter, and to remane with the samyn quhill the morne at vj houris, and than the vther (*blank*) with sum honest nychtbour, with tua officeris, sic as the said baillie sall deput, to haue the charge of the said day wache quhill vj houris at evin, and than Dauid Somer, baillie of the northeist, with the lik nowmer and ordour to releif thame; and this ordour to be keipit amangis the hale baillies quhill vther ordour be taikin as said is, and siclike that all the porttis of this toun be closit day and nycht, the West Port and Nethir Bow except, and the keyis thairof deliuerit to the dene of gild, and the saidis West Port and Nethir Bow to be closit at ix houris at evin, and the keyis deliuerit to the baillies of the quarteris, viz., Dauid Somer and maister Jhonn Spens, and nocht to be oppinnit quhill (*blank*) houris in the mornyng, at quhat tyme thair sall be enterrit fyve men to euerye ane of the said porttis to keip the samyn with the porteris quhill the closing of thaim at nycht.

The prouest baillies and counsale foresaid ordanis Alexander Park, thesaurer, to caus big mend and compleit the sloppis and hollis in the pairttis of the toun wallis, and in speciall the new wall at the college, sua that [na] pairt of the samyn be clymable nor passable fra this furth; with certificatioun and he failye till do the samyn with all posseble deligence the danger skayth or inconvenient may follow thairupoun salbe laid to the said Alexanderris charge, and that becaus he hes bene diuers tymes chargit heirto of before and as yet the samyn vndone.

Toun wallis, Park.

### 18 *August* 1564.

The prouest [bailies and council,] vnderstanding that be the command of the kirk, Jhonn Knox and Jhonne Craig, ministeris, ar instantlie to depairt, the tane to the north and the vther to the south pairttis for preiching of the evangell in tha pairttis, and that it is appoynttit that Christopher Gudeman, minister of Sanct Androis, sall abid and remane in thir pairttis to thair returnyng, and in thair places to minister and preche;

Minister, Gudman.

184   EXTRACTS FROM THE RECORDS   [1564.

*Minister, Gudman.*

quhairfor thay ordane maister Jhonn Spens [and four others] to pas to the said maister Gudman, offer him in thair names all honorable intertenement, and caus the stewert of Jhonne Knox hous to keip table to him vpoun the townis expenssis, and ordanis the said Alexander Park to pay the samyn ouklie.

25 *August* 1564.

*Villa, Pennycuk.*

[The bailies, council and deacons of crafts] ratefeis and apprevis the act and ordinance maid the ix day of August instant betuix the gude toun and the persoun of Pennycuke tuiching the Kirk of Feild, and ordanis the appoyntment thairintill contenit tobe endit with all deligence, and the saidis dekynnis gyf thair full consent and assent thairto.

*Youngar.*

The baillies and counsale foresaid, vnderstanding that George Younger, furrour, hes bene he himself with ane seruand allanerlie be the space of xv dayis vpoun Werdye Mwre, and is at this present hale and feir of his persoun, quhairfor thay grant and gyf licence to the said George, efter he be clengit, to pas to sum quyet hous vtwith the toun for the space of viij dayis before he enter within the said toun, and thairefter being of gude helth to resort to the said toun.

*Mariners.*

The bailles and counsale foresaid, efter avisement with the Quenis Maiesteis writing grantit in fauouris of the schippis to lose thair guddis vpoun the Inches, appoyuttis the schippis of James Logan, Thomas Symsoun, (*blank*) Scott of the Wemys, (*blank*) Litiljhonn and (*blank*) Blyth, to Inchekeyth; the schippis of Robert Sandis, the grewhound, George Hay, to Sanct Columbeis Inche; the Ducheman and Robert Hog to Crawmond Inche; and ordanis Mertyne Vddert pursevant with the saidis letteris to the saidis Inches, and charge the keipairis thairof to resaue the saidis schippis conforme to the saidis letteris, and Alexander Park, thesaurer, to gyf to the said Mertyne xl s.

*Villa, commoun passenge, West Port.*

1 *September* 1564.

The bailies and counsale foresaid, efter ressonyng vpoun the narrowing

of thair commoun passages, and in speciall the hie passege quhilk ledys Villa, com-
fra the West Port to the Commoun Mwre throuch the raw and streit callit moun passage
[blank], fyndis the said commoun passege sua narrowit be bigging and West Port.
furthsetting of choppis vtouth the sydwallis of the biggit landis of the
said streit hard to the calsay of the said passege, and in sum pairt within
the samyn, to the greit hurt of the gude toun and expres aganis the act
of parliament, quhairfor thay ordane the procuratour fiscale to rais letteris
conforme to the said act vpoun the proprietaris of the saidis choppis to
heir thaim be decernyt to remove and tak away the samyn within [blank]
dayis nixt efter thay be warnyt, conforme to the said act.

### 8 September 1564.

The bailies and counsale foresaid ordanis ane precept to be maid to Precept,
James Kincaid, fermorar, chargeing him to deliuer to Dauid Somer, baillie, fermorar.
xx li., to be gevin for sustenyng of maister Gudmannis charges.

The baillies and counsale ordanis Alexander Park, thesaurer, to deliuer Gudeman.
to Jhonn Chalmeris the sowme of [blank] pundis for bering of his charges
to Sanctandrois send thair be thame and be the kirk to the kirk of Sanctandrois to impetrat licence to Maister Gudeman to remane heir to the
returnyng of Jhonn Knox minister.

### 18 September 1564.

The baillies and counsale ordanis maister Alexander Logy, George Pest.
Gourlay and Alexander Cuke, to pas to the Newhavin and attend nycht
and day vpoun the lynt and vther merchandice losit thair furth of the
schippis that come laitlie furth of Danskyn, and se the samyn handillit
tryit and purgit, and thairefter mak report to the counsale quhill forther
ordour be tane, and to haue thair charges of the merchanttis expenssis.

### 20 September 1564.

[The provost, bailies, and council, being convened for electing of the new Villa, craftis,
council, John Purves, tailor, presented the names of six craftsmen from which they counsale.
were asked to elect two to be upon the council; but, " for caussis moving thame,"

2 A

Villa, craftis, counsale.

the council refused to accept the persons named, and ordained " the said Jhonn Purves to gyf thame vther vj in tikat, and in case thay war nocht content with thay sex vther sex ay and quhill thay war content, to the quhilk the said Jhonn Purves dissasentit and . . . . . protestit that thay be nocht offendit gyf the hale craftis sutit for remeid at the Quenis Maiesteis hand."]

### 27 September 1564.

Villa, craftis, counsale.

[The craftsmen having desired that two of the craftsmen, whose names were given, should be chosen upon the council, the provost, bailies, and council " declaris and delineris that thay will elect thair counsale and officeris conforme to the act of parliament maid be King James the Thrid tuiching the electioun of officiaris within burgh, quhilk is ane law that thay dar na wayis pretend to alter, quhairiutill is specialie contenit that the auld counsale sall chois the new without mentioun of ony dekyn to haue voit or entres thairintill, and thairfor gyf thay wald nocht gyf in vther tikettis thay wald proceid according to the said act." The deacons of crafts protested against this deliverance.]

### 28 September 1564.

Nota. Dekynnis.

[" This mater of contrauersie being ressonit and persewit be way of complaynt before the lordis of secreit counsale, the saidis dekynnis ar ordanit to present before the counsale of the toun vtheris new tikattis and to observe the said act of parliament."]

### 30 September 1564.

Protestatio. Purves.

[Allan Purves and John Purves produced " ane vther tikat contenyng vther vj personis," desiring the council to elect two of them, " and protestit that this be na periudice to thair auld libertie."

Protestatio. Purves, assasouris.

The dekynnis foresaidis desyrit that William Andersoun, dekin of the candilmakaris, mycht haue voit with thame in electing of officiaris, in respect of thair seill of cause, and the baillies and counsale foresaid refusit, allegeing that occupatioun nocht worthye of ane dekin, and thairfor chargit the said William to remove himself incontinent, and the saidis dekynnis [protestit] for remeid, and forther desyrit the assasouris to be removit and haue na voit in liting or chesing of ony of the officiaris becaus, as thay allegit, they war bot brocht in of polecie to war thame in nowmer, quhilk allegeance and desyre the saidis provost and baillies and counsale refussis Protestatio. and repellis with the rest, and fyndis the saidis assasouris to haue had voit Purves, assasouris. in tymes past and aucht to haue in all tymes cuming.

### 8 October 1564.

[Ale not to be sold dearer than threepence the pint; the fourpence loaf of bread Ale, bread. to weigh twenty ounces.]

### 30 October 1564.

Becaus of the manifest fraud quhilk heirtofore hes bene vsit in wirking, Lytstairis, weving, walking, litting and culloring of clayth within this burgh, it is walkaris, web-statute and ordanit that na fals cullour be brissell, vrsell, aller barkis, or sterris. siclike fraudfull schyftis as drawing, dinging, calking, creiching, flaling or carding of clayth be vsit in tymes cuming, bot that the ordour heirefter to be maid be obseruit and keipit vnder the panys contenit in the samyn, and according to the ordour set furth the xxij of Merche last.

### 3 November 1564.

[William Thomsoun and the remanent litstars in the burgh bound and Lytstaris. obliged themselves] that thai nor nane of thame in ony tyme cuming sall lit ony maner of cullouris of muster de villois, Frenche gray or russattis with brissell or vrsell, nor lit ony blakis with coppruss, gallis, aller barkis or siclike fals colouris, bot the samin to be littit with mader, alme, glew, and sic trew colouris as hes bene and is vsit amangis men of honestie, experience, and gude concience of the said craft, vnder the pane of fiue pound for the first falt, ten pound the nixt falt to be disponit to the commoun werkis, and the thrid and last falt to be banceist the toun and fredome thairof for euer.

Item, for the mair sure tryall of the honestie lawtie and sure wark of the said occupatioun, that thair be maid ane stamp and the tounis armis thairapoun, quhilk salbe gevin in keiping to ane honest trew and sworne nichtboure of experience in making and colouring of claith, quha salbe oursear of all claith littit and maid within this burgh, and sall stamp

| | |
|---|---|
| Lytstaris. | samekill as beis sufficient thairof with the said stamp in leid, and vther wayis nocht, quha sall haue for his laubouris of euerie pece of claith stampit be him as said is tua penneis allanerlie, and that na littister deliner furth of thair hous ony claith littit be thame bot merkit with thair awin merk, vnder the pane of viij s., to be distributtit in maner aboue writtin, sa oft as he faillis but favouris, . . . . . And forder that na maner of man nor woman within this burgh tak vpoun thame the occupationn of litting bot sic as be burgessis and fremen, and befoir thair admissioun that thai mak thair assay of colouris and deliuer the samin to the prouest baillies and counsale of this burgh, and thai to call in befoir thaim the honest nichtbouris with the saidis oursear and tak their jugement of the wordynes of the said assay geuar and of the justnes of the coloure, vnder the pane of banesing of the toun. |

8 *November* 1564.

| | |
|---|---|
| Anent burgessis. | The prouest baillies, dene of gild, and counsale and dekynnis, for certane canssis and considerationnis moving thame, statutis and ordanis that fra this day furth all sic personis as sal happin to be maid burges and fremen of this burgh pay to the dene of gild present and for the tyme the somme of tuentie pound for thair said burgeschip allanerlie, and for thair gildrie the somme of fouretie pound; and this act to indure without preiudice of the richtis granttit to burges barnis contenit in the actis maid of befoir. And siclike concerning prenteissis quhilkis hes bene or sall happin to be heirefter prenteis and bound seruand to merchand or fre craftisman in tymes bigane or to cum, nocht burges barnis, for the space of sevin or five yeiris at the leist, thai to pay for thair burgeschip five pound allanerlie, and for thair gildrie, being wordie thairfoir, ten pound allanerlie, the clerkis dewitie except; providing the saidis prentissis bring with thame the testificatioun of thair maister quhome thai seruit for the said tyme, togidder with thair part of the indentour maid betuix thame and thair said maister, and witnes to approve thair seruice all the tyme thairin contenit befoir the prouest or baillies as said is, and vtherwayis nocht to be resaueit nor admittit. |

### 17 November 1564.

In the actioun and caus intentit be Dauid Somer, procuratour fiscall for the gude toun, aganis Herbert Maxuell tuiching thair passage of xxiij fute braid ledand fra the new well to the Kirk of Feild port, comperit the said Herbert, in presens of the prouest baillies and counsale foresaid, and granttit that be the space of [*blank*] yeris past thair hes bene ane continuall and commoun passage of the breid abone mentiouu ledand fra the new well to the Kirk of Feild port betuix his duelling hous and his vther land now bigand, quhilk confessioun the prouest baillies and counsale forsaid acceptit of; [and they ordained Maxwell to remove the stairs and other buildings which he had erected within the passage.]

*Villa, Maxwell, passage.*

### 25 November 1564.

[The provost bailies and council ordained the dean of guild] to caus big vp and mend the sloppis of the over kirk yaird dike; siclike to close and big vp the south kirk dur entering throuch the said kirk yaird be the Halye Blude He quhilk seruis of na thing at this present bot for ane commoun closit, continuewallie fylit be the wikit; and to mak the entre at the litill dur in Sanct Anthonis He; and siclike to big ane sufficient stane wall fra the eist part of the said south kirk dur direct south to the vther stane wall besyde the sang scule, for stopping of the peple till do thair besynes in sicht of the lordis of sessioun and vther inconvenienttis knawin to the baillies and counsale foresaid.

*Kirk yairde, precept, gyld.*

### 28 November 1564.

[The provost bailies and council,] efter consideratioun and avisement had with the supplicatioun producit before thame be Dauid Somer and the remanent nychtbouris having thair landis and habitationis on lnyth sydis the Quenis hie streit of this burgh be eist the nether tron, bering that be the space of fyve yeris syne or thairby the prouest baillies and counsale for the tyme, vpoun consideratioun of the thraing of mercattis abone the ovir tolbuth, and that the passege vpoun all mercat dayis is sa stoppit be confluence of peple that nane may pas by ane vther, as alsua vpoun consideratioun that the saidis landis and foretenementis be eist Nudryis Wynde ar

*Hyde, woll, skyn merket.*

Hyde, woll, skyn merket.

almaist desolait and nocht inhabitit, beand the farest and braidest pairt of this toun, for laik of merkattis and resort of peple thairto, statute and ordanit that in all tymes cuming thair be merkettis of hyde woll and skyn sould be placyt beneth the said tron in the maist convenient place of the said streit, like as the samyn wes be the space of (*blank*) nixt thairefter quhill be the way and procurment of certane particular personis having thair landis abone the tolbuth the samyn wes drawin away contrair the tenour of the said statute, and to the greit hurt of the nychtbouris foresaid, doun halding of thair waist and brynt landis in tha pairttis, and to the greit hurt of the heritouris thairof, aganis the policie and commoun weill of the hale toun; quhairfor the nychtbouris foresaidis maist humlie requyrit my lord provest baillies and counsale before mentionat, conforme to the said auld statute, to statute of new that the said merkettis of hyde woll and skyn be restorit reponit and brocht agane to the auld place beneth the said nether tron, and thairto be placet all merket dayis in all tymes cuming, vpoun sic panys as thair wysdomes sould think expedient. Quhilk supplicatioun and desyre thairof the provest baillies and counsale foresaid thocht maist ressonabill, and thairfor ratifeit approvit and of new confirmyt the said auld statute in all poyntis, and ordanis vpoun the fyrst merket day that proclamatioun and intimatioun be maid thairof at the over trone and vther places neidfull, sua that nane sall pretend ignorance nor excuse, chargeing the saidis mercattis to be transporttit with all deligence beneth the nether tron as said is, and thair to remane all merkat dayis and na vther place, vnder the pane of escheting of the guddis that in vther places salbe apprehendit, to be applyit to the commoun warkis but favouris, and heirvpoun the said Dauid Somer and remanent nychtbouris askit instrumentis.

### 29 *November* 1564.

Sculemaister.

[The bailies and council, having considered a supplication of "maister William Robertoun, maister of the hie scole," desiring payment of the school mail and his pension for certain years past, found, in respect of the decreet pronounced on 3d October 1562, "that thay ar nocht detbund to the said maister in ony fe or dewtie, scule maile or pentioun, sen the dait of the said decreit."]

[The treasurer ordained to "mak gude and thankfull payment to Robert *Precept, thesaurer.*
Mowbray of Johnne Knokis hous maill induring the tyme of his ollice, as vther
thesauraris hes done of before."]

The provest baillies and counsale foresaid ordanis proclamatioun to *Bowetts.*
[be] maid chargeing all nychtbouris having thair duelling vpoun fore
stairis on the hie stretis and oppin vennellis to hing bowettis, induring this
tyme of wynter, fra v houris at evin quhill ix houris of the samyn, ilk
persoun vnder the pane of viij s.

### 30 *November* 1564.

The provest, baillies, dene of gild, thesaurer and counsale, ordanis *Mynistery.*
Robert Kar, Alexander Clerk, James Lowrye and James Nichole, to travell
amangis the faythful for collecting of the ministeris stepend, and to report
ansuer to the counsale.

### 12 *December* 1564.

[Burdeaux wine not to be bought of a higher price than £36 per tun, and the *Prices of wynis*
same to be sold for 1s. 4d. the pint.] *fra Burdeou.*

### 25 *December* 1564.

The provest baillies counsale and hale dekynnis being convenet *Regina. Pure.*
within the counsall hous of this burgh for taking of ordoure for sustentatioun of the ministeris and pure within this burgh, comperit Adame
Fowlertoun, ane of the burgessis of the samin, and producit the Quenis
Maiesteis writting, vnder hir hienes seill and hir subscriptioun manuall,
quhairof the tenour followis:—MARIE, be the grace of God, Quene of
Scottis: To oure louittis (*blank*) messinger, oure scherefis in that pairt,
conjunctlie and seueralie specialie constitute, greting. Forsamekill as,
vpoun the supplicatioun presentit to ws be the provest and baillies of oure
burgh of Edinburgh in favouris of the pure of our said burgh, quhais
nowmer daylie incressit, we ordanit the saidis provest and baillies to tak
ordour with all and sundrie the inhabitanttis of our said burgh for support
and releif of the said pure; and albeit thai lang maist earneastlie travaillit

Regina. Pure. be all gude persuasionis to moue the harttis of the saidis inhabitanttis to gif of thair abounndance efter thair awin plesour to the help of the pure, yit the maist pairt of them, laiking all pietie and commiseratioun, hes refusit hithertellis to gif ony pairt or portioun of thair gudis to the support of the said pure and sustentatioun of sic as lanbouris in the publict seruice of the kirk, quhilkis presentlie ar chargeabill to ane few nowmer; quhairthrow, seing na thing to tak effect in thai behalfis without oure autorite be interponit thairto: Oure will is heirfoir, and we charge you straitlie and commandis, that incontinent thir oure letteres sene, ye pas and in our name and autorite command and charge the saidis prouest and baillies of oure said burgh that thai, with all gudlie diligence efter the said charge, convene all and sindrie inhabitantis of oure burgh foirsaid without exceptioun, and thair taxt euerie persoun at thair discretioun according to thair abilitie quhat thai sall pay to the releif of the saidis pure and bering of the commoun chargeis of the kirk; and, the said taxatioun beand maid, that the said prouest and baillies caus and compell the personis to be taxt be thame as said is to mak thankfull payment euerie man efferand to the rait and quantitie as thai salbe taxt; and gif neid be that thai poind and distrenye thairfor, sua that the crying of the pure may be stancheit and the wraith of God appeasit, as ye will ansuer to ws thairupoun: The quhilk to do we commit to you coniunctlie and seueralie our full powar be thir our letteres, deliuering thame be yow dewlie execute and indorsit agane to this berar. Gevin under our signet and subscriuit with our hand, at Edinburgh, the xx day of December and of our regnne the xxij yeir. Sic subscribitur: MARIE, R. Quhilk writing beand red, the said Adame desirit the samin to be insert and registrat in the counsall buikis of the said burgh, askit instrumentis vpoun the productioun and deliuering of the samin, and protestit that incaice the said prouest and baillies did nocht execute the saidis letteres in all pointtis that thai wer nocht offendit gif he complenit to the Quenis Maieste and lordis of hir secreit counsale of thair negligence and sleuth.

2 *January* 1564-5.

Craftis, kirk, pure.
The prouest, baillies, and counsale and hale dekynnis, being convenit

within the counsalhous of this burgh, comperit Jhonn Purves, dekin of the Craftis, kirk, talyeouris, and for him self and remanent of the haile craftis oblist him and pure. thame to sustene the haile pure of all occupatiounis within this burgh, sic as craftismen, craftismenis wyflis, seruandis and wedois, vpoun thair awin proper chargeis fra this day furth, sua that the gude toun nor nane resortand thairto salbe trublit with thair purys; and siclike, quhatsumeuer ordour salbe found gude be the prouest baillies and counsale forsaid for sustenyng of the ministerris, that they sall glaidlie heyr and deburse thair ressonabill pairt thairof at thair sychtis; and heirfor requeistit the said prouest baillies and counsale to be myndeful of the saidis ministeris and pure and in case thay wanttit thair ressonable charges that na falt war input to thame heirefter.

The prouest baillies and counsale ordanis maister Robert Glen, Regina, prothesaurer, to pas to Leyth and serche and seik quhair best wynis may pyne. be gottin, and by thre tunnys thairof to be gevin to the Quenys Maiestie, quhateuir the samyn cost.

### 6 January 1564-5.

[The provost, bailies, council and deacons of crafts], all in ane voce, Taxt, pure. consenttis granttis and ordanis that the haill inhabitantis of this burgh be set to certane particulare sowmes be the prouest baillies and counsale, and the samyn to be vpliftit and inbrocht quarterlie, to be distributit for sustenyng of the pure and sic as laubouris in publict seruice of the kirk, and till indure quhill vther remeid may be prouidit.

The prouest baillies and counsale, at the requeist of Alexander Burgen. Guthre, commoun clerk, resauis Richert [blank], Inglisman, arrow makar, thair burges, to gyf him occatioun to remane in the toun for instructing vtheris his occupatioun.

### 17 January 1564-5.

In presens of the prouest baillies and counsale, comperit maister Villa Rober-William Robertoun, maister of the hie seule, and producit the copye of the toun.

Villa, Robertoun.

Quenis Maiesteis writingis, chargeing the provest baillies and counsale to pay to him his yeirlie feis conforme to his gyft and askit instrumentis of the productioun thairof, and siclike my lord provest askit instrumentis that he for himself the baillies and hale counsale requyrit the said maister William to deliuer the principale writingis subscriuit be the Quenis Maiesteis hand to remane with thame, becaus the samyn wes direct to thame and sould be in thair keping, quhilk the said maister William refusit.

### 24 January 1564-5.

Villa, Cok.

[The provost, bailies and council, " induring thair willis, settis and disponis to Thomas Cok, thair officer in Leyth, thair litill new bigit hous vpoun the wallis of the toun at the North Loch," for three merks of yearly mail, and that in consideration of his long service in the town's affairs, and of the discharge of a sum of money due to him.]

Flesh, lentrone.

The provest baillies and counsale ordanis proclamatioun to be maid be sound of bell throuch all pairttis of this toun that na flesche be eittin, nor be the commoun cukis graithit nor sauld, be ony maner of persoun, to na persoun within this burgh, vpoun Fryday and Setterday throuch all the yeir, nor in na tyme of lentren, vnder the pane of xl s. sa oft as thay fale, to be applyit to the commoun warkis, and this without preiudice of the panis contenit in the Quenis Maiesteis actis anent eiting of flesche.

Officiaris sermond.

The provest baillies and counsale foresaid ordanis in all tymes cuming vpoun Soundayis and vther preiching dayis, induring all the tyme of the sarmont, tua of the officeris await at the kirk dur for stopping of the clamour of the pure, tua vpoun the calsay, and the remanent within the kirk for ordering and keiping of the samyn quyet, vnder pane of depriuation of thair offices.

### 3 February 1564-5.

Precept, Maccartney.

The baillies and counsall ordanis maister Robert Glen, thesaurer, to ressaue fra Williame Makcartnay his tua handit suord to be vsit for ane

heiding suord, becaus the auld suord is failyeit, and to gif him five pound **Precept, Mak cartney.**
thairfor.

### 7 *February* 1564-5.

The prouest, baillies, and counsale ordanis this ordour to be obseruit **Ordour in the counsalhous.** in all tymes cumming within the counsalhous the tyme of thair conventionis:—In the fyrst, the prouest and the foure baillies to syt vpoun the snittis abone the rest, nixt vnder thame the dene of gild and thesaurer of the present yeir, nixt thame the dene of gild thesaurer and baillies of the yeir before, and sua furth the remanent merchanttis of the counsale being placit, than the tua craftismen of the counsale; and that na man speik bot ane at anys havand licence thairto of the prouest and baillies before thai speik, vnder the pane of xviij d. to the pure sa oft as thay do in the contrar.

### 21 *February* 1564-5.

[The bailies, council, and deacons of crafts,] all in ane voce, consentis **Pure.** and of new ratifeis and apprevis the ordinance maid in Januar last for sustenying of the pure in all poyuttis, and exhorttis the juges to put the samyn to executioun.

### 2 *March* 1564-5.

The prouest ordanis the baillies to compris the poyndis takin be thame **Prouest baillies.** for sustenyng of the pure this efter nonc and mak penny thairof according to the taxt rollis and deliuer the samyn to the dekynnis to be gevin to the said pure, failling thairof ordanis the officeris to poynd the saidis baillies radiest guddis and mak penny of the samyn incontinent without delay.

### 30 *April* 1565.

It being vnderstand be the prouest baillies and counsale that the **Prouest, Striueling.** Quenis Maiestie wes hielic movit aganis certane principale nychtbouris of this toun vpoun the vniust report maid to hir hienes of the striking and casting of eggis at Sir James Tarbot, preist, apprehendit saying mes in the Cowgait, etc.; for remeid heirof ordanis my lord prouest with tua of the

Prouest, Striueling.

baillies and vtheris nychtbouris, to the nowmer of xl personis, ryde to Strineling to the Quenis grace for metigating of hir Maiestie. And for paying of his and thair chargeis Dauid Kinloch, fyrmorar of the commoun mylnis, now in absence of the thesaurer, to deliuer to Thomas Cok the somme of fiftye pundis quhilk salbe allowit in his compttis.

11 *May* 1565.

Regina. Villa, maister, schole.

The prouest baillies and counsale foresaid ordanis the Quenis Maiesteis writingis vnderwrittin to be registrat in this buke, of the quhilk the tenonr followis :—Prouest and baillies of oure burgh of Edinburgh, greting. Forsamekle as it is humlie menit and schewin to ws be oure louit maister William Robertoun, maister of the grammer scole of the said burgh, that quhair he is lauchfulle pronidit be the abbot of Hallirudhous and convent of the samyn, quha hes the gyft of it, to the said maisterschip of the said grammer scole, for all the dayis of his lyfe, and he vertew thairof he hes bene in peciable possessioun of the vsing of the samyn thir auchtene yeris bipast, without ony interruptioun maid to him be ony persoun, neuirtheles ye, for quhat caussis we knaw nocht, dalie cummerris trublis and molestis the said maister William in the vsing of the said office of maisterschip of the grammer scole foresaid, intending to put ane vther in his place, contrair oure expres mynd and will ; Quhairfor we discharge yow the said prouest and baillies of oure burgh, your officiaris and ilk ane of yow, of all calling intromitting handling or removing of the said maister William fra his said office of maisterschip in ony tyme to cum efter the dait heirof, bot that ye thole him peciablie bruke and joyse the samyn during his lyfetyme, conforme to his said pronisioun, and of your offices in that pairt, be thir oure presentis. Subscrinit with oure hand, at Edinburgh, the xxvij day of Februar the yeir of God j$_m$ v$^e$ lxiij yeris, and of our regnne the xxij yeir. Prouest baillies and counsale of oure burgh of Edinburgh. We greit yow weill. Forsamekle as we ar informyt ye ar addettit to oure louit maister William Robertsoun, maister of your grammer scole, in the sowme of twenty merkis of yeirlie fee to be payit to him euerilk yeir be your thesaurer, as ane act of your bukis maid to him in the xlviij yeir of God proporttis, and siclike that ye ar haldin be vtheris your actis, vse and consuetude obseruit in all tymes bypast be yow and your predecessouris, Regina. Villa, to furnys yeirlie ane sufficient scolehous within oure said burgh, and to maister, schole. pay the male thairof euerilk yeir, conforme to the quhilk ye haue [euerie] yeir sen the first entres of the said maister William to the scole foresaid maid payment to him of the said sowme of xx merkis as for his fe foresaid, and rychtsua hes payit euerye yeir sensyne xx merkis as for the male of the said scolehous quhill the Feist of Witsounday last bipast, sen the quhilk Feist ye haue maid na payment to him, nowther of his fe foresaid nor yet of his scolehous maile, bot haldis the samyn fra him to his greit hurt and expres aganis all equite and ressoun considering he applyis himself to nane vther vocatioun bot to the instructing of your bairnys and vpbringing of thame in virteu: Oure will is heirfor and we charge yow that ye answer the said maister William and mak payment to him of the saidis sowmes restand awand to him be yow fore the caussis foresaid of all yeiris bigane and rychtsua in tymes cuming yeirlie during his prouisioun maid to him of his said seruice, conforme to your actis and consuetudis foresaidis, as ye will answer to ws vpoun your dewtie, quhairthrow that we heir na forther complaynt heirupoun. Subscrinit with oure hand, at Edinburgh, the xx day of December the yeir of God j$^m$ v$^c$ lxiiij yeris. Conforme to the quhilkis writing the prouest baillies and counsale foresaid ordanis maister Robert Glen, thesaurer, to mak gude and thankfull payment to the said maister William of his feis of all termes bigane restand awand him and siclike of the scole males, and the samyn salbe allowit in his compttis.

### 12 *May* 1565.

The prouest baillies and counsale ordanis Jhonn Sym, baillie, maister Precept, Jhonn Spens of the counsale, and Alexander King, aduocat, to pas to the thesaurer. Quenis Maiestie in Striueling for ressonyng aganis maister James Lindesay, Halbert Maxuell, Jhonn Spottiswod and maister Alexander Skene, tuiching the contributioun to the pure, and ordanis the thesaurer to gyf to thame the sowme of [blank] for thair expenssis, and to the said Alexander King the sowme of sex pundis for his panys.

### 31 *May* 1565.

Barroun, Spons.

The baillies and counsale ordanis maister Jhonn Spens and James Barronn to pas to the conventioun to be haldin in Pairth and thair to treit in the caussis of the kirk and commounweill of this burgh.

### 22 *June* 1565.

Wine.

[Proclamation to be made "throuch the toun be sound of bell" that wine shall not be sold dearer than 1s. 2d. the pint.]

### 30 *June* 1565.

[Armour, parliament.]

The counsale ordanis the baillies and officeris to pas to all duelling houssis within this burgh and se that everye fensable persoun, inhabiter of the samyn, be sufficientlie prouidit with armour and wappinnis for seruing of our Souerane at this present parliament, and to caus the officeris of everye quarter put the names of the saidis inhabitaris with thair wappinnis in roll with deligence and present the samyn before the counsale.

### 3 *August* 1565.

Somer, villa.

The baillies, thesaurer, dene of guild [and council,] seing that maister Robert Glen, thesaurer, is nocht of mynd to compleit the toun wall of Leyth Wynde, nochtwithstanding that he hane bene oft and diuers tymes chairgit thairto of before, ordanis all in ane voce that Dauid Somer, maister wark, caus big and compleit the said wall with all deligence.

### 4 *August* 1565.

Extent.

Protestio, Purves.

The baillies, dene of gild and counsale, vnderstanding proclamatioun allrady maid chargeing all maner of man to pas fordward with the King and Quenys Maiesteis in the persute of the erle of Murray and his colleges, and that thay ar subiect be the said proclamatioun to pas with thame, the dyet being lang and the jornay tedious, consentits and granttis that ane vniuersale extent, bayth of merchant and craftisman, be vpliftit and gadderit for rasing and furnessing of ij$^c$ men of weir for ane moneth to pas fordward with thair hienessis in the said jornay. And Allane Purves for him

self, and in name of the haill dekynnis, dissasenttis and protestit that he Protestatio,
nor the saidis dekynnis be na forther subiect nor to the fyft pairt of the Purves.
said extent, conforme to the auld vse and consuetude euir obseruit in
sic caussis.

23 *August* 1565.

The prouest, Archibald Douglas of Kilspindie, [the bailies, council Deprivatio
and deacons of crafts,] beand convenit in the nether counsall hous of this prepositi.
burgh, comperit George Drowmonnd, seruand to my lord of Athole, and
producit the King and Quenis Maisteis writting, of the quhilk the tennour
followis: Rex et Regina. Baillies, counsall, and communitie of oure
burgh of Edinburgh. We greit yow weill. It is oure will, and for diuers
ressonabill caussis and considerationnis moving ws we charge and command
yow, that ye depois and displace the present prouest of oure said burgh,
and in his place that ye elect ressaue and admit oure louit Symoun
Prestoun of that ilk [as] prouest thairof, and radelie ansuer and obey him in
all thingis belanging and appertening the said office as appertenis, as ye will
ansuer to ws thairuponn. Subscriuit with oure hand, at Edinburgh, the
[*blank*] day of August, and of our regnnis the first and tuentie thre yeirs.
The quhilk writing beand red in presens of the prouest baillies counsall
and haill dekynnis foirsaid, the said prouest, of his fre will, resignit and gaif
our in thair handis his said office of prouestrie, and of his fre will dischargeit himself thairof and all that mycht appertene thairto, craifing instrumenttis and documentis that nowther the King nor Quenis Maisteis had
ony just caus of offence to imput to his charge quhairfoir he sould be
deposit ; and further desirit of the saidis baillies counsall and dekynnis gif
ony of thame micht wordalie burdene him with ony sic wrang done
be him the tyme of his office past as micht merit the pvneisment of
depravationn befoir the laufull terme, quha all in ane voce declairit
thai had no falt to lay to his charge, and gif it micht pleis the King
and Quenis Maiesties it wer thair plesoure that he sould jois the
said office quhill Michelmes nixt, quhairapoun he askit instrumenttis
as of befoir and that he obeyit the Quenis Maisteis writting, and sua
removit himself.

Baillies direct to the King and Quene.

The baillies, counsall, and dekynnis foirsaid, ordanis Johne Sym, Dauid Forester and Allane Dikesoun, baillies, maister Robert Glen, thesaurer, James Nicholl and William Fowlar of the counsall, this eftir [none] to pas to the King and Quenis Maiesties desiring to be hard of thame tuiching the dischargeing of Johne Knox, minister, of forder preiching, the deposing of Archebald Douglas, prouest, and to desire licence to remane at hame fra the armie ordanit to convene in this toun the xxv of August instant, and frathine to pas fordward for the persute of the erle of Morray and his complices, and to report thair ansuer the morne.

Woittis concernyng the minister.

The samin day, eftirnone, the baillies counsall and dekynnis foirsaid, being convenit in the counsalhous, efter lang ressoning vpoun the dischargeing of Johne Knox, minister, of forder preiching, induring the King and Quenis Maiesteis being in this toun, all in ane woce concludis and deliueris that thai will in maner of way consent or grant that his mouth be closit or he dischargeit in preiching the trew word, and thairfoir willit him at his plesour, as God sould move his hart, to proceid fordwart in trew doctrine as he hes bene of befoir, quhilk doctrine thai wald approve and abide at to thair lifis end.

*24 August 1565.*

Spens, aduocat.

In presens of the baillies and counsall foirsaid, comperit maister Johne Spens of Condie, aduocat for the King and Quenis Maiesteis, and in thair namis desirit the laird of Craigmiller to be electit prouest conforme to hir hienes writting send with George Drowmound, to the quhilk desire it wes answerit that gyf thai electit befoir the Feist of Michelmes ony maiestrat it micht appear to be preiudiciall to the act of parliament statut for electing of officeris within burgh, and thai abill to incur danger thairthrow, nochtwithstanding thai knawing to be the King and Quenis Maiesteis willis and plesoure thai wald except the said laird of Craigmiller in the office of pronestrie quhill Michaelmes nixt and obey and serue him according to the desire of the said writting, and the said maister Johne Spens askit instrumentis.

The samyn day, Symoun Prestoun of that ilk is maid burges and gild Craigmillar, broder, accepttit and admittit prouest to the Feist of Michaelmes nixt, and prepositus. hes gevin his aith for trew ministratioun of justice, and forder in *communi forma*.

The prouest baillies and counsall granttis and consenttis that ane Extent of jᵐ extent of jᵐ li. be vpliftit of all the inhabitantis of this burgh, and gevin li. for licence [to] remane and bide at hame fra this hoist and armie ordanit to convene at Edinburgh the xxv day of August instant and fra thine to pass fordwart for the persute of the erle of Murray.

Comperit James Johnestoun of Kellebankis and producit the King Regina. and Quenis Maiesteis writting, of the quhilk the tennour followis: Rex Matrell. et Regina. Prouest and baillies of oure burgh of Edinburgh: We greit yow weill. Forsamekill as we ar informit that ye haue detenit and haldin within the tolbuith of oure said burgh Gratran Materall, Frencheman, this lang tyme bigane, at the instance of ane Inglisman for ane allegit cryme committit be him, albeit we are surelie persuadit that he can haue na just actioun thairfoir aganis him bot onlie haldis him in cummer tending to put him to outtar pouertie and rewyne: Oure will is herfoir, and we charge yow that ye put the said Gratran to libertie and fredome furth of the said tolbuith and suffer him depart quhar he pleissis and mak na forder molestatioun nor troubill to him his cautioneris and sonerteis for the cryme foirsaid in tyme cuming, nochtwithstanding ony charge gevin or to be gevin in the contrair heirof, as ye will answer to ws heirupoun. Sub- scriuit with oure handis at [*blank*,] the [*blank*] day of August the yeir of God jᵐ vᶜ lxv yeiris. *Et sic subscribitur*: MARIE, R. HENRIE, R. Quhilk writing, beand red, the prouest baillies and counsall foirsaid ordanit to bo registrat, and the said Gratran to be put to libertie.

### 25 *August* 1565.

The quhilk day, it beand appointtit with my lord the erle of Atholl Ane annuell of that the gude toun sall haue licence to remane at hame fra the hoist and the mylnis.

Ane annuell of the mylnis.

armie abone mentionat, thai deliuering incontinent the soume of ane thousand pound to Capitane Robert Lauder for payment of his men of weir quha man depart the morne with the King and Quenis Maieste, vtherwayis to depart thame selfis, quhilk beand reporttit to the prouest baillies counsall and haill dekynnis thai, willing to do the King and Quenis Maiesteis plesour in this behalf, as alswa for the eschewing of the jurnay, ordanis euerie ane of the counsall to avance xx li. incontinent, the fermes of the commoun mylnis to be inbroucht, and the craftis to deburs thair pairt of the said extent of ane thousand pound, quhilk is ij$^c$ li. ; and becaus na forder money can be gottin at this present thai haue borrowit and borrowis fra oure weilbeluifit nichtbour Alexander Guthre, thair commoun clerk, the soume of foure hundreth merkis and xx li., [and failing payment within twenty days ordained an annual rent of forty merks to be paid him furth of the common mills.]

26 *August* 1565.

Dispensatioun fra the army.

The prouest baillies and counsall ordanis Allane Dikesoun, baillie, maister Robert Glen, thesaurer, and Alexander Guthre, commoun clerk, to pas to the King and Quenis Maiesteis for obtening of the licence for remaning fra the armie abone mentionat quhilk thai obtenit, quhairof the tenour followis: Rex et Regina. We, for certane caussis and consideratiounis moving ws, as alsua vpoun respect of the gude will gratitudis and plesouris offerrit and done to ws at this present be oure louittis the prouest baillies counsall and communitie of oure burgh of Edinburgh, granttis and gevis licence to the saidis prouest baillies counsall communitie and haill inhabitanttis of oure said burgh to remane and bide at hame fra this oure hoist, armie, gadderering, assemblie or conventiounis, ordanit be oure proclamatioun to assembill and convene in oure said burgh the xxv day of August instant and fra thine to pas fordwart and defend ws be the space of xv dayis, providit in feir of weir, eftir thair cumming; commanding heirfoir and alsua dischargeing all and sindrie oure justiceis, justice clerkis, and thair deputtis, oure thesaureris, comptrollaris, scherefis, and all vtheris oure officeris, of all calling, proceiding, arreisting, poinding, vnlawing, troubling, or molesting of the said prouest, baillies, counsall and communitie, inhabitanttis foirsaid, or ony ane of thame, for thair remaning Dispensatioun and biding at hame fra the said hoist armie assemblie or conventioun, fra the army. nochtwithstanding ony oure proclamationnis or chargeis past thairapoun of befoir, dischargeing thame of thair officeis in this part be this present. Subscriuit with oure handis, at oure palice of Halicrudehous, this xxvj day the moneth of August the yeir of God j$^m$ v$^c$ thre scoir fyve yeiris, and of oure regnnis the first and tuentie thre yeiris. *Et sic subscribitur:* MARIE, R. HENRIE, R.

REX ET REGINA. Prouest and baillies of oure burgh of Edinburgh. Payment of We command and charge yow that, incontinent without all delay or sitioun. without continuatioun, ye caus ansuer obey and deliuer to Capitane Robert Lauder the sonne of ane thousand pound granttit be yow for remaning at hame fra oure armie ordanit to convene with ws in the said burgh the xxv day of August instant, qnhais discharge and acquittance salbe als sufficient to yow as ony vtheris that may be requirit, and gif neid be for the mair haistie expeditioun heirof that ye vse quhatsumener ordoure, be wairding or poinding apoun quhatsumener inhabitant within the said burgh, without exceptioun of persoun, that salhappin to be taxt be yow for payment of the samin according for thair parttis for youre releif, as ye will ansuer to ws, be thir presentis. Subscriuit, [at Holyrood Palace, 26 August 1565,] MARIE. R. HENRIE. R.

Followis the copy of the principale instructionis and ordinances gevin be the King and Quenis Maiesteis to my lordis president, clerk of Register, and remanent lordis specifcit in the saidis instructionis:—

Item, thay sall command ane continuall wache to be had and keipit in Edinburgh, alsweill on the day as nycht, bot the nycht wache to be maist stark, and attend that na thing be permyttit to pas furth of the said toun be the quhilk thair inymeis or rebellis may be aydit, nor that na personis resort within the toun quhilk ar suspect without apprehensioun and knaulege to be taikin of thair cuming or depairting. *Sic subscribitur. Ita est.* PETRUS HOWART, notarius, de mandato dictorum dominorum, testantibus meis signo et subscriptione manualibus.

### 28 August 1565.

**Wache.** The proucst baillies and counsale, according to the ordinance aboue writtin, ordanis that nychtlie thair be ane wache of xxxij personis, begynand first at the northwest quarter, to be set in maner following, viz., vj at the brokin wall in Leyth Wynde, iiij at the Gray Freir port, foure at the West port, foure at the Kirk of Feild port, tua at tha Cowgait port, tua at the Nether bow, and the remanent x to be movand throuch all the stretis veseand the vtheris set at the porttis, and to be vnder the charge of ane of the officiaris and sum honest man of the quarter for that nycht, becaus the baillies may nocht walk euerye nycht; and siclik, on the day the hale porttis to be closit except the Gray Freir port, West port and Nether bow, and at all the day quhill the nycht wache agane thare be thre men at the Nether bow, thre at the West port, and tua at the Kirk of Feild in armour and wappinnis.

### 3 September 1565.

**Instructionis.** Followis the copie of the instructiounis presentit this day in judgement be the proucst, subscrinit be the King and Quenis Maiesteis handis, and direct to the said proucst and baillies of this burgh :—

In the first, thair Maiesteis marvellis greitlie how thair rebellis, assisteris and partakkaris, hes laitlie enterit and bene ressauit within thair toun as it apperis be thair negligence or than onrsicht, in respect of the directiounis and prouisiounis left with thame afoir thair Maiesteis departing laitlie, and als in respect of particular writtingis send to the proucst and counsall to that effect, quhairfoir it is thair Maiesteis willis that better heid be taikin in tymes cumming in maner following, assuriug thame gif thai be found negligent thairintill it sall be laid to thair charge as parttakkaris with the saidis rebellis :—

In the first, That the proucst baillies and counsall assembill the haill toun and caus thame quarterlie devide the samin in foure parttis, sua that euerie quarter sall wache and waird for the keiping of the porttis and wallis of the toun for the space of tuentie foure houris.

*Secoundlie.* That ordour be taikin for the performing heirof that Instructioris. thair be foure principall men chosin quha sall answer for the obedience and fulfilling of this first artickle in enerie point.

*Thridlie.* That all the porttis of the said toun be steikit saif, onlie tua quhilk salbe sua keipit that na man enter within the toun except commonn traffikkaris and travellaris knawin to the keiparis thairof, and incace ony vtheris desiris to enter within the said toun that thai be presentit to the prouest and counsall appointit thair be thair Maiesteis.

*Feirdlie.* That the prouest baillies and counsall caus all necesser wiwers be answerit as thair Maiesteis counsall being thair for the tyme hes devisit.

*Fyjftlie.* That, for preseruatioun of thair Maiesteis paillice, that thai caus diligence be taikin be out wacheis in the nicht that na man cum to invaid nor molest thair palice, and incace sa be, that thai with all diligence rescouris the samin with thair haill force.

*Sextlie.* That thai gif thair vter diligence, as thai will answer to the King and Quenis Maiesteis, that na men of weir be vpliftit within thair toun to serve with the rebellis, thair parttakaris or assistaris, aganis thair Maiesteis, and that thai caus mak publict proclamatiounis thairof at the merkat croce, assuring thame that gif ony be liftit allradie or salbe in tyme to cum, thai sall answer thairfoir and be callit at particular dyattis for the samin, as fortefearis and assisteris of the saidis rebellis.

*Seuintlie.* That the prouest caus moustouris to be taikin with all gudelie diligence of the inhabitaris of the haill toun to the effect foirsaid.

*Auchtlie.* Gif thair be ony personis within the said toun that ganestandis ony of thir foirsaidis artickles that thai caus apprehend thame and put thame in ferme custodie within thair tollbuith, or caus the castell ressaue thame, as thai sall think maist expedient.

*Nyntlie.* That na powder nor munitioun be thollit to pas furth of thair said toun to ony thair Maiesteis rebellis.

*Fynallie.* Gif ony of thir foirsadis artickles be contravenit thair Maiesteis will assuritlie lay thame to thair charge with all rigour, and will haue compt thairof.

## 7 September 1565.

**King and Queen's writing.**

In presens of the baillies and counsall, comperit Symon Prestoun of Craigmiller, proueust, and producet the King and Quenis Maiesteis writting vnderwrittin, subscriuit as efter followis, and desirit the samin to be registrat and insert in the tounis buikis of this burgh for his warrand, of the quhilk the tennour followis:—Traist freind we greit yow weill. Forsamekill as we vnderstand thair is presentlie in the theifis hoill of Edinburgh ane souddart of Capitane Stewarttis companie, and ane vther lattin to cautioun to the baillies of the Cannognit, quhilk this berar will deliuer to yow, it is our will that incontinent efter the ressait heirof, for sic crymes as thai haue committit, and the berar will informe yow, ye caus thame baith be hangit to the deid; and this on na wys ye leve vndone, as ye will ansuer to ws and aschew our vtter indignatioun. Doand this ye will do ws greit plesour, for we will nocht in ony wyis that thai eschaip; and ineace ye micht feir or se ony apperance that for the hanging of thame ony vproir will be raisit aganis yow, sua that thair be dainger to haue thame reft furth of youre handis, than and in that cace we charge yow to send thame to ws surelie convoyit with all diligence; and this on na wyis ye leve vndone. Subscriuit with our handis, at Kilsyth, the saxt of September 1565. *Et sic subscrbitur:* MARIE, R. HENRIE, R.

## 12 September 1565.

**Villa, Maioribankis.**

The prouest baillies dene of gild [and council,] efter consideratioun of the gude and thankfull seruice maid be Michaell Marioribank in the sessioun and kirk of God within this burgh, in writing of all thair actis statutis and ordinances, ordanis the said Mychaell to haue of yeirlie stipend and fee the sowme of fourtye pundis, and to be payit him quertelie of the common contributioun.

## 17 September 1565.

**Extent jᵐ li.**

The prouest baillies and counsale granttis and consenttis that ane generale extent of ane thousand pundis be vpliftit of the hale nychtbouris, Extent jm li. for licence to remane and abide at hame fra our Soueranis oistis and armye ordanit to convene the first of October to pas fordwert vpoun the rebellis, etc., to Dumfreis.

### 26 September 1565.

The prouest baillies and counsale and dekynnis, being convenit in Rex, Regina. the counsale hous, comperit maister Robert Creychtoun of Eliott, aduocat to the King and Quenis Maiesteis, and producit thair hienes writting, of the quhilk the tennour followis: Prouest, baillies and counsall of Edinburgh we greit yow weill. Forsamekill as we vnderstand that ye are to cheis yowr new counsall this day, for certane caussis and consideratiounis moving ws, for the weill eis and commoditie of our said burgh foirsene be ws, it is our will and we command yow that ye cheis nominat and woit to be of your counsall Eduard Littill, Duncane Levingstoun, James Curle for the merchandis, Michaell Gilbert and Archibald Leich, furrour, for the craftis, and apoun Friday nixt to cum, according to your auld accustomit vse, put in littis to be your baillies maister Johne Prestoun, Johne Sym, maister Johne Spens and James Nicholl, to be youre dene of gild James Carmichaell, to be youre thesaurer Luce Wilsoun; and apoun Tuysday nixt tocum that ye, togidder with the dekynnis of craftis, cheis woit and elect the saidis personis to be your baillies, thesaurer, and dene of gild as said is; nochtwithstanding this oure charge salbe na wayis hurtfull to youre auld priuelagis in tyme cuming, and this ye faill nocht to do as maist acceptabill seruice vnto ws. Subscriuit with our handis, at our palice of Halierudehous, the (*blank*) day of (*blank*) 1565. *Sic subscribitur:* MARIE, R. HENRIE, R.

### 28 September 1565.

The prouest baillies and counsale, being desyrit of the King and x^m merkis Quenys Maiesteis to avance and len to thair hienessis the sowme of fyve lent vpoun Leyth. thousand pundis vpoun plegis and writtis, efter lang avisement fyndis and deliueris that thair salbe borrowit and vpliftit of the hale inhabittantis of this burgh the sowme of ten thousand merkis to be lent to thair hienes,

| | |
|---|---|
| x<sup>m</sup> merkis lent vpoun Leyth. | haifand for securite of payment agane infeftment of the superiorite of Leyth, and becaus the said sowmes mon be refoundit agane be the gude toun to the lennaris, ordanis the particuler rollis to be registrat, that it may be knawin quhat euerye man hes lent. [Here follow the "Taxt Rollis."] |

12 *October* 1565.

| | |
|---|---|
| Anent annu-allis. | The proues baillies and counsall nominattis maister Johne Prestoun, Andro Stevinsoun and Dauid Somer, for the part of the merchandis, Thomas Reidpeth, Thomas Ewing and Johne Wilsoun, for the part of the craftis, to mak memoriall and put in inventour the chaplanriis, beneficis, landis, annuallis and annualrenttis, and vtheris dewiteis quhilkis pertenit to preistis, munkis, and freiris within this burgh, and to present the samin befoir thame sasone as it may be possibill. |
| Convening of the counsall, and awaitting on be the officiaris. | The proues, baillies and counsall, being convenit for ressoning vpoun the commoun effairis of this burgh, and becaus the haill nowmer of the counsall wer nocht present thai micht nocht decerne nor conclude vpoun diuers actis necessar to be maid for the commoun weill of the samin, and vnderstanding that conforme to the ordoure of this burgh vpoun ressoning and concluding of ony mater of wecht the full nowmer of the counsall sould be present, and that in defalt of thair convening on the dayis appointtit the commoun mater wes deferrit and oursene to the greit hurt of the commoun weill; for remeid of the quhilk the saidis proues baillies and counsall foirsaid ordanis that the proues baillies and counsall convene in the counsall hous of this burgh on Tewisday nixttocum at sevin houris in the mornyng, thair to remane quhill ten houris afoir none, and sua to continew daylie thairefter, the Sounday and tyme of preiching except, quhill Tewisday nixt thairefter, and that thai convene fra thine furth oulklie in the said counsall hous at ten houris befoir none ilk Wedinsday and Fryday without ony werning or the bell ceis, vnder the pane of tua schillingis to be tane of ilk persoun that failyeis and beis absent without he haue leve thairto of the proues and baillies or be furth of the toun in thair necessar besynes; and als gif it happynnis ony |

of the saidis personis to be warnit to cum to the counsall at ony vther Convening of tyme, and beis personallie apprehendit, and comperis nocht within half ane the counsall, and awaitting houre efter the tyme that thai salbe wernit, that he sall pay ij s. as said is; on be the officiaris. and gif ony persoun that failyeis in the premissis and payis nocht the said ij s., it being twyis askit and he refuis, he sall pay for his contempt and disobeydiance, v s., quhilkis siluer sall be gevin to the puiris; and that ane of the gild officeris ilk day keip the north dur outwith the samin thair tyme about and thoill nane to enter without thai be commandit, vnder the pane of pvnesching of thair personis, and the officiaris to keip the vter dur quhilk gangis to the laich tolbuith on the west part of the judgement sait of the samyn; and the saidis haill officiaris to be thair with thair halbarttis, awaiting vpoun the counsale for executioun of sic chargis as salbe appointtit thame, vnder the pane of wairding of thair personis induring the will of the prouest and baillies, without thai obtene licence thairto; and the vter north dur fornent the toure of the auld tolbuith to be lokkit and haldin fast induring the tyme of the counsall, and nane to enter or ische thairat bot the saidis prouest baillies and counsall.

### 14 *November* 1565.

The prouest baillies and counsall ordanis that the panche, pudding Panche and scheipheid merkat be transporttit to the fut of Snawdounis Clois, mercat. quhilk is the fische merkat in symer and thair to remane quhill forder ordour be taikin thairanent.

In presens of the prouest baillies and counsall, Alexander Guthre, [Delivery of common clerk, producit and delinerit to maister Johne Prestoun, dene of charters, etc.] gild, in ane buist, the charter of the superioritie of Leith vnder the greit seill, the precept of the samin vnder the quarter seill, ane reuersioun suillit and subscriuit be Johne Mathesoun of Brouchtoun and Jonet Guthre, his spous, apoun outquitting of ane annualrent of xx li. annalëit be the gude toun to thame furth of thair commoun myluis; item, mair, ane decreit purchest be maister James Quhite aganis the gude toun contenand the soume of iij<sup>c</sup> merkis, the letteris of the foure formes purchest with the samin, togidder with the said maister James acquittance apoun the said

210            EXTRACTS FROM THE RECORDS            [1565.

[Delivery of charters, etc.]   soume ; item, mair, the gift of prebendariis chaplanriis annuallis, etc., quhilk pertenit to preistis [and] freiris, heirtofoir ; all to be put in the chartour hous, and apoun the deliuering thairof the said Alexander askit documenttis.

### 15 November 1565.

Knox, minister.   The provest, baillies and counsale ordanis the sowme of fowre hundreth (*blank*) to be gevin to Jhonn Knox, minister, of the radeast of the annuellis, prebendareis, chaiplanreis, tenementis, propertcis, dewiteis, emolimentis, etc., quhilk pertenit to preistis, monkis, freris, etc., for his yeirlie stipend all the dayis of his lyfe.

### 4 December 1565.

Regina, propyne.   The prouest bailies and counsale ordanis Jhonn Westoun, thesaurer, to by for the King and Quenis Maiestie, aganc Yule, thre twn of the best new wynis with torches and prikettis efter the auld ordour.

Precept, Prouest.   The baillies and counsale, vpoun consideratioun of the greit panis taikin be my lord prouest in the townis effaris, ordanis Jhonn Westoun, thesaurer, to deliuer to his lordschip xij elnis of the best weluot in this toun, to be him ane goun, and ane twn of new wyne agane Yule.

### 14 December 1565.

Wyld melt.   [Proclamation ordained to be made to the lieges of the following prices, "to be keipit quhill Festerannis evin nixt :"—"The couple of best cvnyngis, quhite, quhill Fasterannis evin, vj s., the secundare iiij s., at discretioun of the baillies ; the pair of pertrikis, v s. ; the pair of ploverris, iij s. ; the blak cok or gray hen, ij s. ; the mwre hen, ij s. ; the greit quhawpe, xviij d.; the wyld guse, vj s. viij d.; the wyld duke, xx d.; the pair of telis, xvj d."]

Impositioun, wynis.   [Commissioners appointed to the King and Queen at Linlithgow, " to ressoun determyne and conclude tuiching the impositioun desyrit be the lordis of secreit counsale to be rasit vpoun the wynis to be grantit and gevin to thair hienessis."]

24 *December* 1565.

The provest baillies and counsale ordanis maister Thomas Makcalyeane Commis-
and maister Jhonn Prestoun to convene the morne with the generale kirk, sionaris.
in the counsalhous, and with thame to treit ressoun and conclude vpoun
the caussis of the said kirk.

[After conferring with, and taking oaths of, merchants arrived from Bourdeaux Prices wynis.
concerning the prices of wines, " fyndis the twn of wyne at this present coft as the
first bying xvj crownis of the sone, allowand for the crown efter the price in France
lij s.; summa at the first xli frankis xij sonis; item, of fraucht xvj crownis sone;
item, for vlege vj li.
Proclamation to be made charging all venters of wine not to buy wines to be sold
at higher prices than last year.]

19 *March* 1565-6.[1]

The baillies and counsall ordanis Jhone Westoun, thesaurer, to content Precept,
and pay to Jhone Sym and William Foular, baillies, the sowme of four Sym, Foular,
pundis for the expenssis maid be the saidis twa baillies, thair hors and baillies.
seruandis, in ryding to Dunbar to the King and Quenis Maiesteis, being
thair for the tyme, in this instant moneth of Merche, in effaris and commoun
besyness concernyng this burgh.

20 *March* 1565-6.

[The treasurer ordained to pay to George Gourlay, officer, forty shillings " for his Precept,
expenssis maid vpoun himself and hors in passing at the townis command in thair Gourlay.
effaris to Dunbar in this instant moneth."]

[The treasurer ordained to pay to two persons 6s. 8d. each, " for thair playing Precept,
afoir the towne be the space of thre dayis and convenyng of thame in this instant Clerk.
moneth of Merche the tyme of the perliament."]

---

[1] There are no entries in the Council Record from 11th January to this date.

Precept,
Broun.

[The treasurer ordainned to pay to "Cudbert Broun, tavernar, quha playit on the suesche the xviij day of Merche instant quhen our Soueranis come furth of Dunber to this toun, the inhabitantis thairof being assemblit to meit hir grace, the sowm of sex s. viij d."]

5 April 1566.

Admissio Chalmer.

Sir Symone Prestoun of Craigmiller, knycht, prouest of this burgh, [the bailies, dean of guild, treasurer, council and deacons of crafts,] being conuenit in the tolbuithe of this burgh, comperit maister Dauid Chalmer, ane of the lordis of our Soueranis sessioun, and presentit ane gift maid to him be our Soueranis of the commoun clerkschip of this burgh, vnder the testimoniall of thair graces greit seill, and desyrit the saidis prouest baillies and counsall to admit him and his deputis conforme to his gift, and to the profeitis and commoditeis thairof conform to his prouisioun, and als presentit letteres of our Souerane lordis of sessioun deule execute and indorsit vpoun thame quhair that wer chargit of befoir to do the samyn vnder the pane of putting of thame to the horne, and gif thai falyeit to put thame to the horne, escheit and inbring all the movabill gudis, etc., of the quhilk letteres he declarit that he had supersedit the executioun thir aucht dayis bypast hoiping tham to haue admittit him as said is, quhairof he saw bot delay albeit he had intimat his said gift to thame of befoir, quhairfor he certefeit thame he culd and wald do na les nor put thame instantle to executioun gif thai did nocht the samyn; and maister Jhoue Prestoun, dene of gild, for the haill toun and himself, and in thair names, protestit for remeid of law, and that the admissioun of the said maister Dauid to this office at this tyme preiuge nocht thair priuilegis, he ressoun thai gaif the samyn for the feir of hornyng, and protestit that thai mycht be fre quhensumeuir the samyn vakit to dispone thairvpoun at thair plesour as thai haue done in all tymes past, and allegeit the office culd nocht vaik at this present, bot at the ferrest the dewite thairof induring the tyme Alexander Guthre wes at the horne, and the said maister Dauid in the contrair; quhilkis haill baillies, dene of gild, thesaurer, counsall and dekynnis, with the haill personis aboue speecefeit, except my lord prouest (quha declarit he wald nocht voit nor ressaue him) gaif and grantit and be

thir presentis gifis and grantis to the said maister Dauid Chalmer the said  Admissio
office of commoun clerkschip, with the profeitis commoditeis and dewyteis  Chalmer.
thairof induring the tyme that it sall happin the said Alexander to be our
Soueranis rebell and at hir horne only, wnder protestatioun for remeid of
law as said is, and thairvpoun the said maister Jhone Prestoun, in name
forsaid, askit instrumentis; and the said maister Dauid Chalmer protestit
that his ressait and admissioun wes conforme to his gift presentit this day
and nocht induring the tyme of the said Alexanderis being at the horne,
and that he mycht bruke and jois the said clerkschip conforme to the
samyn in all poyntis and na vtherwayis askit instrumentis.

### 15 April 1566.

In presens of [the bailies, council and deacons of crafts,] comperit  Anent the con-
Sir Symone Prestoun of Craigmiller knycht, prouest of this burgh, and  tinuatioun of the superioritie
produceit and presentit ane writing of our Souerane Lady the Quenis  of Leith.
grace, subscryvit with hir hand and wnder hir signet, of the quhilk the
tenour followis: Prouest baillies and counsall of our burgh of Edinburgh:
We greit yow weill. Forsamekill as we wrait laitlie to yow to delay and
superseid taking possessioun and vsing the jurisdictioun of our toun of
Leithe, be ressoun throw the vrgent and wechty effaris quhilk we haue
now instantle in hand our lasour will nocht permit ws to tak ordour at
this tyme anent the outquiting of our said toun, and we can nocht bot
marvell sa obstinatly to ganestand that our reasonabill desyre and
requeist; quhairfoir it is our will and we requyre and command yow that,
incontinent efter the sycht heirof, ye prorogatt the act and obligatioun maid
anent the redemptioun and outquiting of our said toun and vsing of the
jurisdictioun yit for the space of vther sex monethis nixt efter the presenting of this our letter to yow and mak ane act thairvpoun that we be
nawayis frustrat nor disapoyntit, assuring yow gif ye faill we can nocht
stand content thairwith, bot ye will constrane ws aganis our awin will to
acquite your obstinacie accordingly. Subscryvit with our hand, at Edinburgh, the xiij day of Aprile and of our regne the first and xxiiij yeris

Anent the continuatioun of the superioritie of Leith.

1566. Quhilk wryting, beand red in all thair presens, thai ordanit the samyn to be registrat and insert in thair counsall buke, and the pryncipall to be deliuerit to maister Jhone Prestoun, dene of gild, to be had to the register hous and thair to be kepitt.

Westoun, Steivinstoun.

In presens of the counsall forsaid, Jhone Westoun, thesaurer, desyrit Andro Steivinstoun, baillie, to delyver the first supplicatioun direct to the toun be oure Soueranis for the continuatioun of ony intromissioun with the toun of Leithe quhill Sanct Lukes day nixt to the counsall to be put in register, quha refusit to geve it bot said that he suld keip it him self, quhairvpoun the said Jhone Westoun askit actis of court.

### 8 May 1566.

Presentatio, Henrysoun capellanie. Domini Quintigerni.

The prouest, baillies, counsall and dekynnis gave and grantit, and be the tenour heirof gevis and grantis, to Edwerd Hendersoun the chaiplenry callit Sanct Mungois chaiplenry foundit at the alter of the samyn situat in the paroche kirk of this burgh now vacand in thair handis be deceis of vnquhile Sir James Terbet, last chaiplane thairof, for all the dayis of the said Edwerdis lyfe, with all profeitis, oblationis, emolimentis quhatsumeuir.

Precept.

[The treasurer ordained to pay forty shillings to a locksmith "for certane lokkis furneist and coft be him to the Quenis grace lugeing the tyme hir grace wes in Robesonis innis and furneist at command of the baillies."]

### 17 May 1566.

Precept, Purves.

The prouest baillies and counsall ordanis Jhone Westoun, thesaurer, to content and pay to Alexander Purves, walx maker, ij s. vj d. for ilk pece of tua dosane and allevin torches, extending in the haill to the sowme of iiij li. vij s. vj d., furneist be him to the gude toun at thair command vpoun the ix day of Merche the yeir of God j$^m$ v$^c$ and lxv yeris, to pas to the abbay to vise the Quenis grace immediatle efter the slauchter of vmquhile Seinzeour Dauid Ricio.

OF THE BURGH OF EDINBURGH.

29 *May* 1566.

[The treasurer ordained to pay twenty-four pounds Scots "for half ane tun Precept. wyne deliuerit be him at the tounis command to Sir Symone Prestoun of Craigmiller knycht, thair prouest."]

8 *June* 1566.

[The treasurer ordained to pay to "the bedrellis of Sanct Marie Wynde the Bedrellis. sowme of x s., for the Witsounday terme in the yeir of God j$^m$ v$^c$ and lxvj, quhilk the gude toun gevis yeirly in almes to thame."]

19 *June* 1566.

[The treasurer ordained to pay to William Robertoun, master of the High Precept, School, ten merks for the Whitsunday terms mail of the school and ten merks as $^{magister}_{schole.}$ his fee for that term.]

21 *June* 1566.

The provest [bailies and council] lattis furth of ward and puttis to Dauid libertie Dauid Hoppringill, ypothecar, being input in waird at the instance $^{Hoppringillis}_{restoratioun.}$ of the kirk for marceing of his spous Katheren Creychtoun efter the papis fassoun, he being of befoir adionit to the kirk of God and thair disciplyne, nochttheles the saidis provest baillies and counsall latt him to libertie at the command and charge of our Soveringis writting vnderwrittin, off the quhilk the tenour followis :—Provest baillies and counsall of our burgh of Edinburgh, and all wtheris our officiaris present and to cum. Forsameikill as we ar informit that our louit serwitour Dauid Hoppringill, ypothecar, hes mareit ane woman callit Katharen Creychtoun, donchter to Thomas Creychtoun, our masour, efter the vs and consuetude of our religioun, for the quhilk ye intend to call molest and troubill thame, nochttheles we for ressonabill caussis and considerationis moving ws, hes dischargit and be thir presentis dischargis yow and all wtheris our officiaris of all calling pursewing troubling and molesting or excommunicating of the saidis Dauid, his spous, or ony of thame, arreisting poynding distrenycing warding or intromettiug with thame thair landis gudis or geir in ony wayis, for

| | |
|---|---|
| Dauid Hoppringillis restoratioun. | the said mariage, or ony wther actioun concerning our religioun, and of your offices in that pairt, as ye will answer to ws thairvpoun, be thir presentis. Subscriuit with our handis, at Edinburgh, the secound day of Junii 1566. *Et sic subscritur:* MARIE, R. HENRIE, R. |

### 19 *July* 1566.

| | |
|---|---|
| Precept, bedrellis. | [The treasurer ordained to pay to " the elimosinaris of the Trinotie College the sowme of fyve poundis, for the Wytsoumday terme the yeir of God j$^m$ v$^c$ lxvj, quhilk the gud towne gevis thame in almis."] |
| Malt, ale. | [Ground malt to be sold not dearer than nine firlots for £4, 6s. ; ale to be sold not dearer than fivepence the pint.] |

### 24 *July* 1566.

| | |
|---|---|
| Precept. | [The treasurer ordained to pay four officers " auchtene schilling, for feing of ane boitt and thair laubouris tane in convoying of ane Heiland man, at our Souveranis command and the provest and baillies of this burgh."] |

### 2 *August* 1566.

| | |
|---|---|
| The gift of Pringillis escheit disponit to the provest. | [The bailies and council,] hawing consideratioun of the diligent cure laubouris expenssis and solistatioun that Sir Symoun Prestoun of Craigmillar knycht, provest of this burgh, hes tane this yeir bypast, and as yit takis in setting fordwart of the commoun weill of this burgh and effaris of the samyn, newer being recompansit as yit, and for wther caussis mowing thame, gevis and disponis to the said provest, his airis and assignais, the escheit of all gold, sylwer, cunyeit or uncunyeit, merchandys, elaything, or wtheris gudis quhatsumewer, pertening to wmquhill Thomas Hoppringill, merchand and burges of this burgh, and now to the guid tonne as escheit for his being convict affoir thame for the slauchter of wmquhill Robert Andersoun, with power to the said Sir Symoun to intromett thairwith, to dispone thairvpoun at his plesour, to call and persew thairfoir, and all wtheris thingis to do that the guid towne mycht haife done thairselfis affoir the dispositioun heirof, and transferris thair rycht |

and kyndnes thairof in the said provost his airis and assignais, in recom- The gift of
pance of his labouris and expenssis as said is. Pringillis escheit dispouit to the provest.

The baillies and counsall ordanis Johnne Westoun, thesaurer, to pay Precept,
to Patrik Barroun, officer, the somme of fyftene schillingis sexpenneis Barroun.
debursit be him for making of the skaffald quharvpoun Thomas Hoppringill wes heidit.

### 13 September 1566.

[In presence of the bailies and council,] compeirit maister Johnne Adultrie.
Craig, minister, and presentit to thame our Soveranis writting wnderwrittin, and desyrit the same to be registrat in the buikis of this burgh, the principall to be gewin to him agane; quhilkis the saidis baillies and counsall thocht ressonabill, ordanit the same to be registrat, and the principall to be delyverit to the foirsaid minister, off the quhilk writting the tennour followis: Regina. Forsamekell as we ar informit be faithfull personis that adultre, furneecatioun, oppin harlatrie, and vtheris sic filthe lustis of the flesche, ar committit and sufferit in Edinburgh without ony pwneisment, to the gret dishonoure of oure God, to the sklander of the haill realme, to the manifest contempt of oure lawis and authorite, thairfor we charge and commandis the provest baillies and counsall of our said burgh that ye with all diligence frome tyme to tyme inquyre serche onto and tak all sic publict sklanderaris and filthy personis and pvnische thame according to the act of our last parliament without ony exceptioun of personis, as ye will answer to your God and to our lawis. At Striviling. Gevin vnder our signet, and subscryvet with our hand, the last day of August and of oure regne the twenty foure yeir. *Et sic subscribitur:*
MARIE. R.

Sir Symoun Prestoun of that ilk, knycht, provest, [the bailies and Freiris yairdis.
council,] being connenit in the counsalhous of the samyn, compeirit Johnne Sym. ane of the baillies thairof, and desyrit the saidis provest baillies and counsall that thai wald grant and geve to him *the es commoditie proffeit*

Freiris yairdis. and[1] the keiping of the vmaist yeard quhilk wes sumtyme the Gray Freris of this burgh, for the space of four yeiris nixt and immediatly followand the Feist of Mertymes in the yeir of God j^m v^c thre scoir and sex yeiris, quhilk gcve thai plesit to do, he promeist wponn his awin expenssis to caus big and reparall the myd dyk now cassin downe and dekayit, siclyk as it wes of befoir, and of als greit heicht betuix the buriall place and the said yeard, and als wponn his awin expenssis to strek furth and caus big ane dur and entrie to this yeard in the eist syde wall of the same, quhilk dur salbe patent to all the nychtbouris of this burgh to perimrnic gang rest and pas thair tyme in the yeard foirsaid gratis, and ewery baillie and counsallar, with ony wther honest man of this burgh, that pleissis to mak ane key wponn thair expenssis, to hawe ane key thairof to the effect foirsaid, and the guid towne to hald thair wappinschawin or ony wther conventionis in the same to be appointit be the provest and baillies of this burgh, and als it salbe lesome to mak thair buriall thairinto geve necessitie requyre, and als promessis to mak na subtennent wnder him to the said yeard nor to sett the same to wtheris bot *to vse it he himself and to his proffeit.*[1] [he to haif the kepyn thairof allanerlie[2]] allanerly, and als promeist that at the issche of the saidis four yeiris it salbe lesome to the guid toune to enter to the said yeard, dispone and occupy the same at thair plesour, als frely as thai mycht hawe done afore the gewin of the same in keiping to the foirsaid Johnne, but ony stop impediment or troubill to be maid be the said Johne, or ony wtheris in his name in the contrair, and that he sould purches na maner of lordschipe for obtening of langer possessioun nor perwerting of thair rycht thairto, and desyrit thair lordschip answer heirinto. Quha, efter consultatioun and awysement takyn heiranent, hes gewin and grantit and be thir presentis gewis and grantis to the said Johnne Sym the keiping *es and commoditie*[1] of the said yeard for the space of four yeiris forsaidis wponn the conditiounis abone writtin, quhairwponn the foirsaid Johnne askit actis and instrumentis.

[1] In the original record the words printed in italics are delete, the deletion being explained by the following note written on the margin:— xvij Septembris 1566. Jhone Sym, in presens of the provest, baillies, gild, thesaurer, abl counsall, new, and assessouris, wes content and consentit to the deletioun of thir woundis, ' vse commoditie and proffet.' STEWART."

[2] The words within brackets are substituted for the deleted words which are printed in italics.

### 18 *September* 1566.

The proucst baillies and counsall ordanis Jhone Westoun, thesaurer, to content and pay to James Nicoll, baillie, the sowme of ten pundis for his pniuscheoum of wyne run at the croce the tyme of the Princes birth. [Princes birth.]

### 25 *September* 1566.

The proucst [bailies and council.] being conuenit for chesing of the new counsall, compeirit Jhone Johnstoun, writer, declarand that Johne Knox, minister, had writtin to him that he wes craiflit, at the leist sutit, for his Mertymes termes maill, in the yeir of God j$^m$ v$^c$ and lxv be Robert Scottis spous, desyrit thair wisdomes outher to caus the samyn be payit, other wayis it behuifit him to find the way to satiflie the samyn. [The treasurer ordained to make payment of the sum craved.] [Precept, Scott.]

### 1 *October* 1566.

The proucst, baillies, counsall, new and auld, being conuenit in the tollnuith of this burgh, as at the day of thair heid court, for chesing of thair proucst, baillies, dene of gild, and thesaurer for the yeir in to cum furth of the lytis chosin vpoun Fryday last wes, compeirit Jhone Chesholme, commissar of our Soueranis artalyere, and producit hir graces writing efter specifeit, of the quhilk the tenour followis: Baillies counsall and dekinis of craftis of our burghe of Edinburghe. It is oure will, and we require and pray yow, that ye continew oure weilbelouite Sir Symoun Prestoun of Craigmillar knycht in provest of oure said burghe for the yeir to cum, and of thir personis vnder writtin, being alsua of your awin lites, that ye alsua cheis foure in baillies, viz., Duncane Leuingstoun, Eduard Litill, maister Thomas Fleming, maister Robert Glen, Alexander Clarke, and Alexander Vddart; as liknis that ye continew maister Johne Prestoun in dene of gild and Johne Westoun in thesaurar of oure said burghe for the yeir to cum, as ye will do ws acceptabill plesour, and gif ws occasioun to think that oure requeist is weill acceptit and regardit be yow. Subscriuit with our hand, at Edinburghe, the first day of October 1566. *Et sic* [Elections.]

[Elections.] *subscribitur:* MARIE, R. Quhilk writing being red in presens of thair lordschippis, thai thinkand the samin to be prejudicial to thair previlegis, thocht best to continew the chesing of thair officiaris quhill the Quenis grace wer of new spokin, to se gif thai mycht, be hir graces plesour, cheis thair officiaris conforme to the actis of parliament and auld ordoure.

### 3 October 1566.

Our Soueranis writting.

Quhairof na ansuer wes gottin quhill the thrid day of October, at the quhilk tyme the writting efter following wes producit, and the counsall convenit efter none, and the proveist, [dean of] gild, and thesaurer continewit in thair offices, and the baillies chosyn conform to the writting.

Heir followis the Quenis grace writting mentionat in the act affoir specefeit: Baillies counsall and dekynis of craftis of our burgh of Edinburgh, we greit yow weill. Forsamekill as we wreit to yow befoir, requyring and desyring yow to elect to your provest baillies dene of gild and thesaurer certan persones nominat and contenit amangis your awyn lytis, as in our wther letter mair largely is exprest; quhilk our requeist ye postponit to obey quhill ye knew our plesour, quhilk yisterday in the audience of our counsall be our awyng mouth we declarit to yow, and now can nocht bot merwell wpon quhat motioun ye sould defer and nocht proceid to the electioun according to oure requeist, considdering the personis nominat be ws wer na strangearis bot of thame ye yourself haid schosin in lytis. Quharfoir we hawe thocht guid to writt to yow agane, desyring and requyring yow as of befoir to proceid to the electioun of your officiaris this efternone, according to the tennour of our said wther letter without forther drift of tyme. Geve ye failyie we man luke to that amangis wtheris your proceidingis done in our contempt. Subscrywit with our hand, at Edinburgh. the yeir of God jm vc lxvj. *Et sic subscribitur:* MARIE R.

Anent the cheising of thre of the counsall.

### 4 October 1566.

[The provost bailies and council,] being convenit in the counsalhous of this burgh for cheising of thre merchandis of this burgh to be thre of the counsall in place of my lord provest, maister Johne Prestoun, dene of gild, and Johne Westoun, thesaurer, wes continewit in thair office be wertew of our Soueranis writting foirsaid, and namit Dauid Foster, Alexander Park, or Arthur Grangear to be counsallouris for this present yeir in place of the personis foirsaid and geve thair aythis to vse the office of counsallschip for this yeir intoeum as vs is.

*Anent the cheising of thre of the counsall.*

The provest bailles and counsall foirsaid ordanis Patrik Gowane, belman, Johnne Symsoun and Robert Drummound, keiparis of the kirk of this burgh, to caus soupe and dicht the said kirk ilk oulk anis and to paint it ilk moneth anis, and to keipe the durris thairof the tyme of sermound prayaris and exereys, as vs hes bene in tymes past, and to oppin the durris of the said kirk at sevin houris in the mornyng in wynter and fyve in somer, and to steik the saidis durris at four houris in wynter and sex in somer, and the said Patrik and Robert to await wpoun the counsall in counsall dayis and keipe the counsal hous dur owtwith the samyn.

*Keiparis of the kirk.*

9 *October* 1566.

The provest baillies and counsall forsaid ordanis Jhone Westoun, thesaurer, to caus mak ane dur to the gallois of the Burrow Myre, and to caus mend and heicht the dykis thairof, sua that doggis sall nocht be abill to cary the carionnis furth of the samyn as thai had done in tymes past.

*Dur to the gallows.*

11 *October* 1566.

The provest baillies and counsall statutis and ordanis that in tyme of court the officiaris lat na persoun enter within bar except the provest, baillies, counsall, thair clerkis, officeris, and the partie, pursewar and defender, instantlie callit vpoun, quha hes thair mater in ressoning, with sic vther honest men of this burgh as sall be commandit to be lattin in be the saidis provest and baillies and nane vtheris.

*Ordour tane anent partiis latting in with the bar in tyme of judgment.*

14 *October* 1566.

Statuttis.    The statuttis dewisit and proclamit at the command of Sir Symone Prestoun of that ilk, knicht, pronest, maister Robert Glen, Eduard Littill, Alexander Vddart, and Alexander Clark, baillies, with awise of thair counsall. [Here follow acts as to baxters, farmers of the mills, malt, ale, measures, meal, wheat, fish, poultry, flesh, tallow, candle, stablers, corn market, regraters, vagabonds, middings, swine, removal of "red" or stones from the street, assizes, stands at booth doors and on the High Street, officers and putting of decreets to execution, keeping weapons in booths, blasphemers and slanderers, paying of unlaws, wool, goods weighed at the over trone, keeping neighbourhood in building houses, burgesses remaining in burgh, and convening of the council. These acts are in similar terms to those of previous years already printed.]

Closettis.    Item, it is statute and ordanit that all personis that hes scheildis clenge the samin or euer thai be full, sua that thai brek nocht furth and rin in the streit, vnder the pane of xviij s. to be tane of thame quhome to the scheild pertenis; and attour, gif ony personis happynnis to oppin thair closattis in ane greit weit sua that thair scheildis ryn alangis the streit the tenement salbe poindit for ane vnlaw of xviij s. vnforgevin, and that na maner of persoun hald thair closettis oppin sypeand and rynnand furth bot honestlie couerit, vnder the said pane of xviij s. vnforgevin; and quhen ony scheildis is clengit that the clenger carie the samin honestlie and quietlie in the nycht and nocht to file the streit thairwith.

Furrouris, skynnaris.    Item, it is statute and ordanit that na furrouris duelland within this burgh steip thair skynnis in foir houssis nor hing thame in foir stairis nor yit ding thame on the hie gait nor stairis, vnder the pane of xviij s.

Walkeris.    Item, it is statute and ordanit that na maner of walkeris duelland within this burgh hing thair claiths on foir stairis, nor wesche thame in foir houssis, foirstairis on the Hie Gait, Cowgait, or commoun vynnellis, in tyme cumming, vnder the pane of xviij s. to be tane of ilk ane of thame sa oft as thai failye, and that thair be nane of thair watter careit throw the gait on the day licht vnder the said pane.

Item, foirsamekill as the filthie vyce and cryme of adultrie and  Anent huris.
fornicatioun hes been wickitle vsit within this burgh in the houssis of
syndre inhabitantis thairof, of thair knawlege, be diners personis quhilk
thai hald in thair houssis without regarde of the commandiment of God or
man, only for thair awin avantage; for eschewing quhairof in tymes
cuming it is statute and ordanit that na maner of man nor woman,
indueller within this burgh, hurd hald or ressaue ony sic as committis the
forsaid filthie crymes within thair houssis in tymes cuming, of thair knawlege, bot that thai incontinent thairefter cum to the prouest and baillies
of this burgh and declair to thame the man or woman committer of the
samyn that thai may be pvneist conform to the actis and statutis maid
thairanent, wnder the pane of x li. for the first falt, twenty pund for the
secund, to be vpliftit of the maister of the hous quhair the foirsaid filthines
is committit or sic personis ressauit hurdit or haldin of his or hir knawlege, and banesing of the toun for ewer the thrid falt; and geve maister
or maistres of the saidis houssis be nocht abill to pay the said vnlaw, to be
imprisonat xx dayis within the tolbuith of this burgh and thairefter pvncist
at the will of the magistret.

The provest baillies and counsall namis the personis efter specifeit to  Extent for the
be stentouris of the nychtbouris of this burgh, for the sovme of four  baptysme.
hundreth merkis, to be payit be the merchandis, of the sovme of fyve
hundreth merkis quhilk this townes pairt extendis to of the sovme of
twelf thousand poundis raisit vpoun this realme, and grantit to our
Soueranis for setting fordwart of the babtisme of our Soveran the Prince,
that is to say:—[four persons for each of the four quarters;] and ordanis
the officeris to warne thame to compeir on Wednesday nixtocum to geve
thair aythis to taxt the nychtbouris efter thair conscience and knawlege.

[The tresurer ordained to pay "to James Drummound, trumpetour, fyve schillingis  Precept
for warnyng of the nychtbouris be sound of trumpet the tyme of the proclamatioun  Drummound.
of the actis."]

### 18 October 1566.

It is statut and ordanit be the provest baillies and counsall of this  Nychtbour-
hedis.

Nychtbour-
heidis.

burgh that thai sall convene ilk Fryday at twa efternone in the counsal hous of this burgh, and thair to ressawe awld billis of nychtbourheidis to be gewin in befoir thame, and thairefter to pas and wescy the samyn wpoun the groundis of the land contenit in the clames and geve decreit thairanent for reformatioun conforme to justice, wnder the pane of thre schillingis to be tane of the provest baillie and counsallour being absent and within this burgh without he hawe leife of the provest or baillies, and this without preiudice of the weseing of nychtbourheidis that stoppis men wark instantly bigging quhilk thai ordane to be weseyit as necessitie sall requyre.

22 *October* 1566.

Wyne.

[No new wines of this year to be bought of "ony derrar prices nor that thai may sell the pynt thairof for twelf penneis."]

23 *October* 1566.

Commoun muir.

[Six persons ordered to appear before the council "to answer for breking of thair commoun muir and hoking of the same, making midding thairof to guid thair land, casting of divett and scherettis, thai beand na fremen of this burgh nor hawand entric thairto."]

30 *October* 1566.

Anent the Quenis grace writing.

In presens of the baillies and counsall, comperit Robert Wans, in Leith, and presenttit our Soueranis writting vnderwrittin to thame, off the quhilk the tennour followis: Prouest baillies counsall and communitie of the burgh of Edinburgh, we greit yow weill. In our necessitie we annaliit to yow the superioritie of our toun of Leith, and yit at our desire and requeist ye haif superseidit the putting of your sellis in possessioun of it. It is nocht vnknawin to yow quhat we haue ado, and yit with the first we purpois, God willing, to redeme that thing that we esteme precious and mekill wourth. We ar assurit yit as of befoir ye will nocht spair to gratifie ws samekill as to suspend the possessioun and intromissioun with oure said toun quhill the last day of December nixttocum, quhairinto we pray yow and requeistis yow ernestlie and effectuouslie, as ye will do verray thankfull and exceptabill plesour. This is sufficient gif ye mynde to schaw ony benevolence at onre desire, and gif ye do nocht we man thoill it and provide the nixt best, bot we trest suirlie ye will nocht stand with ws in sic ane mater; quhairupoun we require your ansuer. Subscrinit with oure hand, at Edinburgh, the sevint day of October j$^m$ v$^c$ thre scoir sax yeiris. *Et sic subscribitur:* MARIE, R. Of the quhilk writting the principall wes deliuerit to maister Johne Prestoun in the thesaurer hous. — Anent the Quenis grace writting.

### 13 *November* 1566.

The prouest baillies and counsall ordanis Johne Westoun, thesaurer, to caus mend and reparrell thair bekin beyound thair hevin of Leithe, betuix the hous of Jhone Wardlaw vpoun the southe and the see vpoun the northe. — Precept, beacon.

### 27 *November* 1566.

[The provost, bailies, and council being conveued.] comperit Hectour Trohop, masour, and brocht in the townis mais, quhilk wes weyit in presens of the saidis prouest baillies and counsall, and wes of wecht, silwer, tre, irne and all, twa pund fourteue vnce and ane half. — The wecht of the townis mais.

The prouest baillies and counsall ordanis maister Jhone Prestoun, deue of gild, to caus mend the prik of the sone orloge on the south syde of the kirk in the kirk yard and draw the letteris thairof of new. — Horlege in the kirk yarde.

### [*December*] 1566.

Forsameikill as it is humlie meuit to the prouest baillies and counsall of this burgh be the haill merchandis of the samyn that it hes bene inviolablie obserwit in all tymes bygane past memour of man, lyke as it is yit in dyvers cuntreis, and specialy in France, Flanderis, and Ingland, and hes bene observit within this realme of Scotland alsua, that all scheip war flane throuche to the luggis, sua that na pairt of the skynnis thairof wer diminischit wnto the luggis, nochttheles the flescheouris of this burgh cuttis thair skynnis hard by the craig, at the leist in the mid craig, — Anent the scheip skynnis that the lug be left with the skin.

Anent the scheip skynnis that the lug be left with the skin.

quhairthrow the saidis merchandis wantis samekill of the said skynne at the craig, with the best portioun of the woll thairof, quhilk is the fynest woll of the skyn callit the halslok, and als the saidis flescheouris pullis the haill skyn fra the hals doun to the taill throw all the wambe thairof and cuttis ane tarledder of the skyn thairwith, diminisching thairby bayth the skynnis and the woll in lenth and breid, quhairby the saidis merchandis ar nocht only grytly damnefeit and skaythit, but alsua ar sair mvrmerit be all strangearis quhair thai travell with the saidis skynnis, layand as it wer the falt thairof wpoun the saidis merchandis, quhilk the foirsaidis provest baillies and counsall wnderstandis nocht to be the deid nor will of the honest men of the said occupatioun as thai haife declarit being callit thairto: For remeid quhairof the saidis prouest baillies and counsall hes statnt and ordanit [that all fleshers within the burgh or resorting thereto] flay all thair scheipe in tyme cuming wp throw the haill craig to the luggis, sua that the lug steik with the skyn and neuyer pull the woll of the hals, wambe, nor na wther pairt thairof, nor yit to diminische the samyn be cutting of ony sic pairt as thai call the tarledder wnder the pane of confyscatioun of [the skins, and punishing of the owners and sellers in their bodies and goods.]

Skynnis to be brocht to the merkat with the buik.

[Persons bringing animals to the market to sell, ordained "to bring with thame in all tymes cuming the hyd stikkand with the karkages, and the skynnis with the boukis or laid hard by the samyn quhair the samyn hingis or lyis."]

### 16 *December* 1566.

Precept, extent.

[Edwerd Lytill, bailie of the north-west quarter, ordained to pay to Archiebald Forman, cook, and Agnes Broun, £5, 10s., "for meit and drink furneist to the extentouris of this last taxt be the space of thre dayis quhilk thai wer inclosit in the tolbuith of this burgh the tyme of the setting of the said taxt."]

### 20 *December* 1566.

Commissaris afoir the assemblie.

[The council appointed "James Barroun, merchand, and maister Richert Strang, lawer, thair commissaris and procuratouris to compeir in the townis name in the generall assemble of the kirk presentlie convenit within this burgh."]

[The council and deacons of crafts gave to "Williame Couttis, officer, the beid- Bedrelschip manschip of Sanct Paulis Wark, vacand be the deceis of Jhone Wauchlot, officer," to William Couttis. David Robertsoun, barber, got the promise of the next vacant bedrelship "becaus Robertsoun. he is disapoyntit of this present."]

[The dean of guild instructed "to put ane chenye and ane lok vpoun the Precept, presoun hous at the kirk end ordanit that wemen salbe impresonit in quhilkis lyis prison. in fornecationn or adulterie."]

[Mr William Robertoun, master of the High School, to be paid ten merks for Precept. his fee and other ten for the "maill of the scule."] maister scule.

### 10 January 1566-7.

Compeirit Robert Wans, in Leyth, and producit ane writting of our Leith. Soueranis to delay the taking of ony forther possessioun of the towne of Leyth quhill the last day of Apryle nixtocum, off the quhilk the tennor followis :—(*Blank*) Quhilk writting wes delyverit be William Stewart to maister Robert Glen, baillie, to mak ane bill wpoun to our Soveranis, with the awys of maister Thomas M'Calycoun and maister Richert Strang, and as yit wndelyverit agane.

### 31 January 1566-7.

The prowest baillies and counsall ordanis Hectour Trovp to pay to Anent the Williame Thomsoun, fleschour, the sowme of twelf pundis for the prowestis prowestis ox. ox, and that of his awin consent becaus he intromettit with the dewitie of the faris of Trinitie and Alhallo.

The prowest baillies and counsall ordanis proclamatioun to be maid Playaris in the throuche this burgh be the behman thairof, dischargeing all induellaris kirk. within the samyn, maisteris of scolis or vtheris haifland cure of the youtheid of this burgh, that thay suffer nane of the barnis vnder thair correctioun to frequent to the kirk to play thairinto, as thai will answer to the magistratis, and certefeing thame that sic barnis as salbe apprehendit playand in the said kirk salbe imprisonit at the will of the magistratis

Playaris in the kirk.
efter that thay be quhippit with wandis, quhilk proclamatioun wes maid that samyn day throuch this burgh be the said belman.

Procuratour fiscall.
[The provost bailies and council,] considering the greit hurt incurrit be the burgh of Edinburgh and commoun weill of the samin throw wantting of ane procuratour fiscall to persew and defend in thair commoun actiounis and previlagis, quhilk ar oursene, with the pvneissing of sic as transgressis thair actis and statutis, and haifing consideratioun that Alexander King, procuratour, is maist meit thairfoir, be ressoun he hes be ane lang space bigane bene clerk of thair court and kennis the merceittis of the commoun caussis belanging to this burgh and prevelagis thairof, and hes insistit in the tounis name in persute of the brekkeris of the saidis prevelagis and vtheris diuers actiounis of this burgh, and obtenit decreittis aganis thame with the said burgh, for the quhilkis laubouris he hes had na recompensatioun reward nor payment as yit; quhairfoir thai, willing that he be recompensit for his travellis ellis tane, and that he haif ane yeirlie pensioun induring thair will, to accept the said office vpoun him and to libell thair letteres, clamis, petitiounis, defenssis, ansueris and writtis necesser, in persute or defence of thair caussis and prevelagis foirsaid, and to procure in the samin in tyme cuming, ordanis [the treasurer to pay him ten pounds for past services and ten merks yearly in time coming.]

*11 February* 1566-7.

Precept.
The prowest baillies and counsall ordanis Jhone Westoun, thesaurar, to caus tak away the hevyn wark of the bak dure at the prouestis logeing of the Kirk of Feild and to big vp the samyn dure with lyme and sand.

*26 February* 1566-7.

Chesing of thesaurer.
[John Harwod chosen treasurer in room of John Westoun, "depairtit and deid at the plesour of God."]

*8 March* 1566-7.

Ressait of x<sup>m.</sup> merkis.
In presens of the provest baillies and counsall foirsaid, comperit Johnne Chisholme, comptrollour to our Soveranis arteilyerie, and confest

him to hawe ressawit fra the baillies of this burgh compleit payment of Ressait of the sovme of ten thousand merkis wsuall money of this realme debursit x<sup>m</sup>· merkis. be the towne of Edinburgh wpoun the superioritie of Leyth, and that at our Soveranis command for payment of thair graces men of weir and setting fordwart of artcilyery the tyme thair graces past to the waist countrey.

### 12 March 1566-7.

The quhilk day, delinerit, at the baillies and counsallis command, to Craig, maister Jhone Craig, minister, the writting of the lordis of secreit coun- minister. sall direct to the prouest and baillies of this burgh for taking of ordour and setting of taxt for sustening of thair ministerris, makand mentioun that hir grace had gevyn the annuallis for that effect; and this to schew to our Souerane for obtening of the signatouris of the said annuallis subscriuit.

### 19 March 1566-7.

In presens of the prowest baillies and counsale, comperit Dauid Protestatio, Rowane, maister inellar to our Souerane, and declarit that the castell of Rowane. Edinburgh is to be randerit furth of the handis of my lord Erskyn, and thairfor desyrit the prowest and baillies to pas to our Souerane and seik deliuerance of thair artalyere being within the samyn, quhairof thai had his handwrit, and gif thai did nocht, protestit that he war nocht haldin heirefter to mak compt of thame, becaus it wes incertane to him quha wes to be maid capitane, and thairvpoun askit instrumentis.

### 4 April 1567.

The prowest baillies and counsall ordanis maister Jhone Prestoun, Steking of the dene of gyld, to caus clenge the filthe about the kirk, and to caus steik kirkyaird yet. the gret yet on the est syde of the kirk yaird sua that the laddis get na interes to mak the samyn ane symmar feild and to brek the glas windokkis.

### 11 April 1567.

The prowest baillies and counsall ordanis the belman to pas throuche Bikkeraris.

Bikkeraris. this burgh and discharge the bikeraris, vnder the pane of hanging of sic as ar of age and scurgeing of sic otheris as ar nocht of age, quhilk the said belman proclamit that samyn day and hes yit in his handis.

### 24 April 1567.

Orlage. [The dean of guild ordained " to caus paint the letteris of the orlage."

Three persouis appointed "to talk with the man that hes the orlage to sell, desyrit to be set vp at the Nether Bow, drif it to ane price, and report to the counsall."]

### 7 May 1567.

New wall besyde the Kirk of Feild. [The bailies and council] ordanis Jhone Harwod, thesaurar, to caus big the wall of the toun decayit and fallin doun on the southe syde of the prowest of the Kirkfeildis logeing to be biggit vp of lyme and stane, conforme to the heicht and thiknes of the new wall ellis biggit, and to pas lineallie with the samyn to the wall of the kirkaird of the said kirk, and that he leif na dure nor entre in the said new dik bot that the samyn be maid masse wall, and to gif tuentye fyve pound for ilk rude thairof.

### 12 May 1567.

Salt pannis at Newhavin. [The bailies, council, and deacons of crafts,] all in ane voce, findis gude and consenttis that ane pairt of thair Newhavin be set in tak to Anthonie Hikman, Jhone Achille and Cornelius du Vois, Inglischemen, for the space of fyftie yeris, and that the commoun sele of this burgh be hungyn thairto.

### 16 May 1567.

Ground at Newhavin. [Fourteen persons appointed] to pas to the Newhavyn and vesye the ground desyrit be Anthonie Hikman, Jhone Achille and Cornelius du Vois to be set to thame in tak for making of salt, and to caus met and mesoure the samyn, and to report to the counsall the quantitie and situatioun thairof.

The counsall granttis and gevis to Johne Hepburn, porter of the Hepburn, castell, his burgeschip frie, in hoip of gude seruice to the nychtbouris of burges. this burgh.

### 4 June 1567.

[The provost, bailies, council, and deacons of crafts consented that a portion of Setting of ane their lands lying on the south side of the Newhaven, "contenand twentie thre fall part of thair of lenthe and sextene fall in breid, ilk fall contenand sex elnis Scottis," should be set mak salt. to the three Englishmen before named, for the space of fifty years "to mak salt in." On 18th June three tacks for the periods of 19, 19, and 12 years, respectively, were granted, and are entered at length in the council record.]

### 11 June 1567.

The prowest baillies counsall and dekynnis names Eduard Lytill, [Incoming of baillie, William Foullar of the counsall, and Michaell Gilbert, gold smyth, to lordis to town.] pas to Dunbar to oure Souerane, quha wes thair for the tyme with James Hepburn duke of Orknaye lord Boithwell, admirall, etc., to excus the gude toun and schew thair pairt anent the incuming and entering in this toun of my lordis Athoill, Montrois, Morton, Mar, Glencairn, Home, Lyndesaye, Ruthven, Sanquhair, Sympill, Tulibardyn and Grange, etc. quha had convenit thame self in armis for pvnesing of King Harye Stewartis murthure, putting of our Souerane to libertie, dissolving of the mariage betuix our Souerane and the said Duke and fortefications of James Stewart, Prince of Scotland, and son to the said vmquhile Harye.

The samyn day, the baillies and counsall ordanis Jhone Harwod, thesaurar, to content and pay to Jaques and his peple x s. quha playit afoir the toun the x day of Junii instant the tyme of the incuming of the lordis aboue writting.

### 18 June 1567.

The prowest baillies and counsall, vnderstanding the greit skayth Anent the and dampnage sustenit be the inhabitantis, fremen of this burgh, be burgeses. making of outlandis men, having nother wyf, barnis, familie, stob nor staik

**Anent the making of burgesses.**

within the samyn, burgessis of the said burgh, nochttheles the saidis outlandis burgessis duellis outwith the burgh and passis throw the cuntre, foirstallis skyn, hyde, and other merchandice, and traffectis in selling bying and saling, nochtwithstanding the quhilkis thai eschaip fra taxtis stentis and all otheris portable chargis, and can nocht be apprehendit nor causit pay nor do the samyn be ressoun thai haif nother stob nor staik as said is, incontrair the commonn weill of the samyn, and inlykwys considdering the gret skaithe and dampnage sustenit be the craftismen of the said burgh be making of uther townis prentesis and seruandis lyke fre as gif thai had bene prenteis within this burgh, quhilk is the gret hurt of the said fremen and thair prenteisis, and contrair the commonn weill of burrowis: For remeid of the quhilkis, the prowest baillies and counsall, with consent and awys of the dekynnis of crafts, statutis and ordanis that in tyme cuming na maner of outlandis men be maid burges or fremen of this burgh vnto he be mariit and haif stob and staik within the samyn, sua that he may be apprehendit and compellit to pay taxt and stent and beir his pairt of sic portable chargis as otheris fremen induellaris within the samyn, and that na craftisman be ressauit freman within this burgh bot onle thai that hes bein prenteis within the samyn and thair prenteship fullelie outrun; prouiding allwayis that this act preinge nocht fremennis bairnis nor prentesis being fullele outrun within this burgh, bot thai sall be ressauit but stop or impediment, conforme to the auld vse; and this act to haif strenthe force and effect induring the will of the saidis provest and baillies.

20 *June* 1567.

**Couttis.**

The prowest baillies and counsall ordanis Jhone Harwod, thesaurar, to deliuer to George Couttis, now being imprisonit in the thevis hoill for his contempt done to maister Jhone Craig, minister, the sowme of twelf schillingis sex penneis; and ordanis him to be relevit furth of waird and convoyit to Leithe and boittit thair be tua officiaris; and this in respect of our Soueranis writting obtenit to that effect and of his lang impresonment, and als that thay find him by him self.

2 July 1567.

[The provost, bailies, council and deacons of crafts,] being convenit Superioritie of
in the counsall hous of this burgh, all consentit with ane consent and Leith.
assent that the prowest baillies and certane of the counsall pais vpoun the
ferd day of this instant monetho to the toun of Leithe, hold thair court of
the superioritie thairof as lordis of the samyn vpoun the nychtbouris of
Leithe, and tak possessioun, conforme to thair evidentis. And als ordanit Wappinschaw-
conforme to the actis of parliament that thair be ane generall wappin-ing.
schawing and proclamatioun thairof commanding the nychtbouris of this
burgh to mak the said wappynschawing that samyn day vpoun thair
lynkis of Leithe, ilk nychtbour vnder the pane of ten pund.

[The provost, bailies, council and deacons of crafts,] being convenit For the per-
in the counsall hous of the samyn, comperit nobill and mightie lordis, my sewing of the
lordis erles of Mortoun and Atholl, having with thame the maist honorabill murthure.
and godlie band laitlie maid and subscryveit be ane greit parte of the
nobilite of this realme, bering in effect that thai the saidis lordis altogidder
bindis and obleissis thame, ilk ane to vtheris, vpone the respect of thair
dewite towert thair Souerane, the commoun weill of this thair native
cuntre and honoure of the samyn, that thai altogidder with thair haill
force power and freindis sall persew the crewell myrthereris of the King,
oure said Soueranes husband, to the vtermaist, seik the desolutioun of the
vngodlie mariage maid betuix hir hienes and the erle Boithwell, oure said
Souerane to be relevit of the thraldome bondage ignominie and schame
quhilk scho hes sustenit and wuderlyis throuche the said erles occasionne,
the persone of oure vndoubtit and innocent Prince reposit to full surete
and relevit of imminent dainger quhilk now he standis in, and, finallie,
iustice restoritt and vprichtle ministrate to all the leges and subiectis of
this realme. The quhilk maist godlie and honorabill band, in presens of
the prowest baillies counsall and dekynnis, being red and considerit, thay
all in ane voce approves the samyn and grantis consentis and promittis
thair assistance and fortificatioun to the said lordis in furthsetting persewing and avanceing of the premissis to thair vter power; and for

For the persewing of the Kingis murthure.

assurance heirof hes requeistit and desyritt the rycht honorabill Sir Symon Prestoun of that ilk knycht, thair prowest, for thame and in thair names, with the saidis lordis to subscryve the said band, quhilk salbe als sufficient as gif thai had subscryvit the samyn with thair awin proper handis. And for obseruing heirof ordanis this present ordinance to be insert and registrat in thair counsall buke for the mair sure testificatioun of thair consent as said is.

Band.

Heir followis the copie of the band and oblesing abone specifiit;— Quhair the richt nobill and excellent Prince, vmquhill King Henrie Stewart, the Quenis Maiestie oure Soueranis lait husband, being in his logeing sumtyme callit the logeing of the prouest of Kirkfeild besyde the samyn within this burgh, wes schamefulle and tressonable murthurit, the fame thairof wes in sic sort blawin abreid and dispersit in all realmes and amangis all cristiane nationis that this cuntre wes abhorit and vilependit, the nobillite and haill pepill na other wayis estemit bot as thay had been all participant of sa vnvourthye and horrabill ane murthur, that nane of onye of the Scottis natioun, thocht he wer neuir sa innocent, wes habill for schame in onye forane cuntre to schaw his face, and that nocht without occasioun, seing na maner of just tryall tane nor menit to be takin for the cryme, albeit in all this tyme the murtheraris war weill anewche knawin, for quha culd be ignorant thairof and nocht cleirlie se at behalding the proceding of the erll Boithwell the tyme of the attempting of that odius fact and continewalle seusyne, that war sufficient albeit thair war na other prufe, wes nocht the tryall be him impedit and delayit, and the speciall aithouris of the murthure being requirit to be wardit quhill the tryall of thair caus, houbeit the petitioun wes maist ressonable and nocht repugnant to the lawis, yit culd na part thairof be grantit becaus the cheif murtherar being present maid that staye; and than quhat ane inordinat proces wes ordanitt to clenge and acquit him of that horrable deid all men persaflit, quhen nother the accustomat circumstancis in caussis of tressoun, nor the ordinar forme of justice wes obseruit, bot quhatsumeuir the fader and freindis of the innocent Prince saukleslie murtherit justlie desyrit the contrair wes allwayis done, the said erll the day that he chesit to thoill law being accumpanit with ane greit power, als weill of wagit

men of weir as of otheris, that nane suld compeir to persew him; quhen  For the per-
swa this cruell murthur wes committit and justice smorit and planelie  sewing of the Kingis
abvsit, neuir ceissit he of his wikkit and inordinat pretens, bot, eikand  murthure.
myscheif to myscheif, tressonablie, without feir of God or reverence of his
native prince, quhill on ane forthoucht conspiracie he vmbeset hir
Maiesteis way, tuke and reveist her maist nobill persoun and led the
samyn with him to Dunbar Castell, thair detening hir prisoner and
captive, and in the menetyme procurit doubill sentence of divorce to be
pronuncit betuix him and his lawfull wyff groundit on the caus of his awin
turpitude, and to mak his pretendit mariage (quhilk schortlie followit) vsit
the order of divorce als weill be the ordinar commissaris as in forme and
maner of the Romane kirk, declarand that he wes of na kynd of religioun,
as the samyn vnlawfull mariage suddandlie accompleschit thairefter on
bouthe the fassionis did manifest and testifie, albeit that nother of Goddis
law nor na law maid be man of quhatsumeuer religioun mycht the samyn
mariage lesumlie haif bene contractit; quhilk being endit and he still
proceeding frome ane kynd of iniquitie to ane other, his cruell and ambi-
tious nature being knawin and how na nobill man nor other durst resort
to hir Maiestie to speik with hir or procure thair lesum besines without
suspicioun bot be him and in hir audience, hir chalmar durris being continuallie wachit with men of weir; we (althoucht to lait) begouthe to
considder the estait and tak heid to ourselflis, bot speciallie to the preseruatioun of the lyfe of the fatherles Prince, the onelie soun and rychtuous
air apparent of our Souerane, hir hienes schamefull thraldome and bondage
with the said erll, and with that foirsaw the gret danger quhilk the prince
stoude in quhen, as the murtherar of his fader, the revesar of the Quenis
Maiestie his moder, wes cled with the principall strenthis of this realme
and garnesit with ane gard of wagit men of weir, and how in all appar-
ence he mycht oppres vnprouiditlie and destroy that innocent infant as
he had done his fader, and sua be tyran and cruell deiddis at last to
vsurpe the royall croun and supreme gouernance of this realme, at last in
the feir and name of God, and in the lawfull obedience of oure Souerane,
movit and constrainit be the just occasionis aboue writtin to haif takin
armes to revenge the said cruell and horrable murthure vpoun the said erll

For the per-
sewing of the
Kingis
murthure.

Boithwell and vtheris authoris and devisaris thairof, to deliuer our said
Souerane furth of his handis and of the ignominie schame and sclander
quhilk, being in thraldome with him, scho hes sustenit vnder pretence of
the said vnlawfull mariage, to preserue the lyfe of oure innocent natiue
Prince, and finallie to se justice equallie ministrat to all the liegis of this
realme: Quhairfoir, we the erllis, lordis, baronis, commissaris of burrowis,
and otheris vnder subscriuand, be thir presentis bindis and oblesis ws and
euerye ane of ws to otheris that we sall tak plane trew and vprycht pairt
togidder with our kin, freindis, seruandis, and all that will do for ws in the
avancement furthsetting and persute of the foirsaid querrell, with our
lyflis landis and gudis at our vtermaist, and sall neuer shrink thairfra nor
leif the samyn for ony maner of occasioun that can or is habill to occur
quhill the authouris of the cruell murthure and revesing be condignelie
pvnist, the said vnlawful mariage dissoluit and annullit, our Souerane
relevit of the thraldome bondage and ignominie quhilk scho hes sustenit
and vnderlyis throu the said erllis occasioun, the persoun of the innocent
Prince reposit to full suretie and relevit of eminent danger quhilkis now
he standis in, and fynallie justice restorit and vprychtlie ministrat to all
the liegis and subiectis of this realme. The quhilk to do and faithfulle
performe we promit, as we will answer to Almychti God, vpoun our
honouris trewthe and fedelitie, as we ar nobillmen and luflis the honour
of our natiue cuntrie, quhairin, as God forbid, gif we failye in ony point
we ar content to sustene the spott of periurie infamie and perpetuall
vntrewth, and to be comptit culpabill of the aboue namit crymes, and
inemeis and betrayaris of our natiue cuntrie. In witnes of the quhilk
thing we haif subscriuit thir presentis with our handis as followis, at
Edinburgh, the sextene day of Junii the yeir of God j$^m$ v$^c$ and thre scoir
sevin yeris. *Et sic subscribitur.* *Concordat presens copia cum principale.*
*Ita est.* ALEX$^R$. HAYE.

### 9 July 1567.

Precept for
the monting of
the artalyerie.

[The provost, bailies, and council] ordanis Jhone Harwod, theasurar,
to caus stok band and mont the townis artalyere, now presentle lyand in
the end of the kirk, and to by and caus furnis all thingis necessar thairto,

1567.]        OF THE BURGH OF EDINBURGH.        237

to the effect the samyn may be in reddines preparit and reperallit in cais Precept for
onye forane inemyis wald cum and persew this burgh or nychthouris mounting of the artalyerie.
thairof to do thame harme in thair bodyis or gudis.

                    23 July 1567.

[David Forester appointed by the council to be bailie of the south west quarter Bailie.
till Michaelmas, in the absence of Robert Glen, "quha hes nocht pvncist thame
(the inhabitants of that quarter) for breking of the statuties be this lang space."]

The prowest baillies counsall and dekynnis foirsaid statutis and Defence of the
ordanis that ilk Fryday efter none the counsale convene at tua houris town.
in the counsall hous of this burgh to consult and awys anent the fortificatioun of this burgh and strentheing of the samyn, to the effect that
the inhabitantis thairof may be mair habill to resist quhatsumener thair
vufreindis that is of mynde to persew thame in thair bodie or gudis.

The prowest baillies counsall and deikynnis foirsaid, vnderstanding Ordinance to
the gret and apperand danger quhilk is lyke to rys within this mak ane band
                                                                   betuix the toun
realme be dinisioun of the nobilitie thairof, for the caussis laitlie occurrit, and the castell.
and als considdaring that the inhabitantis of this burgh, thair houshaldis
famile and gudis in sic tumultis ar euer subiect to large grettar danger
nor onye other burgh of this realme, be ressoun thair is certane
wikkit personis awaiting vpoun the spoilye of the samyn gif occasioun
serue, thairfor thai all in ane voce, and with awys and consent of Sir
James Balfour of Pittindrech knycht, clerk of our Soueranis Register and
capitane of the castell of Edinburgh, has thocht and thinkis expedient
that for defence, nocht onlie of the said toun bot alssua of the said castell,
that ane band and liege be maid in writ betuix the said capitane on
that ane pairt and the prowest baillies counsall dekynnis and communite of the said burgh on that other part, for mutuall defence and
support to be maid be ather of thame to otheris aganis quhatsumener that
wald or will persew the said castell burgh or inhabitantis thairof in thair
personis or gudis, the authorite onlie except, and ordanis Alexander
Guthre, thair common clerk, to mak the samyn agane Fryday nyxtocum,

238        EXTRACTS FROM THE RECORDS        [1567.

Ordinance to mak ane band betuix the toun and the castell.
and that day to schaw it afoir the counsall that it may be red and considderit be the said capitane and thame and than fynallie endit conclndit and subscrinit be and vponn laythe the saidis partis.

Town wallis.
The prowest baillies and counsall ordanis the haill houssis and dikkis biggit to thair toun wallis to be castin doun and demoleschit sua that na passage oure the saidis wallis may be had.

25 July 1567.

Band with the castell.
[Alexander Guthrie, common clerk, presentet the bond he had been instructed to prepare between the captain of the castle and the town. The council approved of the bond, and instructed the clerk to sign it on their behalf.]

Commissioun for coronatioun of the King.
The prowest baillies and counsall forsaid nemmis and constitutes Nycoll Vddart, Michaell Gilbert and Robert Abercrummye of the counsall, thair commissioneris to pas to Strineling, and thair to consent and vse the office of commissioneris of this burgh at the coronatioun of oure Souerane, James Stewart, Prince of this realme; and ordanis ane commissioun to be maid to thame to that effect, subscrinit with thair clerk and selit with their seill of caus, *et promiserunt de rato.*

Ane wache.
The prouest baillies and counsall ordanis ane wache to be maid nychtlie within this burgh induring thair will, becaus thair is monie and diuers men of weir and men wanting maisteris within the samyn.

30 July 1567.

To poynd thame that set nocht furth fyres.
The prowest baillies and counsall ordanis the officiaris of this burgh to pas poind and distreinye the inhabitantis of this burgh that set nocht out thair fyris vpoun the tuenty nyne day of Julij instant quhan our Souerane James Stewart, Prince of Scotland, wes crownit, for ane vnlaw of ten pund; and ordanis xl s. to be payit of ilk ane of the saidis personis and applyit to the commoun warkis of this burgh.

1 *August* 1567.

The provost baillies counsall and dekynnis, being convenit in the counsalhous, efter lang resonyng vpoun the present troublis within this realme, and the apperand danger to cum vpoun this toun this nixt wynter be men of weyr and vther idill pepill, quhilkis makis commoun passagis in and out oure thair wallis, and in speciall at that pairt of the wall at the Blackfreris to Sanct Marye Wynde vnbigit: For remeid heirof, and eschewing of vther inconvenientis apperand, thay all in one voce, George Smyth, allegit dekyn of the tailycouris except, fyndis gude consenttis and grauttis that that pairt of the toun wall abone mentionat, with all deligence possabill, be compleitlie biggit and endit of the heicht and thiknes of the new wall joynit to the samyn; and for performyng of the samyn that ane extent of ane thousand pundis be sett and vpliftit alsueill vpoun the landis of thame that duellis without the burgh havand landis within the samyn as vpoun the landis and guddis of the inhabitanttis. *(margin: Town wallis. Extent of jm li. Protestatio, Smyth.)*

[The provost, bailies, council, and community entered into a contract with Thomas Jaksoune and Murdo Walker, masons, by which it was provided that] the said Thomas and Murdo sall, with all deligence possibill, begin and big the toun wall, samekill as is vnbiggit thairof, compleitlie, fra the new wall, at the Blakfreris to Sanct Marie Porte, of the heicht and thiknes of the said new wall, viz., sex futes thik at the ground and fyve futes thik ascending vp to the battelling plane on baithe sydes weill pinnit and harlit, the said battelling of fyve quarter heich or thairby, and the haill heicht of the said wall fra the ground vp to be and contene sewin elnis heicht; and the said Thomas and Murdo to furneis sand, lyme, stane, masoneis, layaris, quarrouris, barromen, scaffalding, and all vther necessaris for the said wark . . . and sall nocht tak doun the auld dike presentlie standand vnto the time the said new wall be past ane mannis heicht with the mair; and sall forther, efter the avise and appointment of my said lord prowest and sic vtheris as salbe nominat with his lordschip, big at sic partes of the said wall as salbe fund maist convenient and necessar blok housis, flankouris, mvrdreis hoillis and vther defenssis necessar. *(margin: Villa, town wall, contract, masouneis.)*

8 *August* 1567.

Precept thes- aurer.
[The treasurer ordained, " with all deligence possebill, to caus big vp and mend the toun wallis and sloppis thairof, mend the Kowgait port, the wall at the castell bank, the gallous wallis, the ovir trone and the calsayis vtouth the West Port."]

13 *August* 1567.

Grange, artailye.
The prouest baillies and counsale and dekynnis ordanis the thesaurar to len to the laird of Grange sa mekill of the townys monitioun for seruing of him towert Orknay, taking his obligatioun to rander the samyn agane, quhairof the said thesaurer salbe dischargit.

20 *August* 1567.

Ipoticaris.
The prouest baillies and counsale, vnderstanding the hale ipoticaris of this burgh to be the principale ventaris and sellaris of spices, quhilk apertenis principallie to the brethering of gild and nane vtheris, quharfoir thay ordane maister Jhonn Prestoun, dene of gild, to caus all the ipoticaris of this burgh to desist and ceis fra venting of spices in commoun, vtherwise than in thair medicinis, failling heirof to close and lok vp thair durris ay and quhill thay becum fre burgessis and gild brether.

27 *August* 1567.

Landis and annuallis.
The prouest baillies and counsall namis, deputis and ordanis Robert Cuninghame, [and seven others,] to tak triall and to mak inventure of the annuallis sumtyme pertening to the chaplanis and mortefeit to the kirk and now to the ministerre and pure; and names maister Nicholl Chesholme to be collectour of the money that sall happin to be restand of the saidis annuallis or houssis belanging to the ministerre.

Swescheouris, slauchter of the King.
The baillies and counsall ordanis Jhone Harwod, thesaurar, to pay fyvetein shillingis to the thre swescheouris that playit afoir the toun the xxij day of August the tyme of the halding of the assys vpoun the laird of Skyrling, Richardtoun and Capitane Edmistoun for the alledgit slauchter of the king.

11 September 1567.

The provest baillies and counsale of this burgh, with awys and con- Chisholme, sent of maister Jhone Craig, minister, and haill kirk of this burgh of collectour. Edinburgh, hes maid constitute and ordanit, lykeas be thir presentes thay mak constitute and ordanis thair weilbelouit nychtbour, maister Michaell Chesholm, burges of the said burgh, thair collectour generall in and to the vplifting and inbringing of all malis, fermes, dewiteis, annuallis, annualrentis, daill syluer, obeittis, anniuersareis, and otheris dewiteis quhatsumeuir quhilk heirtofoir pertenit or wes knawin to perten to quhatsumeuir chapillis, kirkis, colledgis, prebendareis, chaiplanereis or alteragis within the said burgh and libertie thairof, foundit be quhatsumeuir persoun or patroun thairof in ony tyme past, and alssua to vplift and inbring the malis, fermes, emolimentis, annuallis, annualrentis, proffettis and dewiteis of all landis, tenementis, houssis, biggingis, craftis, orcheardis, kirkis, kirkyairdis, quhilkis in tymes past pertenit to preistis, monkis, freris, chanonis, nonis, and otheris of that ordour, lyand within the said burgh, fredome and libertie thairof; gewand grantand and committand to the said maister Michaell thair full fre and plane power for the saidis maillis, dewteis, annualrentis, emolimentis, fermes, proffettis, anniuersareis, obeit syluer, and otheris dewiteis quhatsumener of the saidis kirkis, colledgis, chaipellis, chaiplanereis, nonreis, houssis, biggingis, yairdis, kirkyairdis, orchardis, kirkis and chaipellis, the tymber, stanys thairof, intromettit with be quhatsumener persoun or personis, to call and persew the samyn, to vplift and inbring to the vtilite and proffett of the ministeris, ministare, pure and hospitallis of the said burgh, and all and sindrie otheris thingis till do that to the office of collectorie pertenis or salbe knawin to pertene; prividing alwayis the said maister Michaell be haldin yeirle to mak compt rekning and payment of his intromissioun of the premissis to the provest baillies counsall and kirk foirsaid to the effect aboue speceifiit. And this present gift and office to haif strenthe or effect induring thair willis allanerlie. And the said maister Michaell, in presens of the saidis provest baillies and counsall, acceptit the said office in and vpoun him and promist to do his dewite thairin as he wald answer to God and thame.

1 *October* 1567.

Lokkis of the new well.

The baillies and counsall, sittand in the counsalhous, comperit Alexander Uddart and delinerit the four lokkis of the new well, with tua keyis to the samyn sernand thir four lokkis, to Alexander Clerk, baillie of the southeist quartar.

3 *October* 1567.

Blakfreris, hospitale.

The baillies and counsale ordanis officeris to charge Walter Bynning, paynter, Nychole Fyldour, Jhonn Gilbert, goldsmyth, and all vtheris that hes intromettit with stanys or tymber of the Blakfreris to restore the samyn agane in thair awin places, for biging of the hospitale, with all deligence, with certificatioun and thay failye thair personis salbe wairdyt quhill the samyn be done, and ordanis cast doun the said Bynningis yaird biggit vpoun the freir kirkyaird.

The vnlaw of sic as drawis blude in thair fechting.

The prowest baillies and counsall, having considderatioun of the gret and manifest wrangis and oppressionis committit dalie be certane nichtbouris of this burgh, and otheris resortand thairto, aganis otheris, quhilkis, haifling nother feir of God nor man, daylie invadis otheris with fensable wappinnis, sic as sweirdis, quhingaris, battonis and vtheris instrumentis bellicall, sumtyme committing slauchter mutilatioun or lamyng ather of other: For remeid of the quhilk and stancheing of sic horrable oppressioun, the saidis prowest baillies and counsall statutis and ordanis that quhatsumeuer persoun within this burgh in tyme cuming drawis blude of ane other be way of violence, with quhatsumeuer kynd of wappin, battoun, stane or otherwys on set purpois, or is conviet of bludewyte, that the drawar thairof, or being conviet of bludewyte, sall pay ane vnlaw of fyve pund, vnforgevin, to the commoun warkis of this burgh, without preiudice of the panis of imprisonment, satisfactioun of the pairtie, or other actis maid anent trublance of befoir.

### 10 *October* 1567.

The baillies and counsall ordanis maister Robert Glen and Alexander Kirk. Guthre to vesye the kirk and faltis thairof and to report to the counsall, that the samyn may be remedit.

### 7 *November* 1567.

[The treasurer ordained] " to caus mak and deliuer to ilk ane of the *Officiaris of* tua sernandis of Leithe ane buttoun of sylner, haiffand the tounis mark on *Leyth.* the samyn, viz., the castell and ane schip, togidder with ilk ane of thame ane halbart."

### 10 *November* 1567.

[The bailies, council and deacons of crafts,] being convenit in the *Prestoun,* counsalhous of this burgh, comperit Sir Symon Prestoun of Craigmillar, *prouest, gift of the Trinitie* knycht. prouest of this burgh, and schew and declarit to the saidis baillies *College to* counsall and dekynnis that he had obtenit and impetrat at my lord *Edinburgh.* regentis handis the gift of the Trinite College, kirk, houssis, biggingis, and yairdis adiacent thairto, and lyand contegue to the samyn, to be ane hospitall to the pure. and to be biggit and vphaldin be the gude toun, and the elimosinaris to be placit thairinto be the prouest baillies and counsall present and being for the tyme, and nochtwithstanding that he hes lauborit the samyn it wes nocht his mynde to laubour it to his awyn behuif bot to the gude tounis as said is, and thairfore presentlie gaif the gift thairof to the gude toun and transferrit all rycht and titill that he had or mycht haif thairto in the guid toun fra him and his airis for euir *ad perpetuam remanentiam.*

The prowest baillies and counsall foirsaid namit and constitute *Foullertoun,* Adam Fullartoun, baillie, maister of wark to the hospitale to be foundit *maister of wark, college.* in the Trinitie Colledge, with power to him to cheis his officiaris and warkmen as he sall think gude.

14 *November* 1567.

Foullertoun, villa.

The prouest baillies and counsall ordanis Adam Foulertoun, maister of wark of the Trinite College, to caus, with all deligence possibill, conforme to the devise takin be thame, enter to the bigging of the hospitall in the said college, and to transport and intromet with the townis tymmer lyand in the freris yardis, and to apply the samyn to the werk of the said hospitall, and siclike to mak money of the lime and stane in the saidis freir yardis to be warit vpoun the said hospitall as said is.

20 *November* 1567.

Freir yairdis, sett.

[The council disponed to certain persons, in feu farm, the lands "sumtyme pertening to the Blak freris and now to the toun of Edinburgh, for the interes syluer and yeirlie annual vnderwrittin, to be payit to thair hospitale and sustening of the pure thairof."]

10 *December* 1567.

Ansenyeis.

[The bailies, council, and deacons,] being convenit in the counsall hous of this burgh, ordanis [*blank*] ansenyeis of quhite and blak taffateis to be maid, haiffand the Kingis armes on the ane syde and the castell of Edinburgh on the other side, and to be payit of the superexcrescence of the last taxt maid and rasit for bigging of the wall at the Blakfreris.

Anent the striking of swesche.

The prouest baillies and counsall statutis and ordanis that na swesche nor tabroun be strekkin within this burgh without command and licence obtenit thairto be the saidis prowest or baillies, or that onye playaris on siclyke instrumentis pas to honest menis houssis or yettis to play, except onlie our Soueranis men of weir now instantlie being within this burgh, vnder the pane of breking of the swesche and pvnesing of sic as playis thairwith fra this day furth.

24 *December* 1567.

Making of burgessis.

The baillies and counsall ordanis that euerye man at the making of him burges sall obleis him self to haif jak, speir, swerd, buklar and steill bonet, for serving of the baillies and gude toun quhen thai haif ado, and to keip the wappinschawing with the nychtbouris vnder sic panis as may be laid to thar charge. <small>Making of burgessis.</small>

### 18 *February* 1567-8.

The baillies counsale and dekynnis disponis the dewteis and renttis of the alterege of Sanct Anthone, now vacand and being in thair handis be deces of vmquhile Sir James Young, last chaplane thairof, to maister Mychaell Chisholme, collectour of the hospitale, and ordanis the dewteis of the wynis pertenyng to the said alterege, viz., ane choppin of ilk puntioun to be rowpit and lattin to thame that biddis maist thairfor, and to be applyit to the said hospitale. <small>St Anthonis alterege.</small>

### 20 *February* 1567-8.

[The treasurer ordained "to deliuere to Mungo Bradie, goldsmyth, cautinare and suertie for Jhone Knox hous maill, the sowme of x merkis."] <small>Jhone Knox.</small>

### 3 *March* 1567-8.

[The provost, bailies, and council, at the desire of the chaplain of St James' altar in St Giles' Kirk, consented, as patrons of that altar, that a tenement situated at the head of the Over Bow should be set in feu, the purchaser paying to the chaplain during his lifetime, "and efter his deceis, to the hospitall foundit be the gude towne in the Trinitie College, the sowme of twelf merkis yeirly feu maill." <small>Villa,St James' altar, hospital.</small>

### 19 *March* 1567-8.

[Certain fines for selling wines above the fixed price "to be applyit to the hospitale."] <small>Hospitale.</small>

[The bailies and council,] efter inspectioun of the peyr bulwark and havin of Leyth, and seing the samyn rewinous, dekeyit, and sall nocht fale haistelie to fall doun gyf mair haistye help be nocht prouidit, and siclik the hale calsayis betuix and Leyth to be brokin, the greit wyndois of Sanct Gelis Kirk to be blawin doun, the maist pairtt of the rufe tyrvit be the last greit wynd, sua that the pepill sall nocht convene thairintill at <small>Reparatioun of the peyr, calsayis and kirk.</small>

Reparatioun of    preching and prayer, and the hale kirk dekey gyf in like maner the
the peyr, cal-    samyn with all deligence be nocht reparit and helpit, and knawing thame
sayis and kirk.
                  selffis to haue na commoun gude before the hand, and to be greitlie superex-
                  pendit and thair commoun renttis thirlit, sua that it sall nocht be able to
                  thame to help repair and big the saidis warkis according to thair honour
                  and commoun weill, except the merchanttis and craftismen may be persuadit
                  to spair the proflit of the commoun mylnis, for this present yeir allanerlie,
                  quhilk is appoyntit in pairt of payment of thair sowmes debursit vpoun
                  the superioritie of Leyth sa fer as the samyn will extend, and to this
                  effect ordanis officeris to warn the haill dekynnis to compeir before thame
                  the nixt counsall day for registering of thair consent to the premissis.

Masonis,          Adam Foullertoun, baillie, confest him to have ressaueitt fra Thomas
Foullertoun.
                  Jacksoun and Murdo Walker, masounis, the sowme of four scoir pundis for
                  the lime, sand and stanis lyand in the Blakfreir kirk yard before thair
                  intere to the bigging of the town wall, quhilk he hes warit vpoun the
                  bigging of the hospitall.

                                    24 *March* 1567-8.

Villa, Guthrie,   In presens of [the bailies and council,] comperit [the deacons of crafts,]
bulwark, lent
money.            and efter rype avysement and deliberatione amangs thameselfis and with
                  thair haill craftis, concludis grantis and consentis, for themselfis and haill
                  craftis, that thair fyft pairt of the money avaneeit be thame vpoun the
                  superioritie of Leyth for this present yeir, [beginning Martinmas 1567 and
                  ending Martinmas 1568,] be avansit and debursit be Alexander Guthre,
                  commoun clerk, vpoun the reparatioun of the peyr and bulwark of Leyth,
                  the calsayis betuix and thair, and vpoun the warkis of Sanct Gelis kirk,
                  as at lenth is contenit in thair act of the daitte *decimo nono instantis Martii;*
                  provyding alwayis thai be nocht forther astrictit be this thair consent to
                  want thair money langar nor for this present yeir abone mentionat; and
                  siclyke, the baillies and counsall foirsaid, takand the burding vpoun thame
                  for thameselfis and haill merchantis of this burgh quhilkis hes lent and
                  avansit money vpoun the said superioritie of Leyth, grantis and consentis

that the rest of the haill money of the common mylnis for the said yeir be  Villa Guthrie,
avansit and debursit vpoun the saidis warkis be the said Alexander, bulwark, lent money.
deduceand the annuellis and necessar expenssis vpoun the reparation of the
saidis mylnis, provydand as is befoir prouydit.

### 27 *March* 1568.

The baillies and counsall ordanis Adame Fowlertoun to accept the  Foullertoun.
charge vpoun him of the bigging of the kirk windokis, and all vther workis
necessar within the kirk, and assignis to him the dewite of the burgeschipis
and gildschippis of all sic as he may find that occupeis the fredome of this
burgh to the payment of the charge of the said wark, and quhat he beis
forther superexpendit ordanis Alexander Guthrie to mak him payment
thairof of the readiest of the dewite of the mylnis.

### 7 *April* 1568.

[The bailies and council, "efter consideratioun of the pouertie and auld decrepit  Freir Leis.
aige of freir Andro Leis, blak freir," instructed the collectors of "the saidis freris
renttis" to pay him yearly £16 during his lifetime.]

### 9 *April* 1568.

The prouest baillies and counsale, vnderstauding be complaynt of the  Commissaris to
dekynnis and commonetie that be licencis allegit granttit be my lord Glasgow for discharging of
Regenttis grace to cary victuellis furth of the realme, thair is greit victuellis.
apperance of skantnes and derth, quhairfor thay ordane Alexander Clerk,
baillie, maister Mychaell Chisholme, James Young of the counsale, Alexander
Guthre and Thomas Aikinheid, dekyn of the skynnaris, to pas to my said
lord Regenttis grace in Glasgow for dischargeing of the saidis licences,
and ordanis the thesaurer to recompance thame thair expenssis.

### 13 *April* 1568.

The prouest baillies and counsale ordanis Andro Selater, baillie, and  Collectoris,
William Litill, of the counsale, to travell amangis the nychtbouris of this hospitale.
burgh of the north pairt of the toun, Jhonn Adamsoun and Nychole Vddert
for the south, and to inquyre quhat thay will grant of thair liberalitie to

| | |
|---|---|
| Collectoris, hospitale. | the biging of the hospitale, and the samyn to collect and inbring to be applyit vpoun the said hospitale. |

### 20 April 1568.

| | |
|---|---|
| Beidmanschippis. | [The council gave "tua beidmanschippis, vacand be deces of James Tollnith, barbour, and (blank), to Dauid Robertsoun, barbour, and Henry Bawtie, masoun."] |
| Burges, etc. | [Andro Hagye " maid burges and gild broder gratis, at the requeist of my lord erle of Mar."] |

### 8 May 1568.

| | |
|---|---|
| Wilsoun, dekyn of the smythis dischargit. | The prowest baillies and counsall, after avisement with the supplicatioun producit befoir thame be the deikin and brether of the hammermen craft, bering that the multitude of thair said craft had, by the consent of the honest men thairof, electit and chosin Jhone Wilsoun, pewderer, to be thair deikin for the yeir intoeum, beand ane man of na religioun, expres contrer the tenour of the act of parliament laitlie maid, and thairfore desyrit the said Jhone to be deposit and ane other to be input in his place, as at mair lenth is contenit in thair said supplicatioun; quhilk beand red and considderit, the said Jhonne Wilson beand personallie present and confessand himself nocht [to] be adiunit with the kirk of God, nother to haunt nor frequent preiching nor prayer, thai all in ane voice, conforme to the said act of parliament, dischairgis the said Jhone of his office of deikinschip, and ordanis ane other to be electit in his place quhill he communicat and is of the kirk of God, and thairvpoun the said brether of hammer craft askit actis. |
| Extent vc li. | [The provost, bailies, and deacons of crafts] consentis and grantis that ane extent of fyve hundreth pund be vpliftit of the haill nychtbouris of this burgh for monting of the munitioun and defence of the toun as neid sall requyre. |

The prowest baillies and counsall ordanis ane walpinschawing to be maid of all the nychtbouris of this burgh on Wednisday nixt, ilk persoun vnder the pane of twenty s. vnforgevin.

## 12 May 1568.

The prowest baillies and counsell ordanis ane wache to be made Wache. nychtlie of ane hundreth men, and on the day of twenty foure men, and that nane be chargit, nother compeir vpoun the said wache, but the principallis of euery hous, except thai be passit the dait of thre scoir of yeiris, and thais to furnisch habill and sufficient men weill arnit for thame, ilk persoun vnder the pane of auchtein s.

The prowest baillies counsell and deikinis ordanis twa sweschis to pas Sweschis. nychtlie throch the touh, bayth Hie Street and Kowgait, at aucht houris at evin and siclyke at fyve houris in the morning.

## 19 May 1568.

The baillies and counsall ordanis writingis to be maid to the magis- Villa. tratis of Campheir in fauouris of George Kinkaid and the vtheris factouris Campheir. Scottismen dwelland thair, willing thame to travell at all handis neidfull for thair quietnes and securite in this time of trowbill.

The prowest baillies and counsall ordanis the dekynnis vnderwrittin [Army.] to avise with thair craftis and report ansuer on Friday nixt quhether thay will pas furth with my lord Regentis grace, efter the tenour of the proclamatioun ordanit to convene at Beggar the x of Junij nixt, or furneis men or money.

## 2 June 1568.

The prouest baillies and counsall ordanis Adame Fowlertoun, Jhone [Army.] Harwod, Alexander Guthre and James Young to pas to my lord Regentis grace, and in thair names desire licence to the gude toun to remane at hame from the armie, and to report ansuer.

## 4 June 1568.

At the requeist of my lord Regentis grace writing, William Leich, Leche burges, ane of the grumeis of his graceis chalmer is maid burges and gild brother fr. gilde. and the dewite thairof gevin him gratis,

Extent jn li.

The prowest baillies counsall and haill dekynnis consentis and grantis that ane extent of j^m li. be vpliftit of the haill nichtbouris of this burgh, for furnesing of the men of weir to pas fordwert at this present armie with my lord Regentis grace, vnder the chargeis of Adame Fowlertoun, baillie, and ordanis the counsall to be extentouris of this extent.

### 17 July 1568.

North Loch.

[The bailies and council,] vnderstanding that thair North Loche is dry and passable layth be man and hors at the west end thairof; for remeid quhairof thay ordanit Jhoun Harwod, thesaurer, to fie xxiiij werkmen with spaid, schule, and matok, for casting of the fowseis at the heid of the said loch, and to geve to everilk ane of the said werkmen ij s. in the day, to be vplifted of the nychtbouris conforme to the stent roll, passand be ordour throw all the quarteris of the toun, geve neid sall requyre, viz., everilk nychtbour to furneis ane man for ane day, and makis Eduard Hendersoun maister of wark induring thair will.

[Wells.]

The baillies and counsall ordanis the thesaurer to caus theik and cover the Stok wall, Muse wall, and Sanct Michaellis wall, and ordanis the kepar of the West port to keip the said Stok wall, the portar of the Greyfreir port the Muse wall, the porter of the Kirk of Feild the new wall, and the porter of the Cowgait port Sanct Michaellis wall; and thes wallis tilbe oppinit for seruing of the nychtbouris at fyve houris in the mornyng and tua efter none in somer, to be closit at xij houris opinit at tua and cloisit at four for all nycht.

### 28 July 1568.

Maister of scole.

The baillies and counsale ordanis maister Alexander Guthre to ryde to Sanctandrois for maister Thomas Buchquhennane to be maister of thair hie scole.

### 6 August 1568.

Villa, thesaurer, touu warkis.

The prouest baillies counsale and dekynnis, being convenit in the counsale hous, eftir lang ressonyng vpoun the apperand troublis to be maid be the lordis of the south and north and west countreis betuix and the nixt parliament, and hering that thay pretend with all thair forces to cum to this toun, ordanis Johnn Harwod, thesaurer, with all possabill deligence, to caus ranforce the blokhoussis of the toun wallis, byg and mend quhair myster is at the saidis wallis, and to big ane stane wall at the eist end of the North Loch, cast fowseis, and repair all vther thingis neidfull for strenthing of this toun.

*Villa, thesaurer, toun warkis.*

### 11 August 1568.

The provost baillies and counsale ordanis the hale dekynnis, being personallie present, to convene thair craftis, bayth maister, taskman, prentise and seruand, and tak inquisitioun be thair aithis quhat will be thair pairttis in this present troublis, to enroll thair names and report thair depositionis the morne eftermon, as they will ansuer vpoun thair vtermaist charge.

*Craftis.*

The provost baillies and counsale ordanis Jhonn Harwod, thesaurer, to borrow Walter Cant and William Logannys artailye and to becum oblist for deliuering of the samyn agane or the avale thairof.

*Villa, artailye.*

The provost baillies and counsale ordanis ane strang wache to be set nychtlie for keiping of the toun, and that euerye man walk be his awin persoun without exceptioun bot of sic as ar aigit or seik, vnder the pane of xviij s. vnforgevin, and this wache be ordour throuch the toun to indure quhill the end of the parliament.

*Villa, wache.*

### 26 August 1568.

[The provost, bailies, and council,] efter lang ressonyng with maister Thomas Buchquhennane concernyng the instructing of the youth of this toun, knawing him to be maist abill and qualifeit thairfor, for thame selflis and in name and behalfe of the hale counsale and dekynnis, havand thair command and consent thairto, appoynttis and aggreis with the said maister Thomas in maner following, that is to say: for the first yeir, in case it be knawin to thame that the said maister Thomas, with the fiftie

*Maister scole.*

Maister scole. merk thay haue grantit him of yeirle pensioun, with the dewitc of the barnis, quhilk is iiij s. of ewerie barne, be nocht worth thre hundreth merkis for the said first yeir or thairby, thay sall caus thair thesaurer, present or for the tyme, to gif vnto him vther fifte merkis quhilk salbe j<sup>e</sup> merkis for the samyn first yeir, and yeirle thairefter according to thair appointment to be maid fifte merkis as said is.

Vddert, villa. The baillies and counsall ordanis writingis to be direct to the haill borrowis for thair consent to ane taxt to be maid for satisfeing of Nicholl Vddart of the sowmes debursit be him in doungetting of the x siluer deneris of ilk tun wine in Burdeaux, and to register thair ansuer with deligence.

### 5 September 1568.

Guthre, Inglis, villa. The proucst baillies and counsale ordanis Alexander Guthre and Jhonn Inglis, masoun, to ryde to Dunbar and vesy the stanys thairof laitlie castin doun, and gyf thai be found meit and convenient for the wark of the schore of Leyth to by the samyn.

### 5 October 1568.

Regent, villa, continuatio prepositi et ballinorum. The copye of my lord Regenttis writing producit be Capitane Mailuill:—Counsale and dekynnis of the burgh of Edinburgh, we greit yow hartlie weill. Being, as ye knaw, in radynes to pas in Ingland for that commoun caus that is sa deyr to ws all, we haue had speciall thocht and consideratioun of tua thingis belanging your toun, that is of the electioun of the magistratis the appoyntit tyme now approching, and of the publict ordour to be obsernit anent the plaige quhairwith God hes presentlie veseyit the samyn, that in sa fer as mannis pairt and dewtie is the occasioun of forther infectioun may be cuttit of be all gude menys, amangis quhilk we fynd na mene mair apperant to proflit nor that tha samyn magistratis that hes begyn the ordour, and presentlie takis cair for the preseruatioun thairof, remane and be continewit in thair offices, be ressoun vtheris to be electit, perauenture refusing to accept, or at leist delaying, the leist tyme protractit may be the occatioun of rycht greit skayth, or than sic as salhappin to tak the office vpoun thame throuch laik of experience may omyt the maist necessar thingis that in sa strait ane tyme ar requisit to be done. Ye ar nocht ignorant of the cair deligence and gude will of your present prouest, and of Alexander Clerk and Adam Foullertoun, baillies, in all commoun seruices sen thay war placet be yow in that charge, and thairfor it is best, be oure aduise and openioun, and we will effectuallie desyre and pray yow in your electioun now approching to continew the prouest and the tua baillies aboue writtin for the yeir to cum, quhairin we dont nocht bot ye sall greitlie avance and further your commoun weill in monye respectis, and thairwithall we will think that in this as diuers vtheris wayis ye do ws werray thankfull and acceptable plesour. God in this your present actioun and all vtheris comfort and conduct yow. At Temptalloun, the xxvj of September 1568. Your rycht assurit freind, JAMES, Regent. Quhilk writing, in presens of the baillies and hale counsale, being red and considerit, thay all in ane voce granttis consenttis and obeyis the samyn, bot, for obseruing of the ordour, willis the said prouest and baillies to be electit of new and to be continewit for the yeir to cum, vnder protestatioun this be nocht preiudiciall to the princlegis grantit in the act of parliament concernyng the electing of officeris within burgh. *Regent, villa, continuatio prepositi et balliuorum.*

### 13 *October* 1568.

The baillies and counsall ordanis proclamatioun to be maid that na maner of persoun tak vpon hand to pas to the Borrow Muir for veseing of the seik, or quhatsumeuer vther caus, befor xj houris afore none, at quhilk time euerie day thair salbe ane officiar appointit to remane at the West Port for conveying of thame that hes ado on the said muir, and of all sic as sall pas with him do thair besines in his presens and return agane with him; and siclike na maner of persoun tak vpoun thame the charge of keping of seik without licence had and obtenit of the baillie of thair quarter, vnder the pane of deid. *Pest.*

### 15 *October* 1568.

Statutes for the baillies of the Mure and ordouring of the pest as efter followis :-- *Pest.*

| | |
|---|---|
| Pest. | Item, in the first, for ordouring of the said mure and pepill infectit thairvpoun, for clenging of thair claythis and clengeing of houssis within the toun, that Jhone Steuart, wobster, and Robert Fleming, cordiner, be electit baillies of the said muir and suorne for doing of thair office treulie, conforme to the statutes vnderwrittin and panis contenit in the samyn, [they receiving for their labouris £8 monthly]. |

Item, that Jhone Leggat and Alexander Frencshe haue the charge of of the bureing of the deid, and with thame Jonet Wylie and Agnes Broun, and thay to haue the monethly wages following:—[John Leggat and Alexander Frensche, £5 each; and Jonet Wylie and Agnes Broun, £3 each].

Item, that the thesaurer caus mak, with all deligence, for euerie ane of the baillies, clengeris, and the burearis of the deid, ane goun of gray with Sanct Androis cors, quhite, behind and before, and to euerie ane of thame ane stalf with ane quhite clayth on the end, quhairby thai may be knawin quhaireuer thay pas.

Item, that thair be maid tua clois beris with foure feit colourit our with blak, and ane quhite cors with ane bell to be hungin vpoun the heid of the said beir quhilk sall mak warning to the pepill.

| | |
|---|---|
| Villa, Foullertoun. | The baillies, counsale and dekynnis, vnderstanding the greit necessite in this troublis tyme of pest requyris deligent and expert men to tak panys, and seing Adam Foullartoun, baillie the tua yeris past, nochtwithstanding my lord Regentis graces writing for continewing of him, refussis to tak ony forther burding or pane, and will nocht accept the office of baillierie for the yeir to cum, nochtwithstanding he be electit thairto, thay all in ane voce, vpoun the sure experience of the said Adameis habelite and gude seruice, maist ernistlie requeistis and desyris him to accept the said office of baillierie for the yeir to cum as saidis, and faythfulie promissis that thay sall recompance and rewarde him, bayth for his laubouris past and tocum, quhilk promyst the said Adam acceptit and askit instrumentis. |

Item, it is statute and ordanit that how sone ony maner of persoun Statuta fallis seik within this burgh, in quhatsumeuir kynde of seiknes that euer pestilencie. it be, the awneris of the hous inclose thame selflis and cum nocht furth of thair houssis, nowther suffer ony to resort to thame vnto the tyme thai aduertice the baillie of the quarter and ordour be taikin be him, vnder the pane of deid.

Item, that na maner of persoun pas to the mure for veseing of thair frendis thair quhill xj houris before none, in cumpanye with the officer appoynttit for that day, vnder the said pane.

Item, that the buriell be maid in the Grayfreir kirk yaird, lairge and wyde, of deipnes sevin fute and of breid (*blank*) futtis.

Item, that all personis sic as sellis weddis be dischargit, and in speciall sic as sellis wollin and lynning, and uane of thame be fundin makand merket, vnder the said pane.

Item, that na maner of persoun that salhappin pas be the caldrone abstract ony of thair guddis, vnder the pane of deid.

Item, that with all deligence posseble, sa sone as ony hous salbe infect, the hale honshald with thair guddis be depeschit towert the mwre, the deid bureit, and with the like deligence the houssis clengit.

Item, that the clengerris cum nocht within the toun quhill ane officiar pas for thame, and all the tyme of thair besynes the said officer await vpoun thame and gyf attendance that thay haue na commonyng with ony personis be the way, nother interchanging of ony guddis, vnder all hieast pane may be imput to thame.

Item, that na persoun clengit enter within the toun with[out] licence of the baillie, and be convoyit with ane officer to the place appoyntit for thame, vnder the pane of deid; and that thay cum nocht furth of thair houssis for the space of xx dayis efter thair entre within the toun, vnder the said pane; and in the monetyme that [thai] keip cumpany with na clene personis nor thay with thame, vnder the said pane.

[The council and deacons gave "tua beidmanschippis vacand be deceis of Beidman. William Couttis, officer, and Hagy Walkar, to Jhon Richertsoun and Gottersoun, tailycouris."]

| | |
|---|---|
| Chisholme, benefice. | [The council and deacons disponed to Michael Chisholm, "in name of the hospitale, the benefice vacand be deceis of Sir Robert Robertsoun, and ordanis him to collect the dewteis thairof to the pure."] |

*16 October 1568.*

| | |
|---|---|
| Commissio. | The provest baillies and counsale granttis that commissioun be gevin be the lordis of Sessioun to maisteris Thomas Makcalycane, Clement Litill, Alexander Manchane and James Barroun, makand thame baillies deput induring thair willis to juge vpoun the annuall and dewiteis of the kirk of auld, to the vtilite of the ministrie and hospitale. |

*17 October 1568.*

| | |
|---|---|
| Precept, thesaurer, pikis. | [The treasurer ordained to pay to Adam Foullertoun and six others, "euery ane of thame v li., avanceit be thame at thair command to ane man of Hamburgh for certane lang pikis bocht be the counsale fra him."] |

*21 October 1568.*

| | |
|---|---|
| Proclamatioun, burgesses. | [Proclamatioun to be made, charging "all sic as ar burgesses, and hes nocht stob and stuik within this toun, to cum and mak thair remanyng within the samyn within xl dayis nixt heirefter, vnder pane of tynsale of thair fredome."] |

*10 November 1568.*

| | |
|---|---|
| Pest, Forrest. | The baillies and counsale ordanis Jhonn Forrest, cordiner, to tak vpoun [him] the charge of all pepill that sal happin to be clengit of the pest, and appoyntis him the west pairt of thair Borrow Mwre for clenging of thame and thair guddis, with this conditioun gyf falt be found in his clengeing and the pepill clengit infect agane in his defalt that he sall incur the deid thairfor. |
| Extent vc li. | The baillies counsale and dekynnis granttis and consenttis that ane extent be vpliftit of v$^c$ li. for sustenyng of the pure in this present pest. |
| Villa, Lausoun. | Jhone Lausoun of Ilie Riggis produceit befor the baillies and counsall the supplicatioun vnderwrittin, bering, as he wes informit, thair wisdomes had cansit big ane heid dike vpoun his ground and landis of Ilie Rigis and thairthrouch stoppit the watter passege of thair South Loch passing |

throuch his landis in all times past, quhilk will nocht faill be proces of  Villa Lausoun. time mak the said loch to enter at vther partis vpoun his saidis landis and distroy the samyn to his greit hurt, quhairfore he desireit thair wisdomeis to caus reforme the said dike, sua that the watter mycht haue passege as it had of before, and thair ansuer. To the quhilk it wes ansuerit be the pronest baillies and counsall forsaid, thay fand thai had done na wrang in rasing and liging of thair awin dike, vpoun thair awin ground of thair awin South Loch, for halding in of the watter thairof, for serning of the wellis of the Kowgaitt to the furnesing of haill pepill of thair toun and vtheris our Souerane Lordis lieges resortand thairto, and thairfore certefeis the compleneris that thai will proceid according to thair rycht.

### 14 November 1568.

The baillies counsale and dekynnis, efter consideratioun of the greit Villa,Lausoun. ininrie and wrang done to thame be Jhoun Lawsoun of Hierigis and his complices, vpoun Sounday at evin last, within silence of nycht, in the destroying, doun casting, and braik of thair new dike bigit vpoun thair awin ground at the end of the arrabill landis callit Hierigis for inhalding of the watter of thair South Loch for serning of the haill wellis in the Cowgait, etc., ordanis proclamatioun to be maid chargeing all the inhabitanttis of this burgh, merchant, craftismen, and all vtheris without exceptioun, with all deligence possebil, with schole and mattok and spaid, to pas with the baillies to the said South Loch for reformyng of the said wrang, the occasioun thairof, and all vther wrangis within thair boundis and fredome, ilk persoun vnder the pane of xl s. vnforgevin.

### 18 November 1568.

The baillies counsale and dekynnis grantis and consenttis that thair Watche, xviij be lystit xviij men of the maist abill within this burgh, with culvering, to personis. await vpoun the baillies at all tymes neidfull and to keip wache within the toun for saiftie of the nychtbouris houssis and guddis that ar furth of the samyn, and ordanis euerye ane of thame to haue iij li. x s.

| | |
|---|---|
| Wache, xviij personis. | monethlie to be taikin of the hale nychtbouris at the discretioun of the baillies induring the said counsale and dekynnis willis. |
| Villa, demoleshing of houssis on the toun wallis. | The baillies counsale and dekynnis ordanis to demolische and cast doun all houssis jonyt to the toun wallis vtouth and inwith the samyn, sua that the pepill may haue fre passage in the tyme of neid for defence of the toun. |
| Calsay. | The baillies and counsall ordanis the calsay from the Ower Trone to the Castelhill to be maid of new, vpoun the expenssis of the heritouris of the landis on bayth sideis of the gait and within cloissis adiacent thairto, viz., euerie pund maill the annuell xij d., and gif neid beis ordanis officeris to poind thairfor. |

### 19 November 1568.

| | |
|---|---|
| Thesaurer, [Knox.] | [The treasurer ordained "to caus mend and repair the necessaris of Jhone Knox dwelling hous, vpoun the expenssis of Johne Adamsoun and Bessie Otterburne his spous, coniunct fear thairof, and deduce the samyn of thair hous maill, becaus thai haif bene oft tymes requyrit to do the samyn and refussit."] |
| Guthre, villa. | The baillies counsell and dekynnis, vnderstanding the greit necessite of the pvir infectit of the pest vpoun thair borrow mvir for laik of victuallis quhilk can nocht be had becaus thair is na market kepit within this toun, ordanis Alexander Guthre to furnis and delyuer to James Wod, baxter, of the reddiest of the quheit of the commoun mylnis being in his possessioun, and the pryces thairof, viz., fourtie four s. the boll, to be payit to him be the baillies or the said James Wod of the reddiest of the extent grantit for susteining of the pvir. |

### 17 December 1568.

| | |
|---|---|
| Wache. | The baillies and counsale ordanis ane nychtlie wache of xxiiij men, and quha that comperis nocht, being warnyt, to pay ij s. to ane vther to be put in his place, and quha sa evir beis set vpoun the wache and departis before vj howris to pay xviij s. vnlaw. |

[22] *December* 1568.

The baillies and counsale, seing that God of his mercye and gudlnes hes metigat the raige of the pest within this toun, and vnderstanding the monethlie wages payit to the officeris of the mwre to be lairge, thairfor fyndis and delineris that frome the xxv day of this instant December Johnn Stewert, [Alexander] Franche, and the tua wemen with thame, salbe dischargit. — *Officieris of the mwre dischargit.*

1 *January* 1568-9.

The baillies and counsall, vnderstanding the manesing and boist of the lordis of the West Cuntre aganis the toun, ordanis the haill inhabitantis abone the cors gif neids all require, vpoun the warning of the commoun bell or be the drum, to addres thame to Robert Forratt and William Litill, baillies, and the vtheris nychtbouris beneth the tolbuth to Adam Foullertoun and Alexander Clerk, baillies.

7 *January* 1568-9.

The baillies and counsall ordanis the deyne of gild to caus mak ane poupat, portative, to be set vp in the Over Tolbuth for preiching to the papistis, and to caus mend the intres of the polpat in the hie kirk. — *Polpatt.*

The baillies and counsall ordanis that proclamatioun be maid that na oppin tavernis be haldin the time of preiching on the Saboth day, vnder the pane of a vnlaw of fyve li. — *Proclamatio. Sabbathe.*

11 *February* 1568-9.

The baillies and counsall ordanis maister Thomas Bucquhannane, maister of the hie scole, to enter to instructt the yowth of this towne on Mononday nixt, and willis the minister publische the samyn to the pepill. — *Maister schole.*

17 *February* 1568-9.

[The bailies, council, and deacons of crafts] grantis and consentis that ane extent of sex hunder merkis be liftit of the haill nychtbouris of — *Extent, vje merkis.*

Extent, vj<sup>c</sup> merkis.

this burgh for furnissing of certane men of weir to my lord Regentis grace for ane moneth nixt heirafter.

### 4 March 1568-9.

Minister, thesaurer.

The baillies and counsell ordanis Andro Stewinsoun, thesaurer, to pay to Jhone Adamesoun the sowme of fourty merkis for the maill of his hous occupeit be Jhone Knox the yeir past, deduceand thairof the sowme of aucht pund debursitt be the said thesaurar in reparalyng of the said hous in defalt of the said Jhone Adamsoun, being requyrit to do the sam, and als xij merkis xij s. debursit mair be the said thesaurar in reparing of the samyn hous by the viij li. abone mentionat debursit be the said Jhonn.

### 1 April 1569.

Villa, Seynis.

The baillies and counsell, after avysment with thair gyft grantit to thame of the annuellis landis and dewteis quhilk pertenit to the munkis, preistis and freiris of this burgh, for sustening of the ministrie and hospitale, fyndis thai haif oursene thame sellis in omitting of the Seynis furth of thair said gift ; and thairfore ordanis the said gift to be maid our of new, and the four baillies to pas to my lord Regentis grace thairwith to gett the samyn subscryvitt.

### 6 April 1569.

Proclamatio, villa Sanctandrois.

The baillies and counsell, after avysment with ane writting send to thame be the prowest and baillies of Sanctandrois, bering that the cuntrie about thair said toun wes infect with the pest, for the quhilk caus thai haid dischairgit all mercats and fairis, and in speciall the fair callit the Seingyie fair, and thairfore willing that the nychtbouris of this burgh sall nocht tyne thair tyme, willit thame to be aduertist that thai cum nocht to thair said towne for the caussis foirsaid, after avisment as said is the baillies and counsell ordanis proclamatioun to be maid dischairging our nychtbouris to pas thair to the said fairis, with certificatioun to thame that dois in the contrair thai sall haif na entres within this toun before thai be ordorit as suspect personis and pay the vnlaw of ten li. for thair disobedience.

[The deacons warned to appear before the council to consider what portion of Villa, Blak escheat goods should be given to the "sone and air of vmquhill William Smith and Meg. Blak Meg, quha wer justefeit for breking of the lawis the tyme of the pest."]

The baillies and counsell ordanis Jhone Harwod, dene of gild, to Villa, dene of requyre of Dauid Somer the greitt clayth quhilk hang vpoun the bak gild, Prestoun, of thair hie alter the tyme of papistrie, and of maister Jhone Prestoun ane Dornik buird clayth, ane dissone of seruetis, and ane grein clayth; and gif neid be to call thairfore becaus the samyn pertenis to the gude towne.

### 9 April 1569.

The baillies and counsall ordanis Andro Steuinstoun, with all deligence Cliphous. possibill, to caus mak ane chope of tymmer to be set vp besyde the mercatt croce to be ane clypping hous, and ordanis proclamatioun to be maid chargeing all and sindre that hes money to ressaue or deliuer to bring the samyn to the said clipping hous, thair to be nummeritt be Nichole Sym, maister clypper, to the effect the fals money may be clippit and destroyit conforme to the act of parliament, and the said Nicholl gaif his ayth for trew executioun of his office dureing thair willis, and thay ordane him to his awin proper vse the haill fals money clippitt, togidder with 1d. of the pund of the gude money, to be payit be the ressauer for his laubouris.

### 28 May 1569.

The baillies and counsale ordanis fra this furth, induring the tyme of Statuta, symmer, quhan necessitie sall requyre, that the clangeris be everie nycht pestilencie. at the Grayfreir port be nyne houris at evin and remane thair quhill ten quhill the baillies or officieris cum for thame, and thairefter to enter to the clainging of the housis and transporting of the guidis of the housis first infectit, and incontinent, befoir all vther laubouris, to burye the deid gif ony be, and put furth the personis of the infectit housis with thame selfis, sua that nane of thame remane within the toun, and in doing heirof quhill four houris in the mornyng that the suasche strek.

1 *June* 1569.

Villa, Leyth, stanis.

The baillies and counsale ordanis Robert Forret, baillie, to appoint and aggrie with the minister in Leyth for the stanis takin be him fra the kirk of Leyth for reparing of the bulwark.

15 *June* 1569.

Villa, walter yet.

The baillies and counsale ordanis the thesaurer to mak the walter yet in Leyth Wynde patent to the nychtbouris for careing furth of thair fuilye, and to hing on the auld trie yet, mak the lokis, bandis, and barris thairof sufficient in the auld mauer.

29 *July* 1569.

Redar.

The baillies and counsale ordanis Frances Lyntoun to delyver to Jhonn Carnis, redar, the sowme of xix merkis restand awin be him of the annuell of his duelling hous in pairt of payment of the said Jhonnis stepend restand awin to him.

10 *August* 1569.

Annuellis, ministrie.

The counsale ordanis the baillies to put all sic personis in waird as ar decernit be decrete befoir the tovnis commissaris to pay the annuellis of thair landis to the hospital and ministrie, thair to remane vpoun thair awin expenssis ay and quhill the said decreit be satefeit, and that becaus it is provin this day befoir thame be George Gourlay, officer, that he hes chairgit the said personis and thay refusit.

12 *August* 1569.

Cvnynghame, collectar.

In prescus of the prouest baillies and counsale, Robert Cvnynghame, merchand, accepttis vpoun him the office of collectorie for the ministrie induring thair willis, and gevis his aith for deligence in his office.

7 *September* 1569.

Villa, passages North Loch.

The baillies and counsale, vnderstanding that James Nycholsone, writer, and vtheris nychtbouris quhilkis hes thair landis boundit to the

North Loch of this burgh, hes bigit yairdis, and ar of mynde to big hard to Villa, passages the said loch; quhairthronch nocht onlie sall the Kingis lieges be deberrit North Loch. of the auld and commoun commoditie of the loch foirsaid, bot in case the toun at ony tyme heirefter salhappin to be invadit be inimeis the auld commoun passages euer resernit for the defence of the said toun salbe destroyit, quhairfor thay ordane Adam Foullertoun and William Litill, baillies, [and six others,] to pas this efter none and vesye the hale yaird dikis bigit to the said loch, inquyre the names of the heritouris thairof, to the effect reformatioun may be maid, the auld commoun passages restorit, and report to the counsale the nixt counsale day.

### 16 *September* 1569.

The counsale ordanis the foure baillies to convene the dekynnis for Pykis. inbringing of the pikis resauit be thame, lent be my lord regentis grace to the gude toun, and to put in the samyn in the townys mvnitoun hous quhair thay war of before.

### 21 *September* 1569.

The baillies and counsale, vnderstanding that thair is diuers schippis Schippis, pest. arrivit in the raid laitlie cumin furth of Danskin quhilkis ar suspect of the pest, quhairfor thay ordane officeris to pas incontinent and charge the merchanttis, maisteris, marineris and kippage, to pas with thair schippis and guddis to Inchekeyth, Sanct Colmes Inche, and vther places thair-about, and thair lose the guddis being thairiutill and remane thairwith vnder the pane of deid.

### 23 *September* 1569.

The baillies and counsale, being convenit for electing of the new Villa, craftis, counsale for the yeir to cum, comperit Walter Wauhane, dekyn of the lytis. tailyouris, with certane vtheris deaconis, togither with James Young and Dauid Kinloch, prolocutouris for the hale craftis, and desyrit to be hard to resoun for the saidis craftis concernyng the tua craftisman that suld be vpoun the counsale for the said yeir, quhilk wes grantit, and efter lang resonyng it was desyrit be the saidis prolocutouris that the said Dauid

Villa, craftis, lytis.  Kinloch, baxter, and sic vtheris as thai wald joyne to him, to quhome it was ansuerit that nane sic as of thair occupatioun, sic as baxteris, fleschouris, maltmen, quhilkis had the handling of mennis sustentatioun, had bene vpoun the counsale of the toun in ony tyme bypast, nather aucht nor suld be, becaus thai mycht woit and persuade to thair awin particular commoditie, to the greit hurt of the kingis liegis, and siclyke that na cordineris, nor littistaris, nor vtheris of sic rude occupatioun, aucht to be vpoun the counsale, nouther wald thay admit nor resave ony sic; and thairfoir ordanit the saidis dekynnis and thair prolocutouris to geve in ane new tiket of sic vtheris occupatiounis as had bene vpoun the counsale of befoir, with certificatioun and thai failyeit thai wald chuse sic as thai thocht expedient incontinent but langer delay; and the saidis prolocutouris protestit for licence to avyse with thair brethrene and suld report ansuer, quha being remonit and raenterit thai gaif in ane new tikket out of the quhilk was chosin James Norwell and William Harlaw, saidler, counsallouris for the said yeir tocum.

### 7 October 1569.

Personis excommunicat. The baillies and counsale ordanis proclamatioun to be maid chairging that personis excommunicat remove thame selves of this toun within fourtie aucht houris nixt heirefter, vnder the hiest pane can be laid to thair chairge.

### 14 October 1569.

Regent, villa, provest.  In presens of the baillies and counsale, Dauid Forester, baillie, producit my lord Regentis grace writing, delyverit to him be Adam Wanchop, seruand to maister James Makgill, in jugement, of the quhilk the tennour followis:—Baillies counsall and dekynnis of Edinburgh, we greit yow weill. Forsamekill as we vnderstanding that at Michaelmes last ye have electit and chosin the laird of Grainge, capitane of the castell, to be your provest for the yeir to cum, quhilk office he is nocht able to indure, having the charge of the said castell and keping of sic men as ar within the samyn sua that it apperis till ws he doing his dewitie thair

1569.]            OF THE BURGH OF EDINBURGH.            265

ye salbe disappointit of your principal officer, the causis of your commoun  Regent, villa,
weill oursene for him, and our Soueranis liegis within your said toun nocht  provest.
ordorit as thai aucht and suld gif ane vther having les ado war in his
place; quhairfoir we think guid that he be dischairgit for this yeir, and
James Adamsoun, or sic vther able and qualefcit merchant of your awin
toun, electit and put in his place for the said yeir. This we desir yow
to do, and your answer. Quhilk wryting being red and considerit, the
baillies, counsall, thesaurer, dene of gild, and haill dekynnis being convenit, efter lang resonyng, wotis and concludis that thai have fund na caus
quhy the said laird of Grainge suld be deposit of his said office of provestrie for the yeir tocum, and thairfoir ordanis ane wryting to be send to
my lord Regentis grace declaring that for the greit effectioun that thai
knaw the laird of Grainge beris to our Soucrane and his grace thay have
chosin him thair provest, and sen his electioun hes fund na caus quhy he
suld be depryvit, nouther culd thai consent to his depriuatioun, beand a
man of sic honour and fame, without offence committit, and thairfoir
exhorting his grace that he war nocht offendit becaus it is thair mynde
to continew him. And to depesche this wryting with diligence be Hectour
Trolhop, masour, to Kelsow quhair his grace is for this present.

### 21 October 1569.

[Ale, "gud and sufficient drink," not to be sold dearer than fourpence the  Aill, breid.
pint. The fourpence loaf of bread baked by baxters within burgh to weigh
20 ounces, and that baked by baxters without burgh to weigh 24 ounces.]

### 26 October 1569.

The bailies and counsale ordanis Jhonn Legait, maister of the foull  Legait.
mvre, to be clengit and brocht hame according to the ordour, and dis-
chairgis his wagis fra this furth.

### 16 November 1569.

The baillies and counsale ordanis Thomas Henrisoun, thesaurer, to  villa.
geve to Hectour Trolhop the sovme of ten li. for the provest ox at  thesaurer,
Abalownes fair gevin to him be the said provest, allowand thairintill the  custome ox.

Villa, thesaurer, custome ox.

customis gottin in the noult mercat the tyme of the said fair, and decernis fra this furth the said ox to pertene to the provest for the tyme, to be vsit at his plesour, and ordanis na mair to be gevin for the said ox in all tyme cumming nor sall happin to be gottin of the customes of the said fair.

2 *December* 1569.

Villa, candilmakaris.

[The bailies and conncil,] ansucrand to the supplicatioun gewin in befoir thame be Walter Wawane for himself and remanent decanes in fauouris of the candilmakeris, bering that the saidis candilmakeris of ald had grantit to thame be the gude toun and prouest and baillies for the tyme, as thair gift vnder the seill of caus boiris, ane dekin quha had votit with the remanent decanes in the caussis of the commoun weill, quhill of lait, for ane offence committit be vmquhill Johne Young, candilmaker, thair said dekyne was dischargit, and now sen the said Johnis decos thair hes bene na offence committit be thame, quhairfor thai desyrit Johne Clavye, candilmaker, to be authorisit dekyne to haue voit as said is; to the quhilk the baillies and counsall foirsaid dissentit be reasoun that it wes assignit to the saidis dekynnis of befoir to haue brocht with thame sic authentik actis furth of the towne buikis, gif siclyk wer, as mycht be ony testificatioun gif ever thair wes ane dekyne of the candilmakeris of befoir and brocht nane, and forther alledgit thair wes never sic ane thing as ane dekyne of candilmakeris of befoir, and Walter Wawane protestit for remeid.

16 *December* 1569.

Villa, Leith.

[The bailies, conncil] and haill dekynnis, efter lang aduysement and consideratioun takin quhow that, be the oursicht and gentilnes vsit towart the inhabitantis of Leyth sen the superioritie thairof cam in the tovnis handis, the saidis inhabitantis vsit and exercit all kynde of fredome and libertie in wenting of wynis, sailing as friemen and making of opin merchandris, to the greit hurt of the libertie and commoun weill of this burgh, thairfoir thay ordanit for this present, quhill farther ordour be takin, that the baillies and officeris pas to the said toun of Leyth, command and charge all wyne ventaris within the same to desist and ceis fra selling or venting wynis fra this tyme furth, vnder the pane of escheiting of the samyn. — Villa, Leith.

### 30 *December* 1569.

The baillies and counsell, persaving that it hes plesit God of his mereefull gudnes to deliuer this toun of the pest, thay ordane that all sic as ar in the Senys be put to the clene mvre, thair to remane conforme to the ordour, and thairefter brocht into the toun, and that money be provydit for thankfull and compleit payment to the officeris of the mvre for thair panys and seruice. — Villa pest.

### 20 *January* 1569-70.

The baillies and counsale ordanis to caus warne the hale dekynnis aganis Wednisday nixt, that ordour may be taikin with thair avise tuiching the dewitie callit the clerk male, quhilk in tyme of papistrie wes gevin to the perroch clerk, to the effect the samyn may be vpliftit for sustenyng of Jhoun Carnys reder. — Villa, clerk male.

The baillies counsale and dekynnis, efter lang ressonyng vpoun the commoun effaris, and in speciall vpoun sic thingis as war hurtfull to the commoun weill and fredome of this burgh, thay haue found amangis vther inconvenienttis that the making of monye burgessis, and in speciall of sic as ar na burges bairnys and procuris thair fredome and libertie be way of court, or vtherwayis gratis and payis na dewtie thairfor to the commoun gude; quhairfor it is statute and ordanit that the bairnys of all sic as gettis thair fredome gratis in maner foresaid sall nocht haue the libertie of ane fre burges bairne, and this ordinance to indure but renocatioun. — Priuelege of burgessis gevin gratis.

### 25 *January* 1569-70.

The baillies and counsale, efter lang ressonyng vpoun the apperand danger and troublis like to be now, efter the crewall murthur of my lord — Wache.

Wache.

Regentis grace, fyndis gude and ordanis that thair be ane wache in the toun baythe day and nycht induring the counsallis will, in maner following, viz., fra vj houris in the mornyng quhill sevin houris at evin viij men, foure of thame at the West Port and vther foure at the Nether Bow, and the nycht wache, being in nowmer xxiiij personis, to begyn at vij houris at evin and to continew quhill sex in the mornyng, and that thay be relevit be the day wache, and this wache to be of the nychtbouris of the toun conforme to the auld ordour, begynnand at the Northwest quarter; and that thair be chosin foure men of credence and honestie, tua of thame to haue the charge ovir the day wache and tua ovir the nycht wache, quha salbe haldin to answer for the seruice of the remanent; and as ony cumpaneis cumis within the toun ane of thir to cum to ane of the baillies and aduertice thame of the nowmer, and quhat thay ar, and quhair thay luge; and siclike that thair be na porttis oppin induring the counsallis will bot the Nether Bow and West Port allanerlie.

Proclamatio, lang waponis, powder.

The samyn day, the baillies and counsall ordanis proclamatioun to be maid be sound of bell throuch the toun chargeing all nychtbouris that inhabitis foir buithis or houssis vpoun the hie streit that thai haif in reddines lang waponis for redding of pairteis in cas ony troublis be vpoun the gait, and that na powder nor lang waponis be carcit furth of the toun without licence of the prouest and baillies, vnder the pane of escheit; and siclike that the baillies tak inuentour of all the powder that is to sell within this toun and fence and arrest the samyn for serving of the Kingis souldouris and the gude toun.

### 27 January 1569-70.

[Lordis of sessioun.]

The baillies, counsale, and dekynnis, vnderstanding the lordis to remove and skaill the sessioun, thay ordane maister Michaell Chisholme, baillie, Alexander Clerk, Adame Foullertoun, Wilham Harwy of the counsall, Alexander Guthre, clerk, Walter Wawane and Jhonn Wilsoun, dekynnis, to ryde to my lord of Mortoun, chansler, to resort to the toun.

move the lordis to remane and to promys his lordschip assistance [and] [Lords of session.] fortificatioun in the Kingis actionis, his awin, and revenge of the murthure.

The counsall ordanis the baillies to vesie the portis of the toun, the Portis, barris, bandis and lokkis thairof, and se the samyn be suire, and to change artelyearie. the lokkis thairof and put on new lokkis, sielyk to caus ramforce the Walter Yait, to vesie the tounis artelyearie vpoun the wallis and caus mont and mende the sam with diligence be the avys of James Hectour, gwnner.

### 1 *February* 1569-70.

The baillies and counsall namis constitutis and ordanis Alexander Commissaris, Clerk and Adame Foulertoun thair commissaris, grantand and giffand to clerk, Foullertoun. thame thair commissioun and power for thame and in thair names with the lordis of nobilitie to convene, and with thame to conclud the caussis concernying the glorie of God, the Kingis weill, and commoun of the realme.

### 3 *March* 1569-70.

[The bailies and council ratified and approved the commission given to Mychael Chancellar. Chisholme and others on 27th January, and "promys as of before."]

### 8 *March* 1569-70.

The baillies counsall and dekynnis, for keiping of gude reull amangis the Villa, gairde lordis of nobelitie, and all vtheris resorting to this toun during the tyme of houssis. this present conventioun, fyndis gude, statutis and ordanis that thair be dalie foure gaird houssis, and in euerye ane of thame tuenty men of the maist honest nychtbouris of the toun in thair awin proper personis, ten of thame with culveringis and moreonys and vther ten with halberttis, pikis, and lang wappynnis; and to enter euerye day at the skaling of the nycht wasche, viz., be sex houris in the mornyng, and remane quhill sevin

| | |
|---|---|
| Villa, gairdc houssis. | houris at evin that the nycht wache enter agane. And of thir gairde houssis to be ane of thame in Gilbert Dikis foreland abone the auld tolbuth, ane vther of thame before the auld tolbuth in Jhonn Symsonis and Frances Tennandis foreland, the thrid in Jhonn Symmis foreland, and the feird in Thomas Thomsonis foreland; and this day wache to indure as said is. |
| Officeris. | The counsale ordanis the officeris to await vpoun thair baillies continuallie the tyme of this conventioun, vnder the pane of deprinatioun of thair offices. |

### 22 March 1569-70.

| | |
|---|---|
| Wache. | The baillies and counsale ordanis the wache to continew as it wes first ordanit quhill forther avisement. |
| South Loch. | The baillies and counsale ordanis Thomas Hendersoun, thesaurer, to vesy the South Loch and mend the samyn quhair the watter rynnis furth. |
| Porttis. | The baillies and counsale ordanis the porttis to be opnit euery mornying be sex houris and closit agane at xij houris quhill tua efternone, and closit agane at vj houris at evin for all nycht, and the porteris continuallie to await thairvpoun, viz., the Kirk of Feild port and Eist port in the Cowgait and keyis to be delinerit nychtlie to the baillies. |

### 24 March 1569-70.

| | |
|---|---|
| Precept, thesaurer, grammer scole. | The baillies and counsale ordanis the thesaurer to pay to maister Jhonne Sandelandis, persoun of Hawik, the sowme of xx li. in compleit payment of all maillis restand awand be the gude toun for the grammer scole in the Freir Wynd, and to deliuer him the keyis of the said scole and gyf the samyn our. |

#### 12 April 1570.

The baillies and counsale, efter avisement with the writing send to thame be the erllis of Huntlie, Argyle, Athole, and lordis of the west countre, gevis for ansuer thair lordschippis salbe wilcum to the toun, and hale nobelitie of this realme.

*Lordis, villa.*

#### 14 April 1570.

The baillies and counsale ordanis the nycht wache to be eikit induring the lordis remanying in this toun, viz., the northwest and northeist quarteris eueryane of thame twa nychtis and the vther tua quarteris eueryane thre nychtis.

*Lordis, wache.*

#### 19 April 1570.

It is appoyntit and aggreit betuix the baillies done of gild and counsale, on that ane pairt, and Robert Creych, knok makar, on the vther pairt, viz., the said Robert bindis and oblissis him to mend and vphald the toun knok, thay furnessing irne allanerlie; for the quhilk caus they ordane the thesauraris present and to cum to pay him yeirlie during his lyfetime, xl s.

*Villa, knok.*

#### 11 May 1570.

[The bailies, council and deacons,] efter consideratioun of the greit charges and soumpteous expensis maid be the laird of Grange, capitane of the castell, protest, vpoun the reparatioun strenthing and fortefeing of the said castell now at the incumming of the Inglis armye, quhilk castell hes bene and lukit for to be the resett and defence of the pepill of this toun and thair guiddis, in consideratioun quhairof thay decerne and ordane Andro Stevinsoun and Alexander Clerk, fermoraris of thair commoun mylnis for this present yeir, to deliuer incontinent to the said capitane, to the suport of his charges, the sowme of tua hundreth pundis, and the samyn salbe allowit to thame in the radicst of the fermes of the said mylnis.

*Prouest, castell, precept, fermoraris.*

## 17 May 1570.

*Wappinschewing.*

The baillies and counsale ordanis proclamatioun to be maid throuch Edinburgh and Leith chargeing all the inhabitanttis of the samyn to gif thair generale mustouris and wappinschewing, in best array with armour and wappinis, throuch this toun vpoun Friday nixt, ilk persoun vnder the pane of x li.

## 26 May 1570.

*Villa, letteres, missiuis.*

The baillies and counsale ordanis the thesaurar to direct the townys missivis to all the burrois makand mentioun of the proclamatioun purchest be the bischop of Glasgow in France dischairgeing the cuming of Scottis schippis thair without the Quenis certificat, requyring thame to support the expenssis of ane man to be send thair for dischargeing of the said proclamatioun, and to report thair ansuer.

## 2 June 1570.

*Villa, Lakprevik, prentar.*

In presens of the baillies and counsale, Nichole Fyldour is becumin cautioun and souertie for Robert Lakprevik, prentar, vnder the pane of j$^c$ merkis, that the said Robert sall nocht fra this furth prent bukis ballettis or ony wark of consequence without the licence of the prouest baillies and counsale; and Lakprevik oblissis him to releif Fyldour.

## 16 June 1570.

*Precepts, thesaurar, Adamesoun.*

The prouest baillies and counsale, with the avyce of the dekynis, ordanis ane writting to be send to the erle of Homtlye for the releif of James Adamesoun, with ane seruand of the prouestis, and the thesaurare to gif him ten pund for his expenssis.

## 12 July 1570.

*Forrester, Foullertoun, commissaris.*

The baillies and counsale makis constitutis and ordanis Dauid Forster, baillie, and Adam Foullertoun, of the counsale, thair procuratouris and commissouris, gevand thame power for thame and in thair names to coupeir in this present conventioun of the nobilitie for the Kingis pairt appoyntit at this burgh xij$^o$ instantis Julij, for electing of ane Regent, etc.

1570.]     OF THE BURGH OF EDINBURGH.     273

The baillies and counsall of the burgh of Edinburgh, sittand in juge- Decreit, ment, in the actioun and caus persewit be Thomas Hendersonn, thesaurare dekynnis of Leyth. of the said burgh, makand mentioun that quhair the said burgh being of auld past memorie of man erected in ane fre burgh of ryaltie, and thairby haveand all prevelegis of ane fre burgh within the boundis thairof, quhilk extendis to the boundis of the fredome of Hathingtoun on the eist, quhilk parte is Edgebukling Bray, and on the west to Almonnd Watter, on the north to the sey, and on the south safar as the boundis of the scherefdome of Edinburgh principall extendis to, and yit the burgessis and commnnitie of the said burgh of Edinburgh, for amplefeing of thair awin prevelegis in the moneth of Maij j$^m$ thre hundreth four scoir xviij yeiris, haifand than the hewin and schoir of Leyth annexit to the said burgh within the fredome and commoditeis thairof, obtenit be dispositioun maid to thame be Robert Logane of Restalrig, knycht, diuers and syndrie previleges for thair eis in bigging of the said port and havin of Leyth, togidder with the haill wayis passages and trans of the toun of Leyth and barronie of Restalrig, for transporting of thair guidis to and fra the samyn, quha alswa for him his airis and assignayis perpetuallie rentit the taverning and selling of wyne, the bakyng of breid to sell, the halding and keiping of marchand buithis, girnelling of quheit, and all vther thingis that wer contrair the libertie and consuetude of the said fre burgh of Edinburgh, swa that nother he his airis nor assignais nor na vtheris in his name or on his pairt sould hald venting and selling of wyne, baking of breid to sell, marchand buithis, girnellis of quheit, be thameselfis nor na vtheris within the toun and landis of Leyth or thairabout, nor yit thole the samyn in ony tyme thairefter to be haldin, as at mair lenth is contenit in the prevelege and rycht maid to the saidis burgessis and commonitie thairvponn; and albeit it be of veritie that the cheif libertie and fredome of ane fre burgh of ryaltie consistes in twa thingis, the ane in vsing of marchandice, the vther in vsing of craftes, resaving of fremen thairto, chesing of dekynnis of craftis, for examinatioun of thame that ar admitted thairto that thai be qualifeit, swa that the leigis of the realme be nocht dissauit of thair occupationes; and that the said burgh of Edinburgh, be vertew of thair previlegis and erectioun of thair burgh as said is and liberteis foir-

2 M

Decreit, dekynnis of Leyth.

saidis obtenit of the said laird of Restalrig, hes bene and yit is in possessioun of thair liberteis and fredomes foirsaidis vsand all thingis concernand ane fre burgh, nochttheles as the said thesaurare is informet and it is of veritie that certane persones induellaris of the said toun of Leyth hes wrangouslie at thair awin hand vsurpet the acceptatioun vpoun thame of the offices of dekynnis of craftes, quhilk is contrair the prevelege and fredome of the said burgh of Edinburgh and rycht maid be the said laird of Restalrig for him his airis and assignais, that is to say : [Here follow the names of the deacons of the smiths, coopers, tailors, baxters, cordiners, fleshers, and websters;] and will nocht desist and ceis thairfra without thai be compellit, as at mair lenth is contenit in the clame gevin in thairvpoun : The richtis ressonis and allegationis of bayth the saidis pairteis, togidder with the depositionis of diuers famous witnes and vther probatioun led and takyne in the said mater at lenth hard sene and vnderstand, and thairwith being ryple avysit, the said thesaurair comperand be Alexander King his procuratour, and the saidis defenderis alswa comperand in jugement to heir sentence gewin, the saidis baillies and counsall, with awys of thair assessouris, decernis and ordanis the saidis persones and euerye ane of thame to desist and ceis fra the vsurping of the saidis names and offices and vsing thairof in ony tyme cuming within the said toun of Leyth or barronye of Restalrig, becaus the said clame being admittted to the said thesauraris probatioun he previt the samyn sufficientlie as efferit, as wes clerlie vnderstand and knawin to the saidis baillies and counsall and thair assessouris,

### 14 July 1570.

Borrowis, Capitane Cokburne.

[A contract entered into between the council, on behalf of the whole burghs, and Captain Ninian Cokburne, whereby the latter was commissioned to obtain the discharge of "ane proclamatioun obtenit and proclamit at the handis of the maist mychti King of France dischargeing all maner of Scottismen with thair schippis gudis or merchandice of all hant resort or tradique within the see townis or vtheris pairtis of his dominionis except sic as sall bring with thame the certificate of our Souerane the Kingis moder or hir lewtennentis to acknawledge only hir and thair authoritie in hir name and nane vtheris."][1]

[1] See printed Records of the Conventions of Royal Burghs, Vol. I. p. 531.

19 *July* 1570.

Forsamekle as the prouest baillies and counsale of this burgh ar certefeit that thair is certane Franche men of weyr arrivit in the raid of Leyth with certane prissis chargit with the guddis of Hollandis, and vtheris freindis to oure Souerane Lord his lieges and realme, of mynd to mak mercatt of thair saidis prissis and guddis in thir pairttis, without onye lauchfull declaratioun of the admarall gyf the schippis and guddis be lauchfull prissis or nocht, quhilk may engender greit inconuenienttis, and alter the freindschip standand with the saidis Hollandis to the greit hurt of oure said Soueranys liegis gyf mair haistye remeid be nocht prouidit, heirfoir I command and charge in our said Souerane Lordis name, my lord Regenttis, and in name and behalf of my lord prouest and baillies of this burgh, that na maner of persoun induellar within the fredome boundis and jurisdictioun of Edinburgh and Leyth trafique by or sell with the saidis Franche men of weyr, or by onye of thair weirfair guddis, vnder the pane of tynsale of all thair guddis movable and banischit the fredome foresaid for evir.

*Proclamatioun, weyrschippis.*

The commissaris of burrois vnderwrittin, convenit at this present conventioun for electing of my lord erle of Levinax Regent, viz. [the commissaris of Edinburgh, Dundee, Perth, Stirling, Glasgow, Ayr, Irvine, Jedburgh, and Haddington], it is statute that in the nixt conventioun the saidis commissaris, or vther that salbe chosin, bring with thame commissioun to propone ressoun and conclude vpoun the commoun weill of burrois and statutis thairfor to mak, and in the menetyme to put in writt sic thingis quhairby thay ar hurt.

*Commissaris of burrois.*

5 *August* 1570.

The bailles and counsale ordanis Thomas Hendersoun, thesaurare, to len to [*blank*] Rutherfourd, baillie of Jedburgh, twa cutthrottis with thair chalmeris and furnessing in support of the said toun of Jedburgh aganis the theifis, takand the said baillies obligatioun vpoun the ressait and deliuerance thairof.

*Jedburgh, cutthrot.*

### 9 August 1570.

Villa, wache.

The baillies and counsale ordanis ane watche to be maid the tyme during my lord Regentis absence, and that na portis be oppin on the day bot the West Port and the Nether Bow, and that thair be put to keip euerie ane of thame on the day by licht thre men, and the baillies to keip the keis in the nycht.

### 11 August 1570.

Craig, minister.

The baillies dene of gyld and counsall ordanis the dekynis to be wairnit to convene the morne at sevin houris in the tolbuith for ressonyng vpoun the commoun afferis and for provisioun to be maid for maister Jhone Craig, minister.

### 15 August 1570.

Proclamatioun, villa.

The baillies and counsall, efter the ressait of my lord Regenttis writting, ordanis proclamatioun to be maid chairging ane stark watch to be nychtlie induring his gracis absence, ilk man to watche in his proper persoun, vnder the pane of fyve pund; and sicklyke that all maner of persoun, induellar within this burgh, without exceptioun, be in reddines in armes and wappounis at the sound of the commoun bell and resort to the baillie of thair quarter and follow sic ordour as he sall appoint for thame, as thai will answer to the Kingis grace and my lord Regentis, and vnder the pane foirsaid; that all hostlaris aduerteis the baillie of thair quarter quhat straingeris resortis to thair houssis, vnder the pane of deid.

### 23 August 1570.

Sabboth, vnlaw, Portuous.

The baillies and counsall decernis and ordanis Patrik Portuous, duelland in the Ovir Bow, to pay fourtie schillingis for brekin of the Sabboth in kairting of twa polkis of woll send to Leyth on Sonnday last, and gyf the said vnlaw to the puir woman in the Seynis, quhilk vnlaw was incontinent payit and deliuerit. Ordanis the cairter to be put in waird induring the counsalis will.

### 24 *August* 1570.

[The bailies, council, and deacons of crafts,] efter lang ressoning vpoun villa, the ministeris stipend and how and quhairvpoun thai sall be sustenit, it ministrie. is thocht guid be the baillies and counsall foirsaid that the auld dewtye quhilk wes payit be the inhabitantis of this burgh to the provest vicare and clerk of the paroche kirk be collectit of new and appoyntit vpoun the said ministrie, and the saidis dekynis desyrit till awys with this quhill the morne, quhilk wes grantit.

### 8 *September* 1570.

The baillies and counsale ordanis the auld hoillis of the Mwse well to Mwse well. be oppin, that the watter may haue passege sua that the nychtbouris landis adiacent be harmeles of the vnder walter rissin be closin of the saidis hoillis.

### 27 *September* 1570.

[The deacons of crafts having given in a "tiket" containing the names of Craftis on the craftsmen from which two were to be elected councillors, the bailies and council counsale. objected to the list " becaus thay had bot alterit the saidis tikettis in the changeing of ane name allenarlie, and thairfor ordanis thame to gif in ane vther new tiket and vther names nor wer given in of before." The deacons thereupon gave in another list, from which two names were selected.]

### 18 *October* 1570.

The counsel ordanis the baillies and dene of gild to discharge the Cramis cramis of the calsay and place quhair thay presentlie stand befoir the northeist dur of the parosche kirk, and to appoint thame the kirk yaird vpoun the south syde of the said kirk alanerlie and na vther place.

The samyn day, thay ordane the said dene of gild to cloise vp the Gildrie. buith durris of all sic as ar nocht gild brether vsing onye merchandrise vther nor cramerye, ay and quhill the counsale be farther avysitt.

### 20 *October* 1570.

Efter lang suting of maister James M'Gill to acceptt vpoun him Protestatio the office of provestrie to the quhilk he was electit on Mychaelmes last, prepositi.

| | |
|---|---|
| Protestatio, prepositi. | efter mony resonis schawin be him quhy he could nocht accept the said office, at leist gif he acceptit the samyn, for the vther charges quhilk lay on him, he culd [nocht] be able at all tymes to do sic seruice to the gude toun as his hert was willing to do, and thairfoir incace he war burdenitt with vther greter actiounis it mycht be the occasioun that he micht [nocht] auaitt on the said office, desyritt that he mycht haif ane president to serue vnder him; to the quhilk it was ansueritt that quhen the tyme or neid suld requyre, he acceptand the said office, thrie suld be nominatt, off the quhilkis ane suld be chosin to support him in his place, and the said maister James askit instrumentis and acceptit the said office. |
| Extent of v<sup>c</sup> pundis. | [The bailies, conncil, and deacons of craftis] grantis and consentis that the nixt stent of v<sup>c</sup> pundis be liftet of the nychtbouris of this burgh, as for the feird pairt of the haill borrowis pairt of the xij<sup>m</sup> pundis granttit be the thrie estaitt for furnesing of certane embassadouris to pas in England. |

25 October 1570.

| | |
|---|---|
| Craftis, ministeris. | [The bailies and conncil] ordanis the deaconis of craftis, presentlie convenit, to convene thair brethrene the morn and inquyre of thair benevolence quhat thai will geve to the support of the ministeris, and to report the ansuer vpoun Fryday nixt. |
| Villa, Nisbett. | The baillies and counsall fyndis guid that Henry Nisbett pas in Ingland with the abbot of Dymfermeling for lowsing of the arrestmentis of the schippis in France, and ordanis the said Henrye to mak him reddie. |

1 November 1570.

| | |
|---|---|
| Craftis, ministrie. | Comperit the dekynis of the craftis, and gaif ansuer to the provest baillies and counsall quhat ilk craft wald perfurnis and gif to the sustentatioun of the ministrie, in maner following:—Skynneris, xx li.; Wryehtis and Masonis, x li.; Tailyeouris, xvj li.; Goldsmythis, vj li. xiij s. iiij d.; Barbouris, iij li.; Jhone Wilsoun smyth, xx merkis; Baxteris, xx merkis; Cordineris, viij li.; Fleschouris, x li.; Wobstaris, xx s.; Bonat-makaris, xx s.; Furrouris (*blank*). |

#### 8 November 1570.

The baillies and counsale, vnderstanding that na apperance is to luikitt for be the laubouris of Capitane Cokburn for the libertie of oure schippis in the pairtis of France, quhairfoir, according to the ordinance maid with the consent of the commissaris of the maist part of the haill burrois of this realme in the moneth of October last, ordanis as of befoir that Henrie Nesbett depairt with all diligence possible with the tovnis wrytingis in name of the haill borrois foirsaid to the King of France, quhairevir he may be found within his hienes dominiounis, and thair, conforme to the saidis wrytingis and articlis gevin him in writ, to crave and desyre the ancient libertie to be grantit to our natioun inuiolablie obseruitt for our pairtis of new.

*Villa, Nysbett.*

#### 15 November 1570.

The baillies and counsale nominatis collectouris for procuring of the beneuolence of the godlie to the support of the ministaris stepend, thir personis vnderwrittin, viz. :—Jhon Harwod and Symoun Marioribankis for the northwest, Adame Foullertoun and Patrik Rig for the northeist, Mr Michaell Chesholme and Nicoll Vddart for the southeist, Mr Jhonn Prestoun and Dauid Forester for the southwest.

*Collectouris, ministrie.*

#### 18 November 1570.

The baillies and counsale ordanis Nicholo Vddart, thesaurare, to caus big ane barrous of tymmer befoir my lord Regentis yaitt, and the samyn sall be allowit in his comptis.

*Thesaurare, Regent.*

#### 29 November 1570.

The maist pairt of the maisteris and principallis of schippis within the toun of Leyth, being convenit within the counsalhous of this burgh, quhair it wes schawin vnto thame the waiknes of the schoir peir and bulwarkis of Leyth on bayth the sydis of the walter, quhilkis sould suddanlie decay be all apperance forevir gif the samyn wer nocht the mair haistelie helpit and remedit, and quhow thai war myndit to caus

*Villa, maryneris, bulwark.*

*Villa, maryneris, bulwark.*

thair nychtbouris the merchanttis and all vtheris resortand with merchandice to the said port of Leyth to pay ane certane dewitye of euerye tvn of guidis for the space of thre yeiris nixt heirefter, quhilk thai dowtit nocht sould be frelie grantit to the helpe of sa guid and godlie actioun, and thairfore sen the mater conceruit thair wellis als hielye as ony vtheris, desyrit thame till convene thame selfis and avys quhat thay wald grant of euerye tun fraucht for the said space and report thair ansuer vpoun Fryday nixt.

1 *December* 1570.

*Maryneris, dewtye bulwark.*

In presens of the baillies and counsall, comperit the maist pairt of the maisteris maryneris of schippis in Leyth, and frelie of thair awin consentis grantit to gif of euerye tun fraucht at the out passing, and siclyk at the incuming, during the space of thre yeiris, xij d., to the reparatioun and support and bigging of the peir and hevin of Leyth; prouyding that this thair consent induce nocht the preperative in tymes cuming, nother thai be compellit heirby to consent to the lyk, nor that efter the ische of the saidis thre yeiris thai be forther chairgit with the said dewtye, and protestit that this thair consent sould nocht hourt vtheris quhilkis had nocht consentit as yit, quhilk offer the provest baillies and counsall forsaid acceptit and grantit thair said protestatioun.

6 *December* 1570.

*Statutis for repairing of the schoir of Leith.*

[The provest, bailies, conncil, and deacons of crafts,] with consent and assent of the maist pairtt of the maisteris skipperis and marinaris of the said toun of Leith, hes statute and ordanitt that for the space of thrie yeris nixt [there shall be collected] tua schillingis of euery tun of gudis enterand within the said portt and hawin of Leith, at the entrie thairof, tua s. of ilk tun at the outpassing, baith of merchanttis friemen and vnfremen and strangeris, and siclike of euerye tunnis fraucht at the incuming xij d. and at the outpassing xij d.; off the schippis cumand frome Noroway and vther pairtis, laidnit with tymmer, of euerie hundreth geistis ane, of euerye hundreth corbellis ane, of euerye hundreth wanescott ane, off euerye hundreth daillis ane, of euerye hundreth rauchteris ane, and siclike

1570.]  OF THE BURGH OF EDINBURGH.  281

of euerye sort of tymmer cumand to the said port and hawin ane, or the availl and price thairof as the remanent salbe said; item, of euerye chalder of victuall that salbe sauld in the said port and haivin of Leith, of the merchant xvj d., and of the skipper and maister aucht penneis, and siclyke of all vther kynd of gudis quhilk ar vsitt to be disponett be chalderis, induring the said space of thrie yeiris alanerlie. *Statutes for repairing of the schoir of Leith.*

In presens of the provest baillies and counsall, sittand in jugement, in the actio in and caus intentit be Thomas Hendersoun, thesaurare and procuratour fiscall, aganis the craftismen and vnfremen occupyaris and induellaris within the vnfre toun of Leyth, . . . the saidis baillies and counsall, with avys of thair assessoris, dischargis the saidis persones of all vsing of the said artificiall craftis in tyme cuming within the said vnfre toun of Leyth, and gif ony of thame will vse the samyn to draw thame to ane fre toun and burghe to the vsing thairof to beir portabill chargis as the rest of the vsaris of thai craftis dois. *Decreit aganis the craftismen of Leyth.*

### 8 December 1570.

The baillies and counsall, vnderstanding that Thomas Cant and Harbert Maxwell, fermoraris of thair commoun myre the yeir past, quha wer actit to gif the sowme of ane hundreth markis thairfor the said yeir, quha gat na proffeit of the samyn be resone the samyn wes flayne be the capitane of the castell for making of gabionis and strenthing of the said castell, quhairfore thai discharge the saidis fermoreris of the said sowme of ane hundreth markis, payand alanerlye for the said yeir [twenty four pounds]. *Maxwell, Cant, charge thesaurar.*

### 27 December 1570.

The baillies and counsall ordanis ane nychtlie wache to be sett of thre scoir of men, and the baillie of the quarter to se the wache sett according to the ordour, and in case the nychtbouris present vnhable persouns to the said wache ordanis the officeris to hyre hable men and put in thair places, and to poynd the saidis nychtbouris for thair waigeis; and siclyke, ordanis the belman and his bruther to ly nychtlie in the steipill *Wache, commoun bell, portis.*

Wacho, commoun bell, portis.

and attend to the commoun bell, and the baillie of the wache to deliuer nychtlie to thame of the vnlawis of the wache iij s.; and siclyke, ordanis the portis of the toun to be all closit, except the Wast Port and Nether Bow; and the keyis thairof nychtlie to be deliuerit to the baillie of the wache and him to answer thairfore.

### 2 *February* 1570-1.

Villa, castell.

[The bailies, council and deacons of crafts,] efter lang resouyng vpoun the commoun effaris and keiping of the toun now in my lord Regentis grace absence, fyndis guid delineris and ordanis that Jhone Sym, Jhone Achesoun, and Mungo Fairlie, baillies, Adam Foullertoun, Alexander Guthrie, Mungo Bradie, Thomas Akynheid and James Inglis, pas vp to the castell this efter none and inquyre of the capitane in case the lordis for the Quenis pairt, or onye vtheris that beiris nocht guid will to the toun, wald resort thairto in multitudes, or with forces, quhat wald be his pairt, and to report his ansuer the morne before none.

### 3 *February* 1570-1.

Villa, castell.

The baillies counsale and dekynnis being conuenit, the personis direct yesterday to the castell reportit ansuer of the capitane quhilk was as followis, that is to say, sa lang as the inhabitantis and nychtbouris of the toun did nocht commit offence aganis the Kingis hous him and his quho had the keiping thairof assuir thameselfis of his fauour, gud will, and assistence gif ony wald meyne to troubell thame be way of dede, and craiffit of the tounschip to keip guid nychtbourheid with him as thay haif done in tymes past.

### 7 *February* 1570-1.

Protestatio, Burgeschippis.

[James Wod, on behalf of the deacons of crafts, "dissasentis that ony alteratioun be maid vpoun the dewtie of burgeschippis or gildrie; or ony hiear prices nor hes bene vsit of befor."]

Statuta Consilii.

[The bailies and council ordained the dean of guild "to execute the auld statutis and hieast prices vpoun burgeschippis and gildrois to be maid conforme to the auld ordinances in all tymes cuming, nochtwithstanding onye protestatioun in the contrair."] *Statuta Consilii.*

### 9 *February* 1570-1.

The baillies and counsale ordanis proclamatioun to be maid chargeing all excommunicat personis to remove thame of this toun betuix and the morne at none, vnder the pane of extreme impresonment, but preindice of the forther panis contenit in the lawis; and that all sic as resettis thame cum and reveill the samyn to the baillies vnder pane of banischement, and siclike that the actis of perliament be execute vpoun fornicatouris but fauouris. *Excommunicat persouns, fornicatouris.*

The baillies and counsale ordanis Jhonne Sym, baillie, and Nichole Vdder, thesaurer, to ryde to my lord Regentis grace in Struieling for satifeing of his grace concernyug the openioun taikin of the gude toun tuiching the capitane of the castellis gaird hous and men of weyr placit be him aboue the Ovir Tron. *Regent, villa.*

### 16 *February* 1570-1.

The baillies and counsale ordanis letter to be maid direct to my lordis erle of Mortoun, abbot of Dunfermeling, and maister James M'Gill. prouest, ambassadouris for the King, presentlie in England, for procuring libertie for our schippis to pas in France, and ordanis Jhonne Fergesoun, younger, to be direct thairwith be post. *Ambassadouris, villa.*

### 14 *March* 1570-1.

The baillies and counsale, vnderstanding that thair is certane schippis of weir arryvit within our soveranis walteris, having with thame certane prissis laidnyt with the guddis of Portingallis, Spanyerttis, or vtheris freindis, and sen trew it is that it has plesit God that the haill subiectis of this realme standis on amytie and freindschip with all forrane nationis, and that alsua be speciall act of parliament all letteres of mark ar dischargit vpoun the saidis Portingallis and Spanyearttis, vnder grat panis, as the samyn at lenth proportis; and seing that nocht onlie the contra- *Proclamatio, schippis, prissis.*

| | |
|---|---|
| Proclamatio, schippis, prissis. | venyng of the saidis actis sall be dangerous, bot as alswa, gyf the guddis of freindis reft and spulyeit be reset within this realme and the spulyearis thairof interteneit and resauit, sall nocht fale to follow sic trowbillis that the hale lieges of this realme salbe banischit all vther countreis or vtherwise thair lyffis and guddis in hasert gyf remeid be nocht proudit : Heirfor I command and charge [that no person within the bounds of Edinburgh and Leith traffic with the goods in the ships referred to]. |

### 30 *March* 1571.

| | |
|---|---|
| Villa, Sym, Lawtye, Dowglas, counsall. | [The bailies and council] disassentis to the putting of Thomas Dowglas to libertie furth of waird laitlie put in the tolbuith for the wounding and muttelating of David Lawtye, writter, bot that he sould remane thair according to the auld statutis of the toun, and Jhone Sym, baillie, confest that he had put him to libertie be ane ordinance and delinerance of the lordis quhilk he had for his warrand and acceptit the danger vpoun him; and the baillies and counsale foresaid protestit that na falt sould be imput to thame for braiking of the auld statutis nor putting the said Thomas to libertye. |
| Extent, borrowis. | The baillies and counsale ordanis ane extent to be sett of twa thousand markis vpoun all the borrowis of this realme for satefeing of Nycholace Vddart of the sowmes debursit be him for the doungetting of ten soulz of the tun of wyne in Burdeaux and for satefeing of Henrye Nysbet and Jhone Fergusoun of thair rewaird and expenssis quhane thay war send to Ingland and France for obtenyng libertie to the schippis to remane thair. |

### 14 *April* 1571.

| | |
|---|---|
| Proclamatio, beir. | The baillies ordanis proclamationn to be maid that na drinking Dutche beir be darrer sauld nor sex d. the pynt. |
| Villa, Regent. | The baillies and counsall ordanis writtingis to be send to my lord Regentis grace be Mungo Bradie of the counsall declairing thair constante obediance and guid mynd toward the King and his grace effairis. |

#### 20 April 1571.

It is found guid that the baillies, counsale, dekynis, and certane honest nychtbouris ryd to Dalkeith to the lord erle of Mortoun, my lord Demfermeling and the prouest to rander thame thankis of thair labouris taikyne in the townis effarris.

*Villa, Mortoun, prouest.*

#### 28 April 1571.

The remanent baillies and counsale ordanis Jhone Sym, Jhonne Adamsoun, maister Jhonne Prestoun, Henry Nisbett, Patrik Rig, maister Richert Strang, Alexander Vddert, Daniel Kinloch, maister Craig, minister, James Young, James Wod, George Smyth, Jhonne Wilsoun, Jhonne Nicolsoun, James Oliphant and Alexander King to pas to the castell and desyre the capitane that all the Kingis lieges may resort to the toun without trouble, and that he suffer nocht the inhabitanttis of this toun to be molestit be the men of weyr rasit be him and the lordis, and to report his ansuer.

*Villa, castell.*

#### 1 May 1571.

The baillies and counsall ordanis writtingis to be sent to Stirveling [be] Mungo Brady to my lord Regentis grace declaring the ordour taikin betuix the tounschip and the capitane, viz., that he nor nane of his sall trubill ony inhabitants of this toun nor vthers resorting thairto that sal nocht be of mynd to trubill nor inquyet him, and forther to declair the said Mungo be credence the guid mynd of the toun toward the Kingis seruice; and ordanis the thesaurer to satiffie him in his charges.

*Regent, precept.*